LIVES

OF THE

PRINCESSES OF ENGLAND

FROM

THE NORMAN CONQUEST.

BY

MARY ANNE EVERETT GREEN

EDITOR OF THE

"LETTERS OF ROYAL AND ILLUSTRIOUS LADIES," "LETTERS
OF QUEEN HENRIETTA MARIA," &c.

VOL. II.

LONDON:

LONGMAN, BROWN, GREEN, LONGMAN, & ROBERTS.

1857.

CONTENTS

OF

THE SECOND VOLUME.

ILLUSTRATIONS.

ISABELLA,

SECOND DAUGHTER OF KING JOHN.

This princess has been frequently placed by our genealogists the third in the list of the daughters of King John and Isabella of Angoulême—but documentary evidence still remains, which proves that she preceded in age her sister Eleanora.[1] The exact date of her birth has not transpired, but it must have taken place some time in the year 1214, since Matthew Paris says that, in 1235, the period of her marriage, she had attained her twenty-first year.[2] At the time of Isabella's birth, a degree of estrangement had

---

[1] See note, p. 3.   [2] Vol. ii., p. 414.

arisen between her parents, and thus a gloom was thrown over her infancy, which the events of succeeding years were not very likely to dispel. The misfortunes that rapidly crowded upon her vicious and unprincipled father were speedily followed by his death, and the royal children were left under the care of the Queen-mother, until her remarriage.

Their early residence was principally in the castle of Gloucester; but, when the troubles that marked the former part of the reign of the young king, Henry III., had passed away, their abode was frequently changed, as the court took up its residence now at the palace of Woodstock, now at the ancient hall of Westminster, frequently at Winchester, Merleberg, Northampton, York, and other seats in different parts of the kingdom,[1] where Isabella spent many of her youthful years.

But few records are extant which throw light on the domestic habits of the children, who at that period comprised the whole of the royal family. A portion of the household account of the first year of Henry III. is still in existence,[2] but the only entry that possesses the slightest interest beyond mere household detail is that of a payment made for a dove, which was purchased at Bourdeaux, and brought over probably as a plaything for the royal children. In the entries for articles of food, payments for fish of almost every description, from sea-wolves to oysters, frequently occur, while those for beef and mutton, and more substantial fare, are rarely found.

Even at this period, Isabella had her own suite of attendants. In 1219, Henry III. granted one penny per day to Margaret her nurse, which was to be paid every day by the hands of the Viscount of Hereford.[3] Paltry as this sum

---

[1] Bartholomew of Norwich. Cotton. MS., Nero, C. v., f. 190, b., et seq.
[2] It forms Roll No. 2644, in the Queen's Remembrancer Office, Carlton Ride.
[3] Rot. claus., 3 Henry III., p. 393.

may appear at the present day, yet, if we multiply it by fifteen, which, according to recent computation,[1] is the proportion which the money of our time bears to that of the period in question, we shall find that her wages amounted to 8s. 9d. a week, or nearly £23 a year.

The attention paid by our monarchs of the olden time to those who had tended their childhood, brings us back in imagination to the tender simplicity of patriarchal days. King John gave four pence a day to the nurse of his son Richard, and many grants were made by him to the nurse of his brother, Richard, the Lion-hearted;[2] and King Henry followed the example, by giving four pence, and then two pence more per day to " our dear nurse Elena," as well as an allowance of fire-wood from the royal forests.[3] Entries also occur for Isabella's cook, valet, and other servants, several of whom were pensioned off in their later years by her brother.[4]

- The first time that the name of Isabella occurs in reference to matrimonial engagements is in the year 1220, when, in the negociations between Alexander of Scotland and King Henry, it was stipulated that she should be substituted in the place of her sister Joanna, should any thing prevent the latter becoming the bride of the Scotch king,[5] an event by

[1] Introduction to the close rolls, by T. D. Hardy, Esq., p. xlv.
[2] The name of this nurse was Hodierna. See printed close rolls, p. 416, b.; and some lands in the parish of Knoyle, in Wiltshire, which were bestowed upon her, still retain the name of Odierne. — Sir Richard C. Hoare's Wiltshire, vol. i., p. 38.
[3] Rot. claus., 3 Henry III., pp. 340, and 355. See also Rot. Lib., 13 H. III., m. 4. Part of Elena's revenues were bestowed, after her death, on Petronilla, the nurse of Prince Edmund. Rot. claus., 36 Hen. III., m. 3.
[4] Patent roll, 19th Hen. III., m. 10 Liberate roll, 24 and 25 Hen. III., in page 15 of Devon's Excerpta, from the Pell rolls. Also Liberate roll, 24 H. III., mm. 10 and 13, in the Tower.
[5] Rymer's Fœdera, vol. i., pt. i., p. 160. Indirect evidence is here afforded that Isabella was the second daughter of King John: otherwise, Eleanora's name would have been placed in this treaty instead of hers, as standing next in age to Joanna. More direct proof is furnished by a letter of King Henry to the Pope, written about 1225, in which he expressly mentions Eleanora as the younger of his two unmarried sisters. Lit. regum apud., Tur. Lond., No. 389. Indeed, wherever the king alluded to his sisters, he

nom eans improbable, seeing that Joanna was then in the
hands of her quondam lover, the Earl of March.

Isabella, however, was never called upon to fulfil this
proviso. Far more· splendid, if not more happy, was the
destiny that awaited her.

It is a curious fact, and one that has hitherto escaped
observation, that negociations took place for the marriage
of Isabella with Henry, King of Germany, son of the Emperor Frederic II., in the year 1225, ten years before her
actual marriage with his father. This appears, from a
letter in the Tower collection, written by the Bishop of
Carlisle to Henry III., when on an embassy in Germany,
one of the objects of which was to bring about this marriage
through the intervention of the Archbishop of Cologne.[1]

The position which the young princess was made to
occupy in these negociations was not a very flattering one.
The commanding influence exercised by the talented emperor caused his alliance and that of his son to be eagerly
courted by the great European powers, and they crowded
in emulation around him, to offer their daughters or nieces,
bribing him to accept them for himself or his son, by out-
bidding each other in the amount of tempting dowries.
The Bishop of Carlisle, who, from his association with the
Archbishop of Cologne, was admitted behind the scenes,
after giving some curiously minute details with respect to
these matrimonial transactions, adds, in speaking of the
emperor, " He indeed thirsts after nothing but the accumulation of money, and we were advised by the Archbishop
to make in all haste such an offer to him as he would not be
likely to reject. The Archbishop of Cologne, whose repre-
sentations of the imperial propensities had drawn forth this
unflattering picture, was, it should be remembered, the

always gave the pre-eminence to Isabella. See Cotton. MS., Julius E I. f.
298, and Harleian MS., 3860.
    [1] See Appendix, I.

confidential friend of the emperor, and therefore the less likely to put his character in an unfair light. The negociations fell through, however, for some unexplained reason, and the King of Germany was married in the same year to Margaret, daughter of the Duke of Austria.[1]

A project was next set on foot for marrying Isabella to the King of France, the far-famed Saint Louis. There is still in existence the rough draft of a treaty between Henry and Louis, which was to be cemented by the marriage of each king with the sister of the other;[2] but this scheme also fell through.

As Isabella grew up she did not remain with her brother, but had a separate establishment of her own. In November, 1229, she went to reside at the castle of Merleberg, which had the previous year been put into repair;[3] and the constable of the castle was ordered by king Henry to allow her to select such of the royal apartments as she chose, for her own use.[4] A friendly connexion still subsisted between Isabella and Henry, for soon after this he sent her word that he had himself defrayed the expenses attending the marriage of her "damsel Katherine."[5] In 1231 and 1232, we find her again an inhabitant of the castle of Gloucester.[6] Several curious entries in the close rolls occur about this time with reference to her. On the 13th of November, 1231, William, the king's tailor, is commissioned to go in his own person to the *fair* at St. Edmondsbury, and there to purchase, besides sundry articles for his master's wear, a tunic, surtunic, and cloak, of blue cloth, furred with miniver, and others of Kentish green, together with a cape of muir furred with doeskin, for the Lady Isabella.[7] The idea of purchasing royal apparel at a fair seems strange to us, but at that period

---

[1] Chron. Augustensis, Freher, vol. i., p. 520. Ricard. St. Germ. Muratori, vol. vii., col. 999. Herman Corner, Echard, vol. ii., col. 856.
[2] Royal Letters, Tower of London, No. 917.
[3] Rot. claus., 13 Hen. III., m. 8.　　[4] Rot. claus., 14 Hen. III., m. 21.
[5] Ibid., m. 13.　　[6] Ibid., 16 Hen. III., m. 8.　　[7] Ibid., m. 19.

almost all commercial transactions took place in these assemblies. The Christmas present bestowed by King Henry on his sister was three dishes and three salt-cellars of silver,[1] and a few months afterwards he gave her a chalice, silvergilt, with two altar-towels for her chapel, besides one surplice and a pair of palls.[2] The provisions for herself and family were to be made by "two or three honest men" of the city of Gloucester;[3] but the king contributed largely to her larder himself by gifts of wine and deer, and also had a tract of one of his fisheries set apart for her use.[4] The entries for Isabella are less frequent in the following year. She is twice named as receiving small presents of venison from the king,[5] and an order occurs that Warin, the chaplain of the king, whom he has sent to be chaplain to Isabella, shall receive adequate support for two horses and two men for his own use.[6] In the summer of 1232, she again removed to Merleberg. As she advanced in age, she seems to have acquired additional importance, for the bailiffs of Merleberg were ordered to allow her the whole of the revenues of the place, and several entries occur for the payment of large sums of money for her expenses.[7]

In 1234 she became an inmate of the Tower of London. It was in the reign of Henry III. that this venerable structure first became a frequent royal residence instead of a mere fortress. "To the lover of antiquity and the inquirer into the manners of the early ages," says Mr. Bayley, in his History of the Tower,[8] "it must be subject of lasting regret that no description has been handed down to us of the domestic apartments of this ancient seat of royalty, and more particularly as no remains of them are now to be traced." Indeed, whoever now visits the interior of the White Tower —some apartments of which are appropriated to the State

---

[1] Rot. claus., 16 Hen. III., m. 18.   [2] Ibid., m. 13.   [3] Ibid., m. 10.
[4] Ibid., mm. 6 and 18. Rot. lib., 17 Hen. III., m. 11.
[5] Rot. claus., 17 Hen. III., mm. 6 and 8.   [6] Ibid., m. 8.
[7] Rot. lib., 17 H. III., mm. 12, 5, 2.   [8] Vol. i., p. 214.

Records and consequently occupied by presses, and the remainder still more disfigured by their appropriation as store-rooms for the board of ordnance—will find that it requires an extraordinary stretch of imagination to recall the times when belted knights and courtly ladies trod the rush-strewn floor of the great painted hall, amidst the rude and luxurious pomp of the royalty of olden times. The royal chapel dedicated to St. John, now known by the name of Cæsar's chapel or William the Conqueror's chapel, is the least altered, and, in the rough simplicity of its Norman arches and columns with their carved capitals, still remains a venerable relic of remote antiquity. This chapel was used for the devotions of the royal household in the reign of Henry III., and he bestowed considerable pains and expense upon it.[1] The other principal apartments were the great hall, which was painted with a history of Antiochus,[2] and the king's chamber of state. The private apartments occupied the remainder of the White Tower,[3] excepting the ground-floor, which was appropriated to the garrison; and they also extended into the Lanthorn Tower and the Cradle Tower, which are supposed to have been built in the reign of William Rufus. In the absence of all authentic information as to the origin of the name of the Cradle Tower, we may hazard a conjecture that it was so called because there were situated the nursery apartments of the royal family.

[1] "In the year 1240, that great patron of the arts, King Henry III., gave particular directions for repairing and ornamenting this chapel, and among other things that were ordered to be made, were three glass windows, one towards the north, with a little Mary holding her child, and two others towards the south, representing the Holy Trinity, and St. John the Apostle and Evangelist. The cross and rood were also to be painted well and with good colours; and there were likewise to be made and painted, where it could best and most properly be done in the said chapel, two fair images—one of them of St. Edward holding a ring and presenting it to St. John the Evangelist."—Bayley's Tower, vol. i., p. 114.

[2] Rot. claus., 36 Hen. III., m. 11.

[3] So called from the custom of whitening its walls, to preserve them.—See Rot. Lib., 25 Hen. III., m. 20; quoted by Bayley, vol. i., p. 107.

When the court was at the Tower, as was frequently the case, Isabella of course formed one of the royal circle, and when the king was absent at the different country residences, where most of his time was spent,[1] she generally remained behind, and he continued to show his kindly remembrance of her by sending her presents of wine, must, &c.[2]

Notwithstanding this apparent cordiality, a considerable degree of mystery hangs over the residence of the princess in this fortress. It was very unusual for one who, as being the elder sister of the yet unmarried king, should have occupied a conspicuous station at court, to be thus kept aloof and so often alone, and the expression used by Matthew Paris, that she was "in vigilant custody,"[3] seems to imply more than a mere voluntary detention. No clue can however now be found to lead to a discovery of the reasons for this honorary imprisonment, if such it should be considered; it must remain in the obscurity in which ages have wrapped it.

In the autumn of the year 1234, however, fresh negociations were entered upon for the marriage of Isabella, but this time it was in a manner rather more favourable to the feminine dignity of the princess, for she was the wooed and not the wooer. Her suitor was no less a person than the Emperor Frederic of Germany, who, having ten years previously rejected her as the bride of his son, yet now, finding that an English alliance would be congenial to his interests, condescended to sue for her hand for himself. Frederic wrote to King Henry, appointing the celebrated Peter de Vineâ his chancellor, procurator of the marriage. His letter opens with a long disquisition on the blessings and advantages of the wedded state, which sounds oddly enough as proceeding from one so notorious for his licentious conduct

[1] Chron. Barth. Norwich, Cotton MS., Nero, c. v., f. 190, b., et seq.
[2] Rot. claus., 18 Hen. III., mm. 2, 19, 16. Paris, vol. ii., p. 414.
[3] Vol. ii., p. 414.

as was the emperor—he goes on to express his intention to marry the said lady, and assigns to her extensive dowry lands with which Peter is to invest her on the conclusion of the arrangements. This epistle bears date the 15th of November.[1] It was followed shortly after by a bull from Pope Gregory on the same subject, and in favour of the match.[2] That Gregory IX. was an active promoter of this union is manifest from a letter he wrote on the occasion to the French king, accompanied by one from Frederic himself, assuring him that the alliance would not prove at all derogatory to the interests of France,[3] for great alarm was excited at the French court by the prospect of so close a connexion between two such powers as England and Germany.

Early in the year 1235, Peter de Vineâ arrived in England, and under his able diplomatic supervision the affair was speedily brought to a decision. He was accompanied by two Teutonic knights hospitallers and several other messengers, and they wended their way to Westminster, where the court was then staying, bearing with them the imperial letters sealed with the golden seal,[4] and made their formal petition for the hand of the princess. Although the matter had been previously negociated, Henry with equal formality demanded three days in which to take the

---

[1] Rot. claus., 19 Hen. III., p. 2, m. 6. Printed, though under a false date, in Rymer's Fœdera, vol. i., pt. i., p. 220.

[2] Dated, December 5th. Rymer, vol. i., pt. i , p. 220.

[3] Red Book, in the Queen's Remembrancer office, f. 171.

[4] Matthew Paris gives us a minute description of this seal, which he says was larger than that of the Pope. The image of the emperor on the obverse side was circumscribed, "Fredericus Dei gratiâ imperator et semper Augustus;" over the right shoulder was written, "Rex Jerusalem," and over the left, "Rex Siciliæ." On the reverse was the city of Rome, circumscribed, "Roma caput mundi tenet orbis frœna rotundi."—Vol. ii., p. 358. Frederic was the first emperor who uniformly adopted the title of semper Augustus.—Heineccius de vet. Sig. p. 106-7. The reverse, as described by Paris, is given in Uredius geneal. Fland., p. 19. In the obverse there is a little discrepancy between the two writers as to the inscription.—See Uredius and Heineccius ut supra. Also, Wilhelmus Heda de episcop. Ultraj., p. 212, and Ludewig reliquiæ diplomat., vol vii., p 515.

opinion of his councillors on the subject. Dazzled by the splendour of the alliance, not a thought was bestowed by the king or his nobles as to the probabilities of happiness for the gentle maiden whose fortunes were thus completely placed at their mercy. The point was soon decided, and an announcement conveyed to the imperial ambassadors that their mission was successful.

Upon this they immediately requested an interview with their future empress. Henry consented, and trusty messengers were despatched to the Tower to conduct the princess to court. All possible pains were taken to set her off to the best advantage : she was arrayed in her richest attire, adorned with jewels, and conveyed to Westminster, where the king her brother and the ambassadors of her future lord were waiting in state to receive her.[1]

The situation of a young lady, thus led into an august assembly for the express purpose of being scrutinized as to her personal appearance, was not the most pleasing in the world, and might well excite the blush of maiden modesty that is said to have mantled her cheek on this occasion ;[2] but Isabella was well fitted to stand the test, for she was exceedingly lovely in person, and after the German knights "had recreated their vision awhile with the inspection of the virgin," says Matthew Paris, "they pronounced her most worthy of the imperial nuptials." The oaths which they had formerly sworn to the king they now confirmed in the presence of Isabella, and then the chief person of the embassy, approaching her, presented her with the spousal ring which had been sent to her by the emperor. As he placed it on her finger, he formally declared her the empress of the whole Roman empire, and instantly the air resounded with acclamations of "Long live the empress !" Isabella, on her part, sent a ring to her lord in token of her acceptance of his troth, after which Peter de Vineâ presented

[1] Paris, vol. ii., p. 414.   [2] Ibid.

to her the imperial letters patent, investing her with the dower lands which she was to possess as Empress and Queen of Sicily. This ceremony took place on the 22nd of February,[1] 1235, and notification of it was forthwith sent to the emperor both by Henry and his own ambassadors.

The English king appears to have been considerably elated on the occasion, for two days afterwards he wrote letters announcing the event to his sister, queen Joanna of Scotland, and to some of the principal persons of the realm, lay and clerical, as well as to the Pope.[2] The legal arrangements were hastened forward, and on the 27th of February the marriage contract was signed and sealed.[3] In it allusion is made for the first time to the *personal* consent of Isabella to the union. The dowry bestowed by King Henry upon his sister was 30,000 marks of silver, of which only a small proportion was to be paid immediately, and the rest at certain fixed periods during the ensuing two years; but it was distinctly stipulated that this sum was to be paid over and above the necessary outlay for plate, jewels, horses, and attire, with which she was to be provided, "according to what it was suitable for such a lady to possess, and for such a lord to receive."[4]

Matters being thus settled, the Chancellor Peter returned to report his success at home, and Frederic immediately despatched an august train of nobles, headed by the Archbishop of Cologne, the chief prelate of the empire, and the Duke of Brabant and Louvain to England, to accompany his expected bride on her journey to her future home. At the same time, the Pope, Gregory IX., wrote to Henry,

[1] Matthew Paris, vol. ii., p. 414, says that it was on the 28th; but the documentary evidence of the close rolls is decisive on the subject. See Rymer, vol. i., pt. i., pp. 223 and 224, where, though the year is miscalculated, the day is given correctly.
[2] Close roll, 19 Hen. III., pt. i., m. 19, dorse and pt. 2. m. 6.
[3] Ibid., pt. 2, m. 7.
[4] Paris, vol. ii., p. 417. The arrangements for the dowry, both as to the amount and the time of payment, were made by the Pope. Martènes Collectio amplissima, vol. ii., col. 1247.

entreating him to allow Isabella to proceed at once to Germany, and not to interpose any unnecessary delays. The ambassadors arrived in the beginning of the month of May, and each of them solemnly took an oath on the gospels that the emperor should both marry and crown Isabella, and treat her with all honour and conjugal affection, and that, in case of his death before these terms were fulfilled, she should be allowed to return safe to England.[1]

The interval occupied by these negociations had been most sedulously employed in equipping the young bride. Henry, on this occasion, indulged to the utmost his love for sumptuous display; and he was the better enabled to gratify his taste, because the Parliament, in consideration of the honour conferred by the alliance, granted a special subsidy of two marks on every knight's fee as a dowry for his sister.[2] We quote from Matthew Paris,[3] who grows quite eloquent in his descriptions. "So great was the preparation made for these nuptials, that it seemed to exceed all royal and even imperial riches. A crown was made for her [the princess] of the most cunning workmanship of the purest and finest gold, and adorned with precious stones. In rings and necklaces of gold set with gems, in caskets and trappings, and other feminine ornaments, in copious treasures of gold and silver, in the splendid equipments of her horses and train which ravished the eyes of the beholder with delight—in all these did the king not only abundantly but superabundantly enrich the departing one. All her innumerable vases, goblets, and dishes were of glittering gold or silver gilt, wrought with such curious devices, that the value of the material was enhanced by that of the workmanship. Her pans and cooking vessels, pitchers and wine cups, dishes and platters were of silver." The account of

[1] Close roll, 19 Hen. III., pt. ii., m. 4.   Rymer, vol. L, pt. i., p. 226.
[2] Madox, History of the Exchequer, vol. i., p. 593.
[3] Vol. ii., pp. 414-15.

the chronicler is fully borne out by documentary evidence. In a memorandum roll of presents, given and received by Henry the preceding Christmas,[1] several entries occur of plate and other valuables presented to the king, opposite to which is a note signifying that they were given to Isabella, the king's sister, to carry away with her. Among these was a table and tablets of Sardinian ivory, which the Countess of Ponthieu had given to the king, and a chess-table and chess-men, enshrined in a casket of ivory, which he had received from the prior of Jerusalem;[2] also twenty-four zones of silk and goldsmiths' work, gifts to the king from Adam of Shoreditch, and other goldsmiths. These bands were at that time, and long after, among the most costly articles of female attire, and were frequently set with jewels of great value.

Another roll in the Tower contains a full and complete

---

[1] Miscellaneous rolls in the Tower. No. 31.

[2] The game of chess was a favourite amusement of the higher ranks at this period. The Cotton MS., Cleopatra, A ix., ff. 4-10, contains a curious poem in old French, on chess, with a strange legend of a game played by two barons in the olden time, one of whom staked his head and the other his daughter on the issue! It is illustrated by several illuminations of the game in different stages, with instructions in prose for playing it—the writing is of the latter end of the thirteenth or beginning of the fourteenth century. In the wardrobe-book of the 29th of Edward I., ff. 150, 151, entries occur for *families* of ivory, jaspar, and crystal, to play chess with, and Edward I. himself often played the game, as alluded to in the copy of the wardrobe-book of 6 Edward I., by Craven Ord, Middlehill MS., No. 1003, fol. 3. The first book ever printed in England was a small treatise of the game of chess, translated from the French by Caxton, and issued from his press, in March, 1474, when it was set up in the Almonry of Westminster Abbey.—(Smith's History of London and Westminster, p. 429, note.) On the Continent, the game was played even earlier than in England. Prince Henry, son of William the Conqueror, afterwards Henry I., whilst on a visit at the court of France, played with the young dauphin Louis, when a quarrel arose, which ended in Louis' throwing his chessmen into the face of his young antagonist, who returned the compliment by a blow with the chess-board, which so enraged the French prince that Henry had to fly the court at once.—(Cron. de Norm., 12mo., Rouen, 1610, fol. 1186.) The origin of the game is ably discussed by M. Freret, in Memoires de l'Academie des Inscriptions et Belles Lettres, vol. v., p. 250. A very ingenious little treatise on chess was written by Ruy Lopez, a Spaniard, in which the author asserts that it is not only a praiseworthy occupation, but even necessary to existence! This treatise was translated into Italian, and printed at Venice as early as 1584.

inventory of the wardrobe of Isabella,[1] giving, with minute exactness, the quantity of material comprised in each article of dress, with the covers and hampers required to pack them in; for in former times, as well as in the present day, the conveyance of a lady's wardrobe was a matter of great difficulty and importance; and in noting, in the old wardrobe accounts, the formidable preparations made for this purpose, one is reminded of Napoleon's impatient exclamation, that he would rather have to convey the baggage of a regiment of his army, than the bandboxes of the empress and her waiting-women.

Isabella appears to have had some anxiety to consult the German fashions in the future arrangements of her apparel, for she carried with her a large quantity of material for dresses not made up. The number of her robes amounted to fourteen, three of which were of silken cloth of gold, and two of the rich embroidered material called Arras,[2] which, from its subsequently being employed for sumptuous hangings, we now associate solely with tapestry—these were furnished with tunics and surtunics of the same, and trimmed with the fur, then so fashionable, called, from its variegated colours, *minute vair*,[3] or *miniver*; two other robes were of scarlet cloth, one of blue, two of green cambric, at that time a very expensive article; the others were of inferior quality, two being of the now despised material called camlet. To these were added a due number of capes, sleeves, cloaks, tunics, and surtunics, and also hose. There is not any mention made of gloves. As yet these appendages seem only to have been worn by knights as a part of their military and hunting accoutrements, although they became common

[1] Rot. miscel., ap. Tur. Lond., No. 12.

[2] So called from being first made at the town of Arras, in Flanders; the place became, in the fourteenth century, so celebrated for its tapestries, that the finest cloths assumed the name of "cloths of Arras," even though not made there. The Italians still call fine tapestries, "Arrazi."—Jubinal, Recherches sur l'Usage el l'Origine des Tapisseries, p. 21.

[3] The word *vair* is still in use as an heraldic term.

for ladies in the succeeding reign. Eight ells of scarlet were bestowed upon the trappings of Isabella's saddle, which, considering the frequency of her journeys on horseback, formed an essential part of her equipment. Among her wardrobe entries, there is one which shows the minuteness of the royal surveillance over her wants—it is for two capes of scarlet, containing 5¾ ells each, one of which was to be lined with silk, and the other furred, to be worn "when she first rose from bed," probably as *robes de chambre*, or dressing-gowns. She took with her two beds, hung with Genoese cloth of gold, and one with arras cloth; and two blankets were provided for them; the whole of her chamber-linen consisted of only two napkins and thirteen towels. She had the requisite furniture for her private chapel, of which such articles as were within the wardrobe department are inventoried on the roll already alluded to; the list comprises linen vests, capes, chasubles, Dalmaticas, and other priestly garments, the napkins for the altar, and a splendid altar-cloth of Genoese cloth of gold.[1] The inventory of her plate and jewels is not in existence, but doubtless they were on the same scale of magnificence.

Neither did the king confine his attention to her own personal wants—he sent six robes to the emperor, one of which was of imperial scarlet; robes were also presented to Peter de Vineâ and the other members of the embassy, and to the *stage players* of the Archbishop of Cologne and the Duke of Brabant. The attendants of the empress, her chaplain, clerk, physician, chambermaids, a knight-templar, whom she employed as messenger, her cook, salterer, washerwoman, and many others whose names are given, though not their offices, were also furnished with robes; she had a complete suite of servants to attend her and minister to her wants in regal fashion, and to take charge of her multiform apparatus—at the head of whom was placed Ralph, the son of the king's seneschal,

[1] Miscellaneous rolls at the Tower, No. 12.

and others from the royal household, with a goodly train of noble matrons and damsels well exercised in all that pertained to their several departments.[1] From this splendid array, however, many of her former female attendants were dismissed, perhaps as not being of sufficient rank to serve her in her new capacity, but ample provision was made for them by her brother.[2]

The Bishop of Exeter, William de Bruvière, was appointed to take charge of the princess and her train; but before their departure a grand farewell entertainment was given by King Henry, on the 6th of May, at Westminster, at which the Archbishop of Cologne, the Duke of Brabant, and the other imperial ambassadors were present. The following day Isabella set forward on her journey, but the parting scene was delayed awhile longer, for the king, Prince Richard, and the whole court accompanied her to the sea-shore.[3] The procession was principally an equestrian one: Isabella herself was a graceful rider, and King Henry had provided so many splendidly equipped horses and palfreys for the royal party, that no less admiration was excited by their beauty, than by the agreeable ease of their riders.[4]

The journey of the first day was to Dartford, thence through Rochester to the abbey of Faversham, and from there to Canterbury, where the party performed their devotions at the shrine of the far-famed St. Thomas of Canterbury, and at length they reached the port of Sandwich. During their progress, the knights had increased to the number of 3,000, yet they did not lack handsome entertainment, for the king had issued his mandates to the neighbouring abbeys as he passed along, that each should furnish accommodation for a certain number of the attendants and

[1] Paris, vol. ii., p. 415.   [2] Rot. pat., 19 Hen. III., m. 10.
[3] Chron. Tewks., Cotton MS., Cleopatra, A. vii., f. 30 b.
[4] Paris ut sup., Chron. Tewksb. ut supra.

horses, who were conducting his sister.[1] Preparations for her voyage were already in progress; orders had been previously sent to the bailiffs of Norfolk and Suffolk to provide ten ships for her passage,[2] and the 11th of May was the day appointed for the embarkation. " Nor were tears wanting," says our chronicler, " when the brother parted from the sister, the king from the empress."[3] It cannot be matter of surprise if tears of unwonted bitterness suffused the eyes of the young Isabella, for, in addition to the sorrow she might feel at her approaching separation from home and friends, her anticipations of future happiness must have been but faint in becoming the third wife of a man whose age so far exceeded her own, and of whose conjugal character she would in all probability have heard rumours that would fill her mind with undefined apprehensions, since it was currently reported that his last wife Yolande, of Jerusalem, had fallen a victim to his resentment. The cause of the discord between the emperor and the princess of Jerusalem was that the emperor formed a violent attachment to a beautiful young cousin of his wife, who had accompanied her to Europe, and whom he compelled to become his mistress, and when the empress resented the injury, he imprisoned her, and her death soon afterwards was strongly suspected to have been caused by poison.[4]

When the last sorrowful adieus had been exchanged, the lady Isabella with all her company of knights and ladies embarked, and, after a tedious sail of three days and nights, they reached the mouth of the Scheldt, and, steering their course along its winding and intricate waters, another day and night brought them to the city of Antwerp, where at

[1] Paris, vol. ii., p. 415.
[2] Rot. pat., 19 Hen. III., m. 11.
[3] Paris, vol. ii., p. 415.
[4] Martin Pole's Chronicle, Royal MS. 13, c. vii., f. 34. Naugelièr, bish. Saint Brien, Middlehill MS. 1852. Cont. William of Tyre, Martène, Col. amp., vol. v., col. 696. Histoire de Jean de Brienne roy de Jerusalem, 12mo., Paris, 1727, p. 351.

length they landed. Here a long train of German nobles, in full military equipment, met their new empress, and joined themselves to the band which was to form her future escort. Nor was it merely as an honorary guard that they were thus appointed. It has already been seen with what a jealous eye France regarded these nuptials which would unite Germany and England in such strict friendship, and the earliest steps of the empress on the continent were fraught with danger, for a scheme had been entered into by the confederates of France to waylay and carry her off. News of this plot had however been communicated to Frederic, and the consequent vigilance of the imperial guards, who encamped day and night around her person, precluded the possibility of its execution.[1]

From Antwerp her journey began to assume a more cheerful character. In all the towns and villages through which she passed, the neighbouring priests and monks came forth to meet her in procession, clad in their most costly garments, and bearing lighted tapers; while the bells rang their merriest peals, and all those who were skilled in music were brought into requisition to salute her with a joyful chorus as she passed.

After a progress of five days thus made, they approached the city of Cologne, which they entered on the 22nd of May.[2] Here preparations were made on a very extensive scale to do honour to the young empress; ten thousand citizens, clad in festive garments, and decked with jewels, went out on horseback to meet her, with garlands and flowers, and when they came up with the procession they parted, and began a mimic fight, spurring on their steeds to execute rapid manœuvres, and showing their skill in darting spears and other missiles at each other. This being

---

[1] Paris, ut sup.
[2] Annales Godefridi St. Pantaleonis, Freher Rer. Germ. Script. Ant., vol. i., p. 400. Paris, vol. ii., p. 415.

over, another pageant drew near, in which we trace the
rudiments of those allegorical and fanciful spectacles that
afterwards became so popular; it consisted of the representation of several ships rowing on the dry ground, which
were borne along by horses concealed under silken drape-
ries: an uncouth device, it must be owned, but its clumsi-
ness was compensated by the delightful music that issued
from the decks of these mimic vessels, for they were filled
with priests, bearing organs and other musical instruments,
which they accompanied in such a manner with their voices,
that we are told " the hearers were ravished with their
melodies." [1]

The entry into Cologne was made on horseback,[2] amidst
such enthusiastic rejoicings that the whole city seemed to
overflow with joy. The principal streets through which
the route lay to the archiepiscopal palace, where Isabella
was to take up her abode, were ornamented in the most
beautiful style : this was done by special command of the
emperor, not merely in token of welcome to his bride, but
to impress the minds of the noble English who formed her
escort with suitable ideas of the wealth of this imperial
city. To the inhabitants, however, the empress herself was
the great object of attraction. The terraces and houses
were crowded with eager throngs waiting to obtain a
glimpse of her; but, to the great disappointment of the
populace, and more especially of the female part, she made
her appearance closely veiled. When Isabella was informed
of their anxiety to behold her, she condescended to gratify
the matrons and damsels of Cologne, whose curiosity,—alas
for the proverbial weakness of the sex!—is distinctly alluded
to by Matthew Paris, and removed the hood and veil by
which her features had been concealed. The graceful

[1] Paris, ut sup.
[2] Chron. de Philippe Mouskes, vol. ii., p. 599, Collection de Chroniques
Belges.

humility of this act, together with the striking beauty of
Isabella's person, combined to excite the warmest admiration, even among the phlegmatic Germans. "They delighted their eyes," says our chronicler,[1] "with the aspect
of her serene beauty, and heaped blessings upon her."
Thus was she conducted in triumph to the stately palace,
which was the residence of the archbishop. But, wearied
as she must have been with the fatigues of her journey,
the loyal zeal of the people allowed her no repose; during
the whole night a chorus of singing girls, accompanying
their voices with their instruments, serenaded beneath her
windows, while a thousand armed men were keeping watch
on the walls and in the city, in case of alarm or danger.[2]

Isabella's stay in Cologne was prolonged to a length very
unusual in a bridal progress. When she arrived in Germany, her intended spouse was engaged in warfare with his
eldest son Henry, the King of Germany, whose repeated
rebellions provoked him to such a degree that when at
length his son, hopeless of successful resistance, threw himself at his feet imploring pardon, instead of granting the
petition, he committed him to the custody of one of his
nobles, to be kept prisoner at Worms.[3] About six weeks
elapsed after Isabella's arrival at Cologne, before matters
were so far arranged that the busy emperor had time to
complete his nuptial arrangements. During this period she
had resided principally with the archbishop, but the latter
part of the time she spent with one of the civic authorities,
the provost of St. Gereo, by whom she was entertained with
the honour due to her exalted rank.[4]

At last, however, a summons arrived from the emperor,
requesting that she would proceed in all haste to Worms.

[1] Paris, ut supra.   [2] Ibid., vol. ii., p. 416.
[3] Schoettgenius Diplom. et Script. Germ. medii ævi, vol. i., p. 51.
Tortinus Rer. Ital. Scriptores, vol. i., p. 106.
[4] Annal. Godefridi Freher, vol. i., p. 400.   Philippe Mouskes, vol. ii.,
p. 519.

Accordingly she again set forth with her train, comprising
the Archbishop of Cologne, the Duke of Brabant, the Bishop
of Exeter, and the other English nobles who attended her ;
and after a journey of seven days, which was conducted as
before amidst much pomp and rejoicing, they reached the
city of Worms, where the young princess was presented to
her plighted lord. She was received by him with great
ceremony and gladness; with her personal appearance he
was delighted beyond measure, nor did her manners gratify
him less, and he is said to have found her pre-eminent in
learning and eloquence.[1] Whether she was equally pleased
with him, our chroniclers have not taken the trouble to
inform us. It might be however that her first impressions
were favourable, for though Frederic was now in his forty-
second year and had been already twice married, he was
strikingly handsome and majestic in his appearance. His
portrait as depicted on his seal is juvenile, with long flowing
hair, his robe clasped with a fibula at the neck, and the
imperial mantle hanging over the right shoulder; but this
was probably taken in his youth. The portraits of him on
his later coins are distinguished by the keen eye and aqui-
line nose, which give a strong expression of acuteness and
penetration to his physiognomy, and his brows are encircled
by the laurel wreath.[2] The emperor's demeanour was
noble and dignified. His earliest associations had been
such as to inspire exalted ideas: he was born heir of the
Sicilian throne in right of his mother Costanza, who is said
to have educated him from infancy for empire,[3] and when
he was only two years old he was elected King of the Romans. The year following, on the death of his father, he
was crowned King of Sicily and Apulia,[4] and had but

[1] Paris, vol. ii., p. 416.
[2] Grævius Thes. Antiq. Siciliæ, vol. viii., table. A classical-looking
portrait of him is to be found in Raumer's Geschichte Hohenstaufen, vol. iii.,
but is of dubious authenticity.
[3] Martin's Chron., MSS., Bib. Reg. 13, c vi., f. 72, b.
[4] Hoveden, p. 449.

reached his seventeenth year, when he was, by unanimous
consent, chosen Emperor of the West. It is not to be
wondered at, that the impress of power was stamped on a
brow that had so long been encircled by the crown.

The marriage of Frederic and Isabella was solemnized
with great splendour on the 20th of July, at Worms,[1] and
the imperial crown was placed on her head by the Archbishop of Mayence.[2]   In the margin of the celebrated original MS. of Matthew of Paris, said to be written with his
own hand, is a drawing of this marriage.[3]   The figures are
only about three inches in height, but, considering the period
of their execution, they are well drawn.   The emperor,
crowned and robed, is in the act of stepping forward with
the plight ring which he holds in his right hand, whilst the
left is uplifted as though in asseveration of his vows.   His
features and attitude indicate eager earnestness; Isabella
also wears a crown—her surtunic, which is full and reaches
to the ground, is confined by a band at the waist: the
mantle, thrown loosely over her shoulders, sweeps the ground,
and is held up by her left hand, while the right is extended
to receive the nuptial ring.   The expression of the countenance is meek, subdued, and sorrowful—the figure of a
medium height, slight and graceful.   Although such a rude
sketch can scarcely be considered a faithful portraiture of
the princess, yet, as the limner was so intimately associated
with the court of Henry III., it may be presumed to be
tolerably correct in general contour.

Four kings, eleven dukes, and thirty earls and marquesses,
besides the ecclesiastical dignitaries, graced the imperial
nuptials with their presence.   One particular circumstance

[1] Chron. Elwayense Freher, vol. i., p. 678. Herman Corner Echard,
vol. ii., col. 863.   Chron. Tewkesbury, Cotton MS., Cleopatra, A. vii., f. 31.
Hoffman's Annals of Bamberg, Ludevig, Rer. Germ. script., vol. i., p. 156,
gives the 8th kalends of August, or the 25th of July, as the date of the
marriage.
[2] Chron. Tewksb., Cotton MS., Cleop. A. vii., f. 31.
[3] Royal MS., No. 14, c. vii., fol. 225.

is noted as connected with the wedding festivities, viz., that the emperor requested the princes and nobles of the court to refrain from squandering their money among mimics and stage-players, as had been their wont on festal occasions.[1] Such an injunction would seem necessary when the love of theatricals was so prevalent that the Archbishop of Cologne and Duke of Brabant had actually brought their stage-players into England, during their recent embassy.[2]

After a residence of nearly a month in the city of Worms, the bridal train, with the whole court, proceeded to Mayence, where for four days the nuptial feastings were renewed with as much pomp as before. On the 14th of August, Frederic held an assembly of the princes of the empire,[3] who were eager to offer their congratulations; and, on St. Timothy's day, the 22nd of August, the whole party attended high mass in the cathedral of Mayence,[4] Frederic appearing in imperial splendour, wearing his royal diadem, and the day was closed by a magnificent fête champêtre which was given by the emperor in the neighbouring country.[5]

It was at this time that Frederic held the celebrated diet of Mayence, at which sixty-four princes and upwards of twelve thousand knights and nobles were present.[6] His first act was marked by a gloomy though perhaps merited sternness. He publicly degraded his rebel son Henry, King of Germany, who, it will be remembered, was once the intended husband of Isabella, from his royal dignity, and sentenced him to perpetual imprisonment, in a castle in Apulia, where he died seven years afterwards,[7] suffocated, it was said, by the squalid filth of his prison-house.[8] The

---

[1] Annal. God., p. 400. [2] See page 15.
[3] Johannis rerum Mogunticarum Scriptores, vol. i., p. 597.
[4] Chron. Elway. Freher, vol. i., p. 678. [5] Ann. God., p. 400.
[6] Heinec. de ant. Goslar, p. 250.
[7] Chron. Wil. Mon. Egmond Matthæus, anal. med. ævi, vol. ii., p. 503.
L'Art de Verifier les dates, vol. vii., p. 341. Chron. Zantifliet. Martène, Coll.
amp., vol. v., col. 70.
[8] Martin Pole's Chron., Bib. reg., MS. 13, c. vi., f. 34. Herman Corner
Echard, vol. ii., col. 863. Yet the letter written by the emperor on his

after proceedings of the diet were however of a character which displayed to advantage the energy and abilities of the emperor, for laws and enactments were made that were likely to exercise the most beneficial influence upon the administration of justice throughout his dominions; they had been drawn up mainly under the personal superintendence of Frederic and his able chancellor Peter de Vineâ, or Weingarten, the Germanic synonym being that by which he was more ordinarily designated.[1]

About this time, the Bishop of Exeter and the other English ambassadors who had attended the empress into Germany, having fulfilled their charge, and seen their royal mistress married and crowned, obtained permission to return home, and took their departure for England. The emperor sent to his brother-in-law, King Henry, many precious gifts unknown in England; amongst them were three leopards, significant of the royal arms of England, which were then said to be three leopards passant.[2] They were afterwards called lions, but the change was merely in name, for certainly the grim-looking brutes, with claws to the full as thick as their bodies, which are depicted on the ancient royal shield, would answer just as well for one or the other, since it would puzzle a zoologist to discover which they were most unlike.

No sooner had King Henry's ambassadors withdrawn, than the emperor thought proper to dismiss almost all Isabella's English attendants of both sexes,[3] and committed her exclusively to the care of Moorish eunuchs and haggard old women, precluding her alike from the society and the mode

death expresses deep sorrow for his fate.—(Vinea's Letters, book iv., No. 1.) One contemporary chronicler asserts that Frederic delivered him from captivity in 1238, and that he died the following autumn.—(Chron., anon., Erfurt, Schannat Vindemiæ litterariæ, vol. i. p. 98.

[1] Kohlrausch, deutsche Geschichte, p. 253.

[2] Paris, vol. ii., p. 416.

[3] They returned to England, and several of them were kindly noticed by King Henry — (See Rot. lib., 21 H. III., m. 10, ibid. 24 mm. 6, 3; also Devon's Excerpta, p. 12.

of life to which she had been accustomed, and condemning
her to an almost monastic seclusion. The reason assigned
for these regulations was, that the empress was likely in
time to become a mother; and that, until that period arrived,
it was requisite that she should be solely in the hands of experienced persons, who would take every possible care of her.[1]

Although purposely avoiding any details respecting the
public career of the Emperor Frederic, familiar as they are
to all the readers of history, a few notices of his private
character may serve to throw light upon his singular
treatment of his wife, and to illustrate the life of the empress Isabella, during the few troubled years in which she,
nominally at least, shared the throne of the Kaisers.

Frederic II. was one of the few free thinkers of his age—
he possessed a mind of extraordinary grasp. His intellectual
abilities were of a high order, and he was distinguished by
a love of justice, and by the strictness with which he
caused it to be administered; never refusing to listen himself to the complaints of the poorest of his subjects. In the
midst of the engagements of an ever-busy life, he contrived
to achieve more in actual attainments in science and art,
than many who devote to it the whole energies of their
existence, and was universally pronounced to be the most
learned prince of his time in Europe.[2] He is said to have
well understood Greek, Latin, Arabic, and French, beside
German and Italian.[3] He wrote a work on Falconry, an
amusement of which he was passionately fond,[4] that gave
proof of the most acute investigation of the nature and
habits of birds.[5] He was also a most liberal patron of the

[1] Paris, vol. ii., p. 416.
[2] Menckenius Bibliotheca Virorum Illustrium, p. 203.
[3] Ricardano Malespini Muratori, vol. viii., col. 953.
[4] One of King Henry's presents to him was his " white gier falcon, and
three others of the best he had." Rot. claus., 20 H. III., m. 6.
[5] This treatise has been several times published, with additions, by his son
Manfred. The edition of 1596 is embellished with a rude wood-cut of the
emperor sitting in state, with two falconers on their knees before him, presenting him with birds.

arts; he established schools and academies in several of the
principal cities of his dominions, and placed over them the
most learned men whom he could collect from different
countries, paying their salaries from his own funds, that
they might be able to afford gratuitous instruction to those
who could not otherwise procure it.   The University of
Naples owed its foundation entirely to him.   He is reported
to have been a poet, too, and to have produced verses full of
feeling, life, and music.[1]   He collected a considerable library
for himself, and had many translations made of valuable
works from Greek and Arabic.   The prophecies of the
celebrated Merlin were also translated from Latin into
French by his order.[2]   The zeal with which he prosecuted
his studies in natural philosophy, and encouraged them in
others, had the happiest effect in forwarding the science of
medicine.[3]   Nor did he stop here; the ceaseless activity of
his mind led him to pry into the inmost recesses of nature;
and, as an easy consequence, he was brought to partake the
wild dreamings of those who professed to acquire, by their
mysterious practices, a strange mastery over the hidden
powers of nature—and the astrologers and alchemists of the
day found in him a patron and a friend.   Among these was
" the mighty wizard, Michael Scott,"[4] whose name has
been rendered so familiar to the ears of every reader, by the
glowing pen of Sir Walter Scott.   This strange being, himself perhaps as much the deceived as the deceiver, found
Frederic willing to enter with enthusiasm into his eager
researches after those unfathomable mysteries, the solution

[1] Kohlrausch's Deutsche Geschichte, p. 251.
[2] A copy of this translation is in the MS., 6772, in the Bibliothèque du
Roi, Paris.
[3] Nicolaus de Janisilla Muratori, vol. viii., col. 495.   Gesta Fred. Imp.
Echard, vol. i., col. 1026.   Thevet vie des hommes illustres, vol. iv., p. 1.
The Arundel MS., No. 295, fol. 1196, contains a curious recipe, said to be
given by the Emperor Frederic, of a charm to cure wounds, but it savours
more of the prevalent superstition of the age than of medical skill.
[4] Ricobald Hist. Echardi Scriptores, vol. i., col. 1170.

of which they fondly deemed might be attained. He was appointed astrologer to the imperial court;[1] and, strange as is the picture which presents itself to the mind's eye, of the kaiser laying aside his imperial robes to share the lonely vigils and magic incantations of the sage, it is no less strange than true; indeed, Frederic did not himself entirely escape the reputation of magical skill.[2] Several of the works of Michael Scott were written at his suggestion, and his work on animals was dedicated to the emperor.[3]

It cannot be matter of surprise that a mind like that of Frederic should discard the trammels of that superstition by which the Church of Rome strove to maintain a dominion, temporal as well as spiritual, over the world. Superstition is the mother of infidelity, and in rejecting an authority which he knew to be founded on a love of power, there seems ground for the fear that Frederic was at heart an infidel. Policy still compelled him to maintain an outward deference to the Romish See, but his true feelings were frequently betrayed in the biting sarcasms in which he indulged. The reports carried to Rome of his keen satires were one main cause of the disagreements and troubles between himself and the holy See.[4] The chroniclers of the day tell us that Frederic was but a lukewarm adherent of Rome, or, rather an ungrateful step-son and bitter persecutor of holy mother Church.[5] Matthew Paris relates a remark which he is said to have made, that

[1] Tytler's Life of Michael Scott, Scottish Worthies, vol. i., pp. 102-3.
[2] Thevet, vol. iv., p. 3.
[3] Dempster Hist. Ecclest. Scotorum, vol. ii., p. 495. This author, who was born in 1579, relates that, when he was a boy, the magic books of Michael Scott were still said to be in existence, but that none durst open them, for fear of the demons which would appear. This popular superstition gave rise to one of the finest passages in the "Lay of the Last Minstrel."
[4] " Sein kuhner Blick traf besonders die Thorheiten seines Zeitalters und er strafte sie oft mit scharfen Spotten; dagegen sah er in jedem, wer, woher, welcher Glaubens er war, nur den Menschen, und ehrte wenn er tüchtig war." Such are the nervous words of Kohlrausch, in his ably drawn character of this monarch.
[5] Martin Pole. MS., Bib. Reg., 13 c. vi., f. 34. Mittarelli Annales Camaldunenses, vol. v., p. 1.

three jugglers, cunning and crafty men, ruled the world, and deluded the universe—Moses, Jesus, and Mahomet.[1] He is also reported to have used some very sarcastic expressions with reference to the personal presence in the eucharist.[2] "Far be it, far be it," exclaims the monk of St. Albans, " from any discreet man, much less a Christian, to have unlocked his lips and tongue, to the utterance of such blasphemies !"

In spite of the consternation of our chronicler, however, truth compels us to acknowledge that, as to the latter part of the charge, Frederic must, on his own confession, stand condemned; for, while he wrote to the Pope denying the remark ascribed to him about the three impostors, he declared he could never be made to believe the dogma of transubstantiation, and more than once openly expressed his ridicule of this doctrine. At the time of his solemn coronation at Rome, an oriental prince, who was with him, inquired the reason of the reverend homage paid both by priests and people to the host. " Their faith is that these wafers are gods," said Frederic—on which the prince very naturally expressed his surprise that the God of the Christians was not consumed, since he was thus eaten every day. On another occasion, when passing with his followers through a field of ripe corn,—" How many gods," he exclaimed, " will be made of this corn in time !"[3] A still more unpardonable offence than his disbelief of transubstantiation, was his open avowal of a wish to reduce the Church to something nearer the purity and simplicity of the apostolic ages.[4]

Unfortunately, in rejecting the superstitions with which the Romish ritual is burdened, Frederic failed to embrace

[1] Vol. ii., p. 482.
[2] For similar accounts see Raynald Ann. Eccles, Anno 1239, Art. 26 and 28.
[3] Heineccius de ant. Goslar, pp. 263-4.
[4] Lambeth MS., No. 419, fol. 56.

that true Christian faith, which, throwing aside all the
superincumbent load of error and ceremonial, taking for its
basis the holy Scriptures alone, addressing itself to the
understanding as well as to the heart, is simple enough to
be intelligible to the meanest capacity, while it is sublime
enough to employ the loftiest, and the emperor seems in
his heart to have thrown away the belief of Christianity
altogether. In judging of his character, however, it should
be remembered that he lived in an age in which learning
and taste were lost in the profitless conceits of the schools,
and in which any one who passed the boundary line of the
learning which was sanctioned by prejudice and superstition
was looked upon with great distrust, and that he is consequently much belied by the Popish writers.[1] Paris, and
several other historians, accuse him of a strong leaning
towards the Moslem faith.[2] Frederic's associations with
the east were intimate, on account of his second marriage
with Yolande, the heiress of Jerusalem, by which he had
become nominal sovereign of that kingdom. He had spent
some time there, and was on the most friendly terms with
several of the oriental princes, and he adopted far more
of the eastern mode of living than was consistent with
European habits and Christian codes of morality.[3] His
palace, thronged with dark-eyed beauties whom he had
brought over in his train, and kept continually near him,
was little better than a harem, and the empress herself,
instead of being the exclusive partner of his home and
affections, occupied a post scarcely more exalted than that
of an eastern sultana.[4] The natural children of the Em-

[1] Heinrich Geschichte des Teutschen reichs, vol. i., p. 290.
[2] Chron. Mailros, edit. Bannat. club, pp. 170-1.
[3] A contemporary chronicler asserts that he was educated, at least
partially, amongst the Saracens, having been sent into the East to escape the
snares laid for him by the jealousy of the Emperor Otho, and that he there
acquired his skill in mechanical arts. Chron. Menconis Matthæus, Analecta
Medii Ævi, vol. ii., p. 171.
[4] Paris, vol. ii., p. 608. Martin Pole, f. 34. Chron. Menconis, ut sup.
Koelerus Entius Frid. imp. filius, p. 4.

peror, Manfred and Entius, were considered as of equal dignity with his legitimate son Conrad, then a boy of seven years of age.[1]

Shortly after his marriage, Frederic was summoned across the Alps, and he left his new-made bride with her step-son Conrad in Germany. Early in the year 1236 Isabella accompanied her husband to Ravenna, where she gave birth to a son, who was named Jordan;[2] but the exultation caused by this eagerly anticipated event was soon after changed into mourning by the death of the young prince, when he was a mere infant. After this time, the empress appears to have been emancipated in some degree from the singular *surveillance* which had been placed over her in the first instance. It might be that Frederic found, on a further acquaintance with his beautiful wife, that her discretion equalled her loveliness, and that he learned to trust her; he seems to have entertained as much regard for her as a man whose mind was wholly divested of all ideas of purity and exclusiveness in attachment can be supposed capable of feeling.

The greater part of the year 1236 was spent by Frederic and Isabella in Italy. He was Italian by descent; Sicily and Apulia had been the kingdoms earliest subjected to his rule, and he seems to have entertained a decided preference for his former dominions, rich as they were in the fairest scenes of nature. But the affairs of the empire were too weighty to leave him much choice as to his place of residence, and he soon afterwards returned with his wife to Germany.

The association between Isabella and her own family was

---

[1] The mother of Entius was Blanche of Montferrat, Marchioness of Lucca. Manfred was by another concubine. Historia Fred. III., imp. Æneas Sylvius, Analecta Monument Vindob., vol. ii., p. 84.

[2] Inveges Annales di Palermo, p. 588. Rocchus Pirrus, Chron. Reg. Sic. Grævius, vol. v., col. 48. Raumer's Geschichte der Hohenstaufen, vol. iii., p. 703, note.

still kept up,[1] because the policy of the emperor required him to maintain those friendly connexions with England, the necessity of which had first led him to seek an English bride; but the intercourse appears to have been conducted in the most formal manner, and little indeed of the heart can be traced in it. In the year 1236, Henry granted a safeconduct to Walter, the ambassador of the emperor and empress;[2] in 1237, a messenger was sent on the part of the empress alone;[3] and soon after, probably on the return of this same ambassador, Henry wrote to Isabella; but the letter is not from the fond brother to the companion and playmate of his earlier years; it is the king of England who addresses the empress of Germany, and not a word occurs breathing of aught more warm than the freezing courtesy of state correspondence.[4] Isabella probably never replied to this epistle, but, if she did, her answer is not preserved.

Henry interested himself in behalf of his imperial brother-in-law, in reference to his quarrels in Lombardy, appealing to the pope and cardinals in his favour,[5] and sending a body of troops, headed by Henry de Turbeville, to assist him. The king was at this time involved in difficulties about the regularly recurring payments of his sister's dowry, which had been stipulated for; having squandered the whole sum granted him by parliament for that purpose, he was obliged to make a two-fold appeal; first, to Pope Gregory, to entreat him to stand surety for the remainder of the money, promising a strict indemnity to the holy See from all loss, and offering to submit to ecclesiastical censure in case of non-payment—and, secondly, to Frederic himself, begging for

[1] Rot. lib., 21 H. III., m. 14. Ibid., 22 mm. 8, 20. Ibid., 25 m. 3.
[2] Dated May 19. Rot. pat., 20 Hen. III., m. 7.
[3] Rot. lib., 21 H. III., m. 14.
[4] Rot. claus., 19 Hen. III., p. 2, m. 1. This roll is a sort of nondescript, as it contains entries for the 20th, and even the 21st of Henry III. The letter is printed in Rymer's Fœdera, vol. i., p. i., p. 229.
[5] Rot. claus., 19 Hen. III., p. ii., m. 1. This was however in the 20th of Hen. III. See previous note.

delay in the period assigned for payment.[1]   In the course
of the following year, however, he contrived to pay off the
whole of the remaining sum,[2] but with great difficulty, for
orders were obliged to be issued, that no money whatever
should be paid from the exchequer, until the emperor's
demands were satisfied.[3]   At the same time, Frederic
was so warmly pressed by ceaseless troubles in the Lombard
states, which were secretly fomented by Pope Gregory—
while, on the other hand, the French king was ready to take
advantage of any disaster—that he was obliged to apply for
assistance to the English monarch,[4] and he entreated that
Prince Richard might be permitted to lead the troops which
Henry agreed to send for his aid against France.   It is
likely that this request was made at the instigation of Isabella, whose heart might well yearn with an earnest desire
to see one of her own relatives again; but the matter being
laid before the English nobles, it was thought inexpedient
that Richard, then the heir presumptive of the crown, should
depart the kingdom, and Henry wrote accordingly, begging
that he might be excused.   No unpleasant feeling was excited by this refusal, however; for, soon after, Frederic sent
a magnificent present to each of his brothers-in-law—to the
king, eighteen valuable horses and three mules, laden with
precious gifts, among which velvets are particularly mentioned.   Richard's present was of a similar character, but
inferior in value.[5]

The spring of the year 1236 was distinguished by an
occurrence, which, if its importance is to be estimated by
the attention it created, deserves at least a passing notice
here.   This was the translation of the body of St. Elizabeth,
one of those royal ladies whose piety had won for her a place

---

[1] Fœdera, vol. i., pt. i., pp. 226 and 228.
[2] Rot. pat., 21 Hen. III., m. 6. Fœdera, vol. i., pt. i., p. 232. Rot. lib.,
21 H. III., mm. 6, 7.
[3] Rot lib., 20 H. III., mm. 9, 10.
[4] Paris, vol. ii., p. 421. Fœdera, vol. i., pt. i., p. 228.
[5] Paris, vol. ii., p. 431.

in the Romish calendar. She was the daughter of Bela, king of Hungary, and widow of Louis, landgrave of Thuringia, and appears to have been a person of a gentle and devout spirit. After the death of her husband, she gave herself up to a religious life, and became eminent for her works of zeal and charity.[1] The ceremony of the removal took place on the 1st of May, and was attended not only by an innumerable concourse of people of the lower orders, but by many chiefs and nobles, at the head of whom was the Emperor Frederic himself, who, whatever his private views might be, had policy enough to fall in with this ebullition of popular fervour. The presence of the empress must be rather conjectured than asserted, since none of our authorities mention her being there. Frederic raised the first stone from the coffin, during the progress of disinterment, and when at length the remains of the royal widow were exposed to the admiring gaze of the crowd, he came forward and placed a golden coronet, from his own treasury, upon the brows of the dead.[2] The body was then deposited in a golden chest, and consigned to the care of the Bishops of Mayence, Treves, and Hildesheim for re-burial, while the holy oil, which was said to have distilled from it, was distributed by the pious monks, and performed, we are told, a variety of miraculous cures.[3]

Immediately after this, Frederic made active preparations for his Italian campaign, and on the 25th of July he took his departure for Lombardy, leaving Isabella in Germany.[4] He was absent from her for some months, but returned in November to spend the winter at home.

The notices preserved of the empress Isabella by the

[1] Chron. Sifrid. Presbyt. Pistorius, vol. i., p. 1043.
[2] Ibid.
[3] Annal. God. Freher, vol. i., p. 401. Addit. Lamb. Schaffnaburg Urstisius, p. 431. Theod. Thuring. de St. Elizab. Canisius Thes. Mon., vol. iv., p. 150.
[4] Rich. de St. Germ. Muratori, vol. vii., col. 1039.

German chroniclers are exceedingly slight, and none of them of that personal or domestic character which would enable us to form an intimate acquaintance with her habits and modes of life; but the probabilities are that, during the frequent absences of the emperor, she lived in quiet but splendid retirement, surrounded only by such menials as the oriental taste of her lord had provided for her. In the February of 1237, she became the mother of a little daughter, to whom the name of Agnes was given, but this child, like the former, died when very young. Frederic wrote a letter to the inhabitants of Palermo on the occasion of its birth, in the conclusion of which he says, " Although the rights of kingdoms and rulers do not rest in females, yet this daughter shall be welcome amongst those of the male sex, since she, a fit harbinger of others to follow, is a most certain pledge of sons, and by the favour of God promises an undoubted progeny of kingly sons to us and to you from the empress our new consort."[1] The inordinate value attached by Frederic to his male offspring, whether legitimate or not, probably made him less heedful of his daughter's early fate.

The emperor passed the year 1237 in Italy, with the exception of a few months, when the dissensions raised against him by the Duke of Austria forced him to recross the Alps, in order to subdue the revolters near home. Having succeeded in this point, he undertook another about which he was deeply interested, namely, the obtaining from the princes of the empire, in full diet, a recognition of his son Conrad, then only nine years old, as King of Germany. The imperial family passed many days together at Vienna amidst festive rejoicings, in which the emperor, laying aside for awhile the weighty cares of royalty, largely participated. He returned to Lombardy at Michaelmas, and remained during the winter,

---

[1] Inveges Annales di Palermo, p. 589. P. de Vin. letters, book iii., No. 71. Rocchus Pirrus Chron. reg. Sic. Graevius, vol. v., col. 48.

having sent for his wife to join him there.[1] He was at this time in frequent communication with Isabella's brother, Richard Earl of Cornwall, whose energetic character was far more consonant to his own, than that of the King of England. He wrote to him on the 4th of December,[2] recounting the successes of his expedition; again on the 11th of February in the following year, 1238, exhorting the prince to fulfil his intention of visiting the Holy Land;[3] and once more on the 3rd of March, upon a topic of more stirring interest. This was the birth of a son, to whom Isabella had given birth on the 18th of February.[4] Frederic oversteps the usual formalities of state etiquette in his warm expressions of exultation on this joyful occasion,[5] and he alludes more than once to the great delight it caused the empress herself, calling upon her brother to sympathize with them both in their joy.

At the time of the birth of this infant, Frederic was absent from home, collecting forces for his summer campaign, nor did he return till more than a month afterwards, as appears from the foregoing letter, and from another that he wrote to the inhabitants of Palermo, announcing the welcome event, both of which are dated from Turin, in the month of March.

Difficulties were now thickly besetting the path of the emperor. His successes in Italy had roused the jealousy of the Holy See, which was increased by his marrying his natural son, Entius, to Adeliza, heiress of the Sardinian throne, and then proclaiming him King of Sardinia, a province to which the Pope had some claim.[6] This, together with former unforgotten causes of discord, brought upon him at length

---

[1] Annal. God. Freher, vol. i., p. 463. Paris, vol. ii., p. 444. Rauch, Rer Austriac. Script., vol. ii., p. 241.

[2] Paris, vol. ii., p. 455. [3] Ibid., p. 466. [4] Ibid.

[5] See also his letter to the inhabitants of Palermo. Epistolæ Petri de Vincis, lib. iii., No. 70.

[6] Ricobald, Echard, vol. i., col. 1174. Henrich, Geschichte des Teutschen reichs, vol. i., p. 283.

the dreaded sentence of excommunication.[1] It was, according to custom, ordered to be pronounced in all Christian countries, and amongst others it was solemnly read at St. Paul's cathedral, London.[2] Whereupon Frederic wrote several indignant letters to his brother-in-law King Henry and to the English barons, expressing his surprise at such a step being allowed.[3] These letters, probably the production of the talented chancellor, Peter Weingarten, are written in a strain of passionate and indignant eloquence.[4]

The energy of Frederic was, however, fully equal to his

---

[1] When the sentence was made known, such was the impression of Frederic's power, that it is said there was not a priest in Germany that could be brought to declare it to him. At last, a Jacobite friar ventured to broach the subject under the guise of fable, as follows:—" Sire," said he, " there was once a lion so fierce and strong that no beast durst attack him ; but, one hot summer day, a fly placed itself between his two eyes and bit him severely. ' Who art thou,' said the lion, ' who darest to bite me?' ' I am a fly,' said the other. ' A fly !' said the lion, ' the most insignificant of beasts ! bite on : if thou wert not the most insignificant beast in existence, thou shouldst pay for it, but I disdain to revenge myself on *thee*.' And, sire," added the friar, " I compare your Majesty to the lion, and myself, in my little estate, to the fly, who pronounce upon you from our holy father the apostle, the sentence which you have incurred by your rebellion against the holy church." " Well," said the emperor, " yet, if it were not for your comparison, and you were in another station, you should repent it." Gray's Scalacronica, edited for the Maitland club, by J. Stevenson, Esq., p. 96.

[2] After the passing of the sentence, Frederic made a point of attending mass and receiving the sacrament, which he had utterly neglected before. Reynaldi Ann. eccles. sub anno, 1239, art. 25.

[3] Fœdera, vol. i., pt. i., p. 237.

[4] The fate of Peter de Vinea, so long the able minister of Frederic, was very melancholy. Having lost the confidence of his master, who suspected him of a design to poison him (Paris, vol. ii., p. 764), he was given up by the emperor to the Pisans, who, for some reason or other, held him in deadly enmity : and they placed him in such rigorous confinement, that, either to escape from present misery or for fear of the future, he dashed out his own brains against the column to which he was chained. L'art de verifier les dates, vol. iii., p. 345. Besides the volume of his published letters, many others are preserved in the Palatine, Barberini, and Vatican libraries. Specimens of his poems may be found in Leoni Allatio's poeti antichi, and Carbinelli's rime antiche. The readers of the Divina Commedia will at once advert to Dante's mention of the unfortunate chancellor in his Inferno, canto xiii., line 58, &c.

> " Io son colui che tenni ambo le chiávi,
> Del cuor di Federigo, e che le volsi,
> Serrando e disserrando, si soávi,
>   Che dal segreto suo quasi ogni uom tolsi:
> Fede portái al glorióso ufizio,
> Tanto ch'io ne perdéi lo sonno e i polsi," &c.

emergencies, and he continued to struggle boldly and successfully with his difficulties. The empress did not remain
with him during the whole of the campaign that ensued.
Wishful that she and her infant should be removed far
away from the bustle and tumult of war, Frederic sent Isabella into his ancestral kingdom of Sicily, choosing for her
an abode near the town of Adrium.[1] Here she spent the
bright vintage months, in a spot where she could luxuriate
at will amidst all the lavish profusion of beauty and fertility
for which the sunny land of Sicily is proverbial.

A curious description is given by a contemporary chronicler of the dress and manners of the Sicilian peasantry at
this period. They must have presented a strange contrast
to those of the more courtly circles, for he tells us that the
men wore a close fitting dress of plates of iron, forming
over the head a hood called maita,[2] and that their other
garments were of unwrought skins. The women wore
tunics of wool, combed, but unwoven. Gold and silver ornaments or embroidery were scarcely known—the married
women were distinguished by the broad vittæ or bands across
the temples, and down both sides of the face and fastened
under the chin. This peculiarity extended also to the higher
ranks.[3] The glory of the men was in their horses, their
arms, and their fortresses, with which every city in Italy
abounded, and luxuries were little esteemed. At table they
were not more refined, the use of separate trenchers was
unknown; the food, consisting of meat cooked with olives,
was served up in one or two large bowls, out of which the
whole family helped themselves, using Nature's own imple-
ments for the purpose: while at supper, candles being unknown, light was afforded by a blazing torch waved in the
hands of one of the party.[4]

[1] Rich. St. Germ. Muratori, vol. vii., col. 1040.
[2] See Du Cange's Glossary, art. Maita.
[3] Heineccius de vet. sig., p. 210.
[4] Ricobald Chron. Echard, vol. i., col. 1170.

In the month of December, 1238, Isabella was summoned
to rejoin her lord; the Archbishop of Palermo was appointed
to be her escort, and under his guardianship she returned
to Lombardy.[1]   The Christmas festivities were celebrated
at Parma, and towards the latter end of January in the
next year, 1239, the emperor went to Padua, where he was
handsomely entertained for several months by the abbot of
the monastery of St. Justina, who, in spite of the thunders
of excommunication which, during this very period, were
hurled upon him from the Vatican,[2] persisted in treating
him with the courtesy due to his exalted rank; he provided
him with a throne and footstool, and other necessary appendages of royalty, and gave him a variety of liberal presents,
among which are noted two sturgeons,[3] a fish that was then
considered a great delicacy.[4]

Isabella did not share in these good things, for she resided
apart from her husband in a mansion at Noenta.[5]   This
might be because a monastery was not considered a fit
place of abode for an empress, but such frequent separations
do not speak much in favour of the affection entertained by
Frederic for his wife.

On account of the spiritual disabilities under which the
anathemas of the Church had placed the emperor, the baptism of Isabella's cherished son was deferred, for his father
was anxious that the supreme pontiff himself should officiate
on so august an occasion, and under present circumstances

---

[1] Rich. de St. Germ. Muratori, vol. vii., col. 1040.
[2] Much of personal rancour blended itself with the political animosity
existing between the Pope and the emperor. Gregory compared his antagonist to the beast mentioned in Revelations, chap. xiii., v. 1 and 2, "like
unto a leopard having on his heads the name of blasphemy;" while Frederic, who, in a trial of satirical skill, was not likely to be behindhand,
compared the holy father to him "on the red horse, to whom it was given
to take peace from the earth, and that they should kill one another." Chap.
vi., v. 4. Kohlrausch, p. 254.
[3] Chron. Mon. Padua, Urstisius, p. 589, printed more correctly in Muratori, vol. vii., col. 678.
[4] Du Cange's glossary, article sturio.
[5] Chron. Padua ut supra.

such an arrangement was of course impracticable, and it remained so during the lifetime of his mother; he afterwards assumed the name of Henry, conferred upon him in compliment to his maternal uncle, Henry III. of England.[1] During the next year or two the Empress Isabella is almost lost sight of, amidst the overwhelming toils and cares which beset the path of her husband. She still remained in Italy, and the gentle gracefulness of her manners, combined with her personal attractions, are said to have produced a deeper impression upon the heart of the emperor.[2] But yet the sentiments with which he regarded her were only those of an eastern despot, who summons his beautiful slave to his presence to wile away a leisure hour, and then dismisses her alike from his sight and his thoughts. At court Isabella seems never to have made her appearance, and though she was surrounded in her seclusion with oriental magnificence and her every want was anticipated, this was but a paltry compensation for that confiding companionship which, as a wife, she had a right to expect, and which she appears to have fully deserved. A friendly correspondence was still kept up between her husband and brother, but in the midst of political business her name is scarcely mentioned.[3]

In the summer of 1241, the imperial court then residing in Sicily, Prince Richard of England landed in that island, on his return from the Holy Land. We have before noticed the degree of intimacy which had arisen between Frederic and his brother-in-law, even when they were at a distance from each other, and he was therefore most cordially welcomed on his arrival. By the emperor's command, his own

[1] The compilers of the new edition of Rymer's Fœdera, who seem determined to misdate every document that has reference to Isabella, have placed the letter, in which Frederic announces to King Henry the *baptism* of his son, under the year 1237, being one year before the *birth* of the prince; while an allusion, in the letter itself, to "our *late* dearest consort Isabella," shows that it was not written till after her death, in 1241. The probabilities are that it should be associated in date with one written by the prince himself to his uncle in 1247, on the same subject.

[2] Paris, vol. ii., p. 548. [3] Rymer's Fœdera, vol. i., pt. i., pp. 236-7, and 241.

seneschal went to meet and receive him, and in the different cities through which he passed he was treated with great honour, the inhabitants coming to greet him with songs and music, bearing in their hands garlands of flowers and palm branches, to do honour to the crusading prince, and to fulfil the wishes of their sovereign. When he arrived at court, he was received with kisses and embraces by the emperor, who ordered for him baths and fomentations and every luxury which his travel-worn condition needed, and they spent many days in mutual colloquies and consultations.[1]

Although Isabella had been so long parted from her own family, yet it never seems to have occurred to Frederic that it would be advisable to admit her to a share of the society of her brother—and when the prince had courteously waited in vain a considerable time in expectation of the empress' appearance, he found himself compelled to make a formal demand to her lord, to be admitted to an interview. His request was granted, not by a summons to Isabella to join the social circle, but by the appointment of a day on which Richard was to visit his sister in her own apartments, where preparations were made for his reception.[2] We are fortunately enabled to accompany the prince into the presence-chamber of Isabella, and thus to obtain a glimpse, the only distinct one with which we are favoured, into what may almost be called the imperial harem.

After the first salutations were over, a number of strange and fantastic games, which had been invented and frequently performed for the amusement of the empress, were gone through, greatly to the wonder and delight of the prince and his English attendants. After divers marvellous plays had been acted, four globes of glass were brought into the apartment and laid on the pavement, and then entered two young Saracen girls of the most exquisite beauty of feature and gracefulness of form, and each ascending two of the

[1] Paris, vol. ii., p. 569. [2] Ibid.

globes, and clapping their hands, they began a dance on their slippery pedestals, spurning the balls with their fairy feet, yet never dismounting from them, bending themselves into the most fantastic attitudes, and sporting with each other in a manner which called forth from the spectators the most rapturous expressions of admiration.[1] Such were the scenes presented in the private apartments of the empress Isabella.

Prince Richard took his departure in a few days, and we have no intimation that he was allowed any further intercourse with his sister. The situation of the empress at this period, for she was again likely to become a mother, might probably be one cause of the strict seclusion in which she was kept. The precautions adopted for her safety were fruitless, however, as far as she was concerned; for but a few weeks after Prince Richard's departure, the imperial mother herself died in giving birth to an infant daughter on the 1st of December, 1241, at the early age of twenty-seven. Although Isabella had been so long absent from England, yet, when her life was drawing to a close, her thoughts and affections clung with fond tenacity to the scenes and associations of her youth, and her dying request to her husband was that he would keep up friendly relationships with her brother King Henry, and assist him by counsel or otherwise whenever he needed it.[2] Her death took place at Foggio, in the region of Naples, and she was interred with imperial honours at the ancient city of Andria.[3] The emperor thought proper that her funeral should be solemnized throughout the whole of Apulia, and wrote the following letter to the justiciary of the province :—

" We have been unable to escape the snares of a concealed foe—since, after having brought numberless regions under

[1] Paris, vol. ii., p. 569.
[2] See letter of Henry to Frederic, Fœdera, vol. i.. pt. i., p. 290.
[3] Rich. St. Germ. Muratori, vol. vii., col. 1048. Matt. Westm., book ii., p. 163. Matt. Paris, vol. ii., p. 578. Palermo regali sepolcri, p. 66.

the yoke of our majesty, and whilst we were possessing peace
and quietness, the misfortune of unexpected death has violently taken away the most serene Augusta, sprung from
royal ancestry. We cannot therefore show gladness of countenance since the death of our consort wrings out for us a
cup of bitterness, and greatly molests and crosses us. Nevertheless, we are unwilling, by the bitterness of our grief, so
to affect our majesty as to offend our Creator, or to let the
immensity of our grief prevent our conferring worthily and
reverently the honour which is fitting and becoming to our
consort, since we are especially desirous that the memory
of such a sharer in our honours should be celebrated throughout the earth. Wherefore we strictly command you to have
her obsequies universally celebrated throughout your whole
jurisdiction, by the whole of the inhabitants in every place,
and chiefly by the clergy and people of the cities—bells
being every where rung—that those assembled in the
churches may especially commend the soul of the Augusta
to the living God, who takes away the spirit of princes. Be-
ware of disobedience, if you wish not to incur the sting of
our indignation.''[1]

Frederic was not present to smooth the dying pillow of
his consort, for he was then engaged in the siege of Faenza;[2]
he wrote to announce the melancholy event to her brother
King Henry,[3] but the communication was made rather tar-
dily, being nearly two months after the decease of the empress. No passionate sorrow is breathed in the epistle
penned by Frederic on this occasion, though he assures the
king that nothing which tender love or warm zeal could do
had been spared to save her, but consoles himself for her
loss in her children. " For by the gift of the Omnipotent,"
adds he, " her royal progeny are still living, who shall rise

[1] Epist. Petri de Vineis, Middlehill MS., 8390, collated with MS. 337.
[2] Raumer's Hohenstaufen, vol. iii., pp. 62-4.
[3] Rymer, vol. i., pt. i., pp. 243-4.

in their father's sight a king and queen, fit emblems of their ancestors. And though the loss of the Augusta our consort and your sister cannot be named without disturbance, nor can anxiety be banished from our inmost breast, yet in her two children the memory of their parent still survives."[1] Even these expressions were, it is likely, but the assumption of that decent exterior of mourning which was due to the rank of the empress. Small trust is to be placed in the love of a faithless and profligate husband; and such Frederic certainly was, and the chroniclers of the day more truly assert that he was little afflicted at Isabella's death.[2] Whether he was ever married again is rather uncertain, owing to the difficulty of distinguishing his mistresses from his wives. Matthew Paris tells us that he was married, and describes his wife as a lady of incomparable beauty.[3]

The feelings of King Henry and his subjects on the arrival of the intelligence of the empress' death, appear to have been deeply excited.[4] Matthew of Westminster, in recording the circumstance, calls Isabella "the hope and singular glory of the English,"[5] but his expression must rather refer to the splendour of her matrimonial connexion, than to any intrinsic personal qualities. If the grief of Henry is to be estimated by the amount of his benefactions in memory of her, it was of the profoundest character: he commanded £206. 6s. 8d. to be paid to friar John, his almoner, to feed the poor for one day, " for the sake of the soul of the empress, formerly our sister "—half of the money

---

[1] Paris, vol. ii., p. 578.

[2] Reynaldus Ann. Eccles. sub anno 1241, art. 87.

[3] Several of the modern German chroniclers assign to Frederic seven wives, but in so doing they commit palpable anachronisms, such, for instance, as that of marrying him, *after* Isabella's death, to Blanche of Lanza, the mother of his son Manfred, although he is mentioned by the historians long before. It seems probable that Constance of Aragon, Yolande of Jerusalem, and Isabella of England, formed the list of his wives, though his illegitimate offspring were very numerous.

[4] Chron. Philippe Mouskes, vol. ii., p. 676. Collect. de Chroniques Belges.

[5] Book ii., p. 163.

to be given at Oxford, and the other half at Ospringe, at the rate of one penny per head. The same sum was to be delivered to " our beloved and faithful William de Haverhill," for the poor in the neighbourhood of London and Windsor, and elsewhere, as to our council may seem fit, and £8. 6s. 8d. additional to the almoner for the same object — thus affording food to upwards of 101,000 paupers, at a cost, according to the proportional value of money in our day, of £6315.[1] Moreover, he established an anniversary for her, at which 4000 poor were annually fed, at a cost of twenty-five marks.[2]

Of the character of Isabella little remains to be said, because there is little in her history which tends to illustrate it. As far as it can be traced, her leading characteristics appear to have been gentleness and humility; and if the retirement in which she lived precluded all possibility of exercising any beneficent influence in public affairs, she has on the other hand escaped the slightest shadow of censure, for the epithets bestowed upon her are never otherwise than laudatory.

Dark and troubled was the career of the emperor Frederic after the death of his English consort. After years of energetic but fruitless strife against the crushing weight of Papal despotism, he was again excommunicated, and in 1245 finally deposed from his imperial authority,[3] and died

[1] Liberate roll., 26 Hen. III., from Devon's Excerpta, pp. 19 and 27. It is curious to remark incidentally that one penny was at that time considered ample allowance for the provision of a day.

[2] Rot. lib., 28 H. III., m. 16 rot. exitus, 28 H. III., Mich.

[3] Hansigius Germ. sacra, vol. ii., p. 342. Frederic was at Turin when the news of his deposition was communicated to him; deeply moved, he ordered the casket containing the imperial insignia to be brought to him, and drawing out the diadem—" Here it is, then," he exclaimed, "that crown that Innocent wishes to deprive me of—but " he added, with desperate energy, placing it once again on his brow, " it is mine yet, and it will cost him some blood before he obtains it."—Paris. vol. ii., p. 679, and Art de verifier les dates, vol. vii., p. 344. The form of his deposition is prefixed to the printed letters of Peter de Vineâ. A sense of its injustice seems to have prevailed extensively, but any expression of it was at once checked by the iron hand of ecclesiastical authority. A poor French curate, before pronouncing in his

in December, 1250, at Fiorenzuola, in Apulia, and was buried at Monreale, in Palermo.[1] He is said to have expressed great penitence in his latest moments, and even to have assumed the habit of the Cistercian order.[2] In his last will he made special provision that the rights of the Church should be respected, and left 100,000 ounces of gold towards the recovery of the Holy Land. Much of mystery however hangs over the closing scene of this illustrious man. By some it is said that his death was occasioned by poison, administered by the hand of his natural son, Manfred; but this suspicion seems contradicted by the fact that after the lapse of six centuries, when the tomb was opened, the body was found perfect, wearing the imperial robe and crown, and exhibiting very slight symptoms of decay.[3] His funeral rites were performed with such secrecy that for years afterwards the opinion prevailed that he was still living,[4] and in 1287 an adventurer who personated him obtained extensive credence.[5] Henry, the son of Frederic and Isabella, a youth of great beauty and promise, did not long survive his father; he seems to have been regarded with considerable interest by his uncle King Henry, and a

church the sentence of excommunication, said, that he knew not the cause of the sentence, but had merely heard that great dissensions had arisen between the pope and the emperor, and that as God only could know who was in the wrong, he excommunicated the one who had been the aggressor and absolved the sufferer. When this tale was repeated to Frederic he was much amused and sent a present to the honest priest: not so his Holiness however, who inflicted a severe canonical penance upon the curate.

[1] Chron. Aug. Freher, vol. i., p. 528. Chron. Lanercost, p. 51. Chron. Mailros, p. 178. Paris, vol. ii., p. 538. Annales Cavenses, Pertz German historians, vol. v., p. 194.

[2] Paris, vol. ii., p. 804. Rauch Rer. Austriac. Script., vol. i., p. 37.

[3] Palermo regali sepolcri, pp. 90-92. Tavola, 2.

[4] Volcmar Abbas, Œfellius Rer. Boicarum Scriptores, vol. i., p. 532. Chron. Aug. Freher, vol. i., p. 528. Chron. St. Peter Erfurt Menckenius, vol. iii., col. 268. His epitaph was as follows:—

"Si probitas, sensus, virtutes, gloria census,
Nobilitas orti possent resistere morti
Non foret extinctus Fredericus qui jacet intus."

Chron. Engel. Leibnitz, vol. ii., f. 1115. Heineccius Ant. Goslar, p. 270.

[5] Gest. Trev. Arch. Martène collect. amp., vol. iv., col. 339-40. Chron. Zantifliet. Ibid., vol. v., col. 121. Chron. Holl. Matthæus annal., med. ævi, vol. v., p. 545.

letter is still extant which he wrote to the king shortly after
his baptism, in 1247, informing him of the performance of
that important and long-delayed ceremony, and also of his
being appointed regent of Sicily during his father's absence
in Italy.[1] There is a childish simplicity about the letter
which renders it probable that it was dictated by the young
prince himself. After his father's death he became titular
King of Jerusalem, but, at the age of sixteen, in the year
1254, he fell a victim, as is generally supposed, to the traitorous artifices of his brother Conrad.[2]

The career of Margaret, the only daughter of Isabella,
whose birth cost her mother's life,[3] was singularly unhappy.
She was married, during the lifetime of her father, to Albert,
marquess of Thuringia and Misnes,[4] and became the mother
of several children; but a passionate attachment entertained
by her husband for his mistress, Cunegonde of Elsemberg,
led him to attempt the life of his wife. She was residing
in a lonely castle in Wortebourg, in Eysenach, when the
murderous emissaries of her husband were sent to perpe-
trate their deed of darkness; but the respect which her
former character had inspired induced one of them to give
her private warning of her impending fate, and she had
just time to escape to a convent at Francfort, where she

[1] Reuber, Script. Germ., p. 756. See also Baluzius Miscellanea, vol. v., p.
194. Frederic's letter to the king, already alluded to, in Vinell's letters, book
iii., No. 21. And Fœdera, vol. I., pt. i., p. 267.

[2] A letter of the hypocritical Conrad, announcing the death of the prince
to King Henry and expressing the most extravagant sorrow, is to be found
in Reuber, p. 755, and in Baluz. Miscel., vol. i., p. 194. Gebauer, in his
Leben des Kaysers Richards, p. 74, note o, tries to argue Conrad's innocence from the passionate expressions in this letter, but the strained unna-
tural style in which it is written rather affords a presumption of guilt, especially considering the advantage Conrad reaped from his brother's death.
He is reported to have employed a Saracen named John as the instrument
of his fratricide, who first administered poison and then completed the deed
by strangling the young prince with a towel.—Raynald. annal. eccles., vol. ii.,
sub. anno 1254, art. xliii.

[3] Tentzel vita Fred. II. Menckenius Rer. Germ. Script. Ant., vol. ii.,
col. 897.

[4] The 16th letter in the 5th book of De Vinell's Epistles relates to this
marriage.

took the veil. The hatred with which she had been regarded by her lord extended to her children, and they experienced the bitterest persecutions from their father, who even attempted to disinherit them in favour of his children by Cunegonde. He failed however in his object; and the posterity of this daughter, the sole descendants of the Empress Isabella, long occupied an honourable standing, though inferior to that which their imperial descent might have been supposed to claim for them among the nobility of Germany.[1]

But far higher destiny awaited her remoter posterity. Her descendant of the fourth generation, Frederic, the warlike, was made elector of Saxony, and his offspring were the progenitors of the noble houses of Saxe Cobourg and Saxe Gotha,[2] so that the blood of the Empress Isabella now runs in the veins of England's Queen, and, through her illustrious consort, of the house of Saxe Gotha, blends in a two-fold stream in those of the royal infants—the hope of the nation—the princes and princesses of England.

[1] Ludewig reliquiæ diplomata, &c., vol. viii., p. 241.
[2] L'Art de verifier les dates, vol. xv., p. 499, and vol. xvi., pp. 160-161.

ELEANORA,

THIRD DAUGHTER OF KING JOHN.

CHAPTER I.

Eleanora's birth—Early education—William Marshall—Eleanora offered to him—Discussions—Marriage—Voyage to Bretagne—Death of Earl William—Eleanora takes a sacred vow—Her dowry embarrassments—Simon de Montfort—Attachment between him and Eleanora—Opposed by the Archbishop of Canterbury—Clandestine marriage—Wrath of the barons—Simon goes to Rome—Eleanora at Kenilworth—Pope confirms the marriage—Simon's return—Birth of Henry de Montfort—Visit of Amelric—Removal to Odiham—Simon is godfather to Prince Edward—King's anger banishes the Earl and Countess—They retire to France—Simon's crusade—Return to England—Gascon expedition—Coolness of the King—Simon and Eleanora retire to Kenilworth—Its situation and strength—Their children—Robert Grostête—Adam de Marisco—Eleanora's dowry—Her visits to Waverley.

Eleanora, the third daughter of King John, first saw the light at a time when troubles were crowding thick and fast around the head of her weak and unfortunate father; and these ominous circumstances at the time of her birth proved but too sad a presage of her future career. The princess received at the font the name of her grandmother, Eleanora of Aquitaine, and she inherited the beauty of person and ardour of disposition of this gay queen of Henry II. Eleanora was scarcely a year old, when the death of her father, King John, in 1216, left her an orphan; and the abandonment of the royal children, by the queen-mother, shortly afterwards, deprived her also of maternal surveillance in her education. Small, however, was the modicum of learning which was considered sufficient for females even of the highest rank, when the business of their life was the endless labour of the spindle and the embroidery frame, or the devotional peregrinations to the numerous repositories of saintly relics, and its pleasures consisted principally in riding and hawking.

The character of the great Earl of Pembroke, who, upon the death of King John, took the helm of government at a time when the throne was shaken to its very basis; and, by his vigorous and well-timed movements, rolled back the tide of foreign invasion, and established the young monarch, Henry III., in his kingdom, is familiar to every reader of English history. He unfortunately only lived for three years to sustain the office of Regent, to which he was elected by the unanimous voice of the nation.[1] He left behind him five sons, the eldest of whom, William, succeeded to his father's title and estates, as fourth Earl of Pembroke; but he did not inherit his firm, unshaken loyalty. At first, indeed, he appears to have warmly espoused the king's cause in the disturbances which arose; for, when the Earl of Albemarle was heading an insurrection, in 1221,[2] he wrote to King Henry, expressing his surprise that he had not been summoned to join the royal standard; and telling him that, although he was now at a distance, and engaged with his own affairs, yet the interests of his sovereign were so much dearer to him than his own, that he wished but to know where and with what proportion of troops he should meet him.[3] The fidelity of Earl William

---

[1] The following curious epitaph was composed for him—
"Sum qui Saturnum sibi sensit Hibernia; solem
Anglia; Mercurium Normannia, Gallia Martem:"
alluding to his being a tamer of the Irish, a favourer of the English, having achieved much in Normandy, and proved an invincible soldier in France.— Dugdale's Baronage, vol. i., p. 602.
[2] Paris, vol. ii., p. 310.
[3] Royal Letters, No. 265, Tower of London.

on this occasion is the more remarkable, since he stood in
the relationship of son-in-law to the rebel Earl of Albemarle ;
but after this, several slight disturbances arose between him
and the government, which are alluded to in the state
documents of the period, and he also espoused the cause of
Prince Richard in his quarrels with his brother.

The influence of this great earl was so extensive and
formidable, that his support was an object of much consequence to the young king and his council of regency ; and,
in order the better to secure it, on the death of his first
wife, Alice de Betun,[1] it was proposed that the hand of the
Princess Eleanora should be offered him. The reasons which
induced the council to devise so unwonted a step are mi-
nutely detailed in a letter written to the pope, in the name
of the king, a few years afterwards,[2] from which it is very
evident that little ardour was shown by the earl in availing
himself of the offer of the royal marriage. This coolness
probably arose from the extreme youth of the princess.
Neither of the unmarried sisters of King Henry was at this
time more than seven years old ; and Eleanora, who was
selected, because, as being the younger, she was considered
of rather less importance than her sister, had scarcely completed her fifth year. The exact age of Earl William has
not transpired, but the charter of dowry granted to him by
Baldwin de Betun, Earl of Albemarle, on occasion of his
first marriage with his daughter Alice, bears date the fifth
year of King John, that is, A.D. 1204, and the earl was at
that time in the prime of life ; therefore he cannot have
been under forty years of age in 1221, when these negociations commenced. Several other matches had been in contemplation for this powerful noble. A sister of the King of
Scotland, and a daughter of the Duke of Brabant, had both

[1] The date of her death is nowhere recorded, but she was living in 1216.
See Pipe roll, 17th John.
[2] See Appendix, II.

been proffered to him; but the council thought that either of these unions would prove injurious to the interests of the realm, by giving a more free access to foreigners. They were anxious, too, to obtain from the earl the royal castles of Merleberg and Lutgershall, which by some means had fallen into his hands, and which he was unwilling to relinquish. To induce him to do so, and also to secure his unflinching loyalty, whilst the throne was still tottering from the effects of the recent commotions, this royal marriage was proposed. The conditions were agreed to, on his part, and the two castles resigned into the hands of the papal legate, to be held by him until the marriage was fulfilled. But the jealousy of some of the English nobles subsequently raised objections to the union. They argued, that the hands of the king's sisters were the most valuable treasures he had to bestow, and should be made available in strengthening the foreign relationships of the kingdom, instead of being thrown away on a subject; and for several years the matter remained in abeyance. The vigorous Earl Marshall was not, however, to be trifled with. Whilst he professed the utmost regard for the welfare of the king and his sister,[1] he declared, at length, that he did not choose to remain any longer unmarried, and procured a papal mandate to the effect that either he should be freed from his obligations to the princess, or that the contract should be forthwith fulfilled.[2] Under these circumstances, the council were compelled to come to a decision. The earl had recently performed a signal service to the royal cause, by recapturing some important fortresses which had been seized by Llewelyn, Prince of Wales. This was pleaded in favour of the match—precedents were also alleged of the princesses of France being married to powerful subjects, and the re-

[1] Letter of William Marshall to Hubert de Burgh, justiciary of England, Original, Tower Collection, No. 620.
[2] Royal Letters, No, 389, Tower.

sult was, that the union was resolved upon. The usual ceremonies were performed on both sides, and Eleanora became the wife of a man almost old enough to have been her grandfather.[1]

The marriage of an English princess with a mere subject was a circumstance very unusual in the annals of royalty, and is in itself a sufficient illustration of the all but regal state of the powerful house of Pembroke. The titles of Earl of Pembroke, Lord of Streguill, Chepstow, Caer-went, Leigh, Wexford, Kildare, Kilkenny, Ossory, and Carlow,[2] accompanied as they were by the essentials, as well as the mere show of power, would not sound insignificantly even in the ears of a maiden of royal blood. The grants of lands made to Earl William by the king, in addition to his extensive hereditary estates, were most munificent. Some of them were situated on the borders of Wales, and with the princes of that country this powerful noble frequently waged an almost even-handed conflict.[3] Others were in Ireland, over which, with the title of justiciary, he exercised an almost viceregal jurisdiction; for all the principal fortresses were placed in his hands, and the then ample revenue of £580 per annum was assigned him from the Dublin exchequer.[4]

Owing to the juvenility of the lady Eleanora, her marriage was for some time merely nominal, and she remained an inmate of her brother's court, while her spouse was engaged in the bustle of active life; nor does the union seem to have been productive of the complete concord which was anticipated; for, in a letter written by King Henry to the Earl

[1] Chron. Dunstaple, vol. i., p. 148, and Chron. Tewksb., Cotton. MS., Cleop. A. vii., f. 9, b., place her marriage in 1224. The Annals of Waverley, Gale, vol. ii., p. 188, Wikes, Gale, vol. i., p. 40, and Chron. Hageneb., Cotton. MS., Vespasian, B. xi., f. 19, b., place it in 1225. The former date is probably correct.

[2] Vincent's Corrections of Brook, p. 413.

[3] Matt. Westm., book ii., p. 282.

[4] See close roll, 9th Hen. III., m. 11, and numerous entries on the patent rolls of the 9th, 10th, 11th, and 14th Hen. III.

of Pembroke, in the year 1226, he reproaches him, though mildly, for failing to meet him in Wales, on account of some false rumours which had reached him, that his conduct was viewed in a suspicious light by the king. Henry assures him of the regard and esteem he entertained for him, and which he has fully proved by the bestowment of his sister, and upbraids him for supposing that, had any suspicions arisen prejudicial to him, he would not have been immediately informed of them. He requires him, however, in case he persist in his intention of departing for Ireland, rather than going into Wales, to deliver up the castles of Cardigan and Carnarvon to the king.[1] This was but a temporary disagreement, however. In general, Earl William was on the best terms with his brother-in-law; and, although he was occasionally absent in Ireland, on the duties connected with his office, or on his own necessary business, yet the repeated mention of his name, as witness or party in almost every record roll of this period, proves that he was a frequent resident at court. His intimate association with the royal family gave him every opprtunity of seeking to possess himself of the affections of his young betrothed, who was fast springing up to maidenhood. That Eleanora should have entertained a tender regard for the man whom, almost ever since her mind had been capable of admitting an idea, she was taught to look upon as her future husband, would not have been extraordinary, especially considering that his rank, his military prowess, and his personal character, all entitled him to respect; but that she should have cherished for her mature spouse a passion as deep and intense as though he had wooed her with all the fervour of impassioned youth, is somewhat singular; and yet after-circumstances fully proved that this was the case.

The period at which the princess Eleanora fulfilled he

[1] Rot. pat., 10 Hen. III., m. 2, in dorso.

marriage-vows was probably the latter part of the year 1229, when she was in her fifteenth year, for an entry occurs in the charter rolls for that year, by which nine manors are confirmed in the possession of her husband, and settled on her exclusively in case she should survive him.[1] This document is dated the 18th of October from Portsmouth, where the royal family were then sojourning, attended by a splendid court, and where a gallant array of troops from England, Scotland, Ireland, Wales, and Galway had been congregated, in order to pass over into France ; the king having been seized with a violent desire, excited by his mother Isabella of Angoulême, to reconquer from the French those provinces which they had taken during the reign of his father. But the necessary arrangements for such an expedition could not be completed at the nod of a capricious youth. Though all the vassals of the crown had been summoned and extraordinary preparations made, the lack of transport ships precluded the possibility of embarking the assembled forces. Henry, in a fit of passion, heaped the most opprobrious epithets upon Hubert de Burgh, his grand justiciary, calling him old traitor, accusing him of receiving bribes from France to delay the expedition, and even rushing upon him with his drawn sword, to inflict some personal damage ; but the Earl of Chester, who was fortunately present at this singular scene, restrained the angry monarch.[2]

The expedition was however necessarily postponed until the following spring, when, as soon as the season would permit, preparations were again made for the voyage. The Earl of Pembroke, whose military talents had been tested in many a hard-fought field, was to attend his sovereign as one of the principal generals of the army, and the youthful countess determined to accompany her lord. The whole party

---

[1] Rot. chart., 13 Hen. III., pars prima, m. 1.
[2] Paris, vol. ii., p. 363.

proceeded to Reading, where they arrived on the 14th of April, 1230,[1] and set sail from Portsmouth on the 30th of that month; but the Princess Eleanora, who had never before braved the perils of the deep, suffered so extremely from sea-sickness, that the king was obliged to put into the island of Jersey, where they landed about nine o'clock on the following morning. Here they spent the whole day, in order to recruit the suffering lady, who was so far recovered that the next morning, at three o'clock, the fleet again set sail, and in about thirty hours landed at St. Malo in Bretagne. There they awaited the arrival of the Duke of Bretagne, and also of Isabella, the queen-mother, who, with her husband, the Earl of March, was appointed to hold a conference with the king.[2]

The issue of the ill-planned and worse-executed Breton expedition was precisely what might have been expected from the frivolous yet headstrong character of the monarch who headed it. Henry took up his principal abode in the city of Nantes, and there spent his time and squandered his money in giving feasts and diversions to his court, till the soldiers, discovering that fighting was not to be the order of the day, took the liberty of selling their horses and arms, in order to provide themselves with the necessary funds to follow their master's example.[3] The movements which had been made in Anjou, Poictou, and Normandy, in favour of the English, being unsupported by the king, were readily suppressed by the vigorous activity of Queen

[1] A curious letter from King Henry to William, Bishop of Carlisle, dated Reading, the 14th of April, is still in existence, in which he commands his royal mantle, crown, sceptre, rod, sandals, and gloves, to be forwarded to Portsmouth in all haste.—Collectanea non impressa, for Rymer's Fœdera, Addit. MS., No. 4753, Art. 26.

[2] Letter of Hugh Neville to Ralph Neville, Bishop of Chichester and Lord Chancellor of England, among the royal letters in the Tower, No. 913. This document, although much defaced, contains several interesting particulars, not elsewhere to be met with, of the Breton expedition, and, as proceeding from the pen of one who shared in it, may be fully relied on.—See also M. Paris, vol. ii., p. 365; and Royal Letters, Nos. 288 and 912.

[3] Paris, vol. ii., p. 367.

Blanche, the regent of France;[1] and Henry, railing upon his allies, his generals, his soldiers, any body or any thing but himself, returned in a fit of disgust to England.[2] At the earnest intercession of the Earl of Pembroke, however, he consented to leave some troops behind, under his command and that of the Earls of Chester and Albemarle; and these lords, freed from the shackles of control under a sovereign who knew nothing of war, if they could not restore, at least did something to retrieve the fortunes of the campaign, for they not only put a stop to the victorious march of the French, who were then about to enter Bretagne, but made occasional successful inroads into Anjou and Normandy.[3]

The following year Earl William and Eleanora returned to England, and after a short stay at court, the earl prepared to go over into Ireland, on business, it would seem, rather of a private than public nature. We have no means of ascertaining with certainty whether Eleanora accompanied him on this occasion, but, as she was seldom absent from his side, the probabilities are that she did so. The very large property possessed by the earl in Ireland would render him desirous of introducing his countess there, especially in those extensive districts which were assigned over for her dower lands. The contrast must have been striking between the polished Bretons, then one of the most civilized people in Europe, and the wild Irish, who were still in a state of semi-barbarism, and who were moreover settling down after a formidable insurrection, raised by the King of Connaught, during the absence of the Earl Marshall. But the residence of the earl and countess in Ireland was not prolonged to any considerable extent, for early in the following year they were summoned to England, on an important occasion.

Fresh honours were about to be heaped on the illustrious

house of Pembroke by the marriage of Richard Earl of
Cornwall, then heir presumptive to the crown, with Isabella,
widow of the Earl of Gloucester and sister of Earl William.
The nuptial feasts were held with great rejoicings, but a
sudden stop was put to the festivities by the death, after an
illness of only a few hours, of the Earl of Pembroke. He
died on the 15th of April, 1231, and was interred in what
was then called the New Temple,[1] near the remains of his
father the great Earl of Pembroke.[2] King Henry was sincerely attached to his brother-in-law, and, with the superstition which formed a strong feature in his character,
attributed his sudden decease to a supernatural cause, for,
on seeing his dead body, he exclaimed, " Alas! is the blood
of Saint Thomas the martyr not yet fully avenged ?"[3]

Intense and passionate was the grief of the widowed
Eleanora, and in the first transports of her sorrow she took
a public and solemn vow, in presence of Edmund, Archbishop of Canterbury, that never again would she become
a wife, but remain a true spouse of Christ, and she received
from him the spousal ring in confirmation of her pledge.[4]
Well had it been for the ill-fated Eleanora if she had kept
that vow. She was dowried with lands so extensive that
there were but few princesses in Europe who might not
have envied her; but these very riches proved a source of
endless annoyance and trouble.

The heir of the late earl William was his brother Richard,
the second of the five sons of the Protector,[5] and on him his

---

[1] Now the Temple Church. One of the bronze recumbent statues in the
entrance of the church is still pointed out as the effigy of the Earl of Pembroke.

[2] MS. Bib. Bodl., Med. 20, f. 109. Matt. Westm., book ii., p. 290. Chron.
Dunst., Hearne's edit., vol. i., p. 203. Paris, vol. ii., p. 368.

[3] Paris, ut supra.   [4] Knighton, p. 2347, Twysden.

[5] The others were Gilbert, Walter, and Anselm, who, by a singular coincidence, all in turn succeeded to the earldom, and all died without heirs. The
reason superstitiously assigned for the blight that thus fell on the family of
the earl is thus given by Matthew Paris. During the Irish wars, two manors,
belonging to an Irish bishopric, had fallen into the hands of the earl of Pembroke, which he afterwards refused to restore. On his death, the prelate

immense estates should accordingly have devolved; but the
king, whose profusion led to poverty, and his poverty too
often to meanness, detained the whole in his own hands for
a short time, under the pretence that the Countess Eleanora,
though little more than sixteen years of age, was about to
become a mother—but when time had proved that this was
not the case, he was still unwilling to relinquish them to
their rightful owner; and, on an absurd charge of traitorous
correspondence with the king's enemies in France, Richard
was commanded to depart the kingdom.   The indignant
earl obeyed, but it was only to fortify himself in Ireland,
where the influence of his family was all-prevalent, and
where a powerful body of troops speedily rose at his bidding.
Henry, as weak in execution as he was rash in purpose,
now took the alarm, recalled the earl, and gave him full
possession of his hereditary estates and dignities.[1]

On her brother-in-law, Richard, the countess-dowager was
naturally dependent for the regular payment of her dower;
for, although it had been settled exclusively on herself, yet
the lands assigned for its discharge were principally situated
in Ireland,[2] in the midst of the Pembroke estates, and consequently under the real, if not nominal power of the earl.
But Richard, who looked upon Eleanora rather as the sister

who then held the See came over to England, and endeavoured to obtain
restitution from William Marshall the younger; but the earl, declaring that
the lands belonged to his house by right of conquest, expressed his determination to retain them.   On which the bishop visited the grave of the father,
uttering over it the most bitter execrations against the spirit of the departed
earl, and not thus satisfied, pronounced the withering sentence of untimely
blight upon all the noble scions of the house of Marshall.   This reached the
ears of King Henry, who remonstrated with the bishop on the subject.
" Sire," said he, " what I have said I have said, and what I have written is
not to be reversed.   The sentence, therefore, must stand.   The punishment
of evil-doers is from God, and the curse which the Psalmist hath written
shall surely come upon this earl, of whom I do thus complain, viz., His
name shall be rooted out in one generation, and his sons shall be deprived of
the blessing, ' Increase and multiply.'   Some of them shall die a miserable
death, and their inheritance shall be scattered, and this thou, O king, shalt
behold in thine own life-time, yea, in thy flourishing youth!"

[1] Paris, vol. ii., p. 369.

[2] See an entry in the fine roll of the 15th of Henry III., vol. ii., p. 109, in
the Excerpta from the fine rolls, by Charles Roberts, Esq.

of the monarch who had so recently injured him, and whom
he had found it so easy to intimidate, than as a near connexion of his own house, was not disposed to treat her with
the consideration due to her rank and her helpless situation.
The magnificent household furniture of the late earl, valued
at a sum equal to more than £6000 of our present money,
which he had bequeathed to his young wife, was appropriated by Earl Richard to his own use, and he was even
ungenerous enough to allow those creditors who had claims
upon his brother to distrain the lands of the widowed
countess, in order to obtain payment of debts which he, as
heir, was bound by every law of honour to satisfy, but the
king interfered to put a stop to so ungracious a proceeding.[1]

Eleanora appears at first to have been too much stunned
by the sense of her loss to pay any attention to her worldly
affairs. The gaiety of the court was uncongenial to her,
and the very day subsequent to that which made her a
widow, King Henry assigned to her the castle of Intebergh,
in Kent, formerly belonging to her husband, as her residence,
and orders were given to the viscount, seneschal, and
servants to receive her with due honour, to put her in
possession of all the goods and chattels of her late lord, and
to provide handsomely for her entertainment, and that of
her family.[2] Henry contributed towards the execution of
this latter clause by ordering three tuns of the best wines
from his cellars in Bristol to be despatched to her,[3] and by
supplying her with venison from the royal forests.[4] He
also issued writs to the sheriffs of the counties in which
those English manors which had been made over to her
on her marriage were situated, ordering their revenues to
be assigned for her use.[5] Instead of the Irish lands,
which constituted by far the largest proportion of her dower,

[1] Rot. pat., 17 Hen. III., m. 6.   [2] Rot. claus., 15 Hen. III., m. 14.
[3] Ibid., m. 15.
[4] Ibid., mm. 14, 12, and 6.   Rot. claus. 16, mm. 8, 6, 18.
[5] Ibid., m. 9.

he merely assigned her a few more English manors, with wardships and other sources of income enjoyed by her deceased spouse, until further arrangements could be made.[1]

In retaliation of the harsh measures adopted by Earl Richard concerning his late brother's debts, Henry ordered that all such moneys as were owing to himself, either as personal debts or as taxes from any part of the estates of the late earl, should be levied on the lands of Earl Richard, and not on those of the dowager-countess.[2] Meanwhile, he appointed commissioners to go over into Ireland, and to associate with themselves other persons well acquainted with the value of land there, in order to form a due estimate of his sister's rights,[3] and it was at length agreed that Earl Richard should pay to Eleanora £400 a-year in lieu of her revenues in Ireland and South Wales, and that, on failure of these payments at regular half-yearly intervals, Henry should distrain his English lands for the required sum—a very necessary precaution, for, in the ensuing year, the king had to avail himself of this provision.[4] This agreement was made without the knowledge or consent of the countess, although it was sealed with her seal. She was only eighteen years old, and, both as a minor and a widow, was under the guardianship of her brother, who transacted all her affairs for her. In this instance, however, he allowed himself to be woefully imposed upon. The revenues of the lands for which he consented to a compromise of £400 a-year were really worth upwards of £1300,[5] and in giving so easy credence to his messengers, who had probably been bribed by Richard Marshall to give a false report, the king very materially diminished his sister's resources.

It seems probable that, during this time, Eleanora continued to reside at Intebergh, for that castle was still retained

[1] Rot. claus., 16 Hen. III., mm. 4 and 12.   [2] Ibid., m. 13.
[3] Ibid., m. 19.
[4] Rot. claus.. 17 Hen. III., mm. 9 in dorso, 8. See Appendix III.
[5] See Appendix, No. V.

in the king's hands, as appears from an entry to that effect, dated August 26, 1233.[1] But, though absent from court, continued proofs of kindly remembrance were bestowed upon her. She was commissioned to receive a reasonable provision of fire-wood from the forest of Sevenoaks.[2] Supplies of venison were sent as usual,[3] and the revenues of sundry fairs and markets were assigned to her.[4] These rural gatherings were at that time considered of such importance, that they were formally proclaimed throughout all the neighbouring districts with great ceremony, and the tax levied upon all goods sold there was a fruitful source of royal revenue.

The countess still found considerable difficulty in obtaining her income regularly, and it frequently ran much into arrear. In the 18th year of Henry III., the justices of Ireland were ordered to pay her 5000 marks out of the estates of her late husband,[5] and £500 from the profits of the sale of his goods and chattels,[6] and in the 19th, Gilbert Marshall, who had succeeded his brother Richard as Earl of Pembroke, gave security for the payment of £750 of debt and arrears.[7] Henry himself behaved very liberally towards his sister, for he remitted all claims for taxes upon her lands in Ireland, both those owing in the time of the deceased earl, and such as might afterwards become due.[8] He also granted to her, in 1237, the castle and manor of Odiham, in Hampshire, to hold as long as she lived.[9] This castle, though small, was, at that period, so strongly fortified as to be almost impregnable; for, when Louis the dauphin invaded England in 1216[10], thirteen men defended it for fifteen days against his whole forces. Other entries occur, granting her presents of

[1] Rot. claus., 17 Hen. III., m. 5.   [2] Ibid., 16 H. III., m. 19.
[3] Rot. claus., 17 Hen. III., mm. 9, 11, 17.
[4] Rot. claus., 16 Hen. III., m. 16, Ibid. 17, m. 6.   See also other entries on her behalf, Ibid. mm. 2 and 15.
[5] Ibid., 18 Hen. III., m. 2.   [6] Rot. claus., 16 Hen. III., m. 5.
[7] Rot. pat., 19 Hen. III., m. 10.
[8] Rot. fin., 19 Hen. III., vol. i., p. 285, Roberts' Excerpta.
[9] Rot. pat., 21 Hen. III., m. 13.   [10] Burton's Antiquities, p. 35.

deer from the royal forests, and remitting the sum of forty
shillings, which she owed to the king.[1]

Notwithstanding her brother's generosity, however, owing
to his mismanagement of her Irish dowry, Eleanora was
frequently deeply involved in debt, and two of her creditors,
one of whom was Ralph, abbot of Tintern, became so im-
portunately pressing in their demands, that Henry, to satisfy
them, gave them his royal word that, in case of the death of
his beloved sister, which he prayed God to forbid, their
claims should be satisfied from her personal estate before
those of any other of her creditors.[2]

King Henry extended his kindly protection even to the
members of his sister's household; he assigned a pension of
ten marks yearly to one of her maidens, until she should be
provided for by marriage.[3] On one occasion, a servant of
the countess had fallen into the clutches of the law, under
the following circumstances: he, along with some of his
fellows, was in one of the royal parks, when they observed
some malefactors committing depredations; they immediately attacked them, and in the strife that ensued, one
of the intruders was killed. The murderer was immediately
committed to prison, and, although the deed was perpetrated
in defence of the king's property, yet so stringently were
the laws against murder enforced amongst the lower orders
of society, that it was not until Eleanora had earnestly inter-
ceded with her brother on her servant's behalf, and he had
sent down a special mandate, that the prisoner was liberated.[4]

[1] Rot. claus., 18 Hen., mm. 15, 16; Ibid. 21 m. 5; Ibid. 22 mm. 5, 10.
[2] Rymer, vol. i., pt. i., p. 212.   [3] Rot. pat., 22 Hen. III., m. 10.
[4] Rot. claus., 22 Hen. III., m. 14. A curious illustration of the severity
with which even manslaughter was punished occurs in the close roll of the
33 of Henry III., m. 5. A little girl, four years of age, called Catherine
Passavant, residing at St. Albans, went to visit a neighbour's child, and, on
opening the door of the house, accidentally pushed her little playmate, who
was still younger than herself, into a bowl of boiling water, by which she
was so seriously injured that she died. On this, the poor little girl, who
had been the innocent cause of the disaster, was taken to the prison of
St. Albans, and closely confined, until an order was obtained from the king
for her liberation.

It is more easy to trace out the pecuniary transactions of the lady Eleanora, during the years of her widowhood, than to elicit any particulars of her private history. After the first outbursts of grief were past, she recovered her natural buoyancy of temper, and with the immediate pressure of sorrow, her monastic inclinations passed away also; for, although she had taken the initiatory, and, as it was considered by many, the decisive, step of assuming the ring and taking the vows of chastity, yet she manifested no disposition to take the veil. She seems to have resided much at the court of her brother, but, at the same time, to have kept up an establishment of her own, probably at her castle of Odiham, and that, too, on a very magnificent scale. We can scarcely otherwise account for her being so frequently involved in debt. At the time of her second marriage, she owed the king the sum of £1000, which he had lent her on interest,[1] which he was afterwards generous enough to remit.[2] Eleanora, during the early part of her life at least, was not famed for prudence or economy, and the extravagant habits which the possession of an independent fortune led her to form were the source of great inconvenience to her in after life.

Between herself and her brother King Henry the most cordial attachment subsisted, for even the state documents that refer to her abound with unwonted epithets of affection. A feeble character will always be found to cling to one of firmer mould, even in circumstances where the support of *mind* can alone be given, and where all power of external aid is absent; and there dwelt in the bosom of the royal Eleanora an ardour and an energy of purpose, whether for good or evil, which presented a strong contrast to the fickle irresolution of her brother.

[1] Madox, Hist. Exchequer, vol. ii., p. 202.
[2] Rot. fin., 28 Hen. III., vol. i., p. 410, Roberts' Excerpta. See also Liberate roll, 22 Hen. III., m. 8, and 21, m. 9.

But we must now introduce to our readers the bold man who exercised so powerful an influence over the future destinies of this princess. ·Simon de Montfort, Earl of Leicester, was the youngest son of the crusading Earl of Montfort, of whom we have already spoken, as leading the armies of the church against the Protestants of Toulouse,[1] and he is thus alluded to in the chronicle of Guillaume de Nangis.[2] " At this time there was in England a knight born in France, noble and valiant in arms, and a very wise man of his age, who was called Simon de Montfort, son of Simon, the old Earl of Montfort, who was a good Christian, and a noble man, and valiant in arms, and who spent much pains amongst the Albigenses to destroy the vice of heresy, and died of a blow of a mangonel in the siege of Toulouse, and passed as a martyr from this world to our Lord."

Though we cannot agree with our monkish chronicler in assigning the martyr's crown to the unrelenting persecutor of the Protestant faith, Nangis certainly does not exaggerate either the noble birth or personal prowess of the Montforts. Their origin has been the subject of much learned disputation, but the most probable opinion is that they descended from William, Earl of Hainault, great grandson of Baldwin, with the iron arm, Earl of Flanders, and of Judith, daughter of Charles the Bold, King of France. This Earl William married the heiress of the house of Montfort, and his descendant, Amalric II., became Earl of Evreux, by his marriage with Agnes, heiress of that house, and a descendant from Richard I., Duke of Normandy.[3] Half the earldom of Leicester devolved upon this powerful family from the marriage of their descendant, Simon III., with Amicia, daughter and co-heiress of Robert Fitz Parnell, Earl of Leicester, in whose right he obtained

[1] See vol. i. of this work, p. 373.   [2] Bouquet. vol. xx., p. 415.
[3] L'art de verifier les dates, vol. xi., p. 471.   Anselme Hist. Geneal., vol. vi., pp. 71-5.

the title of earl, with the hereditary dignity of lord steward of England.[1] At that period, the Montforts were occasional residents in this country, where they enjoyed a high degree of consideration; but their French descent and associations having induced them warmly to countenance the pretensions of the dauphin Louis, at the close of King John's reign, their possessions were forfeited, they were banished the kingdom, and retired to their own domains. Not only the earldom of Montfort, but that of Evereux and Narbonne, with the viscounties of Beziers and Carcassone, formed their proud continental possessions.[2]

On the death of Earl Simon IV., his estates descended to his eldest son, Amalric. The earldom of Leicester, of course, was included amongst these possessions; but, though Amalric made several applications to the king to restore to him the lands and revenues which, since their forfeiture, had been in the hands of the Earls of Chester, he constantly failed in obtaining his suit, on account of the jealous feeling with which, as a French noble possessing extensive continental domains, he was regarded. Finding his efforts unsuccessful, he next renewed his applications in favour of his youngest brother Simon, against whom the same objections could not be supposed to exist;[3] and this time King Henry lent a favourable ear to his petition.[4] He promised to deliver the lands, consisting of the town of Leicester, and the moiety of the earldom, with the office of seneschal, to Simon, as soon as he could get them out of the hands of Ralph, Earl of Chester.[5] This was accomplished the following year, 1231,[6] and in 1232 Simon

[1] This appears from a charter, bearing date March 10th, 1206, in the volume of printed charter rolls.
[2] Chron. Nangis, Bouquet, vol. xx., p 548. Colbert, MS. No. 76, Bibl. du roi, Paris.
[3] Brienne MS., No. 34, fol. 30. Letter of Amalric to Henry III.
[4] Rot. pat., 14 H. III., p. 2, m. 6.
[5] Vincent's corrections of Brook, p. 305. Great Coucher, Duchy of Lancaster's office, vol. ii., fol. 45, No. 3.
[6] Rot. fin., 15 H. III., m. 3. Rot. claus., 15 H. III., mm. 3, 6.

received from his brother Amalric a formal cession of the
rights which he, as the elder, possessed to the honours in
question,[1] for which he paid 1,500 livres, French money.[2]

At this time, Simon was principally a resident on the continent. He made strenuous efforts to obtain in marriage
Jeanne, countess in her own right of Flanders, who, in 1233,
had become a widow. But the hand of this wealthy
heiress was not to be disposed of without the consent of the
French government, in whose wardship she was, and the
queen-regent, Blanche, strongly opposed the suit of Simon.
The grounds of her opposition are not stated, but she probably knew his temperament too well to feel any desire for
so restless a neighbour. In high dudgeon at the affront
thus put upon him by the French queen, Simon quitted
France, and determined to seek his fortunes in England.[3]
The first public mention we find made of him occurs at the
nuptial festivities and coronation of Queen Eleanora of
Provence, in 1236, when he successfully vindicated his
right to the office of steward or seneschal of England, in
opposition to the rival claim of Roger Bigod, Earl of Norfolk,[4] and in that capacity held the golden bason in which
the monarch and his beautiful bride washed their hands at
the conclusion of the banquet—a ceremony which was more
than matter of form when our simple-minded ancestors
were in the constant habit of practically illustrating the

[1] Rot. pat., 16 H. III., m. 6. Fœdera, vol. i., pt. i., pp. 203, 205, 206.
Brienne, MS. No. 34, fol. 27, Bibl. du roi.
[2] Brienne MS. No. 34, fol. 29.
[3] Guillaume de Nangis, p. 548. L'art de verifier les dates, vol. xi.,
p. 482.
[4] The nature and comparative merits of these claims upon so high an office
have been the subject of much learned disquisition. By some the honour is
supposed to be an appendage to the manor of Hinckley in Leicestershire,
which fell to Earl Simon. By others, it is said to have been claimed by him
as a descendant of the great Norman noble, Hugh de Grentesmil. Those
who wish to see this subject fully discussed, may consult Selden's Titles of
Honour, Wilkins' edit., vol. i., col. 687-8. Russell's life of Earl Simon in
Nichols' history of Leicestershire, vol. i., pt. I., pp. 106-7. Cotton MS.
Vespasian, c. xiv., f. 141 b.

good old proverb that "fingers were made before knives and forks."

Earl Simon now paid his court with much assiduity to King Henry, from whom he met with a very favourable reception. The partiality of this sovereign for foreigners formed one of the foibles of his character, and the young earl, handsome in person, and possessing all the accomplishments of a *preux chevalier*, soon became a great favourite with the king.[1] Nor was the kindly feeling with which he was regarded confined to King Henry alone. The intimate access which De Montfort obtained to the court threw him frequently into the society of the Princess Eleanora, and she began to entertain towards him feelings incompatible with the sacred vow she had previously taken. Its shackles had long lain so lightly upon her, that she had learned to forget that, in the eyes of the church, they were as adamantine fetters to bind her to the life of mournful widowhood, which, in her passionate anguish, she had chosen for herself, and she listened but too readily to the whispers of that earthly love which she had sworn to renounce for ever. Nor, it may be presumed, was Simon slow in taking advantage of his position to urge his suit, when the prize to be obtained was a young and lovely princess, who, although she had worn widow's weeds upwards of six years, was now scarcely twenty-three years of age. But the lovers were well aware that their union was likely to meet with serious opposition; not from the king, for his affection for De Montfort led him to sanction their attachment, but on the part of the clergy, who would

[1] The friendly feeling between Henry and Simon is thus alluded to in Harding's rhyming chronicle, fol. 116:—

Symonde, the sonne of Erle Symonde Mounteforte,
Come oute of France for ferdenes of the queene,
To Kynge Henry, whome he gave grete comforte;
He gave hym then, his man for aye to beene, (to be his man for ever),
Of Leicestre the earldom, ferre and clene,
With Stewardship of Engelonde in heritage,
Which is an office of gret privilege.

object to the infringement of Eleanora's vows; and on that
of the barons.   It has already been seen that great discontents had been manifested at the previous marriage of
Eleanora, and, if opposition had been made to her union
with the first noble of the land, the son of the great Protector, it was likely to be far more strenuous when the
bridegroom elect was the younger brother of a French
noble, holding but small possessions in England, and himself one of those foreigners whom the nation regarded with
dislike and mistrust.   On this account their attachment
was carefully concealed.

   But there was one who had taken a paternal interest in
the lady Eleanora ever since she had given herself into his
hands as the spouse of Christ, whose vigilant eye was upon
her, and whose suspicions were excited by her conduct.
This was the learned and pious Edmund, Archbishop of
Canterbury.   He remonstrated seriously and severely both
with Eleanora and her brother, on the sin that would be
incurred should she yield to the fascinations of love, and
violate the vows so solemnly made; but it is hard to convince those whose inclinations are enlisted on the opposite
side, and the only effect produced by his exhortations seems
to have been that of accelerating the union—for, fearing
lest more formidable opposition should be aroused, were
the secret divulged, a private marriage was arranged.[1]
The court was then staying at Westminster, where they
had kept their Christmas, and on the 7th of January, 1238,

---

[1] " A chronicler, who is presumed to have been contemporary with this
event, and who, like most of his class, is accustomed to ascribe the results
of political motives, not very clear perhaps at the time, to some remarkable
object of popular wonder or dislike, attributes the voluntary exile of the
Archbishop of Canterbury to his unsuccessful opposition to this marriage.
The statement is wholly wrong.   However, we are told, in language both
vivid and picturesque, that the prelate, when leaving England, stood upon a
hill which commanded a view of London, and, extending his hands towards
the city, pronounced a parting blessing on his country, and a curse upon the
countess and the offspring of her unholy union.   It is more than probable
that the unfortunate events of after years suggested the insertion of this
story, so creditable to the prophetic powers of St. Edmund."   Introduction

the lovers were united in the most secret manner possible, in the king's private chapel, by his own chaplain, Walter, Henry himself giving away his sister to the bridegroom, who, we are told, " received her right joyfully, not only on account of the abundant love he bore her, but also for the loveliness of her person, the nobleness of her mind, and the honours of her station as daughter to a king and queen, and sister to a king, a queen, and an empress." (Henry III., Joanna, Queen of Scotland, and Isabella, Empress of Germany.) [1]

No fond congratulations, no festive entertainments awaited the new-made bride. For several months the marriage remained a profound secret, but, meanwhile, King Henry treated his sister and her husband with the greatest kindness. He not only forgave Eleanora £60 of debt owing to him by her, but he lent Simon £120, and gave him 400 marks, and, moreover, sent so strenuous a message to the Earl of Pembroke, who had been unusually remiss in his payments to Eleanora, threatening to distrain his lands and chattels, that £200 of dowry arrears were speedily handed over. [2]

Shortly afterwards the court removed to Windsor; but still every precaution was taken by the bride and bridegroom so to guard their demeanour in public as not to betray the secret of their union. A curious proof of this occurs in the list of offerings given to the king's almoner on the 11th of February, in which Simon de Montfort offers one hundred shillings, and several removes lower in the list,

to the household roll of Eleanora, Countess of Leicester, p. xiii., in a volume, entitled " Manners and Household Expenses of England in the 13th and 15th centuries," presented to the Bannatyne club by Beriah Botfield, Esq., and edited by T. H. Turner, Esq.

[1] Matthew Paris, vol. ii., p. 465. Matthew Westm., p. 298. Annal. Waverley, Gale, vol. ii., p. 197.

[2] Rot. lib., 22 Hen. III. On account of the extremely dilapidated state of this roll, part of which is a mere collection of torn loose fragments, no particulars can be traced of the expenditure, if there were any, immediately connected with the marriage. The above entries occur on the 3rd and 6th of February, and 22nd of April.

quite unassociated with that of her lord, stands the name of Eleanora, countess of *Pembroke*, who gave £5.[1]

We cannot but advert *en passant* to an opinion which has been taken up by Rapin and several of our modern historians, most unfavourable to the character of the Princess Eleanora. They intimate that there were powerful reasons for her private and hasty marriage; in fact, that the king consented to it to save his sister's credit, as she was already likely to become a mother. The sole foundation for this opinion is a hasty expression made use of by Henry to Earl Simon, some years afterwards, when, in a fit of passion, he accused him of seducing his sister before their marriage.[2] But the silence of all contemporary writers on the subject affords strong negative evidence that this accusation was unfounded, more especially since the wrath of the monkish chroniclers was so aroused by the violation of Eleanora's sacred vows, that they would not have failed to seize upon a suspicion which would have afforded them a powerful handle against her. It is also disproved by reference to dates, for the birth of her eldest son did not take place until nearly a year after her marriage.

It was scarcely possible that the union of Simon and Eleanora should remain much longer a secret, and when at length it did transpire, the indignation of the nobles was extreme. The king had recently pledged himself to transact no affair of importance without their concurrence, and they justly considered that, in consenting to the marriage of his sister, he had violated his pledge. Their displeasure was further increased by his having, without their advice, promoted another important match: that of Richard Clare, son of the Earl of Gloucester, with Matilda, daughter of the Earl of Lincoln.[3] The cabal of malecontents was headed by the king's brother, Prince Richard, and they seemed

[1] Rot. lib., 22 H. III., m. 7.   [2] Paris, vol. ii., p. 497.
[3] Chron. Lond. Additional MS., 5441, f. 38.

disposed to testify their resentment not only by words but by deeds. They collected a body of troops in Southwark, and made other warlike demonstrations directed against the king and his daring favourite, and it required all the prudent policy of Simon, by bribes and negociations with the leaders of the opposition, to avert the impending storm. He succeeded in detaching Prince Richard from the confederacy, though the nobles were so disgusted with his desertion, that he lost the title of "the staff of fortitude," by which they had hitherto designated him. The king did not in public stand firm to his favourite in this emergency; he lacked the energy to meet such a storm of opposition, although privately his inclination towards him was as strong as ever; and Montfort perceived with regret that clergy and barons alike looked upon him with coolness and distrust. Anxious, if possible, to remove this feeling, he determined on taking a journey to Rome, to obtain from the pope a confirmation of his marriage. This project was favoured by King Henry, who gave him letters to the pope, to forward his cause.[1] He retired from court, and, collecting from his own estates all the money he could extort by taxing, begging, or borrowing, he set out on his journey.[2]

Meanwhile, the Countess of *Pembroke*, as, from the alleged invalidity of her second marriage, she was still called, was left to struggle with the woes and fears of approaching maternity at the castle of Kenilworth. This place had been assigned to her as her residence by King Henry; for her situation at court, whilst by many of its inmates her marriage was considered illegitimate, was so painful, that her pride refused to brook its annoyances. Eleanora appears to have been deeply touched by the humiliating position in which she was thus placed, for she remained in the most

[1] Rot. pat., 22 Henry III., m. 8.
[2] The amount of these exactions may be estimated by the fact that one Simon Curle Vaches, a citizen of Leicester, was alone compelled to pay 500 marks.—Paris, vol. ii, p. 468.

profound seclusion.[1]   She had been, all her life, destitute
of any female friend, to whom she could look up for support.
Her sister Isabella was too nearly her own age to be more
than a mere companion, and was now, moreover, far away
in Germany, while Joanna, the eldest princess, who had never
been more than an occasional visitor in England, had died
only two months after the luckless day which made Eleanora
a bride, thus adding the pangs of sorrow for the dead to
the anxieties she was already enduring, and this too at the
time when, of all others, she most needed the soothing sympathy of a sister's love.   Wearily and sadly must the days
have rolled over in her stately but lonely abode, until the
return of Earl Simon.

His absence was not, however, greatly prolonged.   His
first appeal had been made to his brother-in-law, the Emperor Frederic, the husband of the Princess Isabella, and
he was so far successful as to obtain from him letters,
strongly recommending him to the favourable notice of his
Holiness ;[2] and, armed with these and the credentials of
King Henry, and also other arguments still more *weighty*,
he contrived, by lavishing gifts and promises, to obtain the
fulfilment of his petition, even though he was opposed by
the Archbishop of Canterbury, Eleanora's former spiritual
adviser, who, actuated by conscientious scruples, endeavoured, by telling the whole truth to the pope, to frustrate
his efforts.[3]   But the power of gold proved omnipotent.
Simon returned home, provided with a full dispensation for
his marriage, and with letters from his Holiness to Otho,
the papal legate in England, commanding him to authorize
and ratify it.   With these precious documents, Earl Simon
arrived in triumph at court on the 14th of October, 1238,
where he was favourably received and even appointed to the.

---

[1] " Interea *latuit* apud Konilwarthe Comitissa de Pembroc, gravida, rei
exitus præstolando," is the expression of Matthew Paris, vol. ii., p. 468.
[2] Paris, ut supra.   [3] Paris, vol. ii., p. 471.

office of counsellor to the king;[1] but, remaining there no longer than was absolutely necessary, he hastened to Kenilworth,[2] where he arrived in time to cheer the drooping spirits of his wife, and, by the good news he brought, to cast a gleam of brightness over the birth of their son, which took place very soon after, on Advent Sunday, the 28th of November.

Eleanora, in order to seal the peace with her royal brother, requested him to officiate as godfather to the boy, who received the name of Henry. The Bishop of Chester, who was at that time paying a visit at Kenilworth, on his way to London, performed the baptismal ceremony, but was taken ill the same day, and shortly afterwards expired at the castle.[3]

But there was still a strong party in England, who regarded Eleanora's marriage with the utmost abhorrence. These were the more zealous of the clergy, at the head of whom was one William de Avendon, a Dominican friar, who openly expressed his sentiments on the subject, and strongly reprobated the conduct of the pope; quoting a tractate on vows, by one "Master Peter," from which it appears that a sacred plight ring was considered almost as impassable a barrier as the veil itself against the marriage of the wearer. "But the court of Rome reasoned more subtly than it is given us to comprehend," says Matthew Paris, whose wonted reverence for papal authority struggled hard with his convictions of right in this matter. The opposition of the humbler ranks of the clergy, however, was speedily frowned down by the authority of the papal legate, and gradually died away.

Simon and Eleanora appear at this time to have acted the part of prudence by living a private life at the pleasant retirement of Kenilworth, though the earl paid occasional and necessary visits to court. Meanwhile, they received

---

[1] M. Westm., p. 299. [2] Paris, vol. ii., p. 475.
[3] Paris, vol. ii., p. 481.

several marks of the royal favour. At Christmas, King
Henry sent his sister a present of a robe made of the costly
material called baudekyn,[1] the warp of which was of threads
of gold and the woof silk; it was richly embroidered and
trimmed with miniver fur and feathers; also a mantle of scarlet cloth, a mattress and counterpane for her bed, and several
minor articles, the total cost of which amounted to upwards
of £30.[2]   On the 12th of January, 1239, the king gave
an order that thenceforth the dowry of Eleanora should be
paid to her acknowledged husband, Simon de Montfort.[3]

The following February, Simon received a fresh confirmation of the earldom of Leicester from the king, in presence of his elder brother Amalric, who, having come over
on a visit, renewed the formal resignation he had previously
made of all claims upon the earldom.[4]   The spring of the
year was spent by the earl and countess at Eleanora's castle
of Odiham.   Her now increased establishment demanded
enlarged accommodations, and the gallant de Montfort spent
his leisure hours in the somewhat unchivalric occupation of
superintending the erection of a new kitchen there.[5]   Shortly
after this, Simon, who was still in high favour at court,
was called upon to reciprocate the friendly offices the king
had already performed for him, by becoming in his turn
godfather to the young Prince Edward, who was born on
the 16th of June, 1239; this was not a gratuitous honour,
however, for each of the *nine* godfathers, among whom
were two bishops and Richard Earl of Cornwall, was
expected to present the child with costly gifts.   Nor were
they the only persons taxed on the occasion.   Henry
despatched messengers to all the powerful and wealthy

[1] Or baldekyn, from its being originally imported from Baldach, or Babylon.
—See Glossaries of Ducange and Nares, sub voce.
[2] Rot. lib., 23 H. III., m. 23.   [3] Ibid., m. 22.
[4] Rot. chart., 23 Hen. III., m. 4. Paris, vol. ii., p. 483. Ann. Waverley,
p. 198. Chron. Rishanger, Cotton MS., Claudius, D. vi., f. 68; and Chron.
Tewksb., Cleop., A vii., f. 36 b.
[5] Rot. lib., 23 H. III., m. 9.

nobles of the realm, informing them of the birth of an heir to the crown, and none of these bearers of good tidings were expected to return empty-handed. If the value of the gift presented did not come up to the expectations of the royal beggar, he indignantly rejected it, and sent back the messenger with a mandate on his peril not to return till he had secured a richer booty. The conduct of King Henry on this occasion gave rise to a cutting sarcasm from a Norman jester. " God has *given* us this infant," said he, " but, my lord, the king *sells* him to us."[1]

The Countess Eleanora had not as yet appeared again at her brother's court. She seems to have shrunk, with great reluctance, from meeting her family and friends, even although the stigma cast upon her marriage had been completely removed. But on so joyous an occasion as the baptism of the infant prince, when her husband was to officiate as sponsor, she could not withhold her presence, and therefore accompanied him to court. They were well received by the king; and the palace of the Bishops of Winchester, in Southwark, then unoccupied owing to the temporary vacancy of the See, was assigned to them as a place of residence. Here they remained for upwards of two months, on terms of friendly intercourse with the court.

But a storm was gathering, which burst upon them all the more violently from its being so totally unexpected. The 9th of August was the day appointed for the churching of the queen, and, as was customary, a train of noble ladies assembled to attend her, and among them, of course, her sister-in-law, the Countess Eleanora, who was accompanied by her lord. But no sooner did the king perceive Earl Simon, than he forbade him, in the sternest manner, to advance, or to attempt to join in the solemn feast; reviling him, in presence of the whole court, as an excommunicated man, and accusing him of having seduced his sister, and thus

---

[1] Paris, vol. ii., p. 488.

procured a reluctant consent to his marriage. The earl and countess were struck speechless with surprise at this burst of passionate fury. Confounded and blushing, they hastily retired from the king's presence, took to their barge, and returned to their abode at Winchester palace; but they were speedily followed by the royal messengers, who came to command, and, if necessary, to enforce their immediate ejectment. Overwhelmed with dismay, they hastened once more to Westminster, and by tears and supplications endeavoured to pacify the indignant monarch. But Henry had one quality in common with his Norman ancestors, and that was the fierceness of his wrath when it was fairly roused. He reiterated the reproaches of the morning, and added fresh accusations. — " You corrupted my sister before marriage," exclaimed he, in a tone of vehement passion, "and therefore when I knew it, I gave her to you, unwilling though I was; and in order that her vow might not hinder your marriage, you have been to Rome, and corrupted the court with costly gifts and still costlier promises. And although the Archbishop of Canterbury, who was then at Rome, told the pope the truth, yet your multiplied bribes prevailed; and when you were threatened with excommunication because you could not pay the money you had promised, you crowned your vileness by bringing me through false testimony as your security."[1]

With tearful eyes and downcast hearts, Simon and Eleanora departed, trembling lest personal violence should be added to reproach; and that day's sunset saw them embarked on a fragile bark, with but few attendants and such necessaries only as a few hours sufficed to procure, and sailing for the coast of France. They had not even time to send for their infant son, who was therefore left behind at Kenilworth.[2]

The cause of this wrathful ebullition, on the part of

---

[1] Paris, vol. ii., p. 498.   [2] Ibid.

King Henry, is not named by any of our chroniclers; but he himself seems to reveal the secret when he upbraids the earl for bringing him in as security for his debts. It would appear that this fact had only just come to the knowledge of the king, revealed, doubtless, by claims made upon him for some part of the money to which he thus unwittingly stood pledged; and, unprepared as he ever was to meet even his just claims, he was ill able to brook the advancement of unjust ones, and, heedless of time or place, vented his wrath at the very first opportunity. His indignation would be the more vehement from the fact that Earl Simon was already his debtor to the large amount of £1565. 6s. 8d., besides £15 recently lent to Eleanora.[1]

But the king's anger was subdued almost as easily as it had been excited, and, in the spring of the following year, the earl again returned to England, and was received by the king with his wonted cordiality. The object of Simon's visit was to collect, from his English estates, funds for an intended expedition to the Holy Land. He made vigorous efforts to raise the necessary supplies, but, to accomplish this, he was compelled to sell some of his lands to the canons and hospitallers of Leicester for the sum of £1000. Before Earl Simon took his final departure for the crusade, he revisited his countess, taking with him from England his young son Henry, in order to restore the child to his mother.[2] Eleanora did not accompany him; she remained beyond the sea, where, during the absence of her lord, she gave birth to a second son.[3] The exact residence of the countess, during her exile, is not ascertained with any degree of certainty. The city of Montfort, in the district of Chartres, which was the residence of the elder branch of the Montfort family, was, in all probability, her principal abode, since it is natural to suppose that Simon would seek refuge among his

[1] Rot. lib., 23 H. III., m. 6. [2] Paris ut sup.
[3] Paris, vol. ii., p. 527.

own relations. It must be remembered too that the mother of Eleanora, Isabella of Augoulême, now the wife of the Earl of March, had a home to offer to her daughter; and, though we find no documentary evidence of intercourse between them, yet there is a probability, to say the least, that it did take place during the countess' residence in France.

De Montfort had other reasons than those of a purely religious nature, to induce him to assume the cross, for his brother Amalric was lingering a captive at Babylon, in the hands of the infidels, by whom he had been taken prisoner the preceding year.[1]

No notice is taken by historians of the exploits of the earl during his stay in the Holy Land; yet he must have succeeded, in no ordinary degree, in attracting the regard and admiration of the inhabitants, since the nobility of Jerusalem presented a petition, dated the 7th of June, 1241, to entreat the emperor Frederic II. to appoint him their governor, until the majority of his son Conrad, who was the heir to the throne, in right of his deceased mother Yolante. They sent a formal written engagement, promising to keep and maintain the earl in his office, and to obey him as they would the emperor himself. They prayed Frederic to seal this agreement with his golden seal; and, in token of their good intentions, they appended their own to it.[2] Obstacles, however, arose to the fulfilment of their request. They can scarcely be supposed to have been raised by De Montfort himself, since it is not likely that a petition so consonant to his aspiring views should have been got up without his concurrence; but the emperor knew the energetic character of his brother-in-law too well

[1] L'art de verifier, vol. xii., p. 482. He died on his way to France the following year, and was buried in the church of St. John's, at the Lateran. Ibid. Lansdowne MS., No. 229, f. 120 b.

[2] A copy of this is preserved in the Cotton MS. Vespasian, F. i., fol. 114. It is printed in the learned sketch of Earl Leicester's career, in the introduction to the household roll by Mr. Turner, already referred to, p. xix.

to accede to it. An enterprising governor, in a distant and disaffected province, is often more to be dreaded than a feeble one, and the manner in which Earl Simon had already ingratiated himself with the nobles showed that he might prove but too formidable a rival. On the rejection of the petition, Simon returned to England, whither it is likely his wife accompanied him.

The following year, 1242, was signalized, by the mad scheme of the weak-minded Henry, undertaken at the solicitation of his mother, to rescue the province of Poictou from the hands of the French monarch, by whom it had been granted as an appanage to his brother Alphonso. So strongly was this project reprobated by the English nobles, that they utterly refused to grant the usual supplies, which had, consequently, to be squeezed from the reluctant people by levies of personal contributions.[1] Henry persisted, however, in his wilfulness; and many of the nobles, when they found him thus determined, attended him on the expedition : among their number was the Earl of Leicester. The queen and the ladies of the court accompanied their lords. They sailed from Portsmouth in the month of May, and, on their landing in Guienne, were met by the countess-queen Isabella. She kissed the young king with much tenderness, and said to him, " Dear, sweet son ! you are very good-natured to come to help your mother and your brothers, whom the sons of Blanche of Spain[2] would too wickedly trample and keep under their feet; but, if it be God's pleasure, things shall not come to pass as they expect."[3]

The hopes of the queen-mother were, however, doomed

[1] Paris, vol. ii., p. 582.   [2] The queen-regent of France.

[3] " Quant il fu au port arrivé, la contesse sa mère ala encontre et le baisa moult doucement et luy dist. 'Biau doux fils, vous estes de bonne nature qui venez secourre vostre mère et vos frères, que le fils Blanche d'Espaigne veullent trop malement defouler et tenir soubs piés; mais sé Dieu plaist il n'ira pas si comme il pensent.' " Les grandes Chroniques de France, edited by M. Paulin, Paris, vol. v., p. 268.

to disappointment. The particulars of this luckless and
ill-directed expedition belong to general history. Suffice
it to say that De Montfort fully established his claim to
the title of a valiant chevalier; and at the battle of Xaintes
especially, so unfortunate for the English, he displayed
great prowess, and even rescued the king, who was in
danger of falling into the hands of the enemy, by the efforts
of his personal bravery. On the disgraceful termination
of the campaign, the whole court reassembled at Bourdeaux,
where the queen, the countess of Leicester, and the ladies
of the court had resided during its progress; but, so great
was the dissatisfaction of many of the nobles, that, without taking leave of their royal master, they returned to
England. The Earls of Leicester and Salisbury, and a few
others, still remained true to their sovereign, though the
cost at which they preserved their allegiance was by no
means trifling, for they were left altogether to their own
resources, and obliged to incur large and daily increasing
debts to meet the necessary expenses of their households.[1]

The character of the king is presented to us, at this period,
in a most despicable light; for, while he allowed his faithful followers to suffer from utter destitution of those things
which it should have been his first care to provide, he squandered all the money he could obtain upon foreign parasites.
Among these was the Countess of Bearne, mother of the
far-famed Gaston de Bearne; "a woman," says Paris,
"singularly monstrous in size and prodigious for fatness;"
nor does he represent her mental qualities in a whit more
favourable light, asserting that she came purely to get
what she could out of the king, and, in the end, only returned him evil for good.[2] The Earl of Toulouse and the
king of Arragon were also visitants at the court of Bourdeaux. These two princes still retained their ancient

---

[1] Paris, vol. ii., p. 596.

[2] "Quæ nunquam Regi profuit, imò potiùs offuit, et in fine defuit."—Paris,
vol. ii., p. 594. The point of this passage would be lost in a translation.

animosity to the Montfort family, embittered by so many
years of conflict during the Albigensian wars ; and, by their
frequent insinuations, they endeavoured to prejudice the
wavering mind of the king against Earl Simon.[1] In this
they were but too successful, for the coolness of the king
rendered his situation so unpleasant to him, that he and
his countess took their departure for England.[2]

The alienation of Henry from his valiant brother-in-law
was only temporary. On the king's return to England, in
the autumn of 1243, Simon resumed his former place at
court and council, and indeed appears to have been at the
highest pinnacle of favour. The castle of Kenilworth,
which had before afforded him and Eleanora a temporary
asylum, was now formally bestowed upon them,[3] and ever
after continued to be their principal seat. This stately
building, whose ruins, so fraught with the romantic associations of later years, and venerable with the hoariness of centuries, are still visited by the lovers of the picturesque, was
founded in the time of Henry I., by Geoffry de Clinton, his
treasurer and chamberlain, and had subsequently been a
favourite royal residence.[4] During the recent banishment
of the Earl and Countess of Leicester, in 1240, King
Henry III. and his queen spent a short time there, and
considerable sums were expended in repairing and beauti-
fying it, wainscoting the chapel, and erecting seats therein
for the king and queen, &c.[5] Thus, when the Countess
Eleanora again returned to the proud mansion which had
now become her own, she found a habitation in every respect
well befitting her royal birth, and equally suited to the
martial tastes of her lord ; for Kenilworth was a fortress as
well as a castle. The walls were, many of them, from ten
to fifteen feet thick, and the principal tower, called Cæsar's

[1] Paris, vol. ii., p. 596.
[2] Russell's life of Earl Simon, in Nichols' history of Leicestershire, vol. i.,
p. 212.   [3] Rot. pat., 28 H. III., m. 8.
[4] Dogdale's Hist. of Warwickshire, vol. i., p. 242.
[5] Rot. lib., 25 H. III., m. 16,

Tower, was considered all but impregnable. It was surrounded by a double row of ramparts,[1] and a broad moat,
called the Pool, covering 111 acres of ground, being half a
mile in length, and in some places a quarter of a mile in
breadth, thus affording space for sailing; and it was frequently used for this purpose; for King Henry had given
orders for the construction of a "fair and beautiful boat, to
lye near the door of the king's great chamber,"[2] — the
royal apartments, which were doubtless those afterwards
occupied by the earl and countess, being situated in that
part of the castle which was almost washed by the waters of
the lake. The park that surrounded this princely abode
covered 40 acres of land, and the manors and chase belonging to it extended over 19 or 20 miles more of richly-wooded
country. The castle itself, though not so extensive as it
afterwards became when the Lancaster and Leicester buildings were added to it, was still of very ample dimensions;
the banqueting-hall in particular was capacious enough to
dine two hundred persons, and such an assemblage actually
feasted there in 1277, when Edward I. held his celebrated
feast of the round table, and the beauty and chivalry of
many lands assembled within its ancient walls.[3] The
lower apartments were sometimes used as places of confinement for hostages or state prisoners; the ample dimensions of the castle, and its great strength, rendering it peculiarly adapted for such a purpose.[4] In order that the
inhabitants might be independent of extrinsic services, there

[1] See an order in the liberate roll, of the 25th of Henry III., m. 5, for the
building of a new wall between the inner and outer walls.
[2] Dugdale's Warwick., vol. i., p. 244. The Patent roll of the 15th
of Henry III. is the authority quoted by Dugdale, but no such entry occurs
on that roll. From the nature of it, it would be more likely to be found on
a close or liberate, than on a patent roll.
[3] Dugdale's Warwick , vol. ii., p. 243. Chron. Hayles, Harl. MS., 3725,
fol. 15. A curious description of this round table, with a recapitulation of
the tales told by the courtly guests, is to be found in an old Dutch Chronicle
written in 1316, entitled, Spiegel historial van Lodewyk van Veltham,
pp. 98-106.
[4] Dugd. Warwick., vol. ii., p. 243.

was connected with it a mill to grind corn for their use. A market was held there every Tuesday, for the interchange of commodities amongst the inhabitants of the castle and the neighbouring peasantry; often resorted to, probably, by the Jew pedlars, who might hope to vend their costly wares to the lord and lady of the mansion. Kenilworth was also privileged to hold its own courts of justice. It had its assize of bread, beer, &c., to regulate the prices and weights or measures of these and other provisions; its court baron, for the recovery of debts and punishment of minor trespasses, and its court leet, to judge more serious crimes.[1] From the sentence of this tribunal there was no appeal; for a gallows, which frowned from the walls of the castle, stood ready to execute the last sentence of the law upon the convicted offender.[2] This last appendage is strongly characteristic of the period when might was so often substituted for right, and when a proud baron could, under a show of justice, take summary vengeance on those who had offended him.

Here, then, the lady Eleanora passed the greater part of the few ensuing years, the only period of her wedded life when the halcyon wings of peace brooded for a while over her stormy career. A young family was now springing up around her; and, whatever might be Eleanora's faults, her tender affection, as a wife and mother, is unimpeachable. Henry, her eldest son, was frequently taken to the court of her brother, to be the playmate and companion of his young cousin, Prince Edward. The other sons, Simon, Guy, Amalric, and Richard, as soon as they became old enough, were placed under the tutelage of Robert Grosstête, Bishop of Lincoln.

The intimate association of the Earl and Countess of

---

[1] Court Leete and Court Baron, by John Kiklim, of Gray's Inn Lane, 12mo. London, 1598, fol. 3, b.
[2] Dugdale's Warwickshire, vol. i., p. 247.

Leicester with the above-named prelate is a favourable
feature in their personal character; for the Bishop of
Lincoln was one of the most learned men of the day, and as
remarkable for the grave simplicity of his manners, and
his indefatigable attention to the duties of his sacred calling,
as for his extensive literary attainments.   He was a perfect
French scholar, having spent several years in Paris, in order
to make himself master of what was then the universal language of polished society.   He wrote, in French, a history
of the creation of the world, which is still extant.[1]   His
theological tractates and sermons are numerous,[2] and he
indulged, too, in lighter literature.   He wrote several
poems, one of which, entitled, " le Chastel d'amour," is
an allegory, the castle symbolizing the Virgin Mary.[3]
Whether he was indebted for the sobriquet of Grosstête,
or Greathead, to any physical peculiarity, or whether our
forefathers were phrenologists enough to bestow it on him
from his superior mental qualities, is not recorded.   He was
the confidential adviser of Simon in all cases of perplexity,[4]
and, by his moderate counsels, often succeeded in calming
the irritated feelings of the earl.

His office of tutor to their children, which, although himself of humble birth, he discharged admirably, particularly
in fitting them to fulfil their courtly duties, rendered him a
frequent and welcome guest at the house and table of
Simon and Eleanora.[5]   He also introduced to their notice

[1] See Lacombe's Dictionnaire du vieux langage François, vol. ii., Preface
p. xxxiv.

[2] Several of these are preserved in the Arundel and Burney MSS. A
splendidly illuminated copy of one, entitled Speculum Humanæ Salvationis,
is in the Harleian MS., No. 2838. A list of his works is given in the
Itinerary of William of Worcester, p. 266, Nasmith's edition.

[3] Copies of this poem are still preserved in the Royal MS., 20 B. xiv., and
Harleian MS., 1121, British Museum; also among the Colbert. MSS.,
Bibl. du roi. See Archæologia, vol. xiii., pp. 246-8.

[4] Rishanger's Chron., p. 7, edited for the Camden Society, by J. O. Halliwell, Esq.

[5] The bishop was once questioned by Henry III., how it was that he, a
person of low origin, could so well instruct young nobles. His reply was,

and favour another learned priest, to whom he was himself warmly attached,[1] whom we shall have frequent occasion hereafter to notice. This was Adam de Marisco, nephew of Richard de Marisco, lord chancellor and bishop of Durham,[2] one of the most eminent divines of his time, who took a doctor's degree at Oxford.[3] He seems to have occupied much the same position, in reference to the Countess Eleanora, which the Bishop of Lincoln held with her lord. He was her correspondent, amanuensis, counsellor, and friend. Whether he held nominally the office of her confessor, is not distinctly ascertained. It is probable he might do so, since he belonged to the order of friars minors, from whom, on account of the strictness of their lives, confessors were frequently chosen. At any rate, he discharged some

that he had learned in greater courts than that of the King of England, meaning, in the pages of ancient history. Selden's works, by Wilkins, vol. v., p. 96.

[1] Life of Grostête, by Samuel Pegge, 4to. Lon., 1793, p. 229.

[2] See close roll, 10th Hen, III., m. 6.

[3] This learned man is mentioned with great approbation by several of our ecclesiastical biographers. He commenced his public career as a parish priest, at Wirmouth, in the diocese of Durham; but, anxious to lead a more decidedly religious life, he joined the sect of Franciscans, or friars minors, then the strictest of the monastic orders; and his fame for piety and learning was such, that St. Francis, the founder of the order, sent for him to Italy, where he spent several years. On his return, he greatly assisted the Bishop of Lincoln in his theological studies; and, after having taken his degree at Oxford, he became known by the title of " the illustrated doctor." A MS. of Roger Bacon, quoted by Wharton, Anglia Sacra, vol. ii. p. 344, speaks of him as the Solomon of his day, and one of the greatest scholars in the world: perfect in divine and human learning. In the year 1257, he was sent with the Bishop of Worcester and Hugh Bygod on an embassy into France, to consult with the Earl of Leicester, and Peter of Savoy, about the terms of a peace. Rymer, vol. i., pt. i., p. 359. In 1257, he was nominated to the bishopric of Ely, but failed of procuring a confirmation of his appointment, although he went to Rome on purpose. The pope, to compensate for this disappointment, sent him back with a legantine commission, to inquire into the reported miracles of Richard, Bishop of Chichester, and his consequent claims to saintship. He died shortly after, about the year 1257, or, as others say, 1260. He was the author of several learned theological works, one of which was a book of epistles to Robert Grosstête. Trivet's Annals, p. 205. Stevens' Monasticon, vol. i., p. 130. Fuller's Worthies, vol. ii., p. 287. The Cottonian MS., Vitellius, c. viii., contains a collection of his more familiar letters: possibly it was his own letter-book, since the handwriting is contemporary. Several of those to the Earl and Countess of Leicester will be subsequently quoted.

of its duties with an unflinching firmness almost
amounting to severity. The choice made by Eleanora of
such an adviser speaks well for her discrimination of
character.

The patronage afforded by Simon and Eleanora to literature was very extensive, and it would seem that they paid
some attention to the then arduous and expensive task of
collecting a library; for a chronicler, who wrote a few years
afterwards, describes a book on the life and manners of the
Tartars, containing as many letters as a psaltery, that belonged to the Earl of Leicester, " which," he tells us, " whoever now desires to see, may find it in the book of additions
at St. Albans." [1]

But to return to the general course of history. The star
of Montfort was at this period in the ascendant at court,
and he was treated with great kindness by the king. Eleanora's troubles about obtaining her dowry remittances still
continuing, Henry himself became pledge for the payment of
the £400 a-year due to her for her Irish estates; and, from
this period, we find the orders for its payment in half-yearly
sums occurring in the liberate or issue rolls as regularly as the
recurring periods of Michaelmas and Easter, when it became
due. The guardianship of the castle of Leicester, then one of
the royal fortresses, was assigned to her husband by the king.
Another favour which he conferred was of a more questionable character. The earl and countess had incurred a debt
of £110. 11s. to one David, a Jew of Oxford, and the
monarch took upon himself to remit them this debt, not by
paying it himself, but by the far more convenient mode of
sending word to the *justice* appointed over the Jews (a
woeful misappropriation of term, by the way, with regard
to these officers of the oppressed Israelites), that he had
been graciously pleased to pardon that debt, and that a

---

[1] Chron. John of Oxford, Cotton MS., Nero, D ii., f. 229, col. 2. Chron.
Rish., p. 6.

record of quittance was to be drawn out for it accordingly.[1]

It was but just that some pecuniary compensation should
be granted to Earl Simon, for he had well nigh ruined his
fortunes by the expenses he incurred when in attendance on
the king in Gascony. In order to confer upon him a reward
in some degree proportionable to the value of his services,
the following year Henry sold to him the wardship of Gilbert, the young heir of Humphrey, lord of Umfranville,
who was then only an infant. The sum paid by Simon was
10,000 marks,[2] but so great was the value of the purchase,
that it was even then regarded rather in the light of a gift.
By the iniquitous laws of wardship at that time in operation, the guardian had full power to appropriate to himself
the revenues of the minor, allowing only sufficient for his
support and education. In the case of a female ward, the
emoluments were largely increased by his power of disposing
of her hand in marriage to the highest bidder. By this
accession to their income, and the payment of two other
sums, one of 500 marks and the other of £200, from the
tardy heir of the Pembroke family,[3] the Earl and Countess
of Leicester became, in some measure, liberated from their
pecuniary difficulties.

In the spring of the year 1245, Simon and Eleanora,
according to the ordinary custom of the times, made a
progress to visit several monastic establishments, and,

[1] Rot. pat., 28 Hen. III., mm. 10, 8, and 3. The degree of oppression to
which the unfortunate sons of Abraham were constantly subjected is almost
incredible. Illustrations of it abound in almost every document containing
any detail of royal expenditure. A curious instance occurs in the close roll
of the 41st of Henry III., m. 14. A Jew of London, called Jacob le Evesk,
had been seized with a dangerous malady, which was likely to prove fatal.
In considerate anticipation of such a catastrophe, the king graciously spared
him the trouble of making a will, by sending an order to the *justice* that, in
case of his death, the whole of his wealth, both in money and moveable
property, was to be bestowed on Queen Eleanora. Such was the prejudice
of this queen against the Jews, that she obtained an express order from her
son Edward I. that no Jew should be permitted to live in any of the towers
which were assigned for her dower. Royal letters, No. 1620, Eleanora to
Edward I. [2] Rot. fin., 29 Hen. III., vol. i., p. 436.
[3] Rot. pat., 29 Hen. III., mm. 8, 5, 4.

amongst others, the abbey of Waverley, in Surrey. To the
worthy monks, the coming of a lady of royal birth was
great subject-matter of gratulation, and it is spoken of in
their annals as an affair of much importance. "On Palm
Sunday, which was the 1st of April, the lady Alienora,
Countess of Leicester, sister to the King Henry III., a most
sincere lover of our house, by leave of the pope, most devoutly entered our abbey, having with her her *most pious*
husband, Simon de Montfort, Earl of Leicester, her two sons,
Henry and Simon, and three maidens; at whose entry, a
notable thing happened, for the moment in which her foot
advanced within the church, on the opposite side to the
great altar, where the mass of the blessed Virgin was then
celebrated, the host was raised at the hour of consecration;
nor must this circumstance be ascribed to chance, but to the
divine arrangement, that the holy Virgin, the love of whom
had led her hither, thus offered herself most benignantly to
her." The superstition of the monkish chronicler can
scarcely fail to excite a smile. He goes on to inform us
that Eleanora's offering on this occasion was a precious
altar-cloth, to be placed on the altar at those special seasons
when the relics were brought out; and doubtless she herself
would be favoured with the exhibition of all the bones and
hairs, rags and scrapings of nails, of which the good friars
of Waverley had to boast. The countess was present, we
are told, at the sermon in the chapel, the procession, and
the greater mass, and the kissing of the "wood of God"—
doubtless a piece of the holy rood, or *true* cross of Christ, of
which it has been calculated that amply sufficient was preserved, in the European churches alone, to rebuild Noah's
Ark. "After this, she retired, no little edified," says our
chronicler; "and since then she has sent us fifty marks, and
eighteen more towards the adorning of our church, and by
her help we were enabled to purchase 150 acres of land at
Netham." [1]

[1] Annales Waverlienses Gale, vol. ii., p. 206.

ELEANORA,

THIRD DAUGHTER OF KING JOHN.

CHAPTER II.

Simon's political position—He and Eleanora assume the cross—Simon sent into Gascony—Eleanora's extravagant habits—Good nature—Simon's return—Troubles in Gascony—Eleanora goes over there—Marisco's letters to her—Return to England—Discords between Henry and Simon—Birth of a daughter—Intercourse with Queen Eleanora—Return to Gascony—Simon's seneschalship revoked—retirement into France—summoned by the king—sent ambassador to France—Eleanora's dower demands—Relinquishes her claim to French provinces — Quarrels between Earls Gloucester and Leicester—Simon's influence feared by the king—Arbitration of the French queen—Battle of Lewes—Eleanora's household roll—Her visitors—Domestic arrangements—Charities—Gifts to her daughter—and to her royal relatives—Hauteur of her sons—Desertion of Earl Gloucester—Escape of Prince Edward—Battle of Evesham—Death of Simon and his son—His character—Miracles—Eleanora at Dover—Sends her two sons to France—King angry with her—Interview with Prince Edward—Her banishment—Surrender of Kenilworth—Eleanora retires to Montargis—Visits the French court—Contests with the Earl of March—Murder of Henry of Germany by Simon and Guy de Montfort—Their fate—Eleanora's rights confirmed by Edward I.—Her claims upon the executors of Saint Louis—Her will—Visited by Queen Margaret—Death—Prosecution of her will—Character—Eleanora, the younger—Amalric de Montfort.

We have now to revert, though as slightly as possible, to the beaten track of general history, to furnish those connecting links which are indispensable to a distinct comprehension of the succeeding events in the life of Eleanora. The Earl of Leicester began about this time to assume a more important position in the state than he had previously occupied. In 1244, he was one of a committee chosen to deliberate upon the grant of a subsidy to the king, and, in 1246, his name occurs among those of the other nobles in an appeal to the pope against the enormous exactions of the church of Rome.[1]

[1] Matthew Paris, vol. ii., pp. 639, 700.

In the year 1248, the grand movement for a general crusade, made by St. Louis of France, roused once more the chivalric spirit of Europe. It was preached far and wide, and emissaries were despatched to England, who visited the more influential nobles, to exhort them to share in the holy expedition. On this occasion, Simon de Montfort was not overlooked. Prompted, we are informed, by a desire to make atonement for all his sins, but especially for his marriage, he once more mounted the cross, and determined to accompany the crusading hosts.[1] Now, although Earl Simon had doubtless many sins to atone for, yet, if a pilgrimage to the holy land was to be considered as absolving him from the guilt of marrying one who had taken upon herself sacred vows, he was already free, since, in 1241, he had visited Jerusalem. But this fact is overlooked, or not mentioned by our early chroniclers. Perhaps, were we to attribute his resolution to his restless spirit of enterprise, which, at this time, found no vent in England, we should be nearer the truth. When the Countess Eleanora saw the red cross once more clasped on the bosom of her lord, she determined not again to be left behind, and with eagerness she too flew to assume the sacred symbol.[2] Fired by the example of their lord and lady, the warlike retainers of De Montfort, and even a large proportion of his domestic servants, also took the cross. Matthew Paris, of course, attributes the conduct of Eleanora on this occasion to the impulse of religious feeling, but it accords far better with the general tenour of her mind to suppose that chivalrous enthusiasm had still more to do with it, for she possessed a dauntless and resolute spirit. It might be, too, that, having once known the anxieties of a wife whilst her husband was far away on an expedition so fraught with peril, she shrunk from a second time encountering them, and determined to accompany him,

[1] Paris, vol. ii., p. 742.
[2] " Ad ipsam suspiciendam ociùs avolavit."   Paris, at sup.

and share with him those hardships and dangers which were inevitably associated with a crusading life. Her resolution was not, however, put to the test. Scarcely had Earl Simon taken the vows, than he was despatched by the king to quell an insurrection in Gascony, which he succeeded in doing, and returned to celebrate the Christmas festivals at the palace of Westminster, where he was received with great cordiality by King Henry, amidst the general rejoicing of the people, and where he was most probably joined by his wife and family.[1]

The state of Gascony, the last relic of the splendid continental possessions of Henry II. now in the hands of his degenerate grandson, was most deplorable. The Gascons hated the English rule, and never lost a feasible opportunity of trying to shake it off. When King Henry himself resided amongst them, he had been more than once grossly insulted, although the very great benefits their trade and commerce received through the residence of the English court led them generally to treat him with consideration, in order to induce him to prolong his stay among them.[2] On his departure, Nicholas de Molis, and afterwards William de Bules, were appointed seneschals, but both failed in repressing the turbulent spirit of the people. At length, the king and council determined that the bold De Montfort, whose energetic character and martial prowess well fitted him for the office, should be again sent over. Accordingly, he was duly invested with the office of seneschal, which was granted him by letters patent for six years, with the custody of all the royal castles ;[3] and he took his departure for the continent.

Eleanora did not accompany her husband this time, but remained at her own castle of Kenilworth, a renewed grant of which was made to her for life, without any mention of Earl Simon.[4] The life of the countess was, however, far from an idle one—the whole arrangement of domestic ex-

---

[1] Paris, vol. ii., p. 757.   [2] Ibid., vol. ii., p. 600.
[3] Rot. pat., 32 Henry III., m. 2.   [4] Ibid., m. 3.

penditure devolved upon her, and her office was not a sinecure. The revenues of De Montfort being only those of
half the earldom of Leicester, even with the assistance of
occasional grants from the king, and Eleanora's dowry of
£400 a-year, now regularly paid from the royal exchequer,
besides the revenue of her English lands, were not found
adequate to meet the expenditure of the baronial castle,
with its multitude of retainers, kept up with all the rude
plenty and hospitality of the feudal times, and with a degree
of magnificence all but regal; and the countess had frequently to struggle with an accumulation of pecuniary difficulties. In order to satisfy their uneasy creditors, King
Henry granted the Leicester revenues, first for four, and
then for eight years after the death of Earl Simon, towards
the payment of his debts.[1] But the profuseness of the
sovereign towards his own foreign relations and those of
Queen Eleanora left it out of his power to bestow any
effectual assistance upon his sister and brother-in-law, even
when they were in high favour, although he showed his
willingness to aid them by several small donations.[2]

The minute attention paid by the Countess Eleanora to
every particular of domestic outlay is fully evident from the
details in her household roll hereafter to be mentioned. The
providing of garments for every member of her establishment, attending to her larder, buttery, and poultry-yard,
entertaining the poor, and occasional guests, especially those
of the monastic orders, and her correspondence, which appears to have been extensive, occupied her time, and
afforded scope for her energies. But neither at this time
nor during any period of her life does Eleanora seem to
have remembered that one of the most important principles

---

[1] Rot. pat., 32 H. III., m. 3.   Ibid, 20. m. 4.
[2] In the patent rolls of the 30th of Henry III., m. 2, the annual rental of
£30 for the manor of Wedcumb is remitted to Eleanora, and in that of the
32nd m. 11, a similar remittance is given for £5 from that of Odiham, and
also at m. 3, a gift of 250 marks to Earl Simon.

of good housekeeping is to make the expenditure fall within the income, and she often suffered much inconvenience from the extravagance of her habits. Good nature may have been one cause of her profuseness; for that this formed a prominent feature in her character is evident from a letter written by Adam de Marisco to the Bishop of Lincoln, probably about this time.[1] He states that he has presented the bishop's apologies to the Countess of Leicester, for not having sent to her John of Leicester on the death of H. the cook; but her reply was that, had she the best servants in the world, she would give them up willingly for the sake of the bishop. It is not every notable housewife that would smile away a disappointment in reference to a favourite domestic.

The period of Eleanora's temporary widowhood was not of long duration. While she was busily engaged at home, her spouse was equally busy combating the enemies of King Henry, especially Gaston de Bearne, the son of the "fat" Countess de Bearne, whose personal appearance was so graphically portrayed by Matthew Paris. Before the departure of Earl Simon, the king, with a keen sense of the indignities he had endured from his Gascon subjects, had ordered his gallant brother-in-law to revenge those wrongs by dealing in no very gentle manner with the restless insurgents. This advice was acted upon by the new seneschal, and his conduct so provoked the Gascons that they remonstrated vehemently with the king against his appointment. Henry's appreciation of the value of his services, however, was too strong to permit him to listen to the complainers. The tone of his feelings is best manifested in the commencement of the letter he wrote to Earl Simon on the occasion.—" We give you abundant thanks for the solici-

[1] Cotton MS. Vitellius, c. viii., fol. 37. The utter absence of dates in Adam's Letters renders it difficult to ascertain with certainty when they were written. We give the dates of several with diffidence, and only as probabilities.

tude and also the immense labour which your manliness has so vigilantly expended upon our business in Gascony ; clearly perceiving that your faith and diligence are productive of no small convenience to our land of Gascony, and will bring to all our posterity, in perpetuity, utility and increase of honour. Therefore, we request and exhort your prudence, in which we have as much faith as in ourselves, not to desist from the good undertakings you have begun, but bring all the negociations of the aforesaid land to a happy end, according to the best of your ability, that you may receive from us and our heirs worthy remuneration with all honour."[1]

The good understanding between the King and Earl Simon is further evident from the frequent entries in favour of the earl in the state records of the period, by which it appears that he exercised an almost viceregal authority in Gascony.[2] The whole revenues of Ireland were granted him for the fortification of the province,[3] and all the viscounts or sheriffs in England had special orders to protect his tenants and adherents.[4]

The winter of 1249 was spent by the Earl of Leicester in Gascony. In rogation week, the following spring, he came over for a short time to England, but the breaking out of a fresh rebellion necessitated his speedy return. His efforts to quell it were crowned with success. He took prisoner Gaston de Bearne, the most perverse and troublesome of the rebels, and sent him to the king; but Henry, with a weakness that would be incredible were it not so strongly attested, instead of punishing him, lent an ear to

<hr/>

[1] Rot. claus., 34 Hen. III., m. 20 dorso. Fœdera, vol. i., pt. i., p. 271.
[2] In the patent roll of the 33rd of Hen. III., m. 6, is a ratification of a compromise between Simon and Theobald, King of Navarre. In that of the 34th, m. 9, the executors of Raimond, Earl of Toulouse, are ordered to deliver to him the province of Agennois, and to answer for it to him as they would to the king himself. At mm. 8 and 5, occur several orders for the payment of sums of money for the expenses of the war—the patent roll of the 35th of Henry III. also abounds with entries of a similar character. See Fœdera, vol. i., pt. i., pp. 267, 270, 275.   [3] Rot. claus., 34 H. III., m. 17.
[4] Rot. claus., 34 H. III., m. 20 dorso.

the prayers of his friends, received him favourably, and, at their petition, dismissed him freely and honourably,[1] and even made him magnificent presents.[2]

The post of Earl Simon in Gascony was a critical one, for, in spite of the liberal grants and promises made to him, the real supplies of men and money that he received from England were so utterly inadequate to the necessities of the occasion, that he found it impossible, without further aid, to complete or even preserve his conquests; and, after a series of strenuous but vain efforts, early in the year 1251, he once more made his appearance very unexpectedly in England; not, as he was wont to do, with the gallant bearing of a military chief returning from a successful combat, but with only three attendants, whose soil-worn accoutrements, mean horses, and anxious looks, told how much they stood in need of help.[3] He made his way first to Eleanora, and, with her and Peter of Savoy, proceeded to court. They were met on the road by Eleanora's friend, Adam de Marisco, who remained with her at Reading, while the rest of the party went on to Windsor.[4]

Much sympathy was excited in behalf of the Earl of Leicester; and King Henry, partially roused to a sense of the wrong he had done him in not supporting him in his authority, made an effort to raise supplies for him. Meanwhile, Simon returned to his own estates, to obtain there all the money he himself could muster for the same purpose. The king was not the only person who was inspired with pity for his misfortunes; the feelings of Eleanora were roused on the occasion; for, in spite of the disastrous state of affairs abroad, she resolved to share the toils and perils of her lord, and to return with him to Gascony. A con-

---

[1] Barthol. Norwich Cotton MS., Nero c. iv., f. 195.
[2] Rot. claus., 34 H. III., m. 18.   [3] Paris, vol. ii., p. 810.
[4] Marisco's Letters, Cotton MS., Vitellius, c. viii., f. 34, b. The date of this letter can be distinctly traced to 1251, from the allusions to the residence of the king on certain days, which are easily verified by a reference to the patent rolls.

sultation was held between him and Eleanora, in which
Marisco bore a part, about the disposal of their eldest son
during their absence. The boy had spent much of his time
at his uncle's court,[1] but his parents were not satisfied with
an arrangement which, even though it might be conducive
to his temporal advantage, could not fail to exercise an
injurious influence upon his character; and they determined
to send him, as they had previously sent his brothers, to the
Bishop of Lincoln, that, "while his age was tender, he
might be educated in learning and disciplined in manners."
And, even if the earl remained much longer in England,
the boy was still to be treated according to the bishop's
council.[2] From this proviso, it appears that some uncer-
tainty existed about their proceedings. The movements at
court were tardy and indecisive. Without supplies, it was
impossible for Earl Simon to return to his province, and he
was thus placed in a situation of peculiar difficulty. This is
alluded to in one of Adam's letters to Grosstête, in which
he says the earl and countess greatly desire the bishop's
best advice, and entreat that he will give it them by letter,
since a personable interview is impracticable.[3] They succeeded, however, in steering their way through their per-
plexities; supplies were granted, though not so ample as
the earl could have wished, yet sufficient to enable him to
maintain a respectable appearance; and he and Eleanora
set out for the continent.

On their passage through Flanders, Earl Simon obtained
further help from the Duke of Brabant, who lent him
troops; and, thus armed, he and his countess arrived at
Bourdeaux about the middle of October, 1251, and there
kept the festival of St. Simon and St. Jude, which occurred
on the 28th of that month;[4] after which the earl soon

---

[1] Paris, ut sup.   [2] Letter of Marisco to the Bishop of Lincoln, f. 29.
[3] Cotton MS., ut sup., f. 28 b. The date of this letter also is evidently
1251, from an allusion to the marriage of the Princess Margaret, which was
to take place the ensuing Christmas.   [4] Marisco's letters, fol. 32.

succeeded in reducing the rebels to a temporary subjection.

The conduct of Eleanora, while she occupied so prominent a position, as the wife of the viceregent of Gascony, appears to have been of rather a questionable character. At least, it was such as to bring down upon her the severe reprimands of her ghostly adviser, father Adam de Marisco. The improprieties of which he accuses her are precisely those into which, from her lively temperament, she would be most likely to fall, when placed in a commanding situation; extravagance in personal adornment, over-hastiness of temper, and a want of due subjection to the supreme authority of her lord and master. The epistle of the monk is characterized by good sense and piety, and contains several very apposite scripture quotations. It is too long for insertion—a few extracts must suffice.

After laying down, as a general principle, the duty of perfect subjection in woman, and enlarging upon the evils, tumults, and clamours that must necessarily arise from feminine disobedience, he adds, " Far be it that so execrable a plague should degrade into the destructive gulf of shame a mind elevated by the glory of so many illustrious titles. I entreat the placid grace of the most holy virgin, with the blessed author of peaceful love, that ' the peace of God, which passeth all knowledge, may keep your heart and mind.' Nor wonder, I entreat you, that I follow out sharply so serious an affair with the language of holy men." He next inveighs against all meretricious adornment, quoting St. Paul's exhortation to simplicity of attire. As no Quakerish maxims were extant in those days in reference to dress, and a reproof on the subject is extremely rare, we may infer that Eleanora had fallen into habits of peculiar extravagance. Adam concludes by wishing his heart were transparent, that she might see the anxiety he felt on the subject, and expresses a hope that he may not

have wielded his celestial weapons in vain, entreating her
to pardon the sharp reproof and tender persuasion he has
used, as it is uncertain whether he shall ever again see her
in the flesh. This appeal, eloquent as it is, totally failed
in producing its desired effect, and it was followed by
another, which commences thus :—

" To the excellent lady Alienora, Countess of Leicester,
friar Adam wishes health, and the laudable effects of wholesome counsels. My inmost heart is touched with grief, my
face is suffused with crimson now these many days, because,
from a man of honest fame, I hear no little about the
growing improprieties of your conduct; on which account my
embittered spirit ceases not to bewail, being thus disturbed
in the contemplation of the Saviour, the father of justice,
and the God of all consolation." He proceeds to entreat
her to act carefully, reasonably, and peacefully, after the
example of laudable matrons, especially in her conduct to
her husband, children, domestics, and adherents; assures
her that he and her other friends will labour incessantly
for her safety and honour, whether by their prayers or
otherwise he does not state, provided she will regulate her
conduct by right principles.[1] It is very evident, from the
unquestionable authority of these letters, that the countess
Eleanora was somewhat of a termigant in her temper.
That she sincerely loved her husband and children, is proved
by every public act of her life; for she adhered to Earl
Simon, through all his changing fortunes, with the most
unflinching constancy, taking a very active part in the
support of his cause; and she guarded carefully the interests of her children. But it is one of those anomalies in
the history of mind, which we should scarcely believe did
we not so often witness it, that the same persons who,
inspired by deep affection, watch with jealous vigilance and
resent with keen susceptibility the slightest injury offered

[1] Marisco's letters, f. 57 b. Cotton MS., Vitellius, c. viii.

by another to the beloved object, will yet be utterly reckless of the amount of unhappiness which the capriciousness for waywardness of their own temper may inflict.

Marisco afterwards addressed the countess in a gentler strain, thanking her for the good news she has sent him about her husband, and even praising her care and thoughtfulness, so that we may presume her to have benefited by his counsels.[1]

After the conclusion of a successful campaign, the earl and countess, accompanied by Guy de Lusignan, Eleanora's half-brother, set sail from Witsand, on their way home. A violent wind, however, drove them back to port, and it was not till after they had braved a furious tempest that they landed at Dover. When King Henry heard of their approach to London, he himself went out to meet them, not, we are told, in compliment to his sister and brother-in-law, but to his step-brother, De Lusignan.[2] They spent the Christmas in England, and we find them forming part of the royal circle at court the following spring. They were at Westminster on St. Gregory's-day, March 12th, 1252, probably on a leave-taking visit; for an agreement was then entered into between King Henry and De Montfort, which the latter took an oath by his soul on the holy gospels to fulfil, that, on his approaching return to Gascony, his pecuniary transactions in the province should be laid before commissioners, sent over by the king, and it was agreed that, on which ever side the balance lay, it should be forthwith paid.[3]

The requiring of such a pledge from the Earl of Leicester shows that feelings of suspicion and distrust were aroused in the mind of the king; and when he and Eleanora returned to Gascony, there began that series of harassing discords between the king and his stern and fiery brother-in-law,

[1] Marisco's Letters, ff. 67, b. 68.   [2] Paris, vol. ii., p. 828.
[3] Rot. claus., 36 Hen. III., m. 21 dorso.

which resulted in desolating calamities, both to themselves and the nation.

The Gascons were still making constant complaints of De Montfort's injustice and oppression. It would seem that these complaints were not well founded; for his keeping all the strongholds of Gascony in his own hands, which was the ground of the most earnest remonstrance, was a step not only justifiable but necessary in a province on whose fidelity so little reliance was to be placed; and they had, moreover, been formally placed in his hands by the king's letters patent, on his first appointment to the seneschalship.[1] However, it is consistent with the character of the earl to suppose that there might be more of roughness in his manner towards his troublesome subjects than would be quite agreeable, seeing that he had the authority and even the command of the king to treat them with severity.[2] Henry sent over commissioners into Gascony, to inquire into the truth of these accusations, one of whom was Henry de Wengham, a confidential servant, and another, Roceline de Ros, minister of the Knights Templars.[3] They found the province all in tumult, and Gaston de Bearne up in arms. A truce was negociated, however; and the principal nobles agreed, at the request of King Henry,[4] to come over to England to settle the disputes, but with the proviso that the Earl of Leicester might be present at the pleadings, or at least that he might be kept out of Gascony during their absence; otherwise, they refused to appear.[5] Henry accordingly wrote to summon his brother-in-law to his court.[6] The indignant earl, who ill brooked any aspersions on his character, gladly returned to England, to vindicate himself against his accusers, and the countess accompanied him.

[1] Rot. pat., 32 H. III., m. 2.
[2] See p. 91, infra.   [3] Rot. pat., 36 H. III., m. 13. Rot. claus., 36, m. 13.
[4] Rot. claus., 36 H. III., m. 27, dorso.
[5] Letter of Ros and Wengham to King Henry, in the Tower, printed in "Lettres des Rois," &c., vol. i., No. xc., edited for the French government, by M. Champollion.   [6] Rot. claus., 36 H. III., m. 20, dorso.

Henry was already strongly biassed in favour of the Gascons.[1] He had discovered that De Montfort had bound over some of the Gascons by a solemn oath not to bring any complaints of his government, and this discovery filled his mind with jealous suspicion, which led him to interfere, and annul the oaths of the Gascon lords, and to promise to protect them in their appeals to him.[2] Their statements, particularly those of the Archbishop of Bourdeaux, who was the chief deputy, and their declarations that, if Earl Simon were returned as their governor, they would withdraw their allegiance to the crown of England, had considerable influence over the mind of the king; and when his fearless brother-in-law pleaded his promises to aid him and the obligation of his charter, demanding at least the repayment of the enormous sums he had expended in the Gascon war, Henry angrily refused to keep his word with a " traitor." Simon, in a towering passion at such an imputation on his knightly character, told the king that he lied, adding, moreover—" Who can believe that you are a Christian? — do you ever go to confession?" " I do," replied Henry.—" But what avails confession without repentance and reparation ?" was the angry retort. —" Never," said the insulted king, " did I repent of any thing so much as I now repent that I ever permitted you to enter England, or possess lands and honours here, where in the pride of your heart you thus demean yourself."[3] Had not fear of the nobles, who formed already a powerful party on the side of earl Simon prevented, Henry would have thrown into prison the daring subject who had thus given him the lie to his face. But such was the formidable nature of Simon's influence, that not only was he obliged to refrain from any open manifestation of resentment, but even to restore to him the government of Gascony.

A vivid picture is drawn by Adam de Marisco, in a con-

[1] Rot. claus., 36 H. III., m. 15, dorso.
[2] Ibid., m. 16, dorso, in cedulâ.
[3] Paris, vol. ii., p. 837.

fidential letter to the Bishop of Lincoln,[1] of the close of
these Gascon negociations, in which, of course, he places
Leicester's conduct in the most favourable light. No
pains, he says, were spared, on the part of the embassy, to
prejudice the king and nobles against Earl Simon, while the
latter bore their insults, and the reproaches which in consequence he had often to suffer from the king, with calmness
and magnanimity, merely remarking, that he had never
before known an instance where any person, public or
private, was treated with such manifest injustice. All that
he entreated for was, to be allowed a fair hearing, and to
answer the charges of his antagonists face to face. This he
at length obtained; and, going into the whole course of his
government, in a long and eloquent speech, he triumphantly
vindicated himself from the charges brought against him;
producing letters patent in his favour from the inhabitants
of Bourdeaux, and making it clear that the accusations
against him were those of interested men, who wished to
lead a life of rapine, without the restraints of law; and, as
additional proof of his innocence, he, in the true spirit of
the chivalric age, offered to abide the ordeal of single combat, challenging his accusers to meet him on a fair field,
either in England or Gascony. Either from a consciousness
of the unrighteousness of their cause, or from a fear of the
strong arm of De Montfort, however, they refused the test.

The energy of truth brought, on this occasion, such an
irresistible conviction to the hearers, that Henry was
obliged to confess that the charges were unfounded; and
this declaration was followed by loud applause from Richard,
Earl of Cornwall, and the attendant nobles. It is hard
work, however, to convince a man against his will; and the
following morning the fickle king had again veered round,
and the earl was as much in disgrace as ever. The alterca-
tions had now lasted more than two months, from ascension

[1] Printed in Appendix, No. IV.

day, May 9th, to June 11th, and seemed no nearer a termination than ever. Despairing, therefore, of any appeals
to the justice of the monarch, Simon addressed himself to
his selfishness. He offered, by a private negociation, in
case he were reinstated in his office in Gascony, to exercise
his authority, as mercifully as possible; but if the continued
dissensions precluded pacific measures, promised to take
upon himself and his friends the whole trouble and expense
of the necessary military preparations. If neither of these
propositions met the royal approbation, he offered to relinquish his government on three conditions:—first, that he
should be reimbursed for the insupportable expense he had
incurred; second, that it should be distinctly understood
that his resignation was attended with no disgrace; and,
third, that those friends who had adhered to him in his
troubles should be subjected to no inconvenience for their
fidelity. These proposals were certainly as reasonable as
possible; all, however, that Earl Simon was able to obtain,
was a letter patent, duly signed and sealed, commanding a
truce between the contending parties in Gascony, until the
following February, when the king himself, or Prince Edward,
hoped to arrive there, to settle affairs fully.[1] With this concession, Simon took his departure from court; and, after
spending only a few days with his family, he took leave of them
once again, " relying," we are told, " on him who disappoints
not the hopes of those that trust in him, disciplined to obedience
by what he had suffered, and confiding in the protection of the
Most High," and set sail, on the 16th of June, with his eldest
son Henry, for Boulogne, thence to proceed, without delay,
to Gascony.[2]

Another chronicler, less strongly biassed in Earl Simon's
favour, tells us that he returned to Gascony, burning with
indignation against his accusers, and made them feel the

[1] Rot. pat., 36 H. iii., m. 12.
[2] Cotton. MS., Vitellius, c. viii., fol. 30, b., et seq.

weight of his vengeance.[1] Eleanora was prevented from
accompanying the earl, by the near approach of her confinement.   She felt keenly the indignities her husband
had endured, and she recommended her lord, herself, her
children, and all belonging to her, in the most earnest
manner, to the prayers of the Bishop of Lincoln.[2]   She was
very anxious that her friend Adam should go over to
Boulogue, where the Earl spent a few days preparing for
his journey southward, to advise with him in reference to
his future proceedings and prospects; and, in order to win
her point, took a journey to Oxford, on purpose to visit the
friar, and induce him to yield to her wishes.   She did
not succeed, however.   Father Adam put her off with promises, both verbal and written, to comply with her wishes, if
possible; but, from the tone in which he names the circumstance in one of his confidential letters, it is evident he intended to get off, if he could.[3]

After the departure of Earl Simon, Eleanora retired
almost immediately from court, to her own castle of
Kenilworth, whither she was followed, in a short time, by
father Adam, with whom she held long and familiar dis-
courses, both on temporal and spiritual affairs.[4]   The birth
of her infant, probably her youngest child and only daughter Eleanora, took place about Michaelmas, somewhat pre-
maturely, occasioned, perhaps, by the recent anxieties she
had undergone.[5]   She received, on the occasion, a note of
special congratulation from friar Adam, written in a strain
of devout thankfulness to God, "who had had respect to

[1] Barthol. Norw., Cotton MS., Nero D. II., f. 195 b.
[2] Cotton MS., Vitellius, c. viii., f. 30 b., et seq.
[3] Marisco's letter to friar A., f. 63.
[4] Marisco's letter to the Earl of Leicester. fol. 51. The occasion of the
penning of this letter was, that the earl had taken with him to Gascony
the temporary vicar of the church of Odiham, thus leaving the people
unprovided with a pastor, for which he is sternly reproved by this faithful
priest.
[5] It was not expected till the early part of October, the feast of St. Dennis;
see the letter of Adam just quoted.

her prayer, and not despised her devotion, granting her freedom from perils and anxieties, and the joy of a numerous and promising offspring."[1] As she was still, apparently, at least, on terms of cordiality with the court, a messenger was despatched to inform her sister-in-law, Queen Eleanora, of her safe delivery. The bearer of the news was Peter, the barber of the Earl of Leicester; and the errand was a lucrative one, for he received 40s. (equivalent to £30 of our present money) for his trouble. A nurse, seemingly a person of consideration, for she is styled the *lady* Alice, had been sent to the countess from court, and, during the few following weeks, frequent messengers were sent to inquire after her health.[2] From the circumstance that it was with the queen that this correspondence took place, it would seem that the countess still owed her brother a grudge for his late ungenerous treatment of her husband.

The whole winter was spent by Eleanora at Kenilworth, whither, on the 1st of December, William de Gardin, a confidential servant of the queen, was sent to convey to her a present of jewellery.[3] She, in her turn, at Christmas, sent two of her knights to court, probably bearing tokens of her good will, who each received from the queen a golden clasp, as a new year's gift.[4]

Early in the spring of 1253, she removed to Odiham,[5] and also paid a visit to court to celebrate, with Queen Eleanora, some religious ceremonies, which were to be performed on the feast of the resurrection, March 27th. This latter cir-

---

[1] Letters of Adam de Marisco, f. 57.
[2] The roll from which these entries are extracted is one of a complete series of the household and wardrobe accounts of Queen Eleanora, of Provence, during the years 1252 and 1253, preserved in the Queen's Remembrancer office, at Carlton Ride. The roll in question is the one containing all payments made to messengers, and is marked xxi., 370.
[3] Rot. nunciorum ut supra.
[4] Rot. donorum reginæ Elean. No. vii., 3303.
[5] Where she received a messenger from the queen. Rot. nunc. regin. Elean. anno. 37, No. xxi. 370.

cumstance is ascertained from a sentence in one of Marisco's letters,[1] presumed to be written in this year, to Queen Eleanora; the only French letter which occurs in the whole series, the others being of course written in Latin. The following is a literal translation :—

"Lady,—If you, at this feast of the resurrection, will please to treat with the Countess of Leicester about the salvation of the souls to which, as far as in you lies, you have so blessedly contributed, I hope, in the grace of the blessed son of God, that he, by the virtue of his glorious resurrection, will give his aid, to the glory of his name. May He lead you to the way of eternal salvation! Amen, amen, amen!"

The countess was evidently on the most friendly terms with her sister-in-law, and it is to this period that we attribute another of the epistles of Father Adam, in which he says that the queen and the Countess of Leicester are labouring with anxious and unwearied solicitude to mitigate the irritation of the royal mind against the Earl of Leicester, and he prays that He, in whose hands are the winds and the waves, may controul the heart of the king.[2] But neither the efforts of his sister nor his beloved queen availed with the irascible monarch; and Eleanora soon retired from court, for in Passion week we find her again at Odiham.

His recent quarrels with Earl Simon had left a very unfavourable impression upon the mind of the king. Of this the earl received warning, probably at Eleanora's suggestion, from friar Adam, who wrote to caution him against returning to England, "without great care, much deliberation, and extreme foresight."[3] Even while his seneschal was exerting every effort to preserve for him a province so valuable, Henry secretly fomented the discontents of the Gascon nobles; and, when the Earl was compelled to

---

[1] Cotton MS., Vitellius e. viii., f. 56.
[2] Letter to father Thomas, of York, f. 71.
[3] Marisco's letters, f. 37 b.

return once more to solicit justice, he refused to see or
speak with him. The ill treatment Simon met with is reprobated in the strongest manner by friar Adam, and it
is evident that it was severely felt both by the earl and
countess.[1]

The king finding, however, that in the absence of Simon
the wars still continued in Gascony, and that the rebel
party were becoming every day more formidable, said to
him, assuming his sternest tone, " Return thou who art the
exciter and lover of war; thou wilt find enough of it."—
" I go willingly," replied the earl; " nor will I return to
you, ungrateful as you are, until I have put all your
enemies under your feet." This sudden resolution, taken
by the king probably in a fit of fretful impatience at the
continued annoyance caused him by the Gascon wars, was
acted upon with the utmost promptness; and, without even
staying to take leave of his friends, the earl, accompanied
by his countess and their children, again returned to the
continent. His departure placed his interests in England
in a very critical position. This is hinted at in a letter
from his faithful friend Adam, in which he exhorts him to
put his whole trust and confidence in that God who has
the hearts of kings in his own hands, that he would
bring these doubtful matters to a certain end.[2] The friar
wrote several letters to Eleanora about this time, principally on his detention in England of Gregory Bosell, a
Franciscan monk,[3] whose presence the countess greatly
desired, but who was detained by Adam to fulfil some
literary engagements connected with the lectureship at
Oxford. At length he was sent over at her request.

[1] Letter to Thomas of York, ut sup.
[2] Cotton MS., Vitellius, c. viii., fol. 51. This letter is also without a
date, or any clue by which to identify it with certainty; but the allusion to
the sudden return of the earl to Gascony, as well as the general tone of the
letter, seem to refer it to this period.
[3] He was a theological reader in Leicester, and had obtained considerable
reputation for learning. Parkinson's collectanea Anglo minoritira, p. 61.

The letters do not dwell upon any topics of peculiar interest.[1]

Although the restoration of Earl Simon to his government was seemingly a triumph on his part, yet, in reality, it exercised a prejudicial influence upon his fortunes, by removing him from court, and thus giving his enemies an opportunity of prosecuting their designs against him. They persuaded the king that it was utterly impossible to restore peace to Gascony, so long as a governor so objectionable to the people was permitted to remain; and the fickle monarch revoked the patent by which the seneschalship of Gascony had been granted to him, the only compensation offered being a promise of a sum of money to buy out the remaining years of his patent.[2] It has been frequently asserted that this revocation was occasioned by the king's desire to grant the province to his eldest son Prince Edward; but this idea is not only contrary to the *rationale* of the affair, because Leicester's office of seneschal involved no absolute possession of the province, and could be exercised equally well under the prince as the king, but is also opposed to the testimony of authentic documents; for we find that Gascony was actually conferred upon Edward in the year 1249, several years previous to this period;[3] and the gift was renewed in 1252, when Earl Simon was in England, without exciting any feeling of jealousy on his part. The Prince being at this time only fourteen years of age, his authority was purely nominal.

Though the services of De Montfort were ill appreciated by the sovereign, in whose behalf they had been performed, the reputation that his military talents and firmness of character procured for him in other courts was so

---

[1] Marisco's letters, f. 57.

[2] Matthew Paris (vol. ii., p. 867) says three years still remained; but that cannot be correct, for the patent was granted in 1248 for six years, and, therefore, must have been much nearer its expiration.

[3] Rotulus de donis Vasconiæ, No. 2655. Queen's Remembrancer office, sub anno., 33.

favourable that, on his retiring, as he forthwith did, into France, he was requested and even urged by the government, then left in some disorder by the death of the queen-regent Blanche of Castile, and the absence of the king in the Holy Land, to accept the office of High Steward; but this he steadily refused to do, as wishing to avoid even the appearance of a want of fidelity to his own sovereign. The moderation of Earl Simon on this occasion, so strongly opposed to his conduct in his subsequent career, is ascribed, by Matthew Paris,[1] to the influence which the Bishop of Lincoln, Robert Grosstête, had with him. This judicious prelate represented to him, in lively language, the benefits he had formerly received from the king, especially in the near alliance which he had been permitted to form with the royal family, and entreated him, in consideration of the past, to forgive the present. We do not hear that Eleanora acted as a mediator on this occasion, and the probability is that she did not attempt any conciliatory measures. Her mind appears to have been, to the full, as much estranged from the king as that of her husband; and we shall speedily have occasion to notice, that, after the death of the Bishop of Lincoln, no influence was interposed as a barrier to the designs of Earl Simon. The mention of this prelate, in familiar intercourse with the earl at this period, gives ground for the supposition that, being the intimate friend of Simon, and Eleanora, and the tutor of their sons, he had come over to visit them in the quiet retirement in which they now resided for nearly a year, at a distance from the French court, in the extensive estates of the Montfort family.

Meanwhile, the affairs of Gascony grew worse and worse, and King Henry soon found that the vigilance of his former seneschal had been the true cause of the complaints against him; for, no sooner was the restraint of his presence withdrawn, than the Gascons openly plotted to deliver the pro-

[1] Vol. ii., p. 879.

vince into the hands of Alfonso, of Castile, who claimed it
on the fallacious pretext that it had been granted to his
ancestor, Alfonso III., on his marriage with the Princess
Eleanora, daughter of Henry II.; and, so formidable had
the conspiracy become, that Henry determined to go over
in person to suppress it.   De Montfort had watched these
proceedings, as might be expected, with considerable interest.   He well knew that the unwarlike Henry would be
no match for his rebellious subjects; and, regardless of the
late affronts that had been offered to him, he obeyed the
summons, which he, in common with the other nobles,
received to join their king. [1]   It was conveyed in flattering
terms.   Henry simply asks to speak with him, assuring him
that he shall be at perfect liberty to retire when he pleases;
and that, as the roads are perilous, the Earls of Norfolk
and Hereford and Guy de Lusignan shall escort him.[2]

The Earl accordingly assembled a body of troops in
France, armed, equipped, and paid them from his own
private purse; and, at the head of his small but gallant
band, went to join the king.   The arrival of this "thunder-
bolt of war" was as welcome to the one party as it was dreaded
by the other.   Simon speedily succeeded in restoring order
in the rebel province, which was rendered permanent by
the marriage treaty between Prince Edward and Eleanora
of Castile, since King Alfonso ceded his pretended rights
in behalf of his daughter and her future husband.   Part,
at least, of the expences incurred by Earl Simon, on this
occasion, was reimbursed to him.[3]   Eleanora was also
involved in business transactions with her brother.   During
her residence at the court of Bourdeaux, Henry had been

---

[1] Rot. claus. Vascon., 38 Hen. III., m. 20 in dorso.
[2] Rot. Vascon., 37, Hen. III.. p. i., m. 19.
[3] Rot. pat., 37 Hen. III., m. 11.   An order occurs, dated June 3rd, to the
prior and treasurer of the knights hospitallers of Jerusalem, commanding
them to pay to Simon the rest of the money placed by the king in their
keeping, but the amount is not stated.   There is a similar one on Rot. Vasc.,
38 Hen. III., p. i., m. 16.

sorely perplexed about the payment of 1000 marks, which he owed for the earldom of Bigorre; and his creditor refused to be satisfied unless he could find security better than his own bankrupt credit for the speedy payment. In this dilemma, he applied to his sister for aid; and Eleanora consented to acquit him, and bind herself over as security for the money, which she was soon obliged to produce. Knowing, however, that she was little likely to have her money speedily returned, she made a condition that, in case of its non-payment, the earldom should remain in her hands.[1] An appearance of friendship was again assumed on the part of the English king towards the Earl of Leicester and his family, but there is sufficient room to suppose that fear, and not love, was the real ground of the seeming cordiality. The winter of 1253 they spent at Bourdeaux, whence, on the 20th of August the following year, Simon was despatched to Scotland on confidential business, the purport of which being given by word of mouth, and not committed to paper, has not reached us. He was also employed in negociating a peace with France, which detained him a considerable time in Paris; but, as Eleanora is not mentioned in the transactions, it is uncertain whether she accompanied him.

In 1255, both the Earl and Countess of Leicester were once more in England, whence, in May, the earl again went over to France, partly on the king's business, to confirm the truce, and partly on his own.[2] During this hollow peace between the king and De Montfort, Eleanora's intercourse with her brother was frequent. Whilst her husband was absent, he sent her a present of six deer,[3] a favour which he repeated the following year.[4] But Henry found it more easy to be generous in trifles than just in weightier matters.

---

[1] See rot. claus., 40 H. III., m. 8 dorso. conf. rot. pat., 43 H. III., m. 4.
[2] Rot. claus., 39 H. III., p. i., m. 11 dorso. Letter of Henry to Louis. Carton J., 717, Archives du royaume, Paris.
[3] Rot. claus., 39 H. III., m. 10.   [4] Rot. claus., 40 Hen. III., m. 7.

His sister grew pressing in her demands for payment of
the moneys owing to her; and, wearied with excuses and
procrastinations, her temper became roused, and she angrily
demanded her right.   Henry knew the warmth of her
character, and that, when fairly in earnest, she was not to
be trifled with; yet his exchequer was empty.   In this
dilemma, he wrote to Philip Lovel, his treasurer, ordering
that all the debts due to the king by Roger Bigod, Earl of
Norfolk,[1] should be given to his "dear sister, the Countess
of Leicester," in part payment of the sums owing to her,
and also that, when his brother Richard, whom he had also
made his debtor to a large amount, should have taken as
much money as he pleased from the debts of "Aaron, the
son of Abraham," the remainder should be handed over
to Eleanora; and he entreats his treasurer, at the close
of his letter, not to let his said sister remain unappeased.
This order is dated from Clarendon, July 8th, 1256.[2]
Sorry as was the expedient of making his payments con-
tingent upon the successful gathering in of his debts, it
seems to have proved temporarily successful in calming
Eleanora's wrath; but the 1000 marks must have still
remained unpaid, for we subsequently paid the earldom of
Bigorre in the hands of Earl Simon.

The career of Earl Simon from this period to his death
is so blended with the history of his times, and, therefore,
so familiar to every reader, that the barest outline must
suffice here, more especially as little occurs in connexion
with it to throw light on the personal history of the lady
Eleanora.   The silence preserved respecting her leads us
to infer that she lived principally in retirement at her castle
of Kenilworth.   Her husband, however, did not entirely
absent himself from the royal presence.   On the 11th of
February, 1257, a grant of divers manors was conferred

[1] Roger Bigod, afterwards, in 1258, appointed the Earls of Gloucester and
Leicester co-executors of his will.   Nicolas testamenta vetusta, vol. i, p. 49.
[2] Rot. claus., 40 H. III., mm. 5, 8, dorso.

upon him, the names of Richard, king of the Romans, and the two Lusignans, being found as witnesses; and soon after he received permission, by a deed similarly witnessed, to enclose Shipleigh wood in Northumberland as a park.[1] We may here notice two curious grants made to him by persons in lower rank. One is from John, son of John le Deveneys, who remits to the earl the rent of some lands in the town of Thornton, on condition of his presenting him with a pair of white gloves, value one penny, every year. In the other, Sir William Condray bestows on him lands in the parish of Cottesmore, Rutlandshire, for an annual present of a pair of gilt spurs.[2]

The civil disturbances between the king and his barons, which so long convulsed England with the shocks of civil war, now began to assume a serious aspect. Earl Simon threw the whole weight of his powerful and increasing influence into the scale of opposition against the king and those foreign favourites who made him an easy prey to their grasping covetousness. The year 1258 was famous for the drawing up of the constitutions of Oxford. The Earl of Leicester was appointed by the barons president of the council of twenty-four, who prepared them, and such was the power of the party who supported them, that they compelled the king and Prince Edward to sign them. Any opposition made by any member of the royal family was met in the most summary manner; and when William de Valence refused to deliver up the castles committed to him by the king, Simon told him he should either part with the castles or his head; nor did he rest until he had succeeded in driving him, as well as the king's other half-brother, Guy de Lusignan, from the kingdom. When, however, as matter of form, he was required to swear to these same statutes, he at first refused, from some motive inexplicable,

[1] Great Coucher, in the Duchy of Lancaster's office, vol. i, ff. 160 and 161.
[2] Great Coucher, vol. ii., fol. 46, No. 8, and fol. 51, No. 29. Office of the Duchy of Lancaster.

unless we place it to the score of a superstitious repugnance to take an oath; and when the point was pressed, and he at last consented, he exclaimed, with his usual expletive, " By the arm of St. James, though I take this oath, the last and by compulsion, yet I shall so observe it that none can impeach me!"   The remainder of the year was spent by Earl Simon partly on foreign missions in France or Scotland,[1] and partly at court, where he exercised an almost dictatorial authority.

Early in the following spring, 1259, he was again sent into France on some negociations between Henry and Louis,[2] and the Countess Eleanora went with him. A long series of contests had taken place about the possession of the territory of Agennois, which had been granted by Richard I. to his sister Joanna on her marriage with Raimond of Toulouse. The grand-daughter and heiress of Joanna was married to Prince Alfonso of France, and, on her death, without heirs, that province, according to a previous agreement with the last Earl of Toulouse, Raimond VIII., devolved upon the crown of France. The English king, on the other hand, claimed the restoration of Agennois, and, as it was inherited through his grandmother, Eleanora of Aquitaine, the claim was made not only on his part, but on that of his brother and sister. Henry, however, whose exchequer was always low, made an agreement to resign his rights on condition of the receipt of an annual sum of money, and promised that his two sons, his brother Richard, and his sister Eleanora, should resign in like manner their claims upon the disputed territory.

But the king knew the enterprising character of Eleanora too well to be very sanguine that, as far as she was con-

---

[1] Letter of Henry III., Carton, J., No. 717.   Archives du royaume, Paris. Rot. pat., 42 H. III., mm. 4, 9.

[2] Fœdera, vol. i., pt. i., p. 384.   Rot. claus., 42-47 H. III., m. 11.   His companions in the embassy were John Maunsell, Peter of Savoy, and the Earl of Gloucester.

cerned, he should be able to fulfil his promise. A curious
entry on the roll from which these particulars are extracted
bears witness to his misgivings. After the letters patent of
the agreement between Henry and Louis, the following
note is added:—" Two copies were made of this letter, one
of which makes mention of the King of Germany and the
Countess of Leicester, and the other makes *no mention* of
them."[1]   Provision was thus made for the fulfilment of the
treaty, whether Eleanora chose to be a party or not, and a
private promise was sent to the French king that, if the
Countess of Leicester and her children would not grant their
quittance of the lands, and should afterwards vindicate their
rights, and recover them by a judgment in any of the courts
of France, Louis or his heirs should be indemnified from all
loss by the English king.[2]   Power was thus given to the
Earl of Gloucester and others, who were going as ambassadors
to France, to satisfy Louis, in case of Eleanora's anticipated
refusal, for herself and her children, to ratify the conven-
tion.[3]   It would seem, however, that the French king had
good sense enough to refuse the resignation, unless it were
confirmed by all the parties concerned; and at length
Eleanora gave the required consent,[4] but only on condition
that 15,000 marks of the money which Henry was to receive
from Louis should be placed in the temple at Paris, under the
control of certain persons employed as arbitrators between
herself and Henry, until her dowry demands were satisfied.[5]
In making this arrangement, the countess displayed her
usual tact, for she was relinquishing a merely nominal claim,
while the hold she obtained upon her brother by the power
of detaining his money was of importance to her. She took
this opportunity to press upon him the full payment of her

[1] Conventiones pacis, m. 4. Tower of London.
[2] Rot claus., 42-47 H. III., m. 10.
[3] Rot. pat., 43 H. III., m. 8. Fœdera, i., 385, 386.
[4] Convent. pac., m. 4.
[5] Convent. pac., m. 3. See also Rot. claus., 44 H. III., p. 2, m. 4, dorso,
and letter of Philip III. to Edward I. in Appendix, No. X.

jointure, and the matter was referred to a commission. The arbitrators first fixed upon were Eleanora's brother, Richard Earl of Cornwall, with two other nobles,[1] but they either declined the task, or failed in accomplishing it. The king next selected Richard de Clare, Earl of Gloucester,[2] but the old jealousy existing between him and the Earl of Leicester rendered him objectionable, and Bigod Earl of Norfolk, Bohun Earl of Hereford, and Philip Basset were ultimately fixed upon.[3]

Eleanora laid before these commissioners a complete statement of her wrongs. She declared that the real value of those dowry lands for which King Henry allowed her £400 a-year was 2000 marks, or £1333. 6s. 8d., but that, taking advantage of her tender age while she was altogether in his power, he had entered into an unfair composition for £400 a-year, and had sealed the agreement with her seal without her knowledge or assent,[4] and she strenuously demanded either that the lands should be placed in her hands, and the arrears of the twenty-six years which had transpired since the agreement was made, discharged, or that the sum she specified should be annually paid to her.[5] It is not possible now to ascertain how far these statements of Eleanora were correct. In justice to her brother, however, it must be remarked that the composition made in 1233 was between the countess and the heir of her late husband, not between her and the king, and that it was only in later years that, on account of the delay of the remittances, he became responsible for the sum. Unless, then, we suppose some secret understanding to have existed between the king and the heir of the Pembroke estates, of which there is not the shadow of proof, the utmost charge that can be brought against Henry is that he had suffered himself to

[1] Rot. claus., 42–47 Hen. III., m. 10.
[2] Rot. pat., 43 H. III., m. 8.   [3] Convent pac., m. 3.
[4] See rot. claus., 17 Hen. III., m. 9 dorso.
[5] Convent. pac., m. 4. See Appendix, No. V.

be imposed upon, and not guarded his sister's interest jealously enough.

But, though the points in dispute had been thus clearly brought out, Eleanora did not succeed in establishing her claim, for the entries for the payment of her dowry moneys in the succeeding years are, as before, £200 every half year.[1] She received several additional grants of lands,[2] but they were not sufficient to liquidate the large sums already owed her for arrears.[3]

At this time, Earl Simon, for the sum of 1000 marks, resigned to the king, for seven years, the Earldom of Bigorre, of which he was, as before noted, in temporary possession, in consequence of the bargain made by Eleanora, on condition that the king would marry Simon's niece, Amice de Chabeneys, to some man worth £500 a-year in land, or give her 1000 marks for a wedding portion, "Pur la damoisele marier li quel la damoisele voudra meuz."[4] In this latter negociation, Henry, the eldest son of Simon and Eleanora, now a youth of twenty years, bore a prominent part.

Towards the latter end of this year, Henry paid a visit to the French court,[5] and to prevent all future discussion on the subject which had caused the recent disputes, as well as to cement a permanent peace between the two kingdoms, Eleanora was prevailed upon to give, in her own name and under her own seal, a formal renunciation for herself and her heirs, of all claim to the French territory in Normandy, Anjou, Touraine, and Poictiers. The sweeping terms in which this document is worded seem contrived to place an effectual barrier against the future ambition of the enterprising countess. Eleanora adopts the regal plural in her address. Her signature was affixed on the Thursday after St. Andrew's day, that is to say, the 4th of December,

[1] Rot. lib., 43 H. III., m. 5. Ibid., 44, mm. 8, 2. Ibid., 48, m. 8, &c.
[2] Rot. pat., 43 H. III., mm. 2, 5, 14. [3] Rot claus., 43 H. III., m. 1.
[4] Convent. pac., m. 1. Rot. pat., 43 H. III., m. 1.
[5] Annales luculenti, Cotton MS., Nero D. 11., f. 167 b.

1259, at Paris, in presence of the sovereigns of England and France, and many other persons.[1] At the same time, Earl Simon renounced, in behalf of Alphonso, Earl of Toulouse, brother of the French king, all claim to Toulouse, Beziers, or any part of the territory which had been conquered by his father during the war against the Albigenses,[2] and which had been the subject of long discords between him and the Tolosan earls.[3] This was probably done in compliance with the wishes of his countess, since Joanna of Toulouse, Alphonso's wife, was half cousin to Eleanora.[4] The impression which Eleanora made, during this visit at the French court, upon King Louis, and even upon his queen, Margaret of Provence, although she was sister-in-law to King Henry, must have been very favourable, since, in all her future troubles, they stood her firm friends.

The earl and countess returned to England early in the next year, 1260,[5] with such a cortège of horse and armed retainers, that King Henry, who still remained on the Continent, felt and expressed some serious misgivings as to the future pacific intentions of De Montfort,[6] and not without cause, for the party of the barons, at the head of which were the Earls of Leicester and Gloucester, became daily more formidable, and, under their stern sway, the authority of the king, whose profusion and misgovernment had inflicted a long train of misfortunes on the realm, dwindled away to a mere shadow.

But, after the king's return, a quarrel arose on some trifling

[1] Brienne MS. 28, fol. 83.   Carton, J., 629, No. 13, Archives du roy., Dumont Corps Diplomatique, vol. i., pt. i., p. 212 ; also printed, but very incorrectly, in Martène Thesaurus Anecdotum, vol. i., col. 1084.

[2] Vaisette, Hist. de Languedoc, vol. iii., p. 491, preuves, p. 541.

[3] See Marisco's Letters, Cotton MS., Vitellius, C. viii.

[4] She was the grand-daughter of Joanna, daughter of Henry II. See vol. i., p. 376, of this work.

[5] On the 10th of February, the Earl passed through St. Albans, where he remained all night, and offered a precious baldekin at the shrine.—Matthew Westm., p. 371.

[6] Fœdera, vol. i., pt. i., p. 396. Letter of Henry to Louis.

pretence between Gloucester and Leicester, which, by the disunion it occasioned, promised to be of great service to the royal cause; for De Montfort, exclaiming, " I care not to live and converse among men so unstable and fallacious, and you, my lord of Gloucester, the more eminent you are, the greater is your obligation to obey wholesome regulations," departed in wrath for France.

On the feast of St. Edward, the 18th of March, De Montfort's office of seneschal at the English court was supplied by Henry, son of Richard, King of Germany.[1] But the indignation of many of the nobles against the Earl of Gloucester, as the cause of the absence of their favourite, was such that they even threatened to invade his lands.   Their wrath was, however, speedily appeased by the return of the earl.

There is a singular anomaly in the position assumed by Earl Simon, and unanimously accorded to him by the English nobles; for the great grievance about which they most bitterly complained was the intrusion of foreigners, and yet they chose a foreigner, who had nothing beyond the influence of personal character in his favour, to. be the leader of their armies, the head of their councils, and, in reality, to exercise an all but viceregal authority amongst them.   The stronger the influence of De Montfort became over the sturdy nobles, the more was he out of favour with the king, who regarded him with that mixture of fear and aversion which a knowledge of the strength and unyieldingness of his character was calculated to inspire, when those qualities were enlisted on the side of opposition.   The king, who was the creature of impulse, and acted from the mood of the moment, had not always the policy to conceal from his brother-in-law the nature of the feelings he entertained towards him.

On one occasion, Henry had taken his barge to go up the Thames, then the grand thoroughfare of London, to his

[1] Rot. pat., 44 Hen. III., m. 2.   Rot. claus., 42-47 H. III., m. 8.   This roll is a nondescript, containing entries omitted on the close rolls for six years.

palace of Westminster, when a sudden and severe storm of
thunder and lightning obliged him to land at the first convenient place. This chanced to be near Durham House, the
palace of the Bishops of London, which, during a temporary
vacancy of the See, was occupied by Earl Simon. The earl
went out to meet his sovereign with every mark of external
respect, and bade him not to be afraid of the storm. " I fear
thunder and lightning beyond measure; but, by the head
of God, I fear you more than all the thunder and lightning
in the world !" said Henry. " My lord," answered Simon,
" it is unjust and incredible that you should fear me, your
firm friend, always true to you and yours, the Kings of
England: fear rather your enemies, destroyers, and slan-
derers."[1]   The ideas of the two speakers on the constituents
of truth and fidelity, however, differed widely. The remembrance of the banishment of the Lusignans, Henry's
half-brothers, still rankled in his breast; while Earl Simon
probably looked upon his own conduct on that occasion as
one of the strongest proofs of his fidelity, and such it un-
doubtedly was, if attention to the true interests of the
kingdom, and not to the mere personal fancies of the king,
be the test of loyalty.

In the beginning of the year 1261, the disputes between
the king and his sister and her husband about her dowry
lands were again renewed.   A strong, indirect testimony is
given to the all but regal power of Earl Simon, even at this
time, by the fact that, in order to settle these disputes,
recourse was had, not to the usual tribunals, nor to the
interference of any of the English nobles, but to that of
the King of France ;[2] Henry thus tacitly ceding to the earl
the rank of an independent prince, by calling in a foreign
power to mediate between them. Oaths were taken on both
sides that the arbitration of Louis, or, in case of his declining
to interfere, that of his queen, Margaret of Provence, should

---

[1] Paris, vol. ii., p. 974.   [2] Rot. pat., 45 H. III., m. 15.

be considered final,[1] and the time fixed for the ultimate
settlement of the disputes was the latter end of June.[2]
On the 21st of April, however, Louis wrote to his royal
brother-in-law, expressing his regret that on the arrival of
the English messengers with the terms of an agreement, it
was found utterly impossible to reconcile them with those
proposed by the earl.[3]

Having thus failed in his mediation, Louis turned over
this troublesome quarrel to his queen, and Earl Simon
privately went over to France to add the weight of personal
influence to his cause. The disputes had assumed a more
serious and political character; for, in a letter of Henry to
Louis, dated July 26th, this year, he says expressly that the
points submitted to the arbitration of the queen are those
at issue between himself and his barons, particularly the
Earl and Countess of Leicester.[4] That Henry greatly feared
the influence of his subtle opponent at the French court is
evident from a letter which he wrote in September to Louis,
telling him that he has heard a report that Simon de Montfort has, without his knowledge, gone over to France, and
intreating that the French king will not consent, either at
his suggestion, or that of any other person, to decide anything in his prejudice, in the contest pending between himself and his barons.[5]

The frequent association, in state documents, of Eleanora's
name with that of her husband proves that she was not an
idle or uninterested spectator of these political commotions,
but that she took a share in them, very uncommon to the
ladies of that period. About this time, her two eldest sons,

[1] Rot. claus., H. III., m. 15, dorso.
[2] Rot. pat., 45 H. III., mm. 19, 15. Fœdera, vol. i., pt. i., p. 407. See
Royal Letter, No. 874, from Queen Margaret to Henry. Tower Collection.
[3] Royal Letters, No. 108.
[4] Rot. pat., 45 H. III., m. 6. See also Fœdera, vol. i., p.409.
[5] This letter, which bears date September 25th, 45°, has probably at one
time formed part of the Tower collection. It is now, however, in the Chapter-
house at Westminster, and forms No. 29 of the miscellaneous Exchequer
documents, temp. H. III.

Henry and Simon, received knighthood at the hands of their uncle, King Henry, and, in company with Prince Edward and John of Bretagne, went into Gascony, to merit their newly-won spurs by deeds of valour against the rebels in that province.[1]

From this period, down to that of his death, the history of Simon de Montfort is identified with that of the land, of which, according to the different views of opposing parties, he has been regarded as the patriotic deliverer, or the rebellious disturber.   In the year 1262, the temporary prevalence of the party of the king, and the consequent repeal of some of the constitutions of Oxford, determined Montfort again to retire to France. During his residence there, fresh, though unsuccessful, attempts were made at negociation,[2] and, on occasion of a visit paid by King Henry to Guienne, the contending parties were summoned by Queen Margaret to a meeting at Paris, for the settlement of their differences;[3] but De Montfort, seeing that the absence of the king in Guienne afforded fair opportunity for strengthening his own interests in England, instead of waiting to abide the decision, returned home.   Henry, in a letter, dated October 8th, 1262, from St. Germain des Près, directed to his chancellor and justiciary, informs them of Montfort's arrival, and exhorts them to guard the kingdom against his pernicious attempts.[4]

The king himself returned soon afterwards,[5] and, after some months of fruitless negociation,[6] the barons at length took up arms. That their causes of complaint were numerous and just is undeniable, and it appeared equally certain that they had little to hope from the promises of a prince who

[1] Cotton MS. Nero, D. ii., f. 169.   Matt. Westm., p. 375.
[2] Rot. claus., 45 H. III., m. 12, dorso.   Foedera, vol. i., p. 416.
[3] Letter of Queen Margaret to Henry III., in the Tower.   Printed in M. Champollion's collection, vol. i., No. 108, and in Rymer's Foedera, vol. i., pt. i., p. 422.
[4] Foedera, vol. i., pt. i., p. 436.
[5] On the vigils of St. Thomas, Dec. 20th.   Rot. claus., 47 H. III., m. 15.
[6] Rishanger's Chronicle. pp. 14-16, Camden Society edit.   Foedera, vol. i., pt. i., pp. 436-7.

scrupled not to violate the most solemn oaths when the immediate pressure of necessity was removed. How far they were justified in their warlike proceedings is a more questionable point, and one which it is out of our province to enter upon. Amidst the clang of arms, however, it sometimes happened that anticipations of a more peaceful termination of the contests produced an interval of truce. During one of these intervals, in the summer of 1263, the Earl and Countess of Leicester, with their children, paid a visit to the king in London. They seem to have remained with him for several months, for their safeconduct is dated June 16th, and the earl was still at court on the 21st of September.[1] About this time, Eleanora's nephew, Prince Henry, son of Richard, Earl of Cornwall, and nominal King of the Romans, who had at first joined the party of the barons, disgusted with the idea of carrying arms against his own relatives, and perhaps influenced by a grant of lands, offered him by Prince Edward, came to De Montfort, and said to him, " My lord earl, I can no longer fight against my father the King of Germany, and my uncle the King of England. By your leave, therefore, I will retire from you, but I will never bear arms against you." The earl replied, " I grieve not, Lord Henry, for fear of your arms, but for the inconstancy which I discern in you : go, then, and return in arms against me. I fear you not."[2]

During the commotions that ensued, the Countess Eleanora principally resided in her castle of Kenilworth, where, behind its strong intrenchments, she was safe from any sudden surprise. From the time that the Earl of Leicester first began to anticipate the probability of a bloody termination to the civil contests, he had taken all possible pains to fortify this stronghold.[3] Warlike machines, some of them brought over from the continent, had been erected at great expense,

---

[1] Rot. pat., 47 H. III., m. 8. [2] Paris, vol. ii., p. 992.
[3] Trivet's annals, p. 25.

the walls and towers strengthened, and constantly protected
by a strong garrison; and Earl Simon might well believe,
from the dauntless spirit of the royal Eleanora, that her
presence would add to, rather than diminish, the efficiency
of resistance in case of an attack upon his castellated fortress. Here, with her only daughter, she passed the days,
and long and anxious they must have been, while her husband and sons were engaged in active combat. Frequently,
however, the return of Earl Simon and his retainers, or the
visits of the nobles of his party, afforded animated variety
to her existence. Among these visitants was Llewelyn,
Prince of Wales, a firm ally of the Montforts, between
whom and the younger Eleanora an attachment sprung up,
which was sanctioned by her parents; and their future marriage, as soon as the present commotion had subsided, was
agreed upon.[1]

At length, in 1264, the battle of Lewes, which placed King
Henry and Prince Edward, Richard King of the Romans,
and his son Edmund, prisoners in the hands of Simon de
Montfort, turned the uncertain scale of war.[2] With the
king at his command, Leicester availed himself of the royal
name and seal to obtain all he pleased. His first order,
given a few days after the battle, was to the constable of
Windsor, for the release of his son Simon,[3] who had recently been taken prisoner.[4] By degrees, the strongest
castles of the kingdom, those of Dover, Porchester, Gloucester, Pevensey, &c., were placed in the hands of his sons,
and all the state records of the period abound with entries
in favour of the Montfort family.[5] The Earl of Leicester
was now at the height of worldly prosperity, and he cele-

[1] Rishanger, Cotton MS., Claudius E. III., p. 318 b., col. i. Chron.
Mailros, p. 205.
[2] Paris, vol. ii., pp. 995-6.   [3] Rot. pat., 48 Hen. III., m. 13.
[4] Wikes, p. 60.   Hemingford, p. 582, Gale.
[5] Rot. pat., 48 H. III., mm. 13, 10, 5, 4.   Ibid., 49 H. III., mm. 29, 21,
14, &c.   Rot. lib., 49 H. III., mm. 8, 9.   Fœdera, vol. i., pt. i., pp. 441-3-
4-5-6-9, 454-7.

brated his Christmas with unusual splendour at Kenilworth castle with his wife and family, surrounded by his warlike retainers, of whom he numbered one hundred and forty amongst his domestic servants only.[1] His royal captives probably were amongst the guests, for he treated them with the courtesy due to their high rank, and Kenilworth was the place which he chose as the residence of several of them.

By a most fortunate circumstance, we are enabled accurately to trace out the whole proceedings of the countess during this last and most important year of her wedded life, with a minuteness of detail at which it is rarely the lot of a biographer in so early a period to arrive. The circumstance alluded to is the discovery of the household roll of the Countess Eleanora for the year, which has lately emerged from an obscure French monastery, where it had lain unnoticed for centuries, and has been purchased by the trustees of the British Museum.[2] This curious document, one of the most ancient of the kind now in existence, is written on a roll of parchment about twenty feet in length, and one foot in width, and is still in excellent preservation. To add to the facility of consulting it, it has been printed, along with three other household accounts of later date, in a volume, entitled " Manners and Household expenses of England."[3] Of the digest of its contents presented in Mr. Turner's learned introduction to the household roll of Eleanora, we avail ourselves the more readily, because the work alluded to, being privately published, will be known to comparatively very few.

The entries on this roll commence on the 19th of February, 1265. At this time the countess had left Kenilworth

[1] Matt. Westm., p. 390. Cotton MS., Tiberius, A. vi., fol. 174 b.
[2] It is now enclosed in a case, and forms No. 8,877 of the additional MSS.
[3] Presented to the Bannatyne club by Beriah Botfield, Esq. Edited by T. H. Turner, Esq.

castle. Probably since it had become the prison of her
brother Richard, King of the Romans, and his son, it had
ceased to be a favourite residence with her, and she preferred showing her noble relatives the courtesy which the
ties of kindred demanded, at a distance. Prince Edward
was then in confinement at Wallingford castle, under the
immediate custody of the Countess Eleanora,[1] while the
helpless sovereign was the constant companion of his stern
brother-in-law, who used his name when and as he thought
proper, and it was under patents signed by the king himself that the last remains of the royal party were seemingly
crushed, and the victorious Simon became omnipotent in
England.

We shall find that but a small proportion of time was
spent by Earl Simon in the company of his wife; for, amidst
the ceaseless round of occupations which kept him always
on the wing, he had little time at his own disposal. He
occasionally returned home for a short period, and, when he
did so, the reins of domestic government were immediately
resumed into his own hands; the entries on the household
roll of his wife were suspended, with the remark that for
those days they were made on the roll of the earl.[2] They
seem to have been perfectly independent of each other in
their movements, though on terms of constant correspondence. On the 19th and 20th of February, Eleanora was
at Wallingford castle with her son Richard de Montfort,
and a pretty large retinue, for the horses of the party were
sixty-six in number. On the 21st she removed to Reading,
and, on the following day, proceeded to the castle of Odiham.
This castle and the surrounding manor had been the gift of
the now imprisoned king to Eleanora, and here she spent
several of the succeeding months.

On the 17th of March, she was joined by her son Henry,

---

[1] Chron. Lond. Addit. MS., No. 5444, f. 69 b.
[2] Household roll, p. 14.

who brought with him his two cousins, Prince Edward and Henry, son of the king of the Romans,[1] not however without a strong guard, for the troop consisted altogether of 120 horse. The day but one following the establishment at Odiham was still further increased by the arrival of Earl Simon with 161 horsemen in his train.[2] Simon remained but a fortnight with his wife. He left her on the 2nd of April, and no evidence remains that they ever met again.

During her residence at Odiham, the countess received several visitors, principally of the ecclesiastical order. Her attachment to the abbey of Waverley has been previously noted, and Ralph, the abbot, came twice to see his illustrious patroness.[3] The prioress of Witney and some of the nuns of her convent visited her. These industrious ladies were employed by Eleanora, who herself had little leisure for the exercises of needle-craft, in working a cape for her chaplain, Father J. Angelus, against the approaching feast of Easter.[4] That she was not altogether unversed in this branch of feminine accomplishment appears from the purchase of one ounce of silk, and three ounces of coloured thread for her use. The prioress of Amesbury, Master Nicolas, a physician, Robert de Brus and his knight,[5] Sir Thomas Astley, a Warwickshire knight, the Countess of Oxford, Isabella de Fortibus, Countess of Albemarle, the Countess of Gloucester, and young Amalric de Montfort, who came attended by thirteen horsemen, were all in turn guests at Odiham castle.

It is curious to note the provision made by our ancestors centuries ago for the supply of their tables. A few specimens selected from the household roll will give a fair idea

---

[1] Household roll, p. 13. [2] Ibid., p. 13.

[3] On the 25th of February (see p. 5), and again on the 26th of April (see p. 26). [4] Household roll, p. 18.

[5] " Possibly Robert the Bruce, lord of Annandale, who, with John Comyn and John Baliol, commanded the Scottish auxiliary troops in the army of Henry III. at the battle of Lewes, and were taken prisoners by the Earl of Leicester."—Turner's notes to the household roll, p. 11.

of the whole. Thursday, the 2nd, was the day of Earl
Simon's departure, on which the expenditure at the castle
was as follows :—

"For the countess and her attendants, the Countess of
the Isle,[1] the family of the Lord A. de Montfort, the whole
family of the Earl Simon being present—for the purchase
of bread, 10s. Item, one quarter paid beforehand, and note
that to-day, after the earl had left, six bushels were expended for the dogs of the Lords Henry and Guy de Montfort, and Henry of Germany.[2] Wine, seven quarts, besides
thirty-three quarts, which the earl took with him. Beer,
for one hundred and forty gallons, ten of which came from
Basingstoke, and sixty were expended the preceding Wednesday for the earl before his departure, 8s. 9d., and for
the ten gallons, 7½d. *Brewery :* Two quarters of corn and
five quarters of barley, and two and a half quarters of oats
from the store of the castle. *Kitchen :* one thousand herrings from the store, fishes, 17s., oysters, 2s. 3d., lampreys,
7s. 1d. *Stable :* Hay for forty-four horses, oats, two quarters, seven bushels, bruised.—Sum, 45s. 8½d."[3]

This, however, was in Lent, when fish was the chief
article of the dinner-table, since flesh was not permitted.
On the observance of this point Eleanora was conscientiously
scrupulous, both during Lent and on the Wednesdays and
Fridays of every week. But the coarse taste of our forefathers supplied the deficiency of shambles meat with such
articles of diet as the whale, the grampus, or porpoise, and
the sea-wolf, all of which are mentioned as being served up for

[1] Isabella, Countess of Devon, and the Isle of Wight.
[2] So called after his father's election to the imperial dignity. This prince,
who, it will be remembered, had been a partisan of the Montfort faction,
seems to have been treated by them with kindness and confidence, probably
in the hope of winning him back to their cause. He must have feigned a
willingness to rejoin their party, for they sent him abroad on some commission.—See rot. lib., 49 H. III., mm. 3 and 4, date April 15. It was probably his want of good faith in again abandoning their party that provoked
the young de Montforts, and led to his subsequent atrocious murder.
[3] Household roll, p. 16.

the countess. A variety of other fish is also mentioned, such as salmon, sole, conger eel, cod, mackerel, sturgeon, &c., also shell-fish, such as oysters, crabs, shrimps, and whilks.[1] Of fresh-water fish, darts, eels, lampreys, and crayfish. But the grand staple article was salt herrings, hundreds of which were daily consumed at the table of the countess. Earl Simon seems to have been somewhat more of an epicure in reference to fish than his wife, for, on his arrival at Odiham, a fisherman was despatched with several assistants to fish in the fresh-water ponds at Farnham, where they remained for eleven days, at a cost of 11s. 11d. On those days when meat was allowed, the family of Eleanora did not fail to do justice to it. The following is the entry for Monday in Easter week, April 6th :—

" For the countess and the aforesaid, the countess of the Isle retiring after dinner, bread, three-quarters of ground corn. Bolted flour,[2] 2s. 1½d. For the expenses of the poor through all Lent, without the castle, besides those fed within, eighteen quarters; wine, eight quarts, one sent with the man of the countess (Albemarle) ; olives, 1½d. *Brewery*, reckoned before. *Kitchen:* one ox and a half from the store of the castle; four swine; four sheep; calves, 21d., kids, 7d. *Stable:* hay for thirty-five horses; oats, one quarter; one and a half bushel from the store. *Smithy : 3s.* 0½d. Lights : for the white candles, 5d. ; lights from Wallingford, 20d.—Sum, 9s. 1½d."[3]

Tuesday, the 7th of April. " For the countess and her attendants, Reginald Poliot and his wife — bread, two quarters, two bushels ; wine, three quarts ; beer, for twenty gallons, 15d. *Kitchen :* half an ox ; three swine ; three sheep from the stores : for sheep bought, 3s. 4d. ; calves, 14d. ; kids from the manor, 8d. *Stable :* hay for thirty-

[1] See Todd's Johnson *sub voce* Welk.
[2] " In Northumberland, called ' bouted' bread, and much esteemed."— Notes to the Introd. to the Household roll, p. xxxvi.
[3] Household book, p. 16.

five horses; oats, two quarters, one and a half bushel ground. For spicery: three pounds of pepper, ginger, cinnamon, and galingale,[1] and one ounce of cloves, thirteen pounds of rice; saffron, thirty-eight pounds; three frails of figs, and one of raisins for Lent.—Sum, 5s. 9d.[2]

The term *bread* (panis) is evidently used to denote flour intended for bread, as it is measured by the quarter and bushel from the stores of the castle. "It is probable that the bread generally used in the family was made of the grain called mystelton, a term still in use at the beginning of the sixteenth century, and applied to a mixture of wheat and rye."[3] Some of a finer quality was occasionally used for cakes, or biscuits and tarts. The quantities of wine drunk are but small, and it was probably only served at the table of the countess, while the supplies of beer are enormous. On the 18th of April, five quarters of barley and four of oats were brewed. On the 28th, 188 gallons of beer were bought, and on the 29th, they brewed again seven quarters of barley and two of oats. The cost of beer when purchased was a halfpenny or three farthings a gallon, but the countess generally adopted the more economical plan of brewing at home, and kept a breweress from Banbury [4]—which, it seems, was thus early famed for its ales—to superintend the process which, in those days, was almost entirely managed by women.[5]

To the poor, Eleanora was very bountiful. Besides the entry already mentioned for their food without the castle, on the 14th of April, she fed 800 paupers, who consumed amongst other things three quarters of bread and a tun of cider; and again, a few days after, three quarters of an ox,

---

[1] A species of water-flag, seemingly from the connexion used as a spice.
[2] Household roll, p. 17.
[3] Introd. to Household roll. A note appended to this passage states that in the north of England it is now named maslin, and its price regularly noted in the return of the Hexham market.—Page xxxvi.
[4] Household book, p. 8.   [5] Du Cange sub voce Braisatrix.

for the hall and the poor people, is noted down ;[1] and on the
4th of May, bread and beer for the poor during eight days.
The usual allowance of butcher's meat in the family was
occasionally varied with fowls, geese, capons, &c. Of vege-
tables little mention is made, and of fruits still less—apples
and pears are the only species named, 300 of the latter
having been bought at Canterbury at a cost of 10*d*. The
quantity of spices used was very considerable, but they
were employed to give flavour to the beer, which was brewed
without hops.

Eleanora appears by this time to have been cured of her fondness for dress, for we find comparatively few entries on her roll
relating to her personal adornment, and those few for articles
of an inexpensive kind. The woollen cloth, which was the
general material of attire, both male and female, seems to
have contented her. These cloths were first made with the
nap very long, and, when it was somewhat worn, it was sent
to be shorn, which process was repeated as often as the cloth
would bear it. Accordingly we find the countess sending
her tailor Hicque to London, to get her robes *re-shorn*, at a
cost of 2*s*. A hood of black satin was purchased for her,
price 18*s*.,[2] and also a scarlet robe against Whitsuntide ;[3]
for the festival of the nativity of the Virgin, the purchases
made for her were thirty-four ells of russet for a robe, to
be adorned with a trimming of white lamb's wool. Beneath
the upper robe, she wore, occasionally at least, garments of
leather or sheep's skin—a material which certainly does not
enter into the category of a modern lady's wardrobe—while
the fact that her washing-bills from January to June
amounted to no larger a sum than fifteen pence, does not
give us a very exalted idea of her personal cleanliness.

But, although thus sparing in regard to her own expenditure, the countess was far otherwise with reference to that of
her children and dependants. Her daughter Eleanora in

---

[1] Household book, p. 21.   [2] Ibid., p. 18.   [3] Ibid., p. 25.

particular, who, being the only one of her family constantly with her, may be presumed to have been a special favourite, was treated with every indulgence. For Easter feast, a furred robe of miniver was purchased for her at a cost of 18s.; two pairs of boots, bought against the invention of the holy cross, May 3rd, cost 2s. 4d.; and besides these and several more entries for dress, others occur which prove that her wishes were consulted even in trifles, and sometimes at considerable expense; 15s. was paid for a golden clasp, which she gave to the young son of Lord John de Haye;[1] for twenty-five gilded stars to ornament her chaplet or cap, 2s. 1d. were given,[2] and 2s. 10d. for a gilded plate bought at London for her use. This is the only piece of plate named in the whole roll: four broken spoons are alluded to, but, as they were to be mended *with* eight pennies, it is evident they were of copper and not of silver.

The "Demoiselle," as the younger Eleanora is always styled, was not without her literary tastes either, for twenty dozen of fine vellum were purchased for a pocket breviary to be made for her, and 14s. were paid for the writing of it, which was executed at Oxford.[3] She carried on a correspondence too, but it is questionable whether she acted as her own amanuensis, for the letters of hers which are still in existence in the Tower collection, written at a later period of her life, are evidently penned by a clerk. An entry occurs in the household for the payment of a messenger, bearing a letter from the demoiselle Eleanora to Prince Edward. Now, as such a letter between the young cousins could not have been on business, it is but fair to conclude that it was an effusion of friendly feeling dictated by Eleanora herself. This is the more likely, since they had recently been spending some time in each other's company at Odiham, and the prince may well be supposed to have gladly wiled away the

---

[1] A strong supporter of the Montfort faction. See page 150, infra.
[2] Household book, p. 65. [3] Ibid., pp. 9 and 24.

hours of a close, though not a harsh, confinement in the society of his fair cousin. There are several notices of gifts presented by the countess to other demoiselles, who were probably visitants at the castle, as the companions of her daughter.[1] When she was ill, a horse was despatched to Reading, to bring over a barber to bleed her.[2]

The entries relating to the sons of the countess are, as might be expected, of a different character. They were only occasionally with their mother, but during their absence she constantly corresponded with them, as is proved by sums paid to the messengers who bore her letters, and the care of their hounds and such of their horses as were unfitted for active service was committed to her. Entries occur for food for thirty-four dogs of the Lord Guy de Montfort;[3] and again for forty-six dogs of the Lord Henry and the Lord Guy;[4] for the expenses of a horse of the Lord Simon, staying at Oxford on account of sickness, 3s. 11d. The only mention of any articles of dress for them is a girdle of silk, which the countess bought for her youngest son Amalric.

By far the most pleasing illustration of the personal character of Eleanora, traced in this minute detail of her expenditure, appears in the generous consideration with which she strove, by many delicate marks of attention, to minister to the comfort of her imprisoned relatives. The provision for their necessities did not devolve upon her, and therefore her frequent presents to them may be regarded purely as tokens of good will. A few extracts from the oft-quoted household roll must suffice as instances. A barrel of sturgeon and some whale's flesh were sent to Wallingford during Lent for the use of King Henry. Notice also occurs of the carriage of 108 cod and ling, 32 congers, and 500 hakes from Bristol to Wallingford, of which half were left at Wal-

[1] Household book, p. 27.   [2] Ibid., p. 31.   [3] Roll, p. 36.
[4] It is an odd circumstance that the term used for the food of the dogs is the Latin word *panis*, the same used for the bread or rather corn of the household, from which it seems that they were fed, partially at least, on meal.

lingford, the residence of Prince Edward, probably for his use, and the other half sent to Odiham ;[1] 200 figs were also sent to Wallingford.[2] The King of the Romans, who was at Kenilworth, received a present of spices—20℔s. of saffron, 5℔s. of rice, which by an odd misappropriation of terms was then considered a *spice*, 2℔s. of pepper, 1℔. of ginger, 2℔s. of sugar, &c., and twenty pieces of whale. Eleanora sent him shortly afterwards a quantity of raisins and two measures of wine.[3] His wardrobe too was handsomely provided for: twelve ells of scarlet cloth were purchased for the robes of King Richard against Easter, while his son Edmund had a suit, consisting of robe, tunic, and cloak, of rayed cloth of Paris, at 4*s.* 8*d.* an ell. A satin hood likewise was bought for each.[4] Henry of Germany, by a singular coincidence, was the frequent companion of Guy de Montfort, to whose terrible vengeance he afterwards fell a victim. At this time the cousins were on very friendly terms, and Henry's confinement was merely nominal, as proved by the allusions to his dogs, &c., evidently showing that he was allowed his usual recreations. The only object of real jealousy to the Montforts was Prince Edward. They knew his character well, and his captivity appears to have been far more rigorous than that of his royal relatives.

There are a few other particulars in the household roll of the Countess Eleanora, which, as throwing light on the character of the times, deserve a passing notice. The names of the servants which occur are almost entirely Saxon: Haude and Jacke of the bake-house; Hicke, the tailor; Jacke, the keeper of Eleanora's harriers; Dobbe, the shepherd; Dignon, Gobithesty, and Truebodi, employed as letter-carriers; affording an indication, as strong as it is melancholy, of the utter degradation to which the descendants of the ancient Britons were reduced.

The attention bestowed by the mistress of a large house-

[1] Household roll, p. 5.　　[2] Ibid., p. 11.　　[3] Ibid., p. 32.　　[4] Ibid., p. 25.

·hold to the minutest wants of her servants deserves remark. Entries are made for payments for shoes, hose, and other insignificant articles of dress for the domestics of the countess. The oblations of Eleanora, independent of her gifts to the poor, were about twopence a-day, which, according to an accurate calculation of the comparative value of money,[1] is equal to 2s. 6d. of our present money.

The peaceful tenor of Eleonora's life was at length broken in upon by a circumstance as alarming as it was unexpected to the Montfort party. This was the escape of Prince Edward, the heir of England, from his confinement at Hereford castle. The jealousy that subsisted between the Earls of Gloucester and Leicester has been already noticed. It had been rapidly increasing ever since the battle of Lewes, owing to the grasping nature of Montfort's rule, for he refused to fulfil his previous agreement to deliver up to his companion in arms half of the castles and prisoners taken at or since the battle, bluntly telling him that, if he managed to keep his own lands secure, he might think himself well off. Besides which, the haughty conduct of the young de Montforts, who, in the impetuosity of pride, cast aside all restraints of moderation, highly affronted the Earl of Gloucester. Himself the first in rank among the English nobility, he ill brooked this display of arrogance on the part ·of the sons of an upstart foreigner.[2] He challenged his antagonists to meet him at a tournament at Dunstaple; but the Earl of Leicester, well knowing the fiery passions that were raging on both sides, prohibited its taking place, and thus the breach was rendered still wider.[3] The offended earl

---

[1] See introduction to the printed close rolls, by T. D. Hardy, Esq.

[2] Taxter's Chron., Cotton MS. Julius, A. i., f. 42. Trivet's Annals, p. 222. Knighton Twysden, col. 2451.

[3] Ickham's Chron., Harl. MS., No. 4323, f. 52. The following is the account given by Piers de Longtoft, vol. i., p. 219 :—

"The erle's sonnes wer haunteyn,   The erle gede on a day,
    Did many folie dede   To play him with a knyht,
That teld a knyht certeyn,   And asked him on his play,
    To the erle als thei bothe *gede*   ' What haf I be sight?'
    [went].

determined to avenge these insults by throwing himself into the arms of the opposite party, and accordingly joined himself to Roger Mortimer, and they laid their plans in concert. The first object to be attained was the liberation of some one of the royal family, whose standard might be a rallying point to the party; and Prince Edward, whose energetic character rendered him of far more importance than the king himself, was fixed upon, and, in spite of the vigilance of Montfort, Gloucester succeeded in effecting his deliverance.[1]

The consternation occasioned by this circumstance among the adverse faction was great. No sooner was the news conveyed to the Countess of Leicester, than she determined at once to leave Odiham, which did not afford sufficient protection in case of an attack, and to join her son Simon in the castle of Porchester. She travelled all night, under the guidance of the shepherd Dobbe, whose familiar acquaintance with the country, probably, led to his being employed on this occasion, and reached Porchester on the following morning. She was accompanied, or followed, by her son Amalric and the rest of her family.

" At Porchester, the countess remained until the 12th of June, and then proceeded to Bramber Castle, by way of Chichester, where she dined.[2] From thence to Wilmington, on the 13th; to Winchelsea, through Battle,[3] on Sunday

The knyght ansuerd and said—
 ' In you a faute men fynde,
And is an ille upbraid,
  That ye are nere blynde' [short-
  sighted].
The erle said, ' Nay, perde,
 I may se right wele.'
The knyght said, ' Sir, nay,
 Ye scarce is any dele.
For thou has ille sonnes,
 Foles and unwise,
Their dedes thou not bemones,
 Ne nought welle them chastise,

I rede you gyve gode tent [heed]
 And chastise tham sone;
For them ye may be schent [lost],
 For vengeance is granted bone.'
The erle ansuerd nouht,
 He let that word over go.
No thing thereon he thought
 Tille vengeance fell on the [them].
Ever were his sonnes hauteyn
 And bold for ther partie,
Bothe to knyght and sweyn
 Did they vilanie.
Wherfore wex with them wroth
 Sir Gilbert of Clare," &c.

[1] Chron. Rishanger, Cotton MS., Claudius, D. vi., f. 188, b.
 [2] Household roll, p. 47.   [3] Ibid., p. 48.

the 14th,[1] and arrived at Dover on the following Monday.[2] Her journey from Porchester to Dover seems to have been made in great haste. Many horses and carts were borrowed and hired for the carriage of her attendants and luggage. Among others, the Countess of Arundel lent a chariot and five horses; the prior of Tichfield sent a hackney, which was ridden by a damsel; and a horse belonging to the prior of Southwick carried Hicke, the countess' tailor.[3] Her retinue, altogether, required eighty horses, that being the number provided for at Bramber;[4] and, besides this, a portion of her baggage, or ' harness,' was sent round by sea to Dover, the hire of the boat costing 7s. 7d.[5]

" At Dover, the countess and her women were lodged at the castle;[6] the rest of the household appears to have been quartered in the Tower. She was now in a secure position. Her son Henry was constable of Dover, and warden of the Cinque Ports;[7] and, although at this time he was absent from his charge, the castle was garrisoned by the Leicester faction. She had the command of the sea, and, should the course of events require it, could escape from the country with speed and safety. In her journey along the coast, the countess had not omitted to endeavour to secure the fidelity of the Cinque Ports. During her short stay at Winchelsea, on Sunday, the 14th of June, she gave a dinner to the burgesses, at which two oxen and thirteen sheep were eaten, besides a due proportion of other fare.[8] Some idea may be formed of the number of the guests, when it is found that provision was made for 195 horses; the number in her own train being only 84."....... " Her son Simon, whom she met at Wilmington, escorted her from thence to Dover. On Wednesday, the 17th of June, she entertained the burgesses of Sandwich,[9] and on the next Sunday sent

[1] Household roll, p. 47. [2] Ibid., p. 48. [3] Ibid., p. 49.
[4] Ibid., p. 47. [5] Ibid., p. 39. [6] Ibid., p. 48.
[7] See p. 48, note 2. [8] Ibid., p. 47. [9] Ibid., p. 50.

wine to the ambassadors of the King of France,[1] Sir Drogo
de Hyon, and Friar Boniface; and lodged and rewarded
two monks of Hereford, who had probably brought the ambassadors from that town, whither, it is believed, they had
been to see the earl.[2]

"By the latter end of June, the aspect of the Earl of
Leicester's affairs became very serious. Prince Edward,
having raised a large army, had overrun the counties of
Hereford, Worcester, Salop, and Chester; taken the town
of Gloucester by assault; and was preparing to effect a
junction with the forces led by the Earl of Gloucester.
Before he could engage their united armies, the earl required
to be reinforced; and, on the 24th of June, Simon de
Montfort, junior, marched from Porchester[4] to Tunbridge,[5]
on his way to join his father, whom, it appears probable, he
had agreed to meet at Kenilworth Castle. On this emergency, the household of the countess supplied him with
nine horses, four of which belonged respectively to her
clerk, cook, butler, and farrier.[6] The roll shows that Simon
passed through London,[7] on his road to Warwickshire, with
the double object, perhaps, of confirming the citizens in
their rebellion, and of gathering recruits among them. On
the 8th of June, the Countess sent Sir Fulk Constable and
others, who had recently joined her at Dover, together with
Master William, an engineer, to join him at the capital.
They received 20s. for their expenses."[8]

The expedition of Simon the younger was very successful.
He had mustered twenty banners, and a considerable troop

---

[1] Household roll, p. 51.   She paid their passage back to France, on the
1st of August: p. 66.   [2] Ibid., note 2.
[3] M. Par., vol. ii., p. 855.
[4] The Annals of Waverley say that he raised the siege of Pevensey, for the
purpose of joining his father.   Gale, vol. ii., p. 219.
[5] Household roll, p. 57.   [6] Ibid., p. 58.
[7] On his march, he took and pillaged the city of Winchester.   Ann.
Waverl. Gale, vol. ii., p. 219.   According to the same authority, he
marched from Winchester to Oxford.
[8] Extracted from Turner's Introduction to the Household roll, pp. xxix. to
xxxi.

of soldiers, before he reached Kenilworth. Prince Edward
heard of this movement, and felt the importance of pre-
venting, if possible, the junction of this formidable body
with the army of the Earl of Leicester. He accordingly
set forth on a feigned march to Salisbury; but, making a
short cut across the country, he reached the town of Kenilworth at night, rushed upon the surprised inhabitants, and
made great slaughter of the troops quartered in the town,
taking fifteen of the standards and many noble prisoners.
Simon himself escaped, being safe behind the walls of his
mother's impregnable castle.[1]   The importance of this
movement, in the decisive action that followed, may readily
be conceived. Expecting to join his son's forces, Earl
Simon marched from Hereford, across the Severn, towards
Worcester, and, staying two days near Ramsey, arrived on
the third at Evesham. Scarcely had he reached this spot,
than the floating of banners, approaching from the north,
gave token of the arrival of troops in the direction in which
those of young Montfort were expected. Considerable
excitement prevailed concerning the advancing host, which
was not allayed until Nicholas, the barber of the earl, who
blended some knowledge of heraldry with the medley of
medical and other miscellaneous learning which then apper-
tained to his profession, positively declared, from the bla-
zonry on the banners, that they belonged to the party of
young Simon. The earl, however, had still some vague
suspicions floating in his mind; and he ordered his barber to
mount the steeple of the Abbey of Evesham, to obtain a
more commanding view of the host. On approaching
nearer his enemy, Prince Edward, who had at first displayed
the colours taken at Kenilworth, in order to deceive the Montforts, changed his tactics, and the royal banner of England,
with those of the Earl of Gloucester and Sir Roger Mortimer,
were unfurled to the breeze, and filled the heart of the worthy

[1] Knighton, col. 2452. Twysden.

Nicholas with dismay.[1] " We are dead men," he exclaimed
to his lord, as he communicated his tidings.[2] De Montfort
himself was not sanguine as to the result of a contest with
such unequal forces;[3] but he assumed a cheerful air, and
encouraged his soldiers with confident expressions, telling
them it was for the laws of the land, and the cause of God
and justice, that they were to fight. He himself led one part
of the little host, and his eldest son Henry the other ; and,
to give countenance to their cause, they placed King Henry
among their ranks. As the royalist troops advanced, their
number and martial array struck terror into the heart of
the brave De Montfort. . " By the arm of St. James," he
cried, " they approach in admirable order; they have
learned this style from me, and not themselves"—adding,
mournfully, "let us commend our souls to God, for our
bodies are theirs."[4] His son Henry endeavoured to cheer
him, by exhorting him not to despair so soon. " I do not
despair, my son," replied the earl; " but your presumption,
and the pride of your brothers, have brought me to this
crisis; and I firmly believe that I shall die for the cause of
God and justice."[5]

The fight commenced about two o'clock in the afternoon
of the 4th of August ; but the daring valour of Prince
Edward's troops, and the pusillanimous conduct of the
Welsh soldiers who were in the army of the earl, soon
showed how the scale of conflict was likely to turn. The
earl and his son performed prodigies of valour ; they exerted
themselves to stem the torrent of disaster, and each led
their men to a renewed charge, in which young Montfort,
bravely fighting, fell. The news of his death was forthwith

---

[1] Chron. Evesham MS. in Bibl. Bodl.
[2] Chron. Ickham, Harl. MS., 4323, f. 53.
[3] The Chronicle of Mailros, p. 200, says, that the proportion of the Montfort forces to those of the royalists was only to 2 to 7.
[4] Chron. Rishanger, p. 45.
[5] Chron. Ickham, ut sup. A rather different account is given by G. Nangis. See Bouquet, vol. xx., p. 416.

communicated to his father. " By the arm of St. James,"
he cried, vociferating for the last time his favourite oath,
" then it is time for me to die !" and, grasping his sword
with both hands, he rushed upon his assailants, striking
with such rapidity and vigour, that a witness of the scene
asserted that, had he had but eight followers like himself,
he would have changed the fortune of the day.[1] Wounded,
however, by a blow from behind, he was struck from his
horse, and instantly despatched; and the fate of the battle
was decided. So great was the exasperation of the victors
against the Earl of Leicester, that they revenged themselves
by the mutilation of his dead body.[2] His hand was cut off
by Roger Mortimer, and sent to his countess, at once as a
present, and a token that the great enemy was slain;[3] and
tales, too long to relate, are told of the wonders it performed.[4] The monks of the neighbouring Abbey of Evesham, visiting the late field of carnage, to perform their
kindly offices for the dying and the dead, found and interred in their own abbey the severed and mangled remains of Earl Simon. His limbs, however, according to
the uniform custom of the so-called martyrs of the day,
speedily reunited themselves together again.[5] Such, at
least, was the tradition handed down by some of the worthy
monks of Evesham, who looked upon De Montfort as
a martyred saint; while others, more scrupulous in their
notions, are said to have privately disinterred his body,
and removed it to an unconsecrated spot, because he died
under sentence of excommunication, and attainted of trea-
son.[6] His son Henry was also buried at Evesham.[7] Prince
Edward is said to have shed tears over the remains of his

---

[1] Chron. Lanercost, p. 76. Paris, vol. ii., p. 998.
[2] Ann. Waverl. Gale, vol. ii., p. 220.
[3] Ickham's Chron., f. 53. Others say it was his head.
[4] Chron. Mailros, p. 202-3.
[5] Cotton. MS. Cleopatra, A. I., f. 190, b.
[6] Dugdale's Baronage, vol. i., p. 758.
[7] Guillaume de Nangis. Bouquet, vol. xx., p. 560.

cousin and playmate, and to have himself attended his funeral.[1]

Amidst the clash of varying opinions, it is not easy to form a correct estimate of the character of this extraordinary man. Of his high mental faculties no doubt can be entertained. He who could, in spite of so many and varied impediments, rise to fill the first offices in the state, and take the lead among a band of nobles proverbial for their hatred to foreigners, must have possessed a powerful grasp of mind. Notwithstanding the occasional outbreaks of an impetuous temper, there was about him that stern fixedness of purpose, and unswerving constancy of resolution, which, whether exercised for good or ill, is in itself almost a pledge of success. In the earlier part of his career, his aim seems to have been to acquire a mastery over the mind of the weak king, and rule by him; and when Henry, in the fitful capriciousness of passion, treated him with indignity, and even unkindness, he persevered for years in a course of unshaken adherence to his master; which must have secured for him the esteem of posterity, had not his after-conduct proved that he was incapable of that lofty principle of patriotic disinterestedness which is the spring of true loyalty. When he found himself unable to secure the influence which he hoped for over the mind of his royal brother-in-law, his tactics were entirely changed, and he contrived, in an extraordinary manner, to secure the lead of the opposite party, and carried on his ambitious schemes till the monarch himself was a captive in his hands, and the whole realm at his feet. It should not escape notice that, to sustain his own party, when it was declining through the jealousy of the barons, Montfort had recourse to the support of the knights and burgesses; and, by summoning them to parliament, in 1164, gave the first rude idea, not followed out for centuries, of a popular administration, but

[1] Trivet's Annals, p. 225.

it would be inconsistent with his character to ascribe his
conduct to higher than mere selfish motives.[1] It is a remarkable fact, that all the writers of the day speak of his
character in terms of enthusiastic admiration.[2] Several
curious illustrations of this general feeling in his favour are
preserved among the political songs of the period. A
lament was written for him in the Anglo-Norman dialect,
every stanza of which concludes with the following couplet—

> " Ore est occys la fleur de pris, que taunt savoit de guerre,
> Li quens Montfort, sa dure mort molt emplora la terre"[3]—

which may be thus translated—

> Here slaughtered lies, the flower of price,
> Who knew so much of war;
> Brave Montfort's knight, his woful plight,
> The earth shall long deplore.

The epitaph composed for him compares him to Mars,
Paris, and Cato, for his eminence in war, his personal accomplishments, and his political wisdom.[4] The most marvellous accounts are given of the miracles wrought at his
tomb; although, from the stern manner in which such rumours were suppressed by the opposite faction, they did not
become generally prevalent till the course of years had
weakened the bitterness of party feeling;[5] but that they
were whispered almost immediately after his death, is

[1] Turner's Introduction, p. xxiv.
[2] Amongst a multitude that might be cited, the most interesting are
Rishanger's Chronicle, p. 6, Camden edition, and the Chronicle of Mailros,
pp. 193 and 206, published for the Bannatyne club, where an elaborate comparison is drawn between him and the apostle Simon Peter. The friars
minors composed a service, or litany, for him, embodying the principal scenes
in his history, which is printed in the same volume, p. 282; but this service
was never allowed to be performed during the life of Prince Edward, afterwards Edward I.—Dugdale's Warwickshire, vol. i., p. 245, note d.
[3] Harl. MS., No. 2253, f. 59, printed among the political songs of
Henry III., edited by Thomas Wright, Esq., of the Camden Society. See
also interesting notices of Montfort, in the " Song of the Barons," pp. 61,
64, and 75 to 91 of the same volume.
[4] Nunc dantur fato casuque cadunt iterato,
Simone sublato, Mars, Paris, atque Cato.
Dugdale's Warwick, ut sup.
[5] Paris, vol. ii., p. 998. Guillaume de Nangis, ut sup.

proved by a passage in the *dictum de Kenilworth*, given the following year, where the king is entreated to inflict corporal punishment on those vain and foolish persons who should dare to speak of him as a holy and just person, and to relate miracles concerning him.[1] Among the Cotton. MSS.[2] is a very curious account, written in the subsequent century, of the miracles said to have been wrought through his influence. They are so strongly characterestic of the superstitions of the times, that one or two selected from the one hundred and ninety-three on record are presented as specimens.

Shortly after his death, as one Richard Bayard, of Evesham, was passing towards Stretford, on business of merchandize, with a train of followers, a band of an army appeared coming from Kenilworth, and threw them into such consternation that they were glad to escape the best way they might. In their retreat, they came to the spot where the body of Simon was said to have laid awhile. Peter of Saltmare, one of the party, proposed to offer prayers to the earl, when one William de Beauchamp, who was somewhat of a free-thinker, jestingly replied, " If he is a saint, let him show his saintship, and give us some fresh water, for we greatly need it ; and, seizing the jaw-bone of a horse, he dug in the sand, when, lo! a fountain of fresh water suddenly leaped forth to vindicate the wounded honour of the saint.[3] It was through the medium of this water that most of Simon's miracles were performed. Man and beast, the lame, and blind, and impotent, the sick, with all manner of diseases, gout, asthma, palsy, all the ills, in short, to which frail mortality is heir, here found their cure. On one occasion, a woman of Elmsley, who was sick, sent her daughter to fetch her water from the far-famed spring ; but, as

[1] Cotton. MS. Claudius, D. II., fol. 120.
[2] Vespasian, A. VI.
[3] Appendix to Rishanger's Chron., p. 68. Cotton. MS. Cleopatra, A. I., fol. 191, col. 1.

the maiden was tripping homewards with her pitcher, she was met by some minstrels from the castle, who stopped her, and asked what she was carrying. She said, that it was new beer. " No, no," replied they, "it is water from Leicester's fountain," and insisted on tasting. They, however, found it to be beer, as she had said; but, when she reached home, it had resumed its original state, and the cure of the sick woman was speedily accomplished.[1] The last leaf of this curious MS. contains a form of prayer to be addressed to the earl, written in Latin rhymes, which are worthy of the subject. The strong hold he possessed upon the affections of the monkish orders, who were the sole depositories of the learning of the day, and enjoyed the exclusive monopoly of authorship, may be mainly attributed to his energetic resistance against the oppressions of Rome; their respect, too, was increased by a certain degree of deference which the earl had ever evinced for the ceremonials of religion; " and their gratitude invested with the dignity of a martyr and a saint, a man who perished under the sentence of excommunication."[2]

Having followed her husband to the close of his eventful career, it is now time to return to the lady Eleanora, whom we left residing at the castle of Dover. On Sunday, the 12th of July, some of the burgesses of Sandwich and Winchelsea dined with her, and those of the latter place were again entertained on the 30th. On the 1st of August, she sent a messenger to the earl, and paid the freight of a ship, which brought an engine, probably a mangonel, from Pevensey Castle, which had been previously besieged, and taken by her son Simon,[3] to Dover—a sign that she was providing for the defence of the place in case of attack. On the fourth was fought the battle of Evesham. Ill news

[1] Cotton MS., Vespasian, A. VI. Printed by J. O. Halliwell, Esq., at the end of his edition of Rishanger's Chronicle.
[2] Turner's Introduction, p. xxv.
[3] Rot. lib., 49 H. III., m. 8.

fly apace, and the fugitives of Leicester's party would soon bring the tidings of their disaster to the countess. But the often-quoted Household roll, which generally enables us to trace all letters and messages sent to the countess, by her gifts to the bearers, contains no entry of the ordinary bounty in behalf of the messenger who announced to Eleanora that she was again a widow, and that the head of her first-born son was laid low. The chroniclers tell us that, on resuming the garb of widowhood, her distress was such, that for several days she could not be prevailed upon to taste food; [1] but the entries in the Household roll indicate rather the spirit of energetic resistance to her impending destiny than the prostration of overwhelming sorrow. On the 12th of August, her son Richard arrived by sea from Winchelsea, with a crew of one hundred sailors, ready either to aid in the defence of the castle, or, if expedient, to communicate with France.[2] A letter from Prince Edward was brought to her on the 16th. Probably it was a mandate to surrender, with which Eleanora was not at all prepared to comply. She was not, however, called upon to make good an immediate defence, and she employed the interim in paying the proper respect to her husband's memory.

It is singular that no entry for mourning garments for the countess is found, although twelve ells of black say were bought for her son Richard. On the 19th of August, we find her offering 12s. 9d. for masses to be said for the repose of the soul of her deceased lord, and a similar entry occurs on the 3rd of September.[3] Meanwhile provisions were becoming scarce. One of the last entries for house expenses on the roll, and which is dated the 4th of August, alludes to the obtaining of oxen and sheep by foraging.[4]

Thus situated, Eleanora appears to have given up all serious idea of defending the castle of Dover, for she discharged Master William, the engineer, on the 29th of August,[5] and

[1] Cotton MS. Cleopatra, A. I., fol. 191, col. 2.   [2] Household roll, p. 65.
[3] Household roll, p. 68.   [4] Ibid., p. 84.   [5] Ibid., p. 67.

she determined to provide for the safety of her two sons
who were with her, by sending them to France. On the
13th of September, purchases are noted of different articles
of dress for Richard de Montfort, and on the 18th, 26s. 8d.
was paid for his passage to Gravelinges.[1] The entries for
Amalric do not occur, probably on account of the imperfect
state of the roll, but we learn from undoubted evidence that
he also was sent to France by his mother, and that she gave
her sons treasure to the immense amount of 11,000 marks, to
carry with them.[2] According to the chronicle of Ickham,
part of this money had been stolen by Almaric from the
treasury of the cathedral at York, over which he had for a
short period presided,[3] and the patent of which office, granted
while the king was in the power of Earl Simon, was revoked
immediately after the battle of Evesham.[4] Having secured
her children and her money, Eleanora next tried to convey
away all the furniture, wardrobes, and equipage belonging
to herself and her sons which was within her reach; but in
this she was less fortunate. She hired some French merchant vessels to transport them, but they were seized and
plundered at sea by pirates.[5]

The great point of interest now remaining to Eleanora
was the defence of her castle of Kenilworth; she well knew
its strength and the resolute character of the garrison headed
by her son Simon, and so long as that rallying point of her
party was preserved, there was still room for hope. Her
anxiety on this subject is proved by the number of the
messengers whom she sent to Kenilworth from the 2nd of
September to the 1st of October, when the last entry on the
household roll occurs.[6] We must therefore have recourse
to less decisive testimony as to her future movements.

[1] Household roll, pp. 67, 74.   [2] Rot. claus., 49 H. III., m. 2, in dorso.
[3] Harl. MS., No. 4323, f. 61.
[4] Langtoft, vol. i., p. 222.   Rot. pat., 49 H. III., m. 11, in cedula.   Printed
in Mr. Turner's Appendix, i., p. 87.
[5] Letter of Henry to Louis, dated 2nd October, 1265.—Tower Collection.
[6] Household roll, p. 75.

The severity with which the victorious party of the royalists now prosecuted their schemes of vengeance, was in proportion to the humiliation they had previously been compelled to endure. But it was upon Eleanora and her sons that the weight of the royal displeasure fell. The close relationship subsisting between the parties had not the slightest effect in conciliating matters: it was indeed, as far as might be, disowned by the king, for, in the state rolls, Eleanora bears no other title, after her disgrace, than " Countess of Leicester," the words " our sister," which were formerly appended, being entirely dropped. Nor can this be matter of much surprise. Had Eleanora been a woman of ordinary mind, from whom nothing was to be feared, she might have been permitted, after her husband's death, to retire with impunity into the tranquillity of private life. The part that she had taken in the civil strife, however, was that of De Montfort's wife and not of King Henry's sister, and the well known energy of her character rendered her an object of vigilant attention to the still tottering government. On the 28th of September, Henry wrote to the bailiffs of the port of Dover and the other southern ports, commanding them, as they valued their lives, or had any hopes of future preferment from him, not to permit the Countess of Leicester to pass into France, he having heard that she was preparing to do so, and to carry with her a large sum of money, from which proceeding the most dire mischiefs to king and kingdom are foreboded; and, to prevent the possibility of her escape, they are charged not to allow any one to pass without special license from the king.[1] It was probably the strictness with which this order was obeyed, that prevented the countess for the present from following her sons into France. Henry forthwith sent ambassadors thither, mainly upon the affairs of Eleanora,[2] by whom he sent an insidious letter to

[1] Royal Letters, No. 398, Tower collection. See Appendix, No. V.
[2] Ibid., No. 864.

the King of France, dated the 10th of October, declaring
that he had intended to appropriate the moneys which Simon
de Montfort, his enemy, had in England, to the compensation of some French merchants, who had suffered from the
depredations of English privateers; but, as Eleanora had
sent it beyond seas with her sons, he requested Louis to
adopt such means as were in his power, that the money
might still be so appropriated.[1] There seems something
unmanly and cruel in this attempt to deprive his sister of
her last means of support, under the sentence of banishment, which he was intending to pronounce upon her, by
endeavouring to work upon the self-interest of the French
king. He was, probably, influenced by a fear that she or
her sons would endeavour, with this money, to hire men and
arms in France. All the moneys of the countess which still
remained in England were peremptorily ordered to be deposited in the treasury of the royal wardrobe.[2]

Eleanora met, however, with one more generous foe.
While at Dover, she had an interview, about the middle of
October, with Prince Edward, the result of which was more
favourable than might have been expected. Although the
prince had been recently and deeply wronged by the Montfort
faction, yet he was so moved by pity for the distressed condition of Eleanora, or so wrought upon by the fascination
which she well knew how to exert, that he granted her very
advantageous terms. He wrote, on the 26th of October, to
the Bishop of Bath, the chancellor, informing him that, at
the intercession of his dearest aunt Eleanora, Countess of
Leicester, he has received into favour a number of her adherents, and orders that the sheriffs of the counties where
their several lands are situated shall give them possession
of their estates.[3] A separate stipulation was also made in

[1] Rot. claus., 49 H. III., m. 2, in dorso.
[2] Ibid., m. 6. Turner's Appendix, No. II., p. 88.
[3] Royal Letters, No. 399. Appendix, No. VI. See also rot. claus., 51
H. III., m. 6, and rot. pat., 51, m. 11, dorso.

favour of John de la Haye, the governor of Dover Castle, long the faithful friend of the countess, and a warm partisan of the Leicester faction, that he should be subjected to no forfeiture of his lands, for the part he had taken in the recent transactions, at least not without a fair trial.[1]

Eleanora did not succeed in making terms with the prince on behalf of her sons. Of the two who remained in England, Guy was a prisoner in the hands of the royalists, and Simon was still in active rebellion. The countess was unable to obtain any favour for herself with the king. Henry, implacable in his wrath, pronounced the sentence of perpetual banishment against the sister whom he had once so tenderly loved.[2]

The time when Eleanora left England is not precisely ascertained. One or two of the contemporary chroniclers say that she was in Kenilworth castle during part of the long siege,[3] but they wrote probably on the mistaken supposition that she was there at the time of the battle of Evesham. It seems unlikely that she should have been permitted to return thither from Dover, and the evidence of Paris,[4] that she went abroad soon after the battle, is confirmed by the greater number of the historians of the period. The chronicler of Dunstaple farther says that she sailed with her daughter from Dover, whither she had remained since the earl's death, and retired into France.[5]

From the manner in which Paris speaks of her departure, it would seem that she departed without reluctance. Perhaps she might prefer an asylum amongst her friends in France to a lonely and neglected existence in England, had

[1] Royal Letters, No. 400. Among these letters is a draft of one dated November 5th, from Prince Edward to the Bishop of Bath and Wells on behalf of John de la Haye, according to his contract; and it is followed by an entry dated November 9th, on the close roll, 50th Hen. III., m. 10, dorso, to the same purport. He afterwards joined the younger Simon de Montfort. See rot. pat., 51 H. III., m. 12.

[2] Cotton MSS., Cleop. A. I., fol. 191, and Titus, A. XIII., fol. 57 b. Chron. Anon. MS., 847 Sup. Français, Bibl. du roi Paris, written in 1272.

[3] Cotton MS., Galba E. vii., fol. 171 b, col. 2, Chron. Petrob. Sparke's scriptores, p. 115. Rishanger, p. 51.

[4] Vol. ii., p. 999.   [5] P. 419.

such been offered to her. This is intimated indeed in an inedited contemporaneous chronicle, in which, after detailing the fate of Earl Simon, the author adds, "But the wife of the said Earl of Leicester, desolate and confounded at the death of her husband, would not stay longer in England, but went to transmarine parts; and though she was the sister of the king of England, yet the king accounted her as a stranger on account of the hatred he had borne her husband."[1] It would seem that on her arrival in France she succeeded in interesting King Louis in her favour, for Henry consented that he should act as the mediator of the differences between them,[2] and, relenting from his former stern resolution of forfeiting the whole of her property, he ordered an inquisition to be set on foot to ascertain what sum it was fit and reasonable that she should receive from her dower lands. She was also allowed to have all her remaining goods and chattels.[3]

In the mean time the younger Simon de Montfort assumed the position of leader of the Leicester faction, which was sufficiently strong to create considerable uneasiness in the government. His banner still floated over the castle of Kenilworth,[4] which was his grand point of defence or retreat, and from thence he plundered the neighbouring country and burnt the towns and villages. Collecting all the discontented spirits to his standard, he speedily became so formidable that it was considered expedient for the king himself, with a large army, to undertake the siege of the castle. It was commenced in form on the 23rd of June, 1266,[5] and continued for some time with great vigour. At

---

[1] Liber de gestis Britonum à Bruto usque ad annum 1298, Cotton MS., Cleopatra, A. I., fol. 191, col. 2.
[2] Cotton MSS., Claudius, D. VI., f. 120, and Titus, A. XIII., fol. 55 b. See also patent roll, 50 H. III., mm. 3 and 3 dorso, and 51 H. III., mm. 27 dorso, and 20 dorso.
[3] Rot. pat., 49 H. III., m. 29, date November 18.
[4] Matt. Westm., p. 397.
[5] Chron. Anon. MS. 847, Sup. Franc. Bibl. du roi, sub fine.

length, young Simon, fearing the ultimate result, stole
away privately from the castle to seek assistance in France.

During his absence, offers were made to the besieged of a
very advantageous nature, in case they would surrender,
but they refused, until they had heard the result of his
negociations.   The siege was pressed with renewed vigour.
Simon appears to have failed in his efforts to obtain efficient succour at the French court.   He returned to England, eluding the vigilance of the king's officers, who had
orders to watch the ports night and day to prevent his landing.[1]   Instead, however, of returning to the castle of
Kenilworth, he formed a separate party, among the marshes
of the Isle of Ely, which afforded a strong natural position
of defence.   This course must have been adopted, either
because he found it impossible to enter the castle, on account
of the strict watch that was kept, or, perhaps, because,
trusting to the brave garrison for its defence, he thought it
more advisable to attempt its relief by making a diversion
in another quarter.   Matters were in this position when
the celebrated *Dictum de Kenilworth* was proclaimed on the
last day of October, 1266, by which the besieged were
offered their lives and liberties, and the only penalty they
were to incur was the forfeiture of three, or, at most, five
years income of their possessions.   The only exception to the
offer was the Montfort family, whose case was to be referred
to the King of France.   This was refused, however.   The
garrison, headed by Sir Henry Hastings, declared they had
received the castle from the countess, who had been just
driven from the kingdom, that to her they held themselves
responsible for it, and that nothing should induce them to
give it up, unless she herself commanded it.[2]   But disease
and famine at length accomplished what force of arms had

---

[1] Rot. pat., 50 H. III., m. 18 dorso.
[2] Cotton MS., Claud. E. III., fol. 312, col. 1.   MS. 847, Sup. Franc. sub
fine.

failed in effecting; and, on the 21st of December, the haggard garrison, after having bravely sustained a six month's siege, marched forth with all their banners, arms, and accoutrements, from Kenilworth, and the stately dwelling of the unfortunate Countess of Leicester fell into the hands of the royalists.[1] It was bestowed, along with the earldom of Leicester, upon the king's younger son, Prince Edmund of Lancaster.[2]

Meanwhile, Eleanora was for some time a prey to the deepest despondency. She would neither taste fish nor flesh; her clothing was an under-garment of coarse woollen, worn under those widow's weeds which, having once, in former days, thrown off at the impulse of passion, she was now destined to reassume.[3] In the first impulses of grief she determined to hide her misfortunes and her sorrows in the seclusion of a convent. The one she selected was that of Montargis, in the district of Orleannois, founded by her sister-in-law Amicia de Montfort,[4] the widow of Earl Gauthier de Joigny, and originally belonging to the order of St. Dominic; but which, prior to her entrance, had been changed to that of the friars preachers.[5]

But, though the countess sought refuge in a monastery, she does not appear to have had any intention of taking the veil. Her misfortunes had crushed but not broken her spirit, and she soon began to make efforts to retrieve her fortunes. She interested Queen Eleanora, her former friend, in her favour; and King Henry having consented to appoint the queen arbitrator between himself and the countess, she was permitted to enjoy from her former dower lands the revenue of £500 a year.[6]

[1] Knighton, col. 2437. Matt. Westm., p. 398.
[2] Great Coucher, vol. ii., ff. 2 and 3, Nos. 9, 11, 12, 13, &c. Office of the Duchy of Lancaster. Fœdera, vol. i., pt. i., p. 465.
[3] Wikes, Gale, vol. ii., p. 72.
[4] Chron. Risbanger, Cotton MS., Claudius E. III., fol. 318 b, col. 1.
[5] Gallia Christina, vol. xii., col. 256-7. Amicia de Montfort was buried there.   [6] See Rot. pat., 51 H. III., m. 20 dorso.

Her next object was to secure some provision for her sons. Simon and Guy, having both escaped from the imprisonment to which they had been subjected on the defeat of their party,[1] had joined her.   For this purpose, she availed herself of the friendly relationships which she had contrived to maintain for so long a period at the French court.

When it is remembered that the queens of France and England were sisters, it becomes matter of surprise that Eleanora should have met with so much cordial kindness from the brother-in-law of the offended King Henry, and it must be ascribed to the influence of her personal character, since, after the entire defeat of the Montfort faction, no political motive could induce Louis to interest himself so warmly on her behalf.   In 1267 he again interposed his mediation, and sent over his own butler and two other messengers to negociate affairs between King Henry and the countess and her sons.   The terms he obtained were liberal, all circumstances considered.   Eleanora was, as before agreed, to be allowed £500 a year from her dower lands, to be received by means of a procurator, who was to reside in England, and to make an appeal to the court, in case of any dissatisfaction on her part.   Simon was to receive the value of his father's lands, to be determined by procurators, one appointed by the king, and the other by himself.   Appeal in case of dispute was to be made to Richard, King of Germany; but these concessions were clogged with the condition that Simon should be obliged to sell his patrimonial estates to the English king whenever required to do so—the price to be fixed by the King of France at a low rate, on account of the injuries inflicted on Henry by the Montforts—and also that he and his brothers should give security to dissolve all league with the king's enemies, and never again attempt any hostility towards the king or his children, and also that none of them should ever set a

[1] Cotton MS. Vespasian, A. II., fol. 56 b.   Trivet's annals, p. 226-7.

foot on English ground, unless with an express royal consent. This grant was made on the 24th of May, 1267.[1]

In the June of the same year, we find Eleanora at the
French court, where, strongly supported as she felt herself
to be by the king and queen, she contrived to make out a
claim against her half-nephew, Hugh XII., Earl of March
and Angoulême, for part of the latter province, which she
pretended should have devolved upon her in right of her
mother, Isabella, of Angoulême, and Earl Hugh was summoned to a parliament at Paris to answer the demand.[2]
Considerable light is thrown upon this claim by a letter from
Henry III. to his mother and her second husband, the Earl
of March, dated September 8th, 1242, which is preserved
among the Cotton MSS.,[3] in which he resigns, for himself,
his brother Richard, and his two sisters, Isabella and
Eleanora, all right upon the earldom of Angoulême in
favour of the children of the countess-queen by her second
marriage. From this document, it appears that Isabella's
daughters as well as her sons were originally considered
to have a right to share her estates, which right, though
it had been formally relinquished by them all, herself included, Eleanora did not hesitate to urge when a favourable
opportunity occurred. The argument pleaded by Earl
Hugh, on the other hand, was that the earldom was indi-
visible; but it was proved against him by several precedents,
that appanages had occasionally been granted from it, and
he was actually adjudged to pay to the Countess Eleanora
4000 livres, Angoulême money, a year, with 8000 to be
paid at once in lieu of arrears.[4]

During the few ensuing years, we hear nothing of

[1] Appendix, No. VII., Royal Letters, No. 866, Tower. Rot. pat., 51 H. III.,
p. 2, mm. 20 dorso, 27 dorso.
[2] Letter of Hugh of Lusignan to Henry III. in the Tower collection, No. 146.
[3] Julius E. I., f. 298. Printed in Lettres des rois, reines, &c., vol. i., No. 51.
[4] L'art de verifier, 8vo. edit., vol. x., p. 234. The name of Matilda is by
mistake substituted for that of Isabella, as the mother of Eleanora.

Eleanora and her family. In 1271, Simon de Montfort, taking advantage of the absence of his cousin, Prince Edward, in the Holy Land, ventured to return to England, to pay a visit of affectionate devotion to the tombs of his father and brother.[1] A gloomy and morbid feeling of irritation seems to have pervaded the mind of the young knight, which was stimulated by this visit into a deep, intense desire for vengeance upon those who had contributed to his father's death and his own exile; and the following year chance threw into his way an opportunity of venting his deadly hatred.

In March, 1272, he, with his brother Guy, happened to be at Viterbo, in Italy, when their cousin, Henry of Germany, passed through that town on his return from the Holy Land. While the prince was at his devotions, in one of the churches of that town, the two Montforts surrounded the church with their adherents, and Guy kept watch at the door, while Simon, entering, barbarously murdered the prince, who vainly struggled and implored for mercy. He then committed many indignities on the dead body, to avenge the atrocities perpetrated on the corpse of his father.[2] This deed of vengeance was as unjust as it was ferocious, for both Henry and his father were prisoners at Kenilworth during the battle of Evesham; and was the more reprehensible on the part of Simon de Montfort, because, after he had surrendered himself to the royal party at Northampton, he owed his life to the intercessions of his uncle Richard.[3] The only ground of enmity against his cousin which Simon could plead, was the desertion by the

---

[1] Bartholomew of Norwich, Cotton MS., Nero, c. v., f. 200.

[2] Lansdowne MS., No. 397, fol. 3, et seq. A full account of the murder is given in a letter from Philip of France to Richard, King of Germany, in the Liber de antiquis legibus, Harl. MS., No. 690, ff. 142-3: and it is also detailed in a letter, dated March 13th, from Charles King of Sicily, who was then at Rome with King Philip, to Prince Edward, of which a contemporary copy is in Bodleian MS., 91. See also Villani, Hist. Flor. Muratori, vol. xiii., col. 261, and Gebauer Leben des Kaysers Richards, pp. 274-290.

[3] Rishanger, p. 51.

latter of the cause of the barons in the year 1263, he having previously been intimately associated with the Earl of Leicester. Simon survived this bloody act but a very short time. " Cursed of God like Cain, he became a wanderer and vagabond upon the earth," says an old chronicler,[1] and died in misery the same year at Sienna, in Italy.[2]

In the year 1273, when Edward I. was hastening homewards from the east to claim the crown recently become his own by the death of his father, on his passage through Italy, he made a powerful appeal to the Pope Gregory IV. against Guy de Montfort, who, at his request, was excommunicated,[3] as having been accessory to the murder of Prince Henry, and all those who should receive or assist him were placed under the same sentence. Guy was taken captive by some soldiers of the King of Aragon,[4] and was subjected to a long imprisonment, till he was at length set at liberty by Pope Martin in 1283.[5] Having previously married the daughter and heiress of Earl Aldobrandini, surnamed the red, of Tuscany, he returned thither, and claimed and obtained the earldom in right of his father-in-law,[6] and became the progenitor of the noble house of Montfort in that part of Italy.

Meanwhile, Charles of Blois, Prince of Salerno, son of the newly-elected King of Sicily and Jerusalem, wrote several times to his cousin, King Edward I., of England, entreating the restoration of Guy to the favour of the sovereign, and to the inheritance of his ancestral estates ; but Edward, provoked at the barbarous outrage offered to his house, would consent to no terms gentler than those of

[1] Trivet's Annals, p. 16.
[2] Matt. Westm., p. 401. The Annals of Dunstaple, vol. ii., p. 419, say he died in France.
[3] Matt. Westm., p. 402. Edward paid 30 marks to a messenger to carry the Pope's sentence through Wales, Scotland, and the North of England. Rot. exitûs, 1° Edward I. Pasch.
[4] Cotton MS., Vespasian, A. II., f. 69. Fœdera, vol. i., pt. i., p. 212.
[5] Chron. Rish., Cotton MS., Claudius. E. III., f. 312, b.
[6] Trivet's Annals, p. 240.

perpetual banishment from Europe, or at least beyond the
French mountains, provided he could give pledges for his
good conduct.[1]   Retributive vengeance followed hard after
Guy de Montfort ; for, in the year 1282, he was again
taken prisoner, fighting in the ranks of his friend, Charles
of Salerno,[2] by whom he had been made vicar of Romania
and Tuscany,[3] and died in captivity.[4]

We must now return to the Countess Eleanora.   In the
year 1273, when Edward I. passed through France on his
way to England, she sought and obtained from him, at the
intercession of the French king, Philip III., who had succeeded his father to the French throne, and was an equally
efficient patron of the Countess Eleanora, a deed of confirmation of those rights with reference to her dower, which
she had previously received from his father.[5]   In this deed,
King Edward promises, on condition of her conducting herself well and faithfully, to lay aside all rancour which he
formerly conceived against her, as well as to permit her the
full enjoyment of her rights.   It is dated Melun on Seine,
August 10th, 1273.   The king generously advanced her
the sum of 800 marks, to enable her to discharge the debts
she had been obliged to contract since her arrival in France,
on the condition that he should be reimbursed from the
revenues of her English estates, which was accordingly
done.[6]   He also ordered some still outstanding debts of her
first husband to be collected and paid to her.[7]

A few months afterwards, we find a letter from King
Philip, of France, to Edward I., in which he says that
Eleanora had advanced a claim upon the executors of the

---

[1] The Tower collection contains two letters from Charles to Edward I.,
and one reply from the king, dated 11th April, 1279. See letters 1126-9,
and Fœdera, vol. i., pp. 568, 577, 587.
[2] Ptolemy of Lucca, Murat., vol. ii., col. 1164. Anselme Hist. gen., vol. vi.,
p. 76. Chron. Leodun, p. 287, and Chron. Rot., p. 381. Labbe Bibliotheca
MSS., vol. i.
[3] Matt. West., p. 399.   [4] Nicolas Specialis Marca Hispanica, col. 631.
[5] See Appendix, No. VIII. Chron. Dunst., p. 419.
[6] Rot. claus., 1 Edward I., m. 2.   [7] Ibid.

late King St. Louis, for the 1500 marks which had formerly
been placed in the hand of the French Templars as security
for the payment of her dowry. This money, however, had
been withdrawn eight years before, that is, shortly after
the battle of Evesham, by Henry III., and, therefore, it
was impossible to satisfy her on the subject. Her impor-
tunities made considerable impression upon Philip, for he
entreats Edward, for the sake of his comfort, the exonera-
tion of the executors, and the safety of his father's soul—
which was considered to be endangered by these unsatisfied
claims—to devise some method by which the countess might
be silenced.[1] But we have no record as to how the matter
was settled.

The troublous career of the Lady Eleanora was now
fast drawing to a close, but her energies remained un-
abated. By a document, bearing date January, 1275,
she appointed Nicholas de Whatham, a canon of Leicester, to be her attorney in England, to act in the
courts of Edward I. in her stead, in all pleas or complaints brought for or against her, and this appointment
was confirmed by King Edward.[2] Feeling the monitory
symptoms of approaching dissolution, however, she made a
will, by which she divided her property amongst her children;
and appointed her son Amalric, Simon, vicar of Cley-
broke, Leicestershire, Nicholas de Whatham before named,
and Nicholas de Heyham, her executors.[3] On her dying bed,
she was visited by her long tried friend Queen Margaret of
France, and to her she made her last requests, in which
were, that King Edward would permit the bequests of her
will to be fulfilled, and that he would have pity on her son
Amalric, and restore him to his royal favour.[4]

Amalric and Eleanora seem to have been the only children

[1] See Appendix, No. IX.
[2] Rot. claus., 3 Edward I., m. 25 dorso.
[3] Ibid., m. 13.
[4] Letter of Margaret to Edward I. Appendix, No. X.

of the countess who remained with her to the last. Henry and Simon, her first-born sons, were dead; Guy was a captive in Italy, and Richard was either dead or wandering an unknown stranger. The exact date of her death is not known; for, in the loneliness of exile and widowhood, her sun set behind a cloud of gloom and obscurity. It must, however, have taken place in the spring of this year; for an allusion occurs to it in an order, dated June the 6th, 1275, by which the sheriffs of the different counties in which her lands were situated had orders to deliver up the produce of them to the executors of the *late* Countess of Leicester.[1] The only historian who gives the date of her death is the chronicler of Dunstaple, who places it in 1274;[2] but, supposing the date to be computed by the *legal* year, which did not end till March 25th, and her death to have taken place before that day, in 1275, his account would corroborate the documentary evidence just quoted. It is probable that she died at the nunnery of Montargis, for the chronicler of Lanercost tells us that she was buried there; but her obsequies must have been performed with great privacy and simplicity, for no commemorative tablet or inscription was placed over her tomb, nor does her name appear on the list of illustrious dead who were there interred.

We have now traced, as far as lies in our power, the career of the Lady Eleanora. On a brief retrospect of her character, it must be acknowledged that she was one of the most remarkable women of her time. Gifted by nature with extreme susceptibility of temperament, she yet combined with it an energy of purpose and firmness of resolution rarely to be met with in her sex. But these powers, unregulated by high religious principle, were not always applied for good. It may reasonably be presumed that, had she endeavoured,

[1] Rot. claus., 3 Edw. I., m. 13.
[2] Pp. 420, 429.

in the strife of factions, to exercise that gently-mediating influence which her near relationship to both the contending parties so peculiarly fitted her to assume, she might have materially alleviated the ills from which the country so long and fearfully suffered; but her high spirit rendered her more than once the obstacle to, rather than the promoter of, pacific schemes. In the loneliness and sorrow of her declining years, Eleanora had ample space to repent the follies of her youth. The records of her last days are too scanty to afford any definite information, but charity would lead to the hope that, subdued and sorrow-stricken, she sought, by penitence and prayer, a preparation for another world, when her career in this was drawing to a close. The fate of the younger Eleanora de Montfort, whose loveliness of person equalled her misfortunes,[1] is fraught with romantic and sorrowful interest. The attachment subsisting between her and Llewelyn Prince of Wales has been previously alluded to; and although it was to Eleanora as daughter of the most powerful noble in England that the Welsh prince had pledged his hand, yet, when that daughter was an orphan and an exile, without fortune and without home, the love of Llewelyn remained unchanged, and he eagerly sought the completion of his nuptials.[2] The marriage was performed by proxy early in the year 1275,[3] only a few weeks before the decease of the young bride's mother, the Countess Eleanora, whose last public act was thus to provide for the welfare of her cherished daughter.

The Princess of Wales did not immediately set forth to join her distant lord. Probably the delicate state of her

[1] Matt. Westm., p. 408. Chron. Norw. Cotton MS. Calig., A. IX., p. 139 b. Chron. Rish., Ibid. Claud., E. III., f. 318 b, col. i. Trivet's Annals, p. 248.

[2] Langtoft, vol. ii., p. 236. The loves of Elinor de Montfort and King Llewelyn form a curious episode in an ancient poem, entitled "The famous chronicle of King Edward the First, surnamed Longshanks: also the life of Llewellyn, rebel, in Wales." Written by Peele, 12mo., London, 1593.

[3] Annals Dunstaple, vol. ii., p. 431. Cotton MSS., Nero, C. v., f. 251 b, and D. ii., f. 231 b, col. ii.

mother's health might be one cause of the delay. The death
of the countess, however, soon broke the chain of filial duty
which bound her to France, and she began her preparations
for her departure. Early in 1276, Eleanora set out under the
charge of her brother Amalric de Montfort, to go by sea to
Wales. Besides the escort of knights sent by Llewelyn,
several French knights, with two chaplains and other domestic servants, attended her; and the two vessels in which they
sailed were loaded with every necessary.[1] The reason of the
bridal cortège proceeding by sea was the dread they felt lest
they should be intercepted, if they attempted to pass through
the south of England. A spirit of distrust, the result of constant attempts at aggression on the part of Edward I., had
long subsisted between the sovereigns of England and Wales.
When Llewelyn was summoned to take his place among
the peers at the coronation of the English king, he had
refused to attend without a safeconduct.[2] In his youth,
he had spent many a lonely hour of captivity within the
walls of the Tower of London,[3] and had witnessed the
horrid death of his own father in an attempt to escape from
its frowning battlements.[4] It was no wonder, then, that
he should shrink from exposing himself unprotected in
England. His refusal was attributed, however, to treason-

[1] Chron. Ickham, Harl. MS. 4323, f. 61. Cotton MS., Vespasian, A. II.,
f. 65 b.
[2] Chron. Rish., Cotton MS., Claud. E. III., f. 318, col. ii. Knighton,
col. 2462, Twysden.
[3] Rot. claus., 25 H. III., m. 3. Among the Tower letters is a very pitiful
one, written by Llewelyn, during his captivity, to Henry III. He assures
the king, that during three years he has not had change of dress or linen,
nor even a bed allowed him; and entreats, by God and the souls of his
parents, that the king would think of him, and order him to be better
treated.
[4] Chron. Lond., Addit. MS., No. 5444, f. 46 b. Cotton MS., Vesp.,
A. II., f. 63 b. See also Rot. lib., 25 H. III., m. 4. In the original MS. of
Matthew Paris, Royal MS., 14 c. vii., f. 250, is a curious drawing of the
catastrophe of Griffin, the father of Llewelyn. He is represented in the act
of falling from the Tower, which is scarcely higher than himself, into the
moat beneath; while an immensely thick cord, strong enough to support a
dozen men, dangles from the battlements.

able designs, and gave a pretext for the subsequent wars between the two powers.[1]

Under these circumstances, the progress of Llewelyn's bride to the land of her husband might well be made in fear and secresy. But the precautions taken were unavailing. The young *fiancée* and her guardian were captured off the Scilly Islands by four Bristol merchant vessels, and conveyed forthwith to the port of that city.[2] Bartholomew of Norwich, and other chroniclers,[3] affirm that these vessels were actually commissioned by King Edward to intercept them. At any rate, his appreciation of the service they had performed appears by a gift of 200 marks to their crews;[4] and he is said to have ascribed the circumstance to the special interposition of Divine Providence, which had thus prevented his relation from becoming the wife of his enemy.[5]

Among the Tower letters is one from Amalric de Montfort to some ecclesiastical dignitary in England, but so obliterated, that neither the name of the writer nor the person addressed is legible. It is written in a strain of indignant complaining of the wrongs inflicted upon himself and his sister, and makes an appeal for justice which had but small chance of success when the offending party was King Edward himself. The illustrious captives, after remaining eight days in Bristol castle,[6] were separated: Amalric was placed in solitary confinement first at Corfe and afterwards at Sherborne castle,[7] while his sister was conveyed to

---

[1] Rot. claus., 4 Edward I., mm. 1 dorso, 17 dorso.

[2] T. Wikes, Cron. d'Engleterre, Royal MS., 20 A. xviii., fol. 283 b. The Rev. James Dallaway, in a paper on the city seal of Bristol, printed in the Archæologia, vol. xxi., pp. 80-2, expresses an opinion that the first seal, which represents a vessel sailing up to the castle walls, was granted by Edward I. to the burgesses of Bristol, for their services on this occasion.

[3] Cotton MS., Nero, c. v., f. 251 b. Chron. Petrob., Addit. MS., 6913, f. 235. Guil. de Nangis. Acber spicileg., vol. iii., p. 44. Chron. John Oxford, Cotton MS., Nero, D. II., f. 231 b., col. ii.

[4] Rot. lib., 4 Edw. I., m. 3.   [5] Cotton MS., Vespasian, A. ii., f. 60 b.

[6] Rot. lib., 4 Edw. I., m. 3.   [7] Ibid., mm. 3, 5. Ibid., 7 Edw. I., m. 7.

M 2

Windsor castle, where, if she were not subjected to rigorous captivity, she was detained in a sort of honourable restraint. It has been said that she was placed in the family of the queen, Eleanora of Castile ;[1] but this assertion is disproved by the entries in the liberate rolls, and wardrobe books, containing regular orders for the repayment of sums expended for herself and her family in the " custody " of the king at Windsor,[2] and Llewelyn, in his petitions for her restoration, in which he speaks of her as his wife, expressly says that she is " in the king's prison."[3]

Great was the indignation and bitter the disappointment of the Welsh prince, at finding his plighted bride thus suddenly snatched from him. In the first transports of indignation when the news reached him, he made hostile demonstrations against the English king,[4] and when he was summoned to appear at Parliament, he refused to obey, but at the same time sent messengers demanding peace and the restoration of Eleanora, and offering for her immense sums of money.[5] The king saw his advantage ; he felt that he possessed a strong hold upon his antagonist, and he refused to relinquish Eleanora, except on his own terms.[6] These Llewelyn hesitated to accept. It needed little provocation to rouse the warlike Edward against his rash opponent. He advanced into Wales : county after county yielded to his victorious arms, and Llewelyn was compelled to sue for peace.[7] He was permitted to come under a safeconduct to London, where the terms were finally arranged.[8] The

[1] Chron. Rish., Cotton MS., Claud., E. iii., f. 318 b, col. i.
[2] Rot. lib., 4 Edw. I., m. 1.   Ibid., 5, m. 3.   Ibid., 6, m. 3.   Wardrobe book, 6 Edw. I., ff. 36 b, 45 b, Miscel. roll, No. 44, Tower.
[3] Letters and petitions of the Prince of Wales.   A partially obliterated fragment amongst the uncalendared letters—Tower.
[4] Ickham's chron., fol. 61.   Langtoft says he was like to die for grief.— Vol. ii., p. 230.
[5] Matt. West., p. 468.
[6] Cotton MSS., Vesp., A. ii., f. 65 b.   Nero, D. ii., f. 179.
[7] Trivet's Annals, p. 229.
[8] Barth. Norw., Cotton MS., Nero, C. v., f. 203.   Rot. Walliæ, 6 Edw. I., m. 12, in incedulâ.

price at which Llewelyn consented to purchase the possession of his long-plighted bride tells more favourably for his
love than his patriotism. He promised to hold the moun-
tain-land, for which his British forefathers had bravely
fought and nobly died, as a fief from the hands of King
Edward. Much of it was already in the power of the English, and though he was still permitted to retain the title of
Prince of Wales, yet the island of Anglesey and the lands
in the immediate vicinity of Snowdon were all that were
left him in complete sovereignty, and even these were on
his death to devolve upon the victor king.[1] These conditions were hard, but the stern monarch was inflexible in the
exaction of them : it was only by swearing an oath which,
as it rang through the Welsh mountains and valleys,
thrilled the heart of every son of Cambria with patriotic
sorrow, and woke up the spirit of its bards to strains of enthusiastic indignation and passionate bewailing, that the
ill-omened nuptials of Llewelyn and Eleanora were concluded. They were married at Worcester on the 13th of
October, 1278,[2] in the presence of King Edward and Queen
Eleanora and the whole court. The nuptials were performed
with great magnificence at the expense of Edward, who
himself gave away the bride.[3] The young couple immediately retired to Wales.[4]

The following year, a correspondence took place between
Eleanora and King Edward, in reference to the will of her

---

[1] Trivet's Annals. pp. 250-1. Royal Letters, No. 286.
[2] Cotton MSS., Vesp., A. ii., f. 66. Nero, D. ii., fol. 231 b, col. 3, Chron.
Abercronwey, Harl. MS., 3725, f. 49. Chron. Petrob., Addit. MS., 6913,
f. 239.
[3] Chron. Rish., Cotton MS., Claud., E. iii., f. 319, col. 2. Chron. Rob. de
Barton, Sparke's Scriptores, p. 121.
[4] The liberate roll of this year, m. 1, contains an order for payment of the
conveyance of the harness of Eleanora, wife of our beloved and faithful
Llewelyn, Prince of Wales, from Worcester to Whitchurch. The wardrobe
book of the year also contains some curious particulars about them. A
coverchief was purchased for Eleanora, Princess of Wales, and a messenger
paid for bringing four dogs to the king and two hares to the queen, from
Llewelyn.—Wardrobe book, 6 Edw. I., ff. 34, 44 b.

mother, the Countess Eleanora, which still remained unexe-
cuted. The letter of the "Princess of Wales and Lady of
Snowdon," bearing date October 9th, 1279, is still in existence.[1] She requests the king, since he does not choose that
Nicholas de Watham shall execute the will of her mother,
his aunt, in his kingdom, that he will have all her testa-
mentary estates collected into his exchequer, and a day
fixed when she might come to England, to receive the portion belonging to her, " lest," she adds, " the last will of
the aforesaid lady, your aunt, should lack its proper effect."
She was strengthened in her remonstrances by Queen Margaret of France, who also wrote to the king, urging him,
for God's sake, and that of his own reputation, not to neglect
the dying request of the Countess of Leicester, by retarding
the accomplishment of her will ;[2] but neither petition seems
to have met with much attention. No steps were taken
in reference to the will, till several years subsequently; for
it was not until the year 1281, that her son Amalric, who
was her principal executor, was released from his captivity,
at the intercession of the Archbishop of Canterbury, who
became pledge for his good conduct.[3]

When, however, in 1282, the business was entered into, it
was found that Eleanora had little to bequeath but debt.
All the goods and chattels of which she died possessed were
to be sold to pay a debt of £600 to one Baruncius, a merchant of Lucca, from whom she had largely borrowed.
This debt seems to have been contracted long before, for her
will promised £400 additional to the merchant, provided
King Edward would condescend to *favour* the executors, by
allowing them any part of what belonged to Eleanora in
England, to supply the loss he had incurred through the
said countess, probably from the accumulated arrears of

[1] Royal Letters, Tower, No. 1332. Printed Fœdera, vol. i., pt. i., p. 576.
[2] See Appendix, No. X.
[3] Several documents relating to his liberation are to be found in the
Fœdera, vol. i., pt. i., pp. 602, 3, 5.

interest. £56 were also promised to Henry de Waleys, a citizen of London, for debts which she owed to him.[1] The goods of the countess, however, were, in value, far below the amount of £600; and, three years afterwards, Edward ordered Baruncius' debt to be discharged from his own treasury; with a proviso, that he was to be repaid by those heirs of the Mareschal family, who inherited the dowry-lands of Eleanora in England and in Ireland.[2] Some years after, he also paid to the abbess and nuns of St. Antoine, near Paris, £63 1s. 8d., which she had bequeathed to them by her will, for a debt which she owed them, and for which he had become bound in lieu of paying her a portion of her dowry money;[3] but, so tardy was the king in entirely settling his affairs, that, as late as the year 1292, seventeen years after Eleanora's death, some of her debts, for the payment of which he had similarly bound himself, remained unpaid.[4]

Of Eleanora's children, little more remains to be said. Amalric was, as before named, released from his confinement in England, in 1281. He wrote a letter to King Edward on this occasion, thanking him for his deliverance, expressing his faith and loyalty, and requesting reparation for the manifold losses that he had sustained;[5] but there is little probability that his application would be successful. Soon afterwards, he went to Rome, where, on the death of his elder brother, Guy, he renounced his sacred profession, and was dubbed a knight, but died shortly after.[6] Of Richard, the accounts are at variance. The Annals of Dunstaple

---

[1] Rot. claus., 10 Edw. I., m. 6 in dorso.
[2] Rot. lib., 13 Ed. I., m. 3. These documents are printed by Mr. Turner, in his Appendix to the Household roll, Nos. 6, 7, 8, pp. 90-2.
[3] Writ of payments, 15 Edw. I., p. 98 in Devon's Excerpta.
[4] Rot. exitûs, 20 Edw. I. By writ of privy seal, Michaelmas, 19°, £50, and afterwards 100 marks, were paid to Nicholas de Whatham, to discharge these debts.
[5] Royal Letters, Tower, printed by M. Champollion, vol. i., p. 301.
[6] Trivet's Annals, p. 256. Annales Luculenti. Cotton. MS.. Nero, D. II., f. 182.

say that he died in France, in1271, while Dugdale, quoting from dubious authorities, states that he returned to England, incognito, and became the ancestor of a Leicestershire family, who went by the name of Wellesbourne.[1]

But the melancholy fate of the youngest child of the Countess Eleanora demands a special notice. She struggled for several years to keep up a friendly intercourse between her husband and her uncle, King Edward; and several of her letters to the king, all of a pacific and mediating character, yet remain among the royal letters in the Tower.[2] In 1281, she paid a visit to England, probably with the same object, and took up her abode in the castle of Windsor, where, on the 4th of January, she received messengers from Llewelyn, who were handsomely entertained by order of the king.[3] But her efforts at negociation were all unavailing. The spirit of the Welsh rose too strongly against the galling restrictions laid upon them.   Their ardour was increased by an enthusiastic confidence in a prophecy of the celebrated Merlin, that the crown of Brutus should sometime adorn the brows of a Welsh prince, and they exhorted their lord to stand firm to his own country.[4] A war with England was the inevitable consequence, and Llewelyn, while heading his army, was slain, owing to the treachery of some of his own subjects, in an obscure skirmish, in which he was not even recognised till after his death,[5] and then his head was sent to King Edward, who had it crowned in mockery, with a wreath of ivy, and affixed to the walls of the Tower of London.[6] With his death, and the still more terrible fate

---

[1] The effigies of this Richard Wellesbourne de Montfort are given in Stothard's Monumental Effigies, pp. 36-7.
[2] Translations of two letters from Eleanora to Edward I., are printed in "Letters of Royal and Illustrious Ladies," vol. i., pp. 53-5. One of them, very eloquently written, is in favour of her brother Amalric, and the other relates to the contests between Edward and Llewelyn.
[3] Rot. Walliæ, 9 Edw. I., m. 12, dorso.
[4] Matt. West., p. 411.
[5] Cron. Cambria, Cotton MS., Claud. C. iv., f. 257 b.
[6] The differing opinions that prevailed in reference to this unfortunate

of his brother David in the following year, expired the last spark of Welsh independence, and the whole country fell under the dominion of the conqueror.

The princess of Wales was spared the misery of witnessing the disastrous termination of these contests. She died, shortly after the commencement of the fatal struggle on the 21st of June, 1282, in giving birth to a daughter. Her remains were interred in the church of the Friars minors at Llanvaes, in the Isle of Anglesea,[1] which was also the burial-place of the former Princess of Wales, Joanna, natural daughter of King John. Her infant was brought, a cradled captive, to the English court, and was educated at the nunnery of Lempringham, where she afterwards took the veil.[2]

prince are thus set forth in the jingling Latin rhymes so popular at this period :—

    " Hic jacet Anglorum tortor, tutor Venedorum,
    Princeps Wallorum, Lewlinus, regula morum,
    Gemma coævorum; dux, laus, lex, lux populorum.

    Hic jacet errorum princeps et prædo virorum,
    Proditor Anglorum, fax livida, secta reorum:
    Numen Wallorum, trux, dux, homicida priorum,
    Fex Trojanorum, stirps mendax, causa malorum."
                            Knighton, col. 2463, Twysden.

[1] Chron. Petrob. Addit. MS. 6913, f. 248. Chron. John Oxon., Cotton MS., Nero, D ii., f. 232, col. 4. Barth. Norw. Nero, C v., f. 203 b. Camden's Britannia, vol. iii., 201.   [2] Langtoft, vol. ii., p. 243.

MARGARET,

ELDEST DAUGHTER OF HENRY III.

Margaret's name—Birth—Precarious state of her mother—Her early life—
Betrothed to the Prince of Scotland—Accession of Alexander III.—
Marriage at York—Bridal feasts—Philip Lovel—Alexander refuses homage
—He and Margaret go to Scotland—Harsh treatment of Margaret—Kind-
ness of her parents—Not permitted to visit them—Her mother sends a
physician to see her—His report—Henry's interference—Changes the
government—Meeting of the royal families at Wark Castle—Treaty of
Roxburgh—New regency—Scotch king and queen's visit to England—
Festivities—They intercede for a murderer—Return—Political disputes—
Domestic love—Portrait of Alexander—Prevalence of the Comyn faction—
King and Queen separated—Their letter to England—They visit King Henry
—Court amusements—Birth of a daughter—King Henry's joy—Margaret's
influence with him—Her return to Scotland—Norwegian wars—Birth of
a prince—Margaret's happiness—English commotions—Margaret's letter
to Prince Edward intercepted by De Montfort—Visited by her brothers—
Another visit to England—Prince Edward's farewell visit—Birth of Prince
David—Death of Henry III.—Queen's sorrow—Accidental death of her
favourite knight—She and Alexander present at the coronation of Edward I.
—Homage disputes—Return to Scotland—Queen's delicacy—Death—
Sorrow in England—Death of her sons—The maid of Norway—Alexander's second marriage and death.

The name of Margaret, now so familiar to every English
ear, is French in its origin. It is rendered interesting by
its association with one of the most poetic because the most
simple of flowers, the daisy,[1] and it becomes additionally so
from its frequent recurrence in the annals of early English
royalty. The Princess Margaret, the eldest daughter,
though not the eldest child of Henry III., was indebted for
her name to her aunt Margaret, wife of Louis IX. of France,
who was the sister of her mother, Queen Eleanora of Pro-

[1] Called, in French, *Marguerite*. In the Museum Historico-Philologico-Theo-
logicum, Brema, 12mo., 1728, vol. i., p. 149, is a curious dissertation on the
origin and derivation of the name Margaret.

vence. This queen always manifested a strong, and perhaps an undue, partiality for her own relatives, and one of the most innocent proofs of her regard towards them was the selection of French or Provençal names for her children.

Of the early history of the lady Margaret but few details remain beyond the date of her birth, which took place at Windsor,[1] on the 5th of October, in the year 1240.[2] Her birth seems to have been attended with difficulty, if not danger, for the situation of Queen Eleanora had for some time previously been considered so critical, that special prayers were offered up for her by the Cistercian monks throughout their whole orders,[3] and no sóoner did the news of her safe delivery reach the king than the precentor and choristers of Westminster were summoned to chaunt a *Christus vincit*, in his presence, in commemoration of the gratitude inspired by the event.[4] When his daughter was but a few days old, and before her baptism, the king made her the rather unsuitable present of twelve ounces of gold, accompanied by a similar gift to the queen,[5] who also received £127 for the expenses of her confinement,[6] and on the ceremony of her purification, which took place at Westminster, the king offered for her a splendid gold chandelier.[7]

The particulars of the expenditure of the royal family,

[1] Chron. John Oxford, Cotton MS. Nero, D II., f. 251 b. col. 1.
[2] Chron. Rish., Cotton MS. Claud. D VI., f. 69 b. Cotton MS. Vesp. A II., f. 56 b. Some chroniclers say she was born the latter end of September, but in a state record, quoted note 5, October 5th is named as the date.
[3] Stat. ord. Cist. Martène Thes. Anecd., vol. iv., col. 1478.
[4] Rot. lib. seac., 24 H. III. The liberate rolls thus referred to are a different series from those so often quoted previously. The latter, which are kept in the Tower, are very much larger, and consist of orders for the payment of money which passed through the Chancery, each roll comprising one *regnal* year. The former are comparatively small rolls, containing merely orders upon the Exchequer. There are two for each year, ending at the Easter and Michaelmas terms. They belong to the office of the Comptroller of the Exchequer, but have recently been removed from the Pell Office, Somerset House, to the Rolls House, Chancery Lane. To prevent confusion, the Exchequer Rolls will be referred to as liberate rolls of the *Exchequer*, and the Chancery Rolls simply as liberate rolls.
[5] Rot. lib., 25 Hen. III., m. 22.   [6] Ibid.
[7] Rot. lib. seac., 24 H. III.

which throw such valuable light on their private history, had at this period almost ceased to be registered on the rolls of chancery, as they had been in the reign of King John, and in the commencement of that of Henry III., and formed a separate class of documents called wardrobe accounts; but very few of so early a period are now in existence. On this account, it is impossible to ascertain with certainty the domestic habits of the infant family of King Henry during the frequent peregrinations made by himself and the queen, on the continent. The children did not accompany their parents. Margaret was the constant companion of her eldest brother Prince Edward, whose age only exceeded her own by one year, and they had a separate establishment at Windsor castle. Here they were attended not only by the usual train of nurses, valets, cooks, clerks, and chaplains, but their nursery was also shared by a number of other children; for it was customary to educate such of the heirs of the nobles as were wards of the crown, with the royal children. The female companions of the Princess Margaret were the two infant daughters of the Earl of Lincoln, lately deceased, who, by the king's command, were sent to Windsor to be brought up with her and her sister Beatrice.[1] We find frequent entries of moneys for their expences, of robes ordered for their attendants, of deer, lampreys, and other luxuries sent to them.[2] They do not appear to have been treated with much ceremony by their guardians in the absence of the king and queen. The Archbishop of York was left regent on one occasion; and he gave a singular order, that such deer as were caught in the forest of Windsor and were not good and fat enough to send abroad to the king, should be appropriated to the use of the children.[3] The wine which he provided for them was also so inferior in quality, that

[1] Rot. claus., Vascon., 27 H. III., m. 1.
[2] Rot. lib., 26 H. III., pars 2, mm. 5, 4, 2.   Ibid. 27, mm. 8, 7, 4, 3.   Ibid. 28, mm. 20, 9.
[3] Rot. lib., 26 H. III., p. 2, m. 4.

complaints were made to King Henry, who forthwith sent
a letter, reproving this conduct, and ordering that they should
be served with the very best wine in his stores.[1] King Henry
also ordered "forty-seven ells of good linen-cloth, price 7d.
an ell, to be bought for Edward our dear son and Margaret
our daughter, to make sheets and coverchiefs."[2]

Margaret's name is associated with that of her brother in
an offering made at the consecration of St. Paul's church,
London, in 1242. The royal children were taken by their
parents to the cathedral when they each presented a cloth of
arras, and the king and queen each a cloth of gold.[3]

In the year 1244, when Margaret was a mere infant, the
north of England was invaded by Alexander II. of Scotland,
whose ties to the English court having been broken by the
death of his gentle consort Queen Joanna, daughter of King
John, he was disposed to make good by force of arms his
claims upon those territories which had been so often the
subject of dispute between the Scotch and English crowns.
But King Henry was not willing to incur the perils and expense of a war with Scotland. He had before averted a
similar calamity by the marriage of his sister with the Scotch
king, and he determined again to adopt the same line of
policy. Alexander had an infant son, the heir of his kingdom, and he readily agreed to the proposals of King Henry
to meet him, under a safeconduct, at Newcastle,[4] there to
negociate the terms of a peace, to be ratified by the future
marriage of their children,[5] and meanwhile the custody of
the disputed provinces was yielded to Alexander.

The sudden death of this monarch in 1249 placed the
crown of Scotland on the brows of his son, then scarcely
eight years of age.[6] His inauguration took place almost

[1] Rot. claus., 26 H. III., p. 2, m. 3.　　[2] Rot. lib., 27 H. III., m. 2.
[3] Rot. lib., 26 H. III., m. 17.　[4] Rymer's Fœdera, vol. i., pt. 2, p. 257.
[5] Gray's Scalachronica, p. 100. Chron. Rish., Cotton MS., Claud., D vi.,
f. 73 b.
[6] He was born September 14, 1241. Cron. Mailros, Bannatyne club
edit., p. 154.

immediately afterwards at Scone, and great as was the contempt usually evinced by the rude Scots to the rule of a
minor, it was not seriously opposed, although some futile
pretexts were urged for delay, which were overruled with
some eloquence and more ingenuity by the venerable Earl
of Monteith, Walter Comyn,[1] who eloquently set forth the
dangers of procrastination.[2]   In order to invest with all the
dignity of hereditary grandeur the boy-king, who as yet
could have so little else to recommend him, an aged high-
land bard, with a flowing beard, and hoary locks, attired
in a robe of scarlet, advanced to the royal footstool, and,
bending the knee, he chanted in the Gaelic tongue, to the
great delight of the assembled multitudes, the names of
all the ancestors of King Alexander III., commencing,
" Benach de re Albin Alexander, mak Alexander, mak
William, mak David, &c.," and, " in eloquent meter of his
language, schawing all the kinges of quhilkis he was linialy
descendit" up to Fergus, the first king, and back through
the endless genealogies of the Scoto-Irish to Iber Scot, the
first Scotchman, who was descended from Nevil, king of
Athens, and Scota, daughter of Pharsala Cenchres, king
of Egypt![3]   At the conclusion, he was " plesantly rewardid
for his labours,"[4] not, however, we should presume, by the
juvenile monarch himself, who may be considered to have
behaved to admiration if he manifested neither fear nor
impatience at the endless list of crackjaw names thus voci-
ferated into his ears.

The new position now occupied by Alexander did not
affect his relationships with the English court, except per-

[1] Fordun, vol. iii., pp. 757-8.
[2] These dangers were not imaginary ones, for Henry III. had actually
written to the pope, representing Scotland as an English fief, and entreating
him to prohibit the coronation of Alexander until his own consent as feudal
superior had been obtained ; but this was refused. Hailes, Hist. Scot., vol. i.,
p. 162. Fœdera, vol. i., pt. 1., p. 277.
[3] Fordun, vol. iii., pp. 760-1.
[4] Ballenden's Boethius, f. 99.

haps by accelerating the period of his marriage; for King
Henry, who was entertaining a project of going on a crusade to the holy land, thought that he should best secure
the tranquillity of his dominions on the side of Scotland, by
drawing closer the bonds of union with its monarch.[1]   On
this account the arrangements for the nuptial ceremonies
were made towards the close of the year 1251, and the
Christmas of that year was fixed upon for the marriage.
Of all the pageants that distinguished the gay court of
Henry III., none were more magnificent, or recounted with
greater minuteness, than those which took place on this
occasion; the testimony of the chroniclers coinciding with
that afforded by the state-records of the period.

The city of York was again, as on the marriage of Alexander II. with the Princess Joanna, of England, the place
chosen for the meeting of the two courts.   The royal family
advanced in the early part of November as far as Nottingham castle, a favourite residence of our Plantagenet
sovereigns, where they spent nearly a month.   Careful
preparations had been made for their reception here,
and some of the orders issued afford curious illustrations
of the manners of the times.   The queen's chamber, and
wardrobe and the chapel, were ordered to be whitewashed,
and in the chamber, wooden stalls and chairs to be
erected, and iron candlesticks fixed in the wall.   The windows on the south part of the great hall were to be barri-
caded.   In the state-chapel a picture of the history of St.
William was to be painted in front of the altar, and above
it the history of St. Edward.   A private chapel dedicated
to St. Catherine was adorned with pictures of the life of

---

[1] Tytler's Hist. of Scotland, vol. i., p. 5. Many curious entries with reference to this projected crusade occur on the close roll of this year. Amongst
them is one in which the masters of the friars-preachers and friars-minors
are ordered to send men "who are most eloquent in delivering harangues for
the holy cross" to London, to endeavour to swell the number of its votaries.
Rot. claus., 36 H. III., mm. 12 and 16 dorso.

that virgin, and with a representation of the Last Judgment called " *tremendum judicium*." A silver cup, altar
cross, phials, and censers, were also provided for the chapel,
together with a set of books, consisting of a missal, a book
of anthems, a breviary, a gradual, which was a book containing the Psalms from the 118th to the 134th, such as had
been used in the Levitical service, a tropar or book of alter-
nate responses used in chanting mass, a psaltery, and a
hymn-book.[1]

The period of his stay at Nottingham was employed by
King Henry in making preparations for his daughter's
equipment, but on account of her extreme juvenility these
were not very magnificent or costly. Her jewels were to
amount in value to 200 marks; a rich and precious bed was
ordered for her, and also some pieces of plate, a golden chalice
and cup, a silver posnet and pot, and six spoons, &c., with
a pair of basons, two phials, a chalice, and vestments for her
chapel. Instead of dresses, ten pieces of cloth of gold were
given to her, probably that she might consult the Scottish
modes in the form of her attire; but robes of green were to
be made for her two waiting-girls, and one of scarlet, trimmed with miniver, for her governess, Matilda de Cantilupe.
Four saddles were prepared—one of scarlet velvet, with
reins and other harness.[2] Robes of the most costly description were also ordered for the king and queen, for Prince
Edward and several members of the royal suite—that of
Henry being of violet-coloured velvet, embroidered with his
coat of arms, three golden leopards, both in front and behind.[3]

On the 12th of December, the party left Nottingham, and
proceeded by slow stages through Sherwood forest, Worksop,
and Pontefract, to York, which they reached on the 22nd.[4]
The bridegroom probably arrived before them, for as early

[1] Rot. lib., 36 H. III., m. 17.
[2] Rot. claus., 36 H. III., mm. 32, 31, 30, 29. Rot. lib., 36 H. III., m. 7.
[3] Ibid., mm. 30, 31.   [4] Rot. claus., 36 H. III., m. 28.

as the 15th of December orders were issued that he should
be allowed to hunt in the royal forest of Gautriz, as he
was *en route*, and also to have the privilege of carrying
away all the game he killed, as trophies of his juvenile
skill and prowess.[1] The Scotch king was attended by his
mother, Mary de Coucy. Although, on the death of her
husband, she had left her son, and returned to her own
relations, yet she came over to grace the nuptials with
her presence ; and the dowry she enjoyed, as the dowager-
queen of Scotland, added to her ancestral revenues, being
very ample, she was enabled to appear attended by a long
train of French knights, with a degree of magnificence
that excited universal admiration. Alexander was also
attended by the principal Scotch nobility.[2] The Princess
Margaret was not inferior either in the number or rank of
her escorts, for her father and mother, with many of the
English nobles and clergy, accompanied her. Different
quarters of the city were assigned to the visitants of the
two nations, whose houses were provided for them by
appointed marshals ; for, pacific as was their present
meeting, both parties were aware that the sparks of ancient national animosity still slumbered in many a bosom,
only waiting a breath to burst into a flame. Notwithstanding the precautions taken, however, discords did arise, and
fights too, first with sticks, and then with swords, in which
several persons were dangerously wounded, and a few
killed ;[3] but the monarchs interfering, with their guards,
succeeded in appeasing the strife.[4]

The knighting of King Alexander was considered an
indispensable pre-requisite to his marriage ; and it was

[1] Rot. claus., ut supra.
[2] Paris, vol. ii., p. 829. Annal. Burton. Gale, vol. i., p. 317.
[3] Paris, ut sup.
[4] Traces of this quarrel may be found in the close roll of the year ; for the
supervisor of the castle of York having incurred the displeasure of Alexander,
was, at his solicitation, deprived of his office by King Henry. See rot.
claus., 36 H. III., m. 26.

arranged that he should receive this honour at the hand of his intended father-in-law. The ceremony was appointed to take place on Christmas-day; and in preparation, King Henry ordered for him a handsome sword, with a scabbard of silk and a silver handle, along with its accompanying belt,—the distinguishing characteristic of knighthood,[1]—and also a pair of silver-gilt spurs to decorate the person of the knight elect. A costly couch was ordered to be presented to him when he performed the preliminary vigils; it being customary to spend the previous night in solitary watchings in some church.[2] Twenty other youths of noble blood shared the honours of the young king, who were all adorned with rich and becoming attire.[3] The earl marshal demanded, as usual, the horse of King Alexander, as the perquisite of his office; " not," we are told, " from covetousness, or regard to its value, but lest an ancient and honourable custom should perish through his neglect." This demand was refused, on the ground that it was simply as matter of courtesy that Alexander had chosen to be knighted by the English king, since the ceremony might have been performed as effectually by any Catholic prince or noble.[4] The day following, being the 26th of December, St. Stephen's-day, was appointed for the nuptials.[5] So numerous were the crowds of spectators who were eager to witness the ceremony, that it was deemed advisable, for the sake of convenience, and probably to avoid any further unpleasant consequences arising from the jealousy between the English and Scotch,

---

[1] Rot. claus., 36 H. III., m. 31.
[2] Rot. claus., 36 H. III., m. 30. From the Introduction to the close rolls, by T. D. Hardy, Esq., p. xl.
[3] Among these was William de Chabeneys, a relation of the king, who was to have three decent robes, a couch, and all other necessary appurtenances for knighthood. Rot. claus., 36 H. III., m. 3.
[4] Paris, vol. ii., p 8 30. Sir Harris Nicolas' Knightage—knights of the thistle.
[5] Cotton MS., Vesp., A. II., f. 54. Paris, vol. ii., p. 829. Fordun, vol. iii., p. 762.

when tumultuously mingled, that the marriage should be performed early in the morning, long before the antici-pated hour, which was accordingly done.[1] The youthful bride of eleven summers was marshalled to the altar by her brother, Prince Edward, and three of his companions, wearing short gowns of rich cloth of gold, embroidered with the arms of England.[2] Of her costume and de-meanour, or that of her still more juvenile bridegroom, no record remains. The day following the marriage, her father bound himself to pay, in the course of the ensuing four years, five thousand marks of silver, as Margaret's wedding portion.[3]

Matthew Paris, who was present at this wedding, launches out into the most eloquent descriptions of the gaiety of the scene. " Such was the diversity of people, English, French, and Scotch, so numerous the crowds of soldiers, adorned with gaudy dresses, and proud of their silken robes and ornaments, that, if all were described, it would beget not only admiration but weariness in the hearers. There were more than a thousand English, dressed in silken quaintises," (a species of robe, so called from its being decorated with some device, or *quaintness*, generally the coat of arms of the wearer[4]) " and yet the next day these were all thrown aside, and they appeared at court in fresh robes ; more than sixty Scotch knights, with many others, who, though they did not bear the title, were equal in every respect to knights, attracted the ad-miration of all."

The bridal festivals were conducted with proportionable munificence and splendour. The whole company were

---

[1] Paris, ut sup.   [2] Rot. claus., 36 H. III., m. 4.
[3] Rot. pat., 36 H. III., m. 14. An aid had as usual been granted to the king for the marriage of this, his eldest daughter, which would far more than furnish her dower. (Madox, Hist. Exchoq., vol. i., p. 594.) This dowry was trifling, in comparison with that bestowed by Henry on his sister, the Empress Isabella, which amounted to thirty thousand marks.
[4] Introd. to close rolls, p. xli.

feasted now by one and then by the other of the kings,
and again by the Archbishop of York, who officiated in
part as master of the ceremonies, since it fell to his lot to
provide residences for the strangers, food for the horses,
provisions for the table, kindling for the fires, &c.; and
very effectually he performed his duties, but at such a cost,
that he had to pay from his own purse 4000 marks, equal
to £40,000 of our money, towards the expences. "Such,"
says Matthew Paris, " was the abundant diversity of the
feasts, the variety and changes of robes, the merriment of
the applauding jesters, and the number of the feasters,
that the hyperbolic narration would beget irony in the
hearts and ears of those who were absent; but one circumstance may, by comparison, afford a test of others—
more than sixty stalled oxen, given by the archbishop,
afforded the *primitiæ*, or first fruits only, of the feasts."

The account of the chronicler is fully borne out by the
entries on the close rolls; for, during several preceding
months, Henry had been accumulating provisions of all
sorts in York. The civic authorities of that city and
the neighbouring towns were to supply their quota of
bread;[1] 200 deer, 300 does, 200 young bucks, and 100
wild boars were to be taken in the royal forests, and sent
thither.[2] A singular entry occurs about these same deer.
Richard Earl of Norfolk was presented with six deer, on
condition that he would afford his aid to catch 200 more![3]
and the seneschal of the forest of Gautriz, where they
were taken, was ordered, as he loved himself, that is, in peril
of his life, to have them at York by Christmas.[4] The
king's fisher was sent to catch fish in the royal fish-ponds,
and to keep them alive in some safe stew until they were
needed, and 230 salmon were provided beside.[5] Supplies
of spicery, wood, and coal, for fuel, and numerous other

---

[1] Rot. claus., 36 H. III., m. 31, in dorso.   [3] Ibid., m. 30.
[2] Ibid., m. 29.   [4] Ibid., m. 30.   [5] Ibid., m. 29.

necessaries too tedious to mention, were likewise furnished.[1]

During one of these joyous seasons of festivity, a strange scene took place. A priest of the name of Philip Lovel, an eloquent and crafty man, who in the former part of his life had exercised important offices in Galway, and therefore become known to Alexander II. and his queen, had recently, and, as it would appear, most deservedly, fallen under the displeasure of King Henry, for bribery in the collecting of taxes. This man artfully contrived to obtain an interview with the young King of Scots, and so moved upon his feelings, that he promised to intercede for him with Henry. Accordingly, seizing a favourable moment, " he came and threw himself before the king with bent knees and joined hands, refusing to be raised, checking jocularity, and almost raising tears in the bystanders, and thus addressed him—' My lord king, your grace knows that, though I am king, and now, by your kindness, made knight, yet I am but a boy, without age or learning, and a pupil likewise; for my father is dead, and my mother left me a tender child, to revisit her distant home beyond the seas. Now and henceforth, therefore, I adopt you as my father, that you may supply to me the place of parents, and give counsel and paternal protection to my youth.' The king, scarcely containing his tears, with suppressed sobs answered — ' Most willingly : ' and the boy, not speaking like a child, added—' By this I shall know and prove you, since of your grace you have heard me, if you bring to pass the first fruits of my desires. Pardon Philip Lovel all his offences; recall him to his former favour; for he once greatly honoured my father and mother and me ; and I have learned from credible persons that he is unjustly accused : forget not that he was formerly apt and obedient to your will.' "[2] Moved by the eloquence of the

<hr />

[1] Rot. claus., 36 H. III., m. 30.   [2] Paris, vol. ii., p. 829.

pleader, and the warm applause of the bystanders, who seconded his petition, King Henry, with more kindness than justice, consented to grant it, and Philip was almost immediately advanced to the office of treasurer of England.[1]

On the conclusion of the nuptials, Henry, with a policy that does more honour to his head than his heart, demanded from his son-in-law the performance of the oft-contested act of homage, by which the feudal superiority of England over Scotland was to be acknowledged. But the gallant boy, though thus taken by surprise, in a moment of excitement, steadily refused: he would pay the customary homage, he said, for the lands he held in England, but as for anything more than this, it was too arduous a matter for him to act in, without the advice of his counsellors, adding, that he was come in peace and amity to England, at the invitation of the king, to contract his nuptial alliance, and that with matters of state he could not now interfere. Henry, balked in his project of surprising the young king into compliance, was not disposed to urge the matter, declaring that " he would not cloud with perturbation so serene a feast, nor molest so young a king, and still younger husband;" so the matter was permitted to lie over.[2]

It was now time for the bridal party to disperse, and Alexander asked and obtained permission to take away his young bride to her future home. Before their departure, Henry presented his son in-law with £109, for his expences while in England,[3] and confirmed to him the lands which Alexander II. had held in Cumberland, and

---

[1] Rot. claus., 36 H. III., mm. 4, 3.

[2] Paris, vol. ii., p. 830. Notwithstanding the precautions taken by Alexander, this conditional homage was afterwards pleaded as a precedent, in the stormy debates on the subject in the latter end of the reign of Edward I.—Chron. Brut. Cotton MS. Nero, A. VI., f. 31 b.

[3] Madox, Hist. Excheq., vol. ii., p. 202.

which, on his death, had reverted to the English king.[1]
He provided an able governess for his daughter, in the
person of Matilda, the widow of William, the second Earl
Cantelupe,[2] a lady richly endowed with the qualifications
necessary for her office. Two English knights, Robert
le Norrey and Stephen Bauzan,[3] with other "discreet and
pleasant men," were appointed to attend her.[4] Arrangements were also made for the government of the kingdom
of Scotland during Alexander's minority. The Earls of
Monteith, Buchan, and Mar, with Robert Bruce and John
Baliol, two of the most powerful nobles, and most nearly
allied to the royal family, were appointed regents, and
were to be aided in their deliberations by a good and
faithful counsellor, to be sent over from England.[5] To
these men, therefore, the persons of the young king and
queen were committed.[6] They travelled by way of New-
castle-upon-Tyne, where they took up their abode in the
princely castle of the English king, the governor of which
had orders to receive them handsomely, and provide them
with wine, flesh, and fish, as long as they should think
proper to stay.[7] On their arrival in Scotland, they were
conveyed to the castle of Edinburgh, which was assigned
as their residence.[8] How the youthful queen was received
by her new subjects, we are not informed. Her name,
which would remind them of their much-loved Queen
Margaret, the Atheling, the wife of Malcolm IV., who
was alike the ancestress of both Alexander and Margaret,[9]

[1] Rot. claus., 36 H. III., m. 26.   [2] Paris, vol. ii., p. 831.
[3] They do not seem to have remained with her. See rot. claus., 36
H. III., mm. 2, 5.
[4] The governess and two gentlemen are named in the patent roll, 36
Hen. III., m. 14.
[5] Paris, vol. ii., p. 831. Fordun, vol. iii., p. 763.
[6] Chron. Otterbourne, Hearne's edit., p. 78.
[7] Rot. claus., 36 H. III., m. 27.
[8] Wyntown's Chron., vol. i., p. 384.
[9] Through Matilda of Scotland, the queen of Henry I, who, it will be
remembered, was the daughter of Margaret the Atheling.

would be likely to operate in her favour; the more so
since the recent translation of the bones of her illustrious
ancestress had vividly recalled to the memory of the
people the many virtues which adorned the character of
Saint Margaret.[1]

At present, however, Margaret had little association with
the Scotch.   Disputes arose between her English attendants and the servants who were placed around her by her
guardians,[2] which rendered her situation very uncomfort-
able. She was kept under a guardianship, almost amounting to imprisonment, in the castle of Edinburgh, which
stands on a sea-girt precipice, rising 300 feet perpendicu-
larly from the level of the water,[3] where she could walk
but little, and where riding was out of the question; and
she was thus precluded those pleasant horseback scampers
in which she had greatly delighted, among the green fields
of her own land.   As the climax of her woes, she was
not permitted any freedom of intercourse with the spouse
who had, even at that early age, made a deep impression
on her affections. This last deprivation she seems to have
felt the most keenly, since it formed the principal subject
for the complaints which she sent to the English court.
Probably no unkindness was intended, on the part of the
Scottish lords, but Margaret was a petted child, accustomed to the luxuries and refinement of her father's court,
nursed in the lap of tenderness—for Eleanora of Provence
was a most affectionate mother, and the contrast of her
present situation was so irksome to her, that she made

---

[1] Her conjugal love was not only as strong, but stronger than death; for,
at the translation of her body, it was found impossible to stir it an inch
beyond the tomb of King Malcolm, until, at the suggestion of a holy
man, *his* bones were also dug up, and permitted to accompany hers in its
approaching honours, upon which the coffin was easily moved. Fordun,
vol. iii., p. 760.

[2] Tytler, Hist. Scot., vol. i., p. 11.

[3] Scotia depicta, J. Claude Nattes, plate xxxi.   The ancient palace of
Edinburgh occupies the eastern end of the square formed by the present
castle.   Maitland's Hist. Edinb., p. 161.

frequent applications for redress,[1] especially to Queen
Eleanora, with whom she maintained continued intercourse, as appears by the numerous orders for payments
to messengers from her.[2] The maternal feelings of the
queen were strongly excited in behalf of her suffering
daughter. She contented herself for awhile by sending
messengers with letters and occasional presents to her;[3]
forty-eight shillings were also given to Isabella de Valet,
formerly the nurse of Margaret,[4] and King Henry gave
her a still more substantial proof of regard, by presenting
her with all the fines recently raised by his justiciary in
Cumberland;[5] but to the desolate young girl, wealth was
a poor compensation for the tender sympathies of domestic love.

In the spring of 1253, an effort was made to bring the
young queen back to England, under the pretext of a visit
to her mother. Henry wrote to King Alexander, stating
that he was about to depart for Gascony, leaving Queen
Eleanor regent of England, and that the queen, who
was advanced in pregnancy, greatly desired the solace
and recreation of her daughter's society. He therefore
earnestly entreated Alexander to allow Queen Margaret
to go over into England, and to remain with her mother
until after her confinement, and until the ceremony of her
purification had been performed. William Archbishop of
York and other messengers were sent to urge this request,
and the archbishop was commissioned to take charge of
Margaret, and conduct her to England, in case it proved
successful.[6] But, although a safeconduct was actually
granted to her,[7] with the proviso for her return, when

[1] Paris, vol. ii.; p. 908.
[2] Rot. nunc. regin. Elean., 36 and 37 H. III., No. 370, Queen's Remembrancer Office.
[3] Rot. regin. Elean., No. 370 and No. 3294, Queen's Remembrancer.
[4] Roll of the secret expenses of Queen Eleanora, No. 3290.
[5] Rot. claus., 37 H. III., m. 10.   [6] Ibid., m. 9, dorso.
[7] Rot. pat., 37 H. III., m. 13.

required, the design does not appear to have taken effect. Indeed, it was scarcely likely that the regency would be induced to allow such a step, since, knowing the dissatisfaction felt by the young queen, they might naturally apprehend that, in spite of the pledges made, it would be difficult to allure her back again, if she were permitted to go home.

The following year was passed by Henry and his queen in Gascony, but they despatched English messengers to Scotland in February, " on urgent business,"[1] and in August, Simon de Montfort, Earl of Leicester, was sent over on a secret mission,[2] the direct purport of which has not transpired; but it was doubtless to inquire into the situation of Queen Margaret. The result seems to have been unfavourable; for at length Queen Eleanora became so seriously uneasy, particularly about the health of her daughter, that she determined to send over a confidential physician of her own, one Master Reginald, of Bath, to keep a strict surveillance over Margaret, and also over her husband, for whom she entertained a maternal affection.[3] When this man arrived at Edinburgh Castle, bearing letters of credence from the English king and queen, courtesy compelled his admission. He was introduced to a private interview with Margaret, and was struck with the extreme pallor of her countenance, and the perturbed sadness of her demeanour. On his proposing to her the usual inquiries relative to her health, "It is fitting," answered she, " to lay open the secrets of the body to a physician, as those of the soul to a priest;" and forthwith entered upon an explanation of her circumstances, and particularly of the mode of her treatment by her stern governors. The indignation of Master Reginald was greatly excited by the complainings of the sick and pining

[1] Rot. claus., 38 H. III., m. 14, dorso.   [2] Fœdera, vol. i., p. 320.
Paris, vol. ii., p. 907.

child. He vehemently reproached her guardians and the
magnates of the kingdom, who had the supervision of
affairs, and even accused them of the crime of *lèse-majesté*,
in thus wantonly trifling with the health of their queen.
A few days afterwards, the physician was seized with
sudden and violent illness : dark suspicions were naturally
afloat as to the nature of his attack ; the sufferer himself
attributed it to poison, administered by the deadly animosity of the chiefs whom he had provoked. If so, their
object, which was to prevent his report being carried to
the court of England, was frustrated ; for his decease was
not instantaneous ; and he had time to despatch letters to
the English king and queen, telling them that he had
come to Scotland under a fatal star ; that he had seen
their daughter faithlessly and inhumanly treated by the
Scots ; and that, because he had remonstrated, they had
prepared a bitter death for himself.[1]

The parental feelings of Henry and Eleanor were as
might be expected, strongly roused by such an appeal.
Henry even entertained thoughts of dissolving the marriage immediately ; and he privately sent two of his trusty
adherents, Richard Earl of Gloucester and John Maunsell,
into Scotland, to ascertain the real situation of the young
queen, and the best mode of relieving her.[2] On arriving
at Edinburgh, they found the castle and its royal inmates
so carefully guarded, that the only way in which they
could obtain access was by assuming the liveries of the
servants of Robert Bruce, the guardian, and thus entering
the castle privately. Their followers, who dropped in
gradually after them, adopted the same policy, so that the
English party was soon strong enough to master the garrison, in case of detection. They speedily found their

[1] Paris, vol. ii., p. 907.
[2] Rot. pat., 39 H. III., m. 4. Rot. claus., 39 H. III., m. 7, dorso. Paris.
vol. ii., p. 908. Fœdera, vol. i., p. 326.

way to the presence of the queen, and she told them, with sobs and tears, that she was a complete prisoner in that sad and solitary place; that she was permitted no household of her own; and that even her favourite maidens, whom she wished to have to attend upon her, or sleep with her, were not allowed to do so; and, above all, that she was denied the loving society of her spouse. So vehement was her irritation against her tormentors, that she entreated that the king her father would come with an army into Scotland, and inflict upon the country the miseries of war, rather than leave her unrevenged.[1] The earls gently soothed her with kind words and still more welcome promises of speedy redress. They formed a powerful party among the nobility of Scotland, being furnished with ample authority by King Henry to receive in his name all who chose to join the English party against those "who had done such mischief to King Alexander, and showed themselves rebels to his dearest daughter, Queen Margaret;"[2] and with this assistance, they triumphantly released the king and queen, and conducted them in safety to Roxburgh Castle: after which, they dismissed the former regency, as a preparatory step to the formation of a new one, composed entirely of men of their own party.[3]

Henry had already anticipated this event, and under pretext of a desire to visit the King of Scots and his daughter, "whom he had not seen for a long time, and whom he desired with the greatest desire of his heart to behold,"[4] he advanced northward, and summoned the military force of all England to join him, secretly vowing deadly vengeance against those who had maltreated his daughter, especially Bruce and Baliol. Being wishful, however, to lull the jealous suspicions of the Scots, which were strongly ex-

---

[1] Paris, vol. ii., p. 908.   [2] Fœdera, vol. i., p. 326.
[3] Tytler's Scotland, vol. i., p. 13.   Chron. Mailros, p. 181.
[4] Rot claus., 39 H. III., m. 7, dorso.

cited by his interference, he gave it out that, although he was going towards Scotland, to gratify his earnest wish of seeing his son-in-law and his dearest daughter, yet that he would do nothing prejudicial to the interests of the king or kingdom.[1]

The great point now was to settle a time and place in which an interview could be arranged between the King and Queen of Scotland and King Henry and his queen; for Eleanora, with all the yearning love of a mother, had undertaken this long journey with her husband, that she might once more behold her beloved and injured child. On the 16th of August, Henry ordered nine deer to be taken for the use of his dear daughter, the Queen of Scots.[2] But considerable delay and hesitation occurred before the preliminaries for the interview could be satisfactorily arranged. On the 25th, Henry issued a declaration, likely to propitiate the Scots, assuring them that nothing that had transpired at the time of the marriage of Alexander and Margaret should ever be prejudicial to Scottish liberty.[3] On the 26th of August, he sent her and Alexander a safeconduct to come to him,[4] and on the 28th, the Earls of Gloucester, Albemarle, &c., were commissioned to escort them to the king.[5] But Henry had not crossed the frontiers, and it was deemed more prudent by the Scots that the meeting should take place in Scotland. At length, however, Wark Castle was decided upon as a suitable place for the rendezvous, and there, accordingly, King Henry, and his queen, took up their residence;[6] but, finding still some demur existing about venturing the persons of the young king and queen into England, in spite of the safeconduct, Guy de Lusignan and William de Valence, Henry's halfbrothers, with Richard de Clare, Earl of Gloucester, and

[1] Fœdera, vol. i., p. 327.   [2] Rot. claus., 39 H. III., pars i., m. 5.
[3] Rot. pat., 39 H. III., date Newcastle, Aug. 25th.
[4] Ibid., 39 H. III., m. 3.   [5] Ibid.   [6] Ibid.

other nobles, were sent to urge on their journey, and they
pledged themselves that neither the king nor queen should
tarry at all in England, except with the consent of the
Scottish nobles.[1]   A safeconduct, in which was included a
renewed promise to attempt nothing contrary to the interests of Scotland, was sent them, bearing date September 5th.[2]   King Henry arrived at Wark on the 6th of the
same month.

> " Thydder the Kyng of Scotland
> And the quene, wyth hym passand,
> As on Tryst and purpos set,
> On a day togydder met,
> Wyth mony folk on ilke syde.
> Of Ingland the Quene was there that tyde ;
> There the kyngis made bydyng
> By cownsale thare and long spekyng
> There was made sich Ordynans,
> That was grete grefe and displesans
> To of Scotland the thre Statis,
> Burgers, Barowns, and Prelatis."[3]

The first provision of the ordinances that gave so great
offence to the Scotch, was that Queen Margaret should be
treated with proper attention and respect, and that her
intercourse with her husband should be no longer re-
stricted; but the political arrangements that followed
were less unobjectionable. The former regents having been
deposed, and deprived of all power,[4] the government was
placed in the hands of those who were known to be devoted to the English interests, and who were to hold the
reins during the seven years that still remained to elapse
before Alexander was of age;[5] while King Henry reserved
to himself the title, so dangerous when conferred on
the sovereign of a more powerful state, of " principal
counsellor to the King of Scotland." So great was the
" displeasans" excited by this treaty, that some of the
most loyal among the Scotch nobles refused to sign it,

[1] Fœdera, vol. i., p. 327.   [2] Ibid.
[3] Wyntown's Chron.. vol. i., p. 385. See also Chron. Mailros, p. 181.
[4] Fœdera, vol. i., pt. i., p. 328.   [5] Ibid.

lest it should undermine the bulwarks of that national independence for which they had so long striven.

King Alexander's visit at Wark was not of long duration. During his stay, the articles agreed upon were drawn up into a treaty; but, as he did not wait till it was completed, King Henry paid him a visit at Roxburgh Castle, where, on the 20th of September, Alexander formally affixed his signature to it. The monarchs visited the abbey of Kelso, where they were received in solemn procession, and heard high mass together, after which King Henry returned to Wark.[1] The pleasure experienced in the late family reunion had been greatly damped by the illness of Queen Eleanora, who was so extremely indisposed that, in consideration of her situation, Queen Margaret was permitted to remain behind a while after the departure of her lord, on a pledge being given by King Henry, that no attempt should be made to take her further south than Wark, and that she should be surrendered to her husband, or his knights sent for the purpose, as soon as the queen-mother was well enough to return home.[2] After enjoying the society of her fond mother for a short time, on the recovery of Queen Eleanora, Margaret was sent back to Scotland, and once more took up her abode in the castle of Edinburgh;[3] not in her former state of

---

[1] Chron. Mailros. p. 181. The chronicler gives August 15th as the date of King Henry's visit; but this must be incorrect, since it did not take place till after the interview at Wark, which was the 2nd week in September. It is also disproved, by an examination of Henry's movements, which, as proved from a collation of dates in the patent, close, and liberate rolls, were as follows: August 11th to 17th, he was at York; 18th, at Newburgh; 19th, Allerton; 22nd and 23rd, Durham; 25th to 30th, Newcastle; September 2nd, Alnwick; 4th and 5th, Chillingham; 6th, to 22nd, Wark or Carham, which is within a few miles of Wark. At Carham, (not *Carlisle*, as misprinted in the Fœdera, vol i, pt. i., p. 329) the treaty was drawn up on the 16th, on which day the king was at that place; and, as there is no record of his whereabouts from the 18th to the 20th, probably that was the time that he went into Scotland, deeming the signing of the treaty of sufficient importance to render it worth his while to use his personal influence to accomplish it. He confirmed the treaty on the 21st.

[2] Fœdera, vol. i., pt. i., p. 327.   [3] Wyntown, vol. i., p. 386.

captivity, however.   Whatever might be the political ten-
dency of the recent treaty, for the queen it produced a
most agreeable revolution.   She was now comparatively
her own mistress, enjoying unrestricted the society of her
husband, to whom she was passionately attached, and
surrounded entirely by her father's friends.   The steps by
which she had obtained this emancipation were certainly
of a questionable character.   That a queen should invite
the attacks of a foreign army upon the land of her adoption, so as even to threaten its independence, seems, at
first sight, to reflect severely upon her; but then it must
be borne in mind that Margaret was scarcely fifteen years
of age, that she had received nothing but harsh treatment
at the hands of the Scotch, and therefore the feelings of
an English princess must have been in her heart much
stronger than those of a Scottish queen; and her child-
like appeal to her father for assistance in her troubles was
too simple, too natural, to deserve severe reprehension in
one who could not be supposed to be alive to the political
bearings of her conduct.

The principal persons now at the head of the Scotch
government were Patrick Earl of Dunbar, and Malice
Earl of Stratherne.   The latter of these noblemen was
specially commissioned by King Henry to repair to his
daughter, and remain near her person, and not to suffer
her to be taken against her will to any place which she
disliked, and he promised faithfully to guard his " dearest
lady the Queen of Scots " in all which concerned her
person, convenience, and state.[1]   A familiar intercourse
was carried on between the courts of England and Scotland.   Almost immediately upon Henry's return to England, he granted Queen Margaret some fines which had
been recently incurred in those parts of Cumberland which

[1] Letter of Malice to Hen. III., in the Tower Collection, No. 852. Foedera,
vol. i., pt. i., p. 371, where it is mis-dated 1258.

she held in her hands, and he also sent messages to the
sheriffs of the northern counties to be ready to march with
all their forces to assist King Alexander against his rebel
subjects, in case such aid were needed.[1]   It scarcely need
be added, that by these stigmatized *rebels* were meant
those true-hearted Scotchmen who deplored and might
venture to resist the predominance of English influence.

Early in the year 1256, Prince Edward paid a visit to
his sister,[2] and shortly after, the King and Queen of
Scotland accepted an invitation to visit their royal parents
in England,[3] to celebrate with them the fête of the Assumption of the Virgin, August the 15th.   It was now
nearly five years since Margaret had left her native country,
and her longing eagerness to revisit the scenes of her
childhood is strikingly described by Matthew Paris.   It
was not merely her parents that she wished to see, dearly
as she loved them; it was the fields and the woods, the
rivers and the meadows of England, its cities and churches,
on which she longed once more to gaze, and once more to
be associated with English hearts and English manners.
She communicated her enthusiasm to her youthful spouse,
who had never before been farther south than the city of
York; and right joyous was their progress, as they wended
their way with the three hundred knights who formed
their train.[4]

King Henry had made splendid preparations for their
reception.   The palace of Woodstock was the place designed for the celebration of the fête, and he had taken
care to have it well provided for the occasion : besides the
usual supply of food, large quantities of spicery, such
as saffron, sugar, cinnamon, ginger, cloves, rice, &c.,
were ordered to be in readiness ;[5] and two pipes of white

[1] Rot. claus., 40 H. III., m. 3.
[2] Ibid., m. 9, dorso.
[3] Rot. pat., 40 H. III., m. 8.
[4] Paris, vol. ii., p. 930.
[5] Rot. claus., 40 H. III., m. 6, dorso.

wine were " to be spiced with cloves, after the counsel of
Robert de Hampedlers," and sent to Woodstock.[1]   Though
Woodstock was then furnished with all the splendour of
a royal residence, Henry sent for hangings of cloth of
gold, rich tapestries, a state bed which had been presented
to him by the countess of Provence, chapel furniture and
plate, wax lights, costly linen, and magnificent table plate
—one piece of which is specified as " the great cup of
York"—probably a memento of the bridal feasts there—
to add to its decorations.[2]

When the train of the Scottish king and queen was
discerned in the distance, King Henry hastened to show
his respect by going to give them the meeting; but no
sooner did he approach, than the girlish queen, heedless
of the forms of state etiquette, rushed into her father's
arms, and he folded her in a long and fond embrace,
which was afterwards shared by her spouse; and then
they indulged in that free intercourse, to which their long
separation from each other was calculated to add a peculiar
zest.[3]   They proceeded together to the palace, where,
doubtless, Margaret met with an equally warm reception
from her mother, and her sister and brothers.   The guests
assembled to do honour to the Scottish king were so
numerous, that the palace, extensive as it was, was quite
inadequate to contain them; the groves and lawns of the
romantic park were studded with tents for their accommodation; and not only so, but all the neighbouring villages, and even the city of Oxford, were filled with guests,[4]
and the Assumption festival was observed with a splendour rarely before witnessed.[5]

At length the exhaustion of the adjoining districts began to remind the revellers that it was time to disperse;

[1] Rot. claus., 40 H. III., m. 7.   [2] Ibid., m. 6.
[3] Paris, vol. ii., p. 930.   [4] Ibid., p. 626.   Matt. Westm., p. 363.
[5] Ibid., vol. ii., pp. 930-1.   Lib. de ant. leg., Harl. MS., No. 690, f. 41.

and, fearing lest their large trains could not travel conveniently together, they parted, and took different routes to the metropolis. King Henry had given orders for London and Westminster to be richly ornamented with tapestry, beautiful silken cloths, robes, crowns, and other symbols of rejoicing ; and, these preparations being completed, Prince Edward came out to meet his father and the King and Queen of Scotland, and conduct them to the palace of Westminster. Their entry was made on Sunday, the 27th of August ;[1] and the following day the whole party, including the two kings and queens, and all the attendant nobles and knights, the Bishop of London, and many of the citizens, were invited to a splendid entertainment given by John Maunsell, provost of Beverley, Henry's favourite and confidant, at his mansion of Tothill : his house could not, of course, contain all the guests—whose number was so great, that 7000 dishes were needed for one course alone ; but ample tents, of regal purple, were spread out for the remainder, and the feast afforded as much ground for satisfaction as for surprise, being the first on record given by a mere priest to so many crowned heads.[2]

To crown the favours which he had heaped upon his son-in-law, King Henry bestowed upon him the manor of Huntingdon, which had been previously possessed by several of his ancestors ;[3] and, soon after, he ordered 300 marks to be delivered to the queen, not, however, as a direct present from himself, but from her husband, for they were to be deducted from the stipulated payments of

[1] Chron. Lond., Addit. MS., 5444, f. 54.   Liber de ant. leg., ut sup.
[2] This prelate, who occupies a conspicuous place in the State records of Henry III., though he was never advanced to any ecclesiastical dignity, was yet so favoured by the king, that the benefices he enjoyed are said to have brought him an income of 18,000 marks, equal to £180,000. But he incurred the indignation of the party of the barons, and, after many reverses of fortune, he at last died abroad, poor and in misery, in 1268.—Chron. Mailros, p. 214.
[3] Paris, vol. ii., p. 931, gives the 17th of September as the date of this gift, but the charter itself bears date Woodstock, August 16th, 1256.

her dowry.[1] He provided Margaret with an English chaplain, whose salary of 60s. a year was paid by himself, who was to officiate constantly by offering up prayers on her behalf at the church of her patron saint, Margaret, at Westminster. To Alexander the king gave a parting present of 500 marks, which, although entered as a gift, was probably only an instalment of the promised dower.[2]

During this visit, the protection of Alexander and Margaret was sought and obtained by the wife of a notorious malefactor, whose husband was just about to suffer the extreme penalty of the law. The name of this miscreant was William de l'Isle, a substantial and wealthy landed proprietor of Lincolnshire, who, under the influence of an avaricious temper, had seized a herd of beautiful cattle belonging to one of his neighbours, and then, by the most infernal tortures, compelled the herdsman who had them in charge to pretend that his master had obtained them by theft. The matter was, however, brought to a trial, at which the whole truth came out, and the culprit was sentenced to death; but his wife, in an agony of despair, rushed to court, and, by her passionate pleadings, her tears, and her sobs, so wrought on the compassions of the young king and queen of Scots, to whom she appealed to mediate on her behalf, that, listening only to the voice of pity, they interposed for her husband, and obtained his pardon; "for the king," says Paris, "unwilling to grieve them, granted him safety of life and limb, though very unwillingly, and by a sort of constraint, seeing that the man was manifestly guilty. But it happened, according to the words of the apostle, that by the faithful wife the unfaithful husband may be saved."[3]

In the middle of September, Mary de Coucy, the mother

[1] Rot. lib., 40 Hen. III.. m. 2.   Issue roll, 41 Hen. III., p. 37, Devon's Excerpta.   See also issue rolls, 42 and 47 Hen. III., Easter.
[2] Issue rolls, 41 Hen. III., pp. 34 and 36, Devon's Excerpta.
[3] Paris, vol. ii., pp. 931-2.

of King Alexander, joined the royal party, and remained
till the early part of November, when she seems to have
accompanied her son on a visit to Scotland.[1]

The kindness with which Alexander had been treated in
England produced its natural effect upon a young and
generous spirit. He became strongly attached to his
father-in-law; and this feeling, constantly cherished by his
wife, led him on his return to Scotland to manifest a preference for the English, which was peculiarly obnoxious
to his own subjects, whose susceptibilities were already
keenly alive on the subject. Accordingly, we find jealousies speedily springing up between him and some of his
nobles, increased by the presence of John Maunsell, who
was sent into Scotland under pretence of advising the
king, but in reality to keep up the English interest.[2] The
sheriffs of all the northern counties had strict orders to
be at Maunsell's command, in case he should need their
assistance against the rebels of the King of Scotland, and
he was ordered to act in the place of the English king in
providing, ordering, and disposing the affairs of the King
of Scotland.[3] His interference was, however, so obnoxious to the Scottish nation generally, that the unwelcome
favourite was quickly recalled.

The King of Scotland and his queen had now taken up
their residence at the castle of Roxburgh, and from this
place Alexander wrote to King Henry on the 4th of February, 1257. He assures him of the jocund and prosperous state of himself and Margaret, and hopes to hear the
same of the King of England and his dear mother the
queen; but the chief subject of the letter is the arrangement of a peace with the Earls of Monteith, Buchan, Mar,
&c. Patrick, Earl of Dunbar, the head of the English
faction, is the witness of this letter.[4] The discords here

---

[1] Rot. pat., 40 Hen. III., m. 3. Ibid., 41, m. 17.
[2] Fœdera, vol. i., p. 347.   [3] Ibid., p. 353.   [4] Ibid.

alluded to continued the whole summer, the emissaries sent by King Henry to settle affairs [1] effecting little or nothing. The party of the Comyns was still very powerful: [2] there were three earls and thirty-two belted knights of that family, the least considerable of whom had under his command ten or twelve robust chiefs, and among them many daring and resolute spirits, that ill brooked their present state of humiliation. The result was a constant series of struggles between the parties. The state of affairs is alluded to by King Henry, in a letter to Mary de Coucy, the Queen-mother of Scotland, who, in the summer of 1257, asked permission, along with her second husband, John de Brienne, son of the King of Jerusalem, to pass through England, on her way to Scotland. It was granted by Henry, but only on condition that both would pledge themselves not to do anything against the king, the queen, or the council whom Henry has placed over them, " between whom and the former council discord has arisen."[3]

But amidst external commotion, great domestic harmony appears to have been enjoyed by Alexander and his queen. They were now springing up from childhood to youth, and Margaret already began to display that loveliness of feature for which she was afterwards distinguished. Alexander, too, if we may trust the delineation of him on his seal, was graceful and pleasing in person. His privy seal is a characteristic one, for so troublous a reign; instead of a sceptre and orb, the usual emblems of sovereignty, the right hand wields a sword, and the left the sceptre, while the orb, the symbol of peace, is omitted altogether: besides the usual legend, is an outer one, conveying council which few monarchs ever had greater need to adopt—" Be wise as a serpent, and simple as a

[1] Fœdera, vol. i., p. 362.   [2] Fordun, vol. iii., p. 765.
[3] Rot. claus., 41 Hen. III., m. 8, dorso. Fœdera, vol. i., p. 357.

dove." The face of the king, as there depicted, is juvenile, and very pleasing: the robe, cut round at the neck, is bound at the waist by a belt; the short, clustering locks are confined by a coronet.[1] In his great seal, the figure and attitude are somewhat similar to the last, but the features somewhat older, and more formed: the expression of the countenance is commanding, yet sweet.[2]

The only circumstance worthy of notice connected with Queen Margaret's history for this year, is the bestowal upon her by her husband, with her brother's consent, of a manor in the forest of Inglewood, the revenues of which were to be assigned over for her chamber expences.[3]

The following summer, 1258, the king and queen removed from Roxburgh Castle to Kinross, where they were sojourning, when an event transpired that changed the face of affairs. The Comyn faction had now become so powerful—having received the additional support of the queen-mother, who, in spite of her promises of non-interference, given to Henry, joined their side[4]—that they felt themselves to possess strength enough successfully to combat the English party. But, as in all commotions that arise during a minority, each party is desirous to assume the show of right, by availing themselves of the name of the king to sanction their exercise of the regal functions, they were very anxious to possess themselves of the person of Alexander. Accordingly, by a daring and successful nocturnal enterprise, they seized the king without ceremony, while he was asleep, and before morning had conveyed

---

[1] Liber Mariæ de Melros, Plate I., No. 1.

[2] Anderson's Diplomata Scotiæ, p. 36. The seal engraved in Tytler's Scottish Worthies, frontispiece to vol. i., although used by Alexander III., in the early part of his reign, was really the seal of Alexander II., as will be seen on comparing pp. 30 and 36 in Anderson's Diplomata; but, having been misused, it was broken up, and the seal here described substituted. Fordun, vol. iii., p. 763. An examination of the seals of our three first Edwards and of the early Stuart kings of Scotland, will show that the same great seal was often made to serve for several successive reigns.

[3] Rot. claus., 41 Hen. III., m. 2.   [4] Fœdera, vol. i., pt. i., p. 378.

him and the queen to Stirling, and made themselves masters of the kingdom.[1] Alexander was placed in honorary confinement, and was again separated from his queen, lest her influence should, as it was natural to expect, be exerted in favour of the opposite faction.[2]

Great consternation pervaded the English court when the news of this revolution arrived. Henry endeavoured, by a series of manœuvres, first to carry off the young king to England, and, that failing, by negociations to gain time for the assembling of an army, before any decisive measures were taken.[3] But the Scottish regency were on their guard, and by the skilfulness of their arrangements and the rapidity with which they collected their troops, they completely frustrated these designs, and extorted a reluctant acknowledgment of their newly assumed powers from King Henry,[4] who promised not to disturb them, since they had taken upon themselves the government of Scotland, so long as they should rule " for the good and honour of his very dear son, the illustrious King of Scotland, and of his well-beloved daughter, the queen their lady."[5]

Amidst the strife of contending factions, little detail remains of the private history of the monarch himself, and still less of that of his wife. Whatever might be Alexander's feelings with reference to the recent change, to her it was probably matter of regret, since it removed the power from the hands of her father's adherents. Their friendly relationships with the court of England still continued to all appearance the same.

In the year 1259, Henry III., anxious to see his daughter, and wishful, perhaps, to secure a permanent influence over the unfolding mind of her husband, sent a pressing invi-

---

[1] Wyntown, vol. i., p. 386.

[2] Paris, vol. ii., p. 957.   [3] Tytler's Scotland, vol. i., p. 19.

[4] Chron. Mailros., p. 182. Fœdera, vol. i., p. 371.

[5] Fœdera, vol. i., p. 378. Rot. claus., 42 47 H. III., m. 22, sub anno 43.

tation to the King and Queen of Scots to visit him. But
the regents were unwilling to permit such intercourse;
and pleading the length and laboriousness of the journey,
with the difficulty attending the sovereign's leaving his
kingdom, the invitation was declined.[1] King Henry still
continued to manifest his usual tender affection for his
daughter. This year, he sent her a present of 100 marks
through the Viscount of York.[2] The following year, 1260,
he renewed his solicitations that Queen Margaret and her
spouse should pay him a visit, and with more success.
Alexander was now old enough to express an opinion, and
have a will of his own : he had, some time before, so far
escaped the thraldom of the regents, as to secure the
loving companionship of his young wife, and he now resolved to comply with the request of his father-in-law.
His pretext for visiting England was, that he wished
to obtain a full confirmation of the manor of Huntingdon,
and also to procure payment of the 4000 marks which
were yet owing as Margaret's dowry.[3] Probably, however, he urged the visit from a still stronger motive—the
desire to gratify his wife by an arrangement so congenial
to her feelings.

Such, however, was the jealousy of the government,
that the most extraordinary provisions were made, to
guard the king and kingdom from any injury that might
accrue from this visit. But the principal care was to
provide for the return of Queen Margaret. Her situation
now promised an heir to the crown of Scotland; and, full
of the trembling expectations of approaching maternity,
she was extremely anxious that she might be permitted to
await the birth of her infant in her own land, and with the
queen her mother. Her wishes were warmly seconded by

[1] Matt. Westm., pp. 365, 6. Tytler's Scotland, vol. i., p. 21.
[2] Rot. lib., 43 Hen. III., m. 6.
[3] Annal. Iucul., Cotton MS. Nero, D. ii., f. 169 b.

Henry and Eleanora; but the Scottish nobles were naturally reluctant that the first-born of their sovereign should be a native of England, and they feared also lest Henry should detain the child in his own hands. Margaret, in her great anxiety to be allowed to go to England, had concealed from them the expected period of her *accouchement*;[1] but their suspicions were aroused, and they demanded from King Henry the strictest pledges, that in case the queen, by her husband's consent and theirs, awaited her confinement in England, both mother and infant should be at perfect liberty to return to Scotland within forty days afterwards, or at latest by the ensuing Easter. These arrangements were made with minute attention to every possible contingency of life, health, &c., so anxious were the Scottish nobles to secure the safe return of the queen, and especially of the expected heir. It was likewise agreed that no state affairs should be treated of during the visit that might prove at all prejudicial to the kingdom of Scotland.[2] The safeconduct was to be available till the following February, with a proviso of extension for any of the party that might be taken ill in England, to remain till they were well, and that none of them should be " scrutinized or persecuted," either about their own business, or that of the State.[3]

At length, Alexander and Margaret commenced their journey, accompanied by the Bishop of Whitherne,[4] who had strict orders to guard and attend the person of the queen. They arrived at Berwick on the Sunday after Michaelmas, where they were received by John Maunsell, who then held the temporalities of the vacant bishopric of Durham; and he, according to the king's positive order,

[1] Matt. Westm., p. 377.
[2] Rot. pat., 44 H. III., m. 3. Fœdera, vol. i., p. 402.
[3] Rot. claus., 42-47 H. III., m. 8.
[4] A See now extinct, belonging to the archbishopric of Glasgow. In Latin records it is called " *Candida casa.*"

conducted them through the whole of the bishopric; and wherever they chose to abide, in castle, forest, or manor, he was to permit them so to do, and to entertain them with all the courtesies, civilities, and honours due to them.[1] As they advanced southward, Prince Edward, the Archbishop of York, the Earl of Winchester, and others, met and accompanied them, and the sheriffs of Northumberland, York, Nottingham, Leicester, Northampton, Buckingham, Bedford, and Hertford, were ordered to supply them with all necessaries, at whatever cost, during their passage through their respective counties.[2] Margaret, in her delicate situation, was not able to travel with the rapidity of her husband and brother. They therefore preceded her by several days, leaving her in charge of the Bishop of Whitherne; and she journeyed by slow stages as far as St. Albans, which she reached at the time of the vesper service. Here she was met by her younger brother, Prince Edmund, welcomed into the city with a stately procession, and entertained with great honour. The following morning, she set forward to London, accompanied by her trusty friend, the bishop, who never left her side till he had conducted her to court, and presented her to her parents; they received her with great joy, and bestowed many rich rewards on her protector.[3] The presence of their eldest daughter was more than ordinarily welcome to the king and queen; for they had recently parted with the Princess Beatrice, on account of her marriage with the heir of Bretagne, while their youngest and loveliest flower, the Princess Catherine, had been torn from them by death.

The festivals held in honour of the King and Queen of Scots were very magnificent; Richard Earl of Cornwall,

[1] Rot. claus., 44 H. III., pars i., m. 5, dorso.
[2] Rot. claus., 44 H. III., mm. 4, 3. Fœdera, vol. i., p. 402.
[3] Matt. Westm., p. 377. Annal. lucul., ut sup.

titular ·King of Germany, with his queen, sharing the
honours with them.[1] Such was the gay profusion of
the feasts, that the neighbouring country was exhausted
by the intolerable expence; for, from the impoverished
state of Henry's exchequer, his sumptuous entertainments
often fell heavily on the lower classes. The King of
Scotland was always an expensive guest; for, by an arrangement of long standing, as soon as ever he crossed
the Humber, he was allowed 100 shillings a day, equivalent to £75 of our present money, for his private expenses.
£300 were paid to Alexander on this score, on the present
occasion, thereby determining the length of his visit,
which, from the time of crossing to that of recrossing the
Humber, was sixty days.[2]

One part of the amusements of the festival consisted in
aquatic excursions on the Thames; and Henry ordered the
bailiffs of Dover to send him down a certain boat, decorated
with embroidered banners, provided not only with twelve
honest men of Dover to row it, but with beautiful youths
to play on trumpets and other instruments, that this boat
might ply on the river, for the recreation of the party.[3]

King Alexander spent nearly two months in England, and
entered into satisfactory arrangements with his father-in-
law, in reference to the dowry of his wife and other business matters. He then bid adieu to his royal relations,
committing to their charge his young queen, whom, in
compliance with her own entreaties and their wishes, he
consented to leave behind, and took his departure for
Scotland. He journeyed by way of St. Albans, where he
offered rich altar cloths, and was splendidly entertained.[4]
Henry sent one of his own servants, called William le
Graunt, to attend him; but this man had well nigh paid

---

[1] Matt. Westm., ut sup.
[2] Rot. lib., 45 H. III., m. 18. ′ See also Annal. lucul., ut sup.
[3] Rot. claus., 44 H. III., m. 5, dorso.   [4] Matt. Westm., ut sup.

a heavy penalty for his courteousness. As they were passing through the forest of Sherwood, he, relying on the illustrious rank of his fellow-traveller to protect him, ventured to shoot several deer in this former haunt of the prince of outlaws. But so strict were the game laws then in operation, that he was summoned to answer for his offence before the king's forester; and it was only on the special interference of the monarch that he was saved from the infliction of a heavy penalty.[1]

On the departure of her husband, Queen Margaret gladly retired from the festive throngs that had crowded the palace of Westminster to the quiet retreat of Windsor Castle, where she remained with her mother in great retirement, except that during the Christmas week they joined the royal circle, when the king came to Windsor to celebrate his Christmas festival.[2] We find an order from the king, that as the queen and his dearest daughter, the Queen of Scots, are about to stay at Windsor, where there is at present lack of wine, the Viscounts of Oxford and Northampton shall send messengers, to travel day and night, with some measures of wine, to supply the want.[3]

The winter of this year was remarkable for brightness and mildness; but, in the beginning of February, 1261, " when," says our chronicler, " the weather ought to be serene spring, such storms of snow and hail descended, as had not been known for many years."[4] It was amid these troublous scenes of external nature that Queen Margaret gave birth to her long-expected infant, which, however, proved to be a daughter. Such of the Scotch nation as had not been aware of the queen's advanced pregnancy were greatly displeased that the child should have been born in England; but their chagrin was mitigated by the circumstance that it was but a presumptive, and not the

[1] Rot. claus., 45 H. III., m. 13.   [2] Matt. Westm., p. 377.
[3] Rot. lib., 45 H. III., m. 17.   [4] Matt. Westm., ut sup.

apparent, heir of the throne, who had first seen the light in a rival country. King Henry was greatly elated with the birth of this, his first grandchild. The valet of the Queen of Scots, who brought him the happy tidings, instead of merely receiving the usual bounty, was provided for during life by the proud grandfather.[1]

Queen Margaret spent the period of forty days which usually elapsed between the confinement and the ceremony of churching in England; and when that was performed, she returned with her infant, who had received her own name, to her husband, only just in time to escape the troubles that shortly afterwards overtook her parents, when even their personal safety was endangered by the successful attacks of the rebellious barons.[2]

Two circumstances are recorded in connexion with Margaret's residence in England, which deserve mention. In one case, she used her powerful intercession with her father for permission of freedom of traffic in grain between England and Scotland, and at her request some English merchants were permitted to trade in that commodity in Scotland.[3] On the other occasion, her interference was of more questionable propriety, for it was exerted in behalf of John de Branlimston, a notorious robber, to whom, at her request, the king granted a pardon, and the restoration of half his goods and chattels which had been forfeit to the crown; the heinousness of his offences probably precluding the full remission of the penalty.[4] This is not the first instance in which we have seen this queen interposing to arrest the course of justice; but how far her conduct was justified by the peculiarities of the cases cannot now be decided. It was a common expedient of such malefactors as could obtain access to court, to throw

---

[1] Rot. pat., 45 H. III., m. 4. Ibid., 47, m. 12.
[2] Matt. Westm., p. 379.
[3] Rot. claus., 45 H. III., m. 12.   [4] Ibid., m. 13.

themselves upon the mercy of the wife or the children of the monarch; and could they but succeed in procuring their mediation, state etiquette demanded that the request of the royal suppliants should not be refused, unless under very extraordinary circumstances. At a later period, Margaret's petitions were more judicious. She and her husband pleaded several times in behalf of one Baldwin de Weyford, a luckless wight, who, having run into debt, had fallen into the clutches of some usurious Jews. They persecuted him with threats and demands of immediate payment. At the intercession of the Scotch king and queen, however, Henry ordered the extent and value of Weyford's lands to be estimated, and then assigned a reasonable time, within which he could, by economizing his income, pay his debts, and thus delivered him from his annoying creditors.[1]

When Queen Margaret returned to Scotland, her husband had nearly attained the important period of his majority. His mind was far above his years, and he already displayed that manly steadiness of purpose, that intrepid calmness in danger, that firm resolution in difficulty, with those enlightened and independent views in politics, which exercised so happy an influence on his future reign. He divided his kingdom into districts, all of which he visited every year, attending in person to the strict administration of justice, and accessible to the complaints of the meanest of his subjects. " Strengthened and improved by this steady attention to the affairs of government, the character of the king became gradually more vigorous, and his talents in the management of state affairs more conspicuous. Beloved and admired by his own subjects, he was respected by foreign powers; and in his relations with England, whilst he maintained with uniform firmness the independence of his kingdom, he was

[1] Rot. claus., 50 H. III., m. 3.

ever ready to act a friendly part in the difficulties which then disturbed the government."[1]

In the summer of 1261, negociations were set on foot between the courts of England and Scotland, about the dowry of Margaret, £1000 of which were agreed to be paid in the June of the year, and Alexander had rather improvidently sent letters patent, acknowledging beforehand the receipt of the money, to his "dearest mother," as he always styles Queen Eleanora, before he had actually obtained it. It turned out that Henry was unable to raise th whole amount, and 1000 marks, only two thirds of it, were really paid. Of this instalment, Alexander sent a receipt by William de Swyneburn, Margaret's treasurer, but expressed great anxiety that his former receipt for the whole sum should be returned to him by the queen.[2] With this reasonable request Eleanora complied.[3] Queen Margaret herself wrote to her father's chancellor, Merton, recommending to him some private affairs which Swyneburn had to transact for himself in England. Her letter commences as follows :—" Margaret, by the grace of God, Queen of Scots, to the venerable man and her dearest friend in Christ, Lord W. de Mertoun, chancellor of the illustrious King of England, health in Christ, who is the true health of all." The remainder is of mere business character, but it will be noticed that this prologue is written in a strain of piety rather unusual, and which speaks very favourably for its writer. This is the only

---

[1] Tytler's Scottish Worthies, vol. i., p. 55.
[2] Alex. to Hen. III., Royal Letters, No. 846; misdated 1259. Fœdera, vol. i., p. 380. See rot. pat., 45 Hen. III., m. 6.
[3] Rot. lib., 45 Hen. III., m. 5. Memorand. in margin. The Chron. Hageneb., Cotton MS., Vesp., B. xi., f. 25, affirms that this year Prince Edward led an army into Scotland, to avenge the wrongs of his sister, whose life was said to have been attempted by her husband, through the medium of poison, but that the king purged himself from the foul imputation. This absurd and inconsistent story is not mentioned by any other chronicler, and is equally opposed to Alexander's character and the tenour of events.

letter of the Lady Margaret that is known to be in existence.[1]

William de Swyneburn was unsuccessful, however, in his mission relative to the dowry, so he was followed the next year by another messenger of the queen, her clerk, William de Notingham, who brought back abundance of excuses for non-payment: the king had been ill; he had recently lost his treasurer; the sheriffs were tardy in bringing in their accounts, &c.: but, for the present, Alexander got nothing better than apologies;[2] and it was not until the year 1271 that the last arrears were paid.[3]

No coolness, however, ensued between the monarchs; for about the same time we have another very friendly letter from Alexander to his father-in-law, giving favourable accounts of his own welfare and that of his dearest consort, and expressing ardent desires to hear of the welfare of the king, his dearest mother the queen, and their illustrious children—regretting that at present the affairs of his kingdom will not permit him to spare R. de Mowbray, whose presence Henry has requested in England.[4]

The year 1263 was marked by one of those important events which, by arousing the energies and kindling the spirit of a brave and determined people, when under the guidance of a talented leader, impress upon the period a national interest that causes it to be looked back upon with pride and pleasure by many a succeeding generation. This was the celebrated descent of Haco, King of Norway, into Scotland. Contests had long been waged between the monarchs of the two countries, about the rights of sovereignty over the western isles. To support his own claims, the Norwegian king now appeared in Scotland. In vain did Henry III., alarmed at the danger

[1] See Appendix, No. XII., royal letter, No. 851.
[2] Rot. claus., 42-47 H. III., m. 8 dorso. [3] Ibid., 56 H. III., m. 10.
[4] Royal letters, No. 848.

which threatened his son-in-law and his daughter, write to Haco, protesting against his attacking the dominions of his " dear son and ally, the King of Scotland."[1] Equally vain was his appeal to the pope to stop the progress of the northern invader.[2] Haco had collected an army so powerful, that the most energetic efforts of Alexander would have failed in raising a force at all competent to meet the invaders, had they seized their advantage and landed immediately. With admirable skill and presence of mind, however, he made such preparations as were in his power, inspiring confidence into his troops by the calmness of his demeanour, and trusting to his own resources to supply the rest.[3] Aware that, could he succeed in decoying his adversary to trifle away the brief summer of those northern regions, the elements themselves would undertake his cause, he professed the most pacific intentions, and made demands so moderate, that Haco was in hopes that he should win his object without running the hazard of a battle. Month after month passed away in negociations, which ever seemed to be drawing to a close, and yet were never concluded, when the first howlings of the autumn blasts gave fearful tokens to the sea-king of the perils ensuing upon his situation. The Scottish emissaries abruptly broke off the conferences—all treaty was discontinued, and the aged Norwegian monarch saw with vehement indignation that he had been made the dupe of a young sovereign, only just out of his minority. The weather rendered it extremely dangerous for his troops to land; the forces of Alexander were congregated on the beach to oppose them; but, such was the desperate spirit of the Norsemen, that they contrived, with much loss, to effect a landing, and, after a spirited harangue given by

[1] Fœdera, vol. i., pt. i., p. 422, letter from Henry III. to Haco.
[2] Close roll, 46 H. III., m. 12, dorso.
[3] Tytler's Scottish Worthies, vol. i., pp. 29, 30.

each of the leaders to his troops, grounded on the one hand on the justice and righteousness of their cause, and on the other on the desperateness of their situation in case of defeat,[1] the battle of Largis commenced, in which, after an obstinate and bloody conflict, the Norwegians were driven back to their ships.[2] The elements completed the destruction which the sword had begun. Storm after storm scattered and wrecked the remaining vessels; the king himself escaped to one of the Orkney isles, where, his haughty spirit broken by disaster, and his hardy frame worn with fatigue, he soon after expired.[3]

Connected, in point of time, with the defeat of the dreaded sea-king, was another event, still more joyous, which is thus recorded by the chronicler Wyntown:—

> " To Alysaundre the thryd, oure kyng beforn,
> Ane fayre sone that yere was borne,
> In Gedworth[4] towne; Syr Gamelyne,
> Byschope of Saynct Andrews, then
> Baptyzde that Bairn, and Alysawndraye
> Hym callyd, as wes before hys Fadyre.
> And when of that byrth com tythyng
> To Alysawndyr the thryd, oure kyng,
> It wes tauld hym, that ilke day,
> That dede the kyng wes of Norway.
> And swa in dowbil blythenes
> The kyngis hart at that tyme wes."[5]

[1] Ballenden's Boethius, p. 100, b.

[2] Their former sainted Queen Margaret is said to have been the guardian genius of the Scotch in this battle, for she appeared in a vision to a nobleman called Sir John Wemyss, leading a knight who wore the regal circlet round his helmet, and followed by three others, all dazzling in appearance, to whom she pointed as her husband and her three sons, once Kings of Scotland, with whom she was about to hasten to the field of Largis, and procure a glorious victory over the invaders. It may be mentioned, as a curious illustration of the bearing of modern science upon history, that the date of this Norse expedition has been accurately determined, though the chroniclers were a year at variance with each other, by an allusion which they make to a sudden and miraculous darkness which obscured the face of the sun, so that only a bright ring was seen round his orb. It is now ascertained that an eclipse of the sun actually took place in August, 1263, which would be annular in the Orkneys.—Scottish Worthies, vol. i., p. 30.

[3] Johnstone's Norse exped., p. 131. For an animated description of this expedition, the reader is referred to the life of Alexander III., in vol. i. of Tytler's Scottish Worthies.

[4] Gedburgh.

[5] Wyntown's chron., vol. i., p. 389. Chron. Mailros, p. 190. Haco died

If Alexander's heart were "in double blitheness" on this occasion, we may presume that that of his gentle consort was not less elated. Tremblingly anxious as had been her feelings while the destinies of her lord and of the kingdom were hanging so long in critical suspense, it must have been a proud and a happy moment for her, when, after his return home once more, crowned with the laurels of triumph, she placed in his arms the infant heir of all his honours.

A settled peace at this time pervaded Scotland, for Alexander obtained from Haco's successor, King Magnus, a formal renunciation of the disputed islands, in consideration of a small annual rental of 100 marks to be paid by Scotland. The terror of his arms also induced his sole remaining rival, the King of Man, to pay him the long-disputed right of feudal homage.[1]

Queen Margaret was now surrounded by new ties; and, happy in the undivided affection of her husband, she seems to have lost that clinging, exclusive attachment to the friends and the scenes of her childhood, which, during her earlier wedded life, wholly unfitted her, when taken in conjunction with the peculiar political relationships subsisting between the sister countries, for the position of a queen of Scotland. The education of her daughter, the little Princess Margaret, which was conducted under the immediate superintendence of the queen, was of an order so superior to the general scale of female education at the period, as to impress the idea that Queen Margaret herself united considerable learning to the deep piety and

on the 15th, and Alexander was born on the 21st of December; Fordun, vol. iii., p. 769; but, some days elapsing before the news from Orkney could reach the king, both good tidings were received the same day.

[1] Fordun, vol. iii., p. 1771. The charter of homage paid by this island king was seized by Edward I., with all the other ancient Scottish records in the muniment room of Edinburgh Castle, and brought to England. Ayloffe's catalogue of characters, p. 328. The form of peace between the two princes may be found in Johnstone's antiquitates Celto Normanniæ, pp. 52 et seq.

profound humility which marked her matured character.
Indeed, the retired seclusion in which, with her accomplished *gouvernante*, Lady Cantilupe, she had passed the
few first years of her residence in Scotland was well calculated to induce studious as well as pensive habits.   The
Princess Margaret spoke and read both in English and
French ;[1] and it is therefore probable that these accomplishments were possessed by her mother.   The queen
and her consort appear to have also cherished a love of
song ; for, in the wardrobe book of the 6th of Edward I.,
we find mention of a guitar-player, two trumpeters, and
four minstrels of the King of Scots.[2]

The disturbed condition of England, which was now
the prey of contending factions, the king himself being
little better than a tool in the hands of De Montfort and
the barons, prevented the exchange of visits, and all that
freedom of intercourse in which Queen Margaret had previously taken such delight.   During these troublous times,
the movements of the sister queen were regarded with great
suspicion by the barons : they knew her strong attachment to her own family, and they did all that lay in their
power to preclude the interchange of any but the most
formal civilities between the two kingdoms.   Of this, the
following circumstance affords curious proof.   On one
occasion, Margaret had sent a special messenger to her
brother Edward ; but, so complete was the control then
exercised by De Montfort over the royal family, that it
was only through his medium that access could be obtained to the prince.   Edward was seated to receive his
sister's messenger on a chair of state, or throne, the ascent
to which was by several ¦steps.   Simon led the envoy up
to a seat near the prince, and then took his own station, a
little lower down, but keeping his keen eye steadily fixed

[1] Chron. Lanercost, p. 105, edit. Maitland club.
[2] Rot. miscel. ap. Turr., Lond., No. 44.

upon them both, until their colloquy was ended, every word
of which reached his ear; and when the messenger rose to
depart, Simon caused him to walk first, and followed him
closely, lest, in retreating, he should contrive to drop some
missive from Queen Margaret to her brother.[1]

This distrust was occasioned by the fact that King
Alexander had adopted a line of policy as honourable as it
was generous.   Instead of availing himself, as so many of
his predecessors had done, of disturbances in England to
extend his own dominions, or to press his claims upon any
disputed territory, he sent an aid of 5000 men to King
Henry, headed by John Comyn; but, unfortunately, most
of these troops were slain or imprisoned at the battle
of Lewes.[2]   He interfered, at the earnest entreaty of his
father-in-law, to try to effect the liberation of Prince Edward and Henry of Germany from the hands of the
barons;[3] and after the fortunate escape of the prince from
his gaolers, undiscouraged by the recent disasters of his
troops, the Scotch king sent a fresh reinforcement, which
afforded material assistance to the royal cause in the ensuing struggle. These troops were dismissed with honour,
when, after the battle of Evesham and the death of the
Earl of Leicester, their aid was no longer needed.[4] Shortly
after this, Prince Edward, whose energy was indefatigable
in pursuing and scattering the remains of the rebel party,
advanced as far as Alnwick, to combat John de Vesci, who
had retreated to that place; and, having accomplished his
object, he resolved, since he was thus far north, to pay a
visit to his sister, Queen Margaret.   She and her husband
met him at Roxburgh Castle, where they gave him the
most cordial reception, and crowds of the Scottish nobility
flocked to gaze on the young hero, whose military fame

[1] Chron. Mailros, p. 215.   [2] Fordun, vol. iii., pp. 772, 773.
[3] Rot. claus., 49 H. III., m. 8, dorso.
[4] Scottish Worthies, vol. i., p. 56.

was already so widely spread.[1] Little did they dream how fearfully and fatally they themselves were soon to be made to feel his power.

Margaret also received a visit from her brother, Prince Edmund; for on one occasion the king kept the festival of his birthday at Berwick, where he knighted a younger son of the house of Comyn, and among the guests was Prince Edmund, with a long train of knights and household servants.[2]

In 1266, and again in 1267, Queen Margaret, who really seems to have been a sort of city of refuge to English outlaws, sought and obtained from her father the pardon of a criminal accused of murder.[3]

In the year 1268, we find the King and Queen of Scots again in England: they met King Henry and Queen Eleanora at York, where a parliament was held, at which the king's sons and almost all the nobles of England were present.[4] The children of Margaret and Prince Edward also accompanied their parents, so that the English king and queen had the rare gratification of seeing almost their whole family gathered round them. The greater part of the short visit was occupied by Alexander in giving condolences and counsels to his father-in-law, on the state of his kingdom. And well might the Scottish king presume to do this, notwithstanding his inferiority in age, for the prosperous state of his own realms was such, that strangers flocked from far and wide to study the civil polity of the country, to consider its power, and to admire the discretion and wisdom of the king.[5]

A similar visit was paid by the Scottish court the fol-

[1] Fordun, vol. iii., p. 774.   [2] Tytler's Worthies, vol. i., p. 59.
[3] Rot. pat., 50 H. III., m. 22.   Ibid., 51 H. III , m. 13.
[4] Chron. Tewksb., Cotton MS. Cleop., A. VII., f. 193.   Chron. Anon., Cleop., A I., f. 193, col. 2.   Rot. lib., 52 H. III., m. 13.
[5] Fordun, vol. iv., pp. 949, 950. One of his regulations betokens a mind far in advance of his contemporaries. Aware that idleness is the root of much mischief, he commanded every one who did not follow some calling to

lowing year, to London ; and the king gave an order, dated
September 6th, 1269, that "since the illustrious King of
Scots, and his consort Margaret, our dearest daughter, are
coming, for our solace and recreation, to stay with us at
the ensuing feast of Saint Edmund," (November 20th)
they and their attendants shall have safeconduct, and all
men are forbidden, under penalty of life and limb, to molest or injure them in any way.[1]   This meeting was the
last that ever took place between Margaret and her father.

In ,1269, Prince Edward took the cross ; but, before departing on his long and perilous expedition, he paid a farewell visit to his sister, and this time advanced as far as
Haddington. The queen brought with her, to the place
of rendezvous, her little son Alexander, then a blooming
and beautiful boy ; and his simple prattle is said to have
greatly delighted his uncle, for Edward himself had recently become a father, and was therefore the better able
to sympathize in his sister's parental pride. Margaret
felt exquisitely the parting with her brother.   On taking
his last farewell, he left with her one of the knights of his
train, to console her :. one on whom he had probably bestowed special favour, because he boasted of having with
his own hand slain the great rebel, Simon de Montfort.[2]

The following year, 1270, Margaret became the mother
of another son, who was called David ; and being a child
of great promise, he was much beloved, not only by the
queen, but by his father, King Alexander.

The year 1272 at length put a period to the long and
troublous reign of Henry III. When the news of his
death reached Queen Margaret, she was deeply affected ;
sorrow for her father was mingled with anxious forebodings
about her favourite crusading brother, of whom for a long

dig up seven square feet of land every day, thus providing an antidote against
laziness, and greatly improving the fertility of the country. — Scottish Worthies, vol. i., p. 64.
[1] Rot. pat., 53 H. III., m. 4.   [2] Chron. Lanercost, p. 81.

time she had heard no news, and her mind was tinged with
gloomy depression. She was residing at this time in the
castle of Kinchleven, on the banks of the Tay; and one
evening, after supper, wishful to escape the rude hilarity
of the banqueting-hall, so uncongenial to her feelings, she
retired with her confessor, to take a walk along the romantic banks of the river. Her knights and damsels followed her. Anxious to divert the thoughts of their royal
mistress, her attendants began those boisterous sports
which were then common amongst both old and young, and
they succeeded in winning over the queen to participate in
their mirth. The foremost amongst these was Margaret's
favourite knight, the same that had been commended to
her by her brother. He having soiled his hands with mud
in his sports, went down to the river's edge to wash them:
the queen, in her frolic humour, bade one of her damsels
approach him softly from behind, and push him in. He,
being an expert swimmer, laughed heartily at the joke,
and exclaiming, " What care I? I can swim; I ask nothing better," he began to show his skill in aquatic feats,
till on a sudden, approaching within reach of the strong
current of the river, or, as our chronicler calls it, the
whirlpool, he gave a wild scream, and instantly sank. His
little page, who was playing at a short distance, hearing
his master's voice, rushed impetuously into the stream; but
he too disappeared: thus putting a melancholy period to
the evening's diversions, and causing great affliction to the
queen, who had valued the knight for her brother's sake.[1]

It will scarcely be believed by those unversed in monkish legends, that this tale, interesting from the curious
particulars it affords in reference to the domestic habits
of the Scottish queen, is repeated solely to show, in the
so-called *miraculous* death of this knight, the just judgment of Heaven upon him, as having been, or having pro-

[1] Chron. Lanercost, pp. 95, 96.

fessed to be, an agent in the death of that reputed saint, Simon de Montfort!

Not long after this event, Margaret's anxiety was relieved by the arrival of a messenger, bearing letters to herself and the king her husband from her beloved brother;[1] and, in process of time, that brother, now King Edward I., returned to his kingdom. Among the first and the noblest who came to welcome him to his throne, and to grace his coronation, were King Alexander and Queen Margaret. The Princess Beatrice, with her husband, John of Bretagne, was also present; and the loveliness of the two sisters, now in the prime of womanhood, excited general admiration.[2] The coronation ceremony was performed on Sunday, August 19, 1274.[3] Unbounded were the festivities indulged in by all classes of people on this joyful occasion, for Edward was a great favourite with the people, and the suspense caused by his long delay in the East had rendered his return all the more welcome. On the coronation day the conduits in Cheapside ran with red and white wine. The banquet prepared in the great hall of Westminster was decked with all the rude splendour of the period, and when the sovereign took his station on the raised dais, wearing his crown for the first time, a singular scene presented itself. King Alexander, splendidly attired, and mounted on a gallant courser, attended by 100 knights, equally well accoutred, rode into the hall, and, dismounting to pay the accustomed homage to the monarch, flung the reins on the neck of his steed, which, thus set free, galloped out among the crowd; the 100 knights also alighted, leaving their horses a prey to those who were fortunate enough to catch them. This example was followed by Prince Edmund, Earl of Corn-

[1] Issue roll, 1 Edward I., p. 79, Devon's Excerpta.
[2] Matt. Westm., p. 407. Annal. lucul., Cotton. MS., Nero, D. ii., f. 180. Cott. MS., Cleop., A. i., f. 198 b., col. 2.
[3] Sir Harris Nicolas' Chronology of History, p. 310, note.

wall, and by the Earls of Gloucester, Pembroke, and Warren, each with a similar train of 100 knights; so that 500 war-steeds were that day let loose to gratify the joyous mob that thronged the palace gates.[1] Amidst the subsequent rejoicings, the King and Queen of Scots are said to have surpassed all others in the sumptuousness of their entertainments and the costliness of their presents.[2]

Great harmony of feeling, the result of situations and dispositions in some respects strikingly similar, prevailed between the Kings of England and Scotland.[3] It must be confessed, however, that, were a parallel to be drawn between them, the advantage in openness and honourableness of character, and in freedom from injustice, would preponderate greatly on the side of Alexander. Even during these festive seasons, King Edward tried to win over an acknowledgment that the homage just paid by the Scotch monarch was paid *for* Scotland; thus involving the long-contested question of feudal supremacy. But Alexander was both firm and cautious in his dealings with his ambitious brother-in-law; and he distinctly declared, and caused his declaration to be registered, that his homage was solely for the lands he held in England.[4] A firm basis of future intercourse was thus established by Alexander; and, during the remainder of his reign, he ever maintained friendly connexions with Edward, undisturbed by any attempts at aggression, which were so little likely to succeed with a monarch of his sagacity and talent.[5]

On the conclusion of the festivities, Alexander and Margaret, after an absence of five weeks,[6] returned once again

[1] Gray's Scalachronica, p. 100, Stevenson's edit., published for the Maitland Club.

[2] Chron. Lanercost, p. 69.   [3] Trivet's Annals, p. 246.

[4] Tytler's Scotland, vol. i., p. 51.

[5] See letters from Alex. III. to Edw. I., Nos. 1277-1281, 1283, 1294, 1295, 1296, 1298, 1316-20, &c., Tower collection.

[6] Rot. claus., 2 Edw. I., m. 2. The sum of £175 was allowed to Alexander, from the revenues of the vacant See of Durham, to cover the expenses of their journey. Rot. lib., 3 Edw. I., m. 22. Fœdera, vol. i., pt. i., p. 520.

to Scotland. The health of the queen, which, since the
early blight it had received by the hardships of her childhood, had not been strong, was now rapidly sinking, and
it soon appeared that decline was making fearful havoc
upon her frame. Her husband, in the eagerness of
anxiety, summoned prelates and physicians to her bed-
side, but they were of no avail. The higher ecclesiastics,
with whom she was a general favourite, crowded to her
residence, to offer their ghostly succour, but she refused
to see any excepting her own confessor, who was one of
the friars minors, unless in the presence and with the full
consent of her husband. The chastity and humility of her
deportment created much admiration; and the conjugal
affection which had so strongly marked her whole career
remained unaltered to the last. After receiving the sacra-
ments of the church from the hands of her confessor, she
died a tranquil and a peaceful death on the 27th of February, 1275, at the castle of Cupar, in the county of Fife.
Her corpse was interred with great ceremony in the church
of Dumfernline, very near the tomb of the late King David
of Scotland.[1]

The echoes of rejoicings were still ringing through the
stately halls of King Edward's palace, when the tidings of
his sister's fate reached him, which were soon followed
by those of the death of his only remaining sister, the
Lady Beatrice, which took place almost simultaneously;
thus casting an unlooked-for gloom on the late scenes of
revelry.[2] The king ordered anniversaries to be held for
his sisters throughout the whole Cistercian order of
monks;[3] but, on behalf of his favourite sister, Margaret,
he made still further provision. He continued the pension

---

[1] Wyntown, vol. i., p. 291. Chron. Lanercost, p. 97. The author of this
chronicle tells us that he received many of the particulars which he relates
concerning Queen Margaret from her confessor himself.

[2] Annal. Iucul., f. 180.

[3] Stat. ord. Cist. Martène Thes. anec., vol. iv., p. 1478.

of 60s. a year to the chaplain, Walter Tothill, for celebrating services in the church of St. Margaret's at Westminster, "for the soul of his dearest sister, the Queen of
Scots," which had been granted by Henry III. eighteen
years before for prayers for her welfare.[1] A more substantial proof of his regard was afforded by his continuing to
her husband those lands in England, which, as they had
been settled exclusively upon herself, reverted to the
crown immediately on her decease.[2]

Margaret was only thirty-four years old when she died,
but her early fate was happy for herself, inasmuch as it
prevented her from witnessing the calamities which overtook her family. Her two sons, of whom she had been so
fond and so proud, both died in their youth; prince David,
in 1281,[3] when only eleven years of age, and Alexander,
the darling of his father and the hope of the people, in the
year 1283, when he had just become the husband of the
beautiful Margaret, daughter of Guy Earl of Flanders.[4]
Both the young princes were buried in Dumfernline, by
the side of their mother.

The daughter of Queen Margaret, as she grew up,
strongly resembled her mother in the graces of her person
and the qualities of her mind; and the fame of her rare
qualities spreading far and wide, at length reached the
ears of Eric, King of Norway,[5] and led him to sue for the

---

[1] Rot. lib., 2 Edw. I., m. 4. Issue roll, 4 Edw. I., p. 96, Devon's Excerpta. The half yearly payments to Tothill regularly occur in the issue
rolls.
[2] Rot. claus., 3 Edw. I., m. 17.
[3] Fordun, vol. iii., p. 782 :—

> "A thowsand and twa hundyr yhere,
> Foure score oe'r them; to rekyn clere—
> Of Dawy, this thryd Alysawndrys sone,
> Of this lyf all the dayis wer done.
> Dede he was in to Stryvelyn
> And enteryd in Dumfermlyn."
> Wyntown's Chron., vol. i., p. 392

[4] Wyntown, vol. i., p. 395. Fordun, vol iii., p. 781.
[5] Chron. Lanercost, p. 165.

hand of this accomplished princess. Arrangements were accordingly made for a marriage,[1] which was certainly a very politic one, as uniting these two formerly rival crowns. It was regarded with some distaste by the princess herself; but filial and afterwards conjugal duty so influenced her conduct, that she secured the devoted attachment of her husband, and, during the short period of her wedded life, introduced many new and improved customs among the barbarous Norwegians, both as regarded food, attire, and manners. Under her gentle tutelage, too, her husband learned both English and French,[2] and these acquisitions, trifling as they now appear to us, betokened an amount of learning very unusual in that age. This virtuous queen died, however, in 1283, leaving an infant daughter, Margaret,[3] the celebrated Maiden of Norway, at whose early death the posterity of Queen Margaret and of Alexander III. became extinct. The sorrowing monarch had remained upwards of nine years a widower, true to the memory of his English queen; but, when he saw his promising children snatched away one after another by an early death, and when only the fragile life of a delicate female infant was interposed to prevent the evils of a disputed succession, he consented to marry again, in hopes of obtaining an heir to his crown. His second wife was Yolante de Dreux, daughter and heiress of Robert IV., Earl of Dreux, whom he espoused at Roxburgh, in the year 1285; but he survived this marriage scarcely a year.[4]

His death was occasioned by a singular accident. He had been giving a sumptuous feast to his nobility at the castle of Edinburgh. The revellings were prolonged to a late hour, and were all the merrier because of a prediction which had gained considerable credence among the vulgar, that that day was to be the day of judgment. Meanwhile,

[1] Fordun, vol. i., pt. i., pp. 782-3.
[2] Chron. Lanercost, ut sup.   [3] Wyntown, ut sup.
[4] Fordun, vol. iv., p. 949.   Wyntown, vol. i., pp. 398-9.

the night had grown intensely dark; a terrific storm was
howling around, when the king declared his intention of
riding to Kinghorn, where his queen Yolante was then
staying. Vain were the persuasions of the nobles to deter
him from his daring scheme. One of his servants ventured a remonstrance—the king bade him remain behind
if he feared. "No, my lord," answered the man, mournfully, "it would ill behove me to refuse to die for your
father's son!" and he mounted and followed his master.
The monarch and his small train crossed Queen's Ferry
in safety, and reached Inverkeithing; the storm was becoming still more terrible; fresh objections were urged
against his proceeding farther. "You may spare your-
selves this trouble," he replied, smilingly; "give me but
two runners who can show me the way." The road now
lay along the summit of the rocks coasting the harbour of
Pettycur, and in the intense darkness, the steed on which
the king rode stumbled on the brink of a terrific precipice
near Kinghorn,[1] and precipitated his master from its giddy
heights.[2] This fatal accident took place on the night of the
19th of March, in the year 1286, and it plunged the country
over which Alexander had so long and ably ruled into an
abyss of calamities that have scarcely a parallel in the history of any nation. The superstition of the age, ever seeking
to find in sin the direct cause of misfortune, would fain
have attributed his death to some crime on his part, and, for
want of more substantial ground of accusation, attributed
it to the Divine judgment upon him for visiting his wife
during the season of Lent. "But let us not," says an old
chronicler, "question the salvation of this king because of
his violent death, for he who has lived well cannot die ill."

We cannot better conclude this memoir than with the
following stanzas, which are among the oldest extant in the

---

[1] Gough's Camden, vol. iv., p. 114.   [2] Chron. Lanercost, p. 116.

vernacular Scotch, written a few years after the death of
this great and good king.

> "When Alexander our king was dead,
>   That Scotland led in love and law,
> Away was sons of ale and bread,
>   Of wine and wax, of game and glee:
>
> Our gold was changed into lead :
>   Christ, born into virginity,
> Succour Scotland and remedy
>   That sted is in perplexity."[1]

[1] Wyntown's cronikyl of Scotland, vol. i., p. 401, from a contemporary
ballad. The celebrated Thomas the Rimour, of Erceldon, flourished at this
period. On the day before the king's death, the Earl of Mar sent for him,
and asked him what sort of weather there would be to-morrow ; he said there
should be the greatest wind that ever was heard in Scotland, before noon.
The morning, on the contrary, turned out bright and clear. The earl sent
for Thomas, and reproved him for his false prognostics. "This Thomas
maid litil ansuer, bot said, 'Noun is not yit gane.' And incontinent ane
man came to the gate, schawing that the kyng was slane. Than said the
prophect, 'Gone is the wynd that sall blaw to the gret calamite and truble
of al Scotland.' This Thomas wes ane man of gret admiration to the people,
and schew sundry thingis as thay fell. Howebeit thai wer ay hyd under
obscure wourdis."—Ballenden's Boethias, f. 103. This prophetic minstrel
died in 1299. He is said to have followed a hart in the chase, in a forest behind the bower where he usually resided, and never to have been seen more
—King's Early Ballads, p. 188.

BEATRICE,

SECOND DAUGHTER OF HENRY III.

Birth-lands in England—Royal nursery—Wardrobe—Attendants—Visit to Gascony—She procures the pardon of a murderer—Proposed Spanish matches—Plighted to John of Bretagne—Honour of Richmond—Visit to France, and marriage of John and Beatrice—Her dowry—They return to England—Knighting of Lord John—Grant of Richmond—Beatrice goes to Bretagne—Her letters—Children—Difficulties about dowry—Illness of Beatrice—Correspondence—Grant of wardships to Lord John—Crusade of St. Louis—John takes the cross—Gains possession of Richmond—Raises funds—Beatrice determines to go in the crusade—They sail for Tunis—Death of St. Louis—Arrival of Prince Edward—Winter in Sicily—Sail to Acre—Beatrice's residence there—Return to Bretagne—Religious foundations—Relics—John and Beatrice attend the coronation of Edward I.—Her illness—Will—Death—Burial—Earl John's affection—His death—Children of Beatrice.

The Princess Beatrice, second daughter of Henry III. and Eleanora of Provence, was not a native of England, and on account of her early marriage, scarcely half her short life was passed in this country. She first saw the light at the city of Bourdeaux, in Gascony, on the 25th of June, in the year 1242.· Her father was absent at the time of her birth, wiling away his time with characteristic levity in idle disports, in pleasant tents and summer bowers, erected in the meadows near Blaye, on the banks of the Garonne, though the daily expected arrival of the French army might well have aroused him to activity. Queen Eleanora seems, however, to have been attended, during her confinement, by her mother, the Countess Bea-

[1] Paris, vol. ii., p. 594.

trice of Provence, and at her request her infant grand-daughter received her own name.[1]

The infant princess remained a very short time in Gascony. In the month of September following, she returned with her parents to England. They landed at Portsmouth on the 27th of September, and, passing through Winchester, arrived at Windsor on the 6th of October,[2] where the little Lady Beatrice was duly installed into her place in the royal nursery, and she remained there even after the departure of her parents for Westminster.[3] In this ancient abode of English royalty, the infancy and childhood of Beatrice were principally passed, for though the king's children were occasionally taken to London for a short time, yet Windsor was their home. The care of her nurture devolved principally upon her nurse Agnes and her husband, who appear to have discharged their duty with great fidelity, for they subsequently received from the king a pension larger than that bestowed upon the nurses of any of the other children of Henry III.[4]

After the marriage of her elder sister, in 1251, Beatrice of course assumed a more prominent position in the royal household. Prince Edward, now springing up to boyhood, was no longer a resident at Windsor, his father having bestowed upon him the palace and manor of Eltham. Prince Edmund and a niece of the king's, called Mariote,[5] were the principal companions of Beatrice;

[1] Paris, vol. ii., p. 594. Chron. Lond., Addit. MS. 5444, f. 42 b.

[2] Rot. claus., Vasc. 27 H. III., m. 2.

[3] This fact is elicited from an entry in the Gascon close roll of the 27th of Henry III., pt. ii., m. 1, dated Westminster, October 27th, in which the *daughters* of the king are said to be at Windsor Castle.

[4] Rot. pat., 33 H. III., m. 2. The following is a striking illustration of the tenderness with which the royal children were treated. Prince Edmund was a puny, fretful infant; and, when he was about two years of age, King Henry ordered Richard de Harpur to go over to Windsor to *console* Edmund, the king's son, and his wages were to be regularly paid until the child's state was ameliorated.—Rot. claus., 37 H. III., m. 15.

[5] Rot. lib., 38 H. III., m. 2. We have been unable clearly to ascertain who this young lady was, but it is likely that she was a daughter of one of King Henry's half brothers or sisters, several of whom had large families.

five little boys, with their two masters, were kept at
Windsor as companions to the prince.[1] The attendants
named are four ladies in waiting, four serjeants-at-arms,
a clerk, cook, washerwoman, seven valets, besides one for
the king's niece, and five chaplains ;[2] the constable of the
castle presiding over the whole establishment. Tutors
and governesses there were none, and any share of education bestowed on the children must have been mainly
communicated by their chaplains ; the learning of that
period being chiefly confined to the sacred profession.
Their amusements seem to have consisted principally in
rambles among the neighbouring forests, where the boys
exercised their juvenile prowess in the chase, and the
little ladies, if they did not actually join in the sport,
were at least animated spectators. We find a special order
given by the king to his forester at Windsor, that Prince
Edmund shall be permitted to hunt as often as he pleases
in the forest of Windsor, and to carry away whatever he
has shot.[3] But few entries of any interest occur on the
State rolls, relative to the private expenditure of the royal
children. They were supplied with wine[4] and venison[5] as
usual, and with oaks from the king's forests for their fires.[6]
We also find an order for twenty-four silver spoons and
twelve salt-cellars to be sent to Windsor for their use,[7]
for two capes for the daughter and niece of the king,[8] and
for divers purchases to be made for them at the fair
of Pec.[9]

The private accounts of Queen Eleanora afford a few
interesting details with reference to her daughters. In

[1] Rot. claus., 38 H. III., m. 5.   [2] Ibid. Rot. lib., 38 m. 2.
[3] Rot. claus., 38 H. III., m. 3.
[4] Ibid. Rot. lib., 38, m. 4. Rot. claus. 39, m. 22.
[5] Rot. claus., 38. mm, 2, 3, 5. Ibid., 39, m. 22.
[6] Rot. claus., 38, m. 3.   [7] Ibid., m. 7.
[8] Rot. lib., 39, m. 14. Margaret is the name of the princess mentioned
in the roll, but this is evidently a mistake of the clerk, since she was then
in Scotland, and Beatrice at Windsor.
[9] Ibid., m. 5.

1252, although the princess Beatrice had only completed her tenth year, we find that her toilette was matter of considerable interest to her mother. On the 22nd of September, 2*s.* were paid to Andrew the goldsmith, for a jewelled flower for her garland, and 5*s.* for six dozen gold buttons to trim her dress.[1] It is amusing, however, to learn that the cost of making up the robe, so profusely ornamented, was only 4*d.*; while Queen Eleanora's dressmaker's bill for a dress made at the same time amounted to 8*d.*[2] 10*d.* was paid for making doublets for Edmund and Beatrice, and 6*d.* for their gloves;[3] their shoes cost 5*d.* or 5½*d.* per pair, and their boots 1*s.*[4] The queen made her daughter a present of a knife, price 3*s.*, a mirror 7*d.*, and seven dozen of chalcedony buttons, for which the large sum of 46*s.* 8*d.* was paid.[5]

At this time Beatrice had her own suite of servants, although she had had no separate household; we find one of her maidens[6] and the sumpter of her bed, that is the man who had the charge of its carriage from place to place, when she travelled, as recipients of the queen's bounty.[7] The queen was at this period in England, and Beatrice appears to have accompanied her in some of her many wanderings. In the June of 1252, we find her celebrating the feast of St. John the Baptist with the queen at Winchester.[8] Eleanora herself sojourned in her different palaces at Winchester, Clarendon, Merlbergh, and Westminster, but the greatest part of her time was spent with her children at Windsor.[9] Her household expences averaged £5. a day, with from 5*s.* to 10*s.* addi-

[1] Rot. jocalium regin. Elean., No. 3299. Queen's remembrancer.
[2] Rot. garderobæ regin. Elean., No. 3291.
[3] Ibid.
[4] Rot. regin. Elean., No. 3294.
[5] Ibid.
[6] Rot. donorum regin. Elean., No. 3303.
[7] Rot. nunc. regin. Elean., No. 370.
[8] Rot. regin. Elean., No. 3294. Queen's remembrancer.
[9] Ibid., No. 3293. Rot. lib., 38 H. III., m. 4.

tional, bestowed in alms.[1] With the latter end of the
year 1253, the interesting accounts of Queen Eleanora's
expenditure close, and we are thrown upon more general
sources for information.

In 1254, the nursery at Windsor received an addition
in the little Princess Katherine; Queen Eleanora herself
brought her infant there.[2] She was then on the eve of
her departure for Gascony, whither she was accompanied
by her eldest son Prince Edward and her daughter Beatrice.[3] The princess was probably her mother's companion
when the queen went to Burgos, to aid in the celebration
of the nuptials of Prince Edward with the infanta Eleanora of Castile, and afterwards at the gay festivities of
the feast of kings in Paris.[4] The royal family returned
to England early in 1255.

Beatrice had now a companion in her sister-in-law, the
young infanta, who was about her own age. In March,
1255, we find her at court, which was then held at Westminster. Though she was now only thirteen years of age,
she was appealed to, to use her influence with the king
her father in behalf of Ralph Buylly, who had been accused of murder. The case appears to have been a very
aggravated one. The victim being a stranger merchant,
the deed was rendered more atrocious by his unprotected
situation, and by the suspicion that naturally presents
itself that it was committed for the sake of plunder. Yet,
at the instance of his young and innocent daughter, King
Henry not only pardoned the murderer, but restored to him
all his goods which had been seized by the king's justices.[5]

During the next few years, we find but little mention

---

[1] Rot. hospitii regin. Elean., No. 2615, Queen's remembrancer.
[2] Rot. lib., 38 H. III., m. 4.
[3] " Nos vero, cum reginâ vestrâ, ad vos veniemus juxta mandatum ves-
tum et Edwardus filius vester, et Beatrix filia vestra."—Letter of Richard
Earl of Cornwall to Henry III., Fœdera, vol. i., pt. i., p. 296.
[4] Queens of England, vol. ii., pp. 106-7.
[5] Rot. claus., 29 H. III., m. 14.

of the Princess Beatrice; she was now considered old enough to reside constantly at court,[1] and consequently all particulars of her expenses, &c. are merged in those of the king. Robes were ordered occasionally for her use, as well as that of the other members of the royal family :[2] she was also included in the bountiful donations which the king presented every year on festival days to the poor, for the welfare of himself, the queen, and their children. One of these donations may serve as a specimen : on the 2nd of May, 1259, Henry orders his almoner to distribute 150 pairs of shoes, at 8*d.* a pair, among the poor men and women of Windsor, as his and the queen's offering ; and 21 pairs, at 4½*d.* per pair, among the children, as the gift of the royal children ; also an equal number of tunics of three ells each, at 8*d.* an ell, to be similarly distributed against the ensuing feast of Easter.[3] The total of the expense will be found to be £22. 9*s.* 10½*d.*, nearly equal to £350. of our money ; and it must be remembered that similar orders were generally given at least three times every year : viz. at Christmas, Whitsuntide, and Easter.[4] In the noble munificence of their charitable benefactions, our forefathers certainly set an example which it were well if we more extensively followed.

In 1253, when the Princess Beatrice was about eleven years old, a marriage was proposed for her with the son and heir of Peter II., King of Aragon,[5] but the treaty never proceeded far; some unexplained obstacles arose, and it dropped through. Again, in 1256, thoughts were entertained of marrying her to Emanuel, brother of Al-

---

[1] It is evident, from an entry of the close roll of the 41st of Henry III., m. 14, that the Princess Katherine was the only one of the king's children then residing at Windsor.

[2] Rot. lib., 43 H. III., m. 8.   [3] Ibid., 43 H. III., m. 5.

[4] See Rot. claus., 46 H. III., m. 10, &c.

[5] Rot. pat., 37 H. III., m. 12, dorso. Owing to some slight confusion in the numbering of the membranes on this roll, it is quoted in the Fœdera as on membrane 13. Safeconducts for the ambassadors are granted on membrane 11.

phonso IV., King of Castile : her father, being about to despatch ambassadors to Castile, sent his favourite John Maunsell, to consult his brother Richard, Earl of Cornwall, as to what should be said about this marriage. The earl's advice was fraught with worldly prudence. ~ He counselled that the ambassadors should proceed very cautiously; that they should reply to any inquiries made by the Spanish prince, that they did not as yet know what lands the King of Castile had given, or intended to give to his brother, and that it would be most improper to marry the princess to any one who had not ample, competent, and secure possessions. They were instructed to make every inquiry about the expectations of the prince, but not on any account to utter a word that could be construed into a pledge of the marriage.[1] The result of their investigations was probably unsatisfactory, for we hear no more of it.

It was evident that Spain was not the destined home of the Lady Beatrice. Early in 1259, ambassadors arrived from John I., Duke of Bretagne, to solicit the hand of the princess for his eldest son. They were favourably received by King Henry, and still more so by the queen and the magnates of the land, who all regarded the match as a desirable one for the young princess.[2] One obstacle, however, interposed itself. As a condition of the marriage treaty, Henry was requested to restore to the Duke of Bretagne the lands and honour of Richmond, which were his by ancestral right, but which, in the year 1234, had been forfeited to the English crown, when his father, Peter Manclerk, had renounced his English vassalage, and joined the French party in the contests between the two crowns.[3] In 1242, a petition had been made for the

---

[1] Rot. claus., 40 H. III., m. 17. dorso.
[2] Rot. convent. pacis, 43 H. III., m. 1, dorso.
[3] Maurice, hist. de Bretagne, vol. i., p. 167.

restoration of the lands, but King Henry coolly replied, that he saw no possible good that could result to himself thereby, nor had the duke's messenger pointed out any mode in which he might ameliorate his own state by granting the petition, and therefore he refused it.[1] The following year open war broke out between him and the Breton duke, whom this refusal had thrown completely into the arms of France.[2]

On the conclusion of a peace between England and France, King Louis was naturally anxious to compensate his ally for the loss he had sustained; and it was at his instigation, or rather that of Queen Margaret, that the proposal was made for the marriage between young John of Bretagne and Beatrice. Henry was favourable to the request; and the Earls of Gloucester and Hertford, and John Maunsell, were appointed commissioners to arrange the affair,[3] plenary power for its conclusion being given to Queen Margaret, who, as the sister of Queen Eleanora of England, was aunt to the princess.[4] These commissions were drawn out in May, 1259, but the matter proceeded very slowly, because the king, having bestowed the lands of Richmond on his uncle Peter of Savoy,[5] who was then abroad, it was not practicable to arrange about an exchange for them in his absence. Henry wrote, however, to the Duke of Bretagne, informing him of this circumstance, but adding, that he and the queen intended to be in France the latter end of the year, and that they would bring their daughter with them. He requested the duke and duchess, with their son John, to be there at the same time, when Peter of Savoy would also be present, and the negociations could be fully entered into.[6] He

---

[1] Fœdera, vol. i., pt. i., p. 250.
[2] Ibid.
[3] Rot. pat., 43 H. III., m. 11. Fœdera, vol. i., pt. i., p. 382.
[4] Fœdera, vol. i., p. 388.   [5] Rot. chart., 25 H. III., m. 4.
[6] Fœdera, vol. i., pt. i., p. 391.

likewise issued procuratory letters, declaring his intention that the marriage between John and Beatrice should take place, provided some satisfactory arrangement could be made in reference to Richmond.

These letters bore date October 18th; and, on the 7th of November following, the royal party left Westminster, proceeding by way of Canterbury, and embarked from Dover on the 13th;[1] on the 15th, they landed at Witsand, whence they proceeded by slow stages through Boulogne and Beauvais, to Paris, where they arrived in the beginning of December.[2]

The peace recently concluded between England and France, after a series of tedious quarrels, had filled all hearts with exhilaration, and the meeting of the two courts was looked forward to with much pleasure. Louis received his royal relations with every mark of honour, and fitted up apartments for them in his own palace of the Louvre,[3] where, we are told, they held a great feast for many days, and were well served with wines and meats.[4] Among the guests at the palace were the Duke and Duchess of Bretagne, and their son John.

The life of the Lady Beatrice now presented a strange contrast to the quiet retirement in which she had spent her earlier years : this was her first visit to her French relations, and naturally a season of excitement to one so young, which would not be lessened by her being thrown constantly into the society of the youth whom she was taught to regard as the probable sharer of her future fortunes. They were not, as is often the case in royal marriages, mere children, for John had nearly completed his twenty-second year,[5] and was remarkable for the noble

---

[1] Rot. pat., 44 H. III.   [2] Rot. claus., 44 H. III., pars ii., m. 5.
[3] Villeneuve, hist. de St. Louis, vol. iii., p. 25.
[4] Guil. de Nangis, vie de St. Louis, Bouquet, vol. xx., p. 411.
[5] He was born January 3rd, 1238 ; see Morice, Preuves de l'Hist. de Bretagne, vol. i., p. 152.

and classical cast of his features,[1] while Beatrice was glowing in the girlish beauty of seventeen. As the negociations between their parents were fast progressing towards a conclusion, they would, of course, enjoy the unrestrained intercourse which their relative position warranted; and now was laid the foundation of that deep and lasting attachment, which characterized their wedded life. Queen Margaret, who had been the original matchmaker, was delighted with the success of her efforts, and earnestly desired to crown the whole by a speedy marriage between the young lovers. King Henry's previous arrangement had been to return to England immediately after the celebration of the Christmas festivals; but, at the earnest entreaty of Queen Margaret, he consented that the nuptials should be fixed for the 14th of January, and be solemnized in France; and of course he and the queen remained to be present on the occasion.[2]

The preparations for the marriage of Beatrice were almost completed, under the auspices of Queen Eleanora, who took upon herself the task of equipping her daughter.[3] The wedding was to take place at the chateau of the French king at Compiègne, where he and the queen had promised to grace the ceremony with their presence.[4] It was arranged, either as matter of choice on the part of the princess, or of state etiquette, that she should spend the short period that was to elapse before her marriage in retirement; and the abbey of St. Denis was selected for the purpose. Her parents accompanied her thither on the 28th of December;[5] they were welcomed with great honour by the monks, who came in procession to meet

---

[1] This is evident, from the Roman contour of the feature of the portrait statue on his tomb, which is engraved by Maurice, vol. i., plate, p. 224.
[2] Rot. claus., 44 H. III., pars ii., m. 4, dorso.
[3] The total sum expended was £264.   Rot. lib., 44 H. III., m. 2.
[4] Rot. claus., 44 H. III., p. ii., m. 4, dorso.
[5] Ibid.

them, clothed in albes and capes of rich and costly silk; and so delighted was King Henry with his reception that he presented them in return with a splendid chalice of gold and a silver paten of great value.[1]

But a cloud arose to overshadow the gladness of the anticipated festivals. The day but one preceding that appointed for the marriage of John and Beatrice, Prince Louis, the Dauphin of France, a promising youth of seventeen years of age, died suddenly at Paris. His body was brought to St. Denis the following day; and, instead of the merry pealing of bridal bells, the dim aisles of the cathedral echoed with the solemn strains of funereal chantings, as, all night long, the watchers by the corpse of the young prince sang the requiems for the dead. The next morning, King Henry, to do honour to his deceased nephew, himself, with the aid of one of his noblest barons, bore the coffin on his shoulder for a little distance from Saint Denis, and accompanied it to Royaumont, where he assisted in person at the funeral.

On account of the death of her cousin, the marriage of Beatrice was postponed for a week. The French king and queen, now mourners for their first-born, were not in a mood to engage in festivities; it was, therefore, arranged that the proposed journey to Compiègne should be abandoned, and that the wedding should take place at St. Denis, where the princess then was staying. St. Vincent's day, the 22nd of January, 1260, was the day finally appointed; and, notwithstanding the recent calamity which had involved them in the deepest gloom, King Louis and his queen were present on the occasion.[2]

[1] Guil. de Nangis, p. 413.
[2] The Breton chroniclers give December 30th, 1259, as the date of the marriage. Morice, ut sup. We have, however, the authority of King Henry for the date here given. In a letter written by him to Hubert de Burgh, his justiciary, dated January 16th, detailing the causes of his delay in returning to England, he gives several interesting particulars of his daughter's intended marriage. By this letter, we are enabled generally to

With reference to the dowry of the princess, Henry would not consent to restore the lands of Richmond; but he promised to allow the Duke of Bretagne or his son 2000 marks per annum for its value; but, instead of receiving the money direct from the English exchequer, it was to be paid by King Louis, who had pledged himself in more than that amount to the English king, for the lands of Agennois, to which Henry consented to relinquish his claim in favour of his son-in-law,[1] who paid to King Louis the customary homage of a vassal of France for the province which he was nominally to hold.[2]   This arrangement was made only for six years, at the end of which time it was probably hoped that the unwelcome intruder upon the lands of Richmond might be out of the way.   At any rate, Louis wished King Henry, at the expiration of that time, to possess and pay him homage for Agennois as before, and to provide in some other manner for his son-in-law.[3]   Meanwhile, a distinct proviso was made, that, should the King of France fail in his engagement to pay the money regularly, or should it not equal the value of the Richmond estates, John and Beatrice should be fully compensated by King Henry.[4]   On the other hand, the Duke and Duchess of Bretagne made a settlement upon their son and daughter-in-law, which consisted of part of the lands which the Duchess Blanche, who was daughter to the King of Navarre, had received as her dower.[5]

These arrangements being satisfactorily completed, the duke and duchess returned home, leaving their son and his bride awhile longer with her parents.   On the 25th of

confirm, but, in one or two instances, to correct, the account of the wedding given by Guillaume de Nangis, the historian and biographer of Louis; it is to be found on the close roll of the 44th of Henry III., part 2, membrane 4, in dorso.

[1] Rot. claus., 42-47 Hen. III., m. 5.
[2] Fœdera, vol. i., pt. i., p. 392.
[3] Letter of Louis to Henry III.   Cotton MS., Julius, E., I., ff. 58, 59, b.
[4] Morice preuves, i., p. 792.   Fœdera, vol. i., pt. i., p. 413.
[5] Royal letters, Tower.   No. 388.

January, they too left St. Denis, and, passing through
Artois, by Arras and Therouenne, reached St. Omer on the
20th of February, where they remained nearly two months.[1]

Their sojourn was thus extraordinarily prolonged by rumours that filled the minds of the king and queen with
concern. It was reported, that Prince Edward, then in
England, was taking advantage of the general dissatisfaction with his father's government, and plotting with the
barons to supplant him : and it was not until a document,
declaring the groundlessness of this report, had been sent
to the king, formally signed and sealed with the seals of
the Prince Richard, Earl of Cornwall, and the great body
of the nobles, that he was sufficiently re-assured to venture
upon returning.[2] Meanwhile, on the 9th of March, King
Henry wrote a letter to the Duke of Bretagne, in which,
after informing him of the good health of himself and his
family, who were then with him at St. Omer, he proceeds : — " We have retained with us John, your and our
very dear son, alike for his recreation and our own,
although he was unwilling; and we trust you will not
take this ill, but, for our sake, will hold excused the delay which he has made with us against his will, as William de Lexac, his master, will intimate to you more fully.
And because we greatly desire to decorate this same John
with the belt of knighthood, and, most of all, to perform
the ceremony on the feast of St. Edward,[3] which will be
the quinzaines of St. Michael, and which we specially
venerate above the other solemnities of the year ; we ask
you, with the fullest affection, and in all manners that we
are able, that you will be present with us at the aforesaid
solemnity, to your honour and ours and that of your aforesaid son."[4] From this letter, it would seem either that

[1] Rot. claus., 44 H. III., pars ii., mm. 4, 3, 2.
[2] Wikes' chron., Gale, vol. ii., p. 54.
[3] The translation of Edward the confessor, October 13th.
[4] Fœdera, vol. i., pt. i., p. 395.

young John was really anxious to take his bride home
forthwith to Bretagne, instead of remaining with her still
longer at her father's court; or, perhaps, his unwilling-
ness might be partly assumed, in order to elude the jealousy
that would naturally arise in the mind of Duke John on be-
holding his son so completely devoted to his English relations. The consent of the duke was obtained to King
Henry's petition for taking John and Beatrice with him to
England, but we do not learn that he ever acceded to his
invitation to join them there.

The royal family appear to have lived in great retirement at St. Omer; an order for a quantity of Gascon
wine to be sent to them[1] is the only one that gives token
of festivity. Indeed, Henry's funds were too low to
admit of his celebrating his daughter's bridal with the
splendour congenial to his tastes. At this very period,
the greater part of his jewels were in pledge to the King
of France; and he wrote several earnest letters to Hubert de
Burgh, his justiciary, entreating him to send him money
for their redemption, in consideration of the great scandal
and disgrace which were caused by his inability to recover
them.[2] About the middle of April, the royal party prepared for their departure to England. They left St. Omer
on the 15th of April, and, passing through Boulogne on the
18th, on the 21st they reached Witsand, whither vessels
had previously been congregated for their use. After
having waited several days for a favourable wind, they set
sail on the 25th; and, their passage being favourable, they
landed the same day at Dover, and, proceeding through
Rochester, reached London on the 1st of May.[3]

[1] Rot. claus., 44 H. III., pars 2, m. 2.
[2] Ibid. Fœdera, vol. i., pt. i., p. 397. A curious list of these jewels is
given in the Fœdera, p. 410; among them were four crowns, several garlands, clasps, rings, jewelled belts, &c., and also three golden combs, two
golden peacocks, and an *alphabet!* They were not recovered until four
years afterwards. See rot. pat., 48 H. III., m. 2. Fœdera, vol. i., pt. i.,
p. 435.   [3] Rot. pat., 44 H. III., m. 1.

The lady Beatrice and her husband resided entirely at the court during their stay in England. Indeed, had they been otherwise disposed, they could scarcely have afforded to maintain a separate establishment; for King Louis broke the stipulation by which he had bound himself to pay to Earl John the sum due for Agennois; and, when Henry remonstrated with him on the subject,[1] he coolly told him that, since he had received the homage of John for Agennois, it was a business that rested solely between themselves, and that Henry had no business whatever to interfere.[2] King Henry had, therefore, no resource but to leave his daughter undowried, or to provide for her himself. On the 5th of October, he wrote to the Duke of Bretagne, informing him of the health of his queen and children, and also of the duke's son John, and making arrangements for marking out the extent of the honour of Richmond, in order to form a correct estimate of its value,[3] that he might hand over an equivalent, as agreed upon, in case of a failure on the part of the French king; but discussions arose between the parties employed in the business, which lasted for upwards of two years, during which the young couple were left comparatively unprovided for.[4]

Preparations were now made for the ceremonial of knighting John of Bretagne on St. Edward's day, October 13th. The sharers of his honours were to be Prince Edward, Prince Henry of Germany, and the two young Montforts, sons of the great Earl of Leicester, cousins to Beatrice, and eighty other youths, all of noble birth. The ceremony took place at Westminster. It was conducted with extraordinary magnificence, and attended by a large

[1] Fœdera, vol. i., pt. i., p. 413. See, also, letter of Henry to Queen Margaret of France on the subject. Ibid.
[2] Fœdera, vol. i., pt. i., p. 392
[3] Rot. claus., 44 H. III., pars i., m. 4 dorso.
[4] Fœdera, vol. i., pt. i., p. 413.

concourse of the nobility, both from England and the continent.   Prince Edward was the first to receive the belt of knighthood; and being thus, by the laws of chivalry, capable of conferring his newly-acquired honours, he assisted his father in knighting the other youths.   Several of our chroniclers represent the nuptials of John and Beatrice as taking place on the same day;[1] but this assertion is incompatible with the statements already given about her marriage, unless we suppose the former ceremony to have been that of betrothal.   The prejudice that then existed against marrying a young noble until he had been dubbed a knight gives some colour to this supposition; although both the Breton chroniclers and English state documents speak of the ceremony at St. Denis as the *marriage*, and mention no subsequent one.

It was always customary for newly-dubbed chevaliers to seek an early opportunity of shewing that they were worthy of their honours, or " winning their spurs," as it was poetically called; and, therefore, Prince Edward, with his brother-in-law, John of Bretagne, and his cousins Henry of Germany and the Montforts, set off forthwith to display their prowess at a tournament that was to be held at Paris, in honour of the marriage of Robert of Artois, youngest son of the French king, to Amicia de Courtenay.[2]

Beatrice did not accompany her lord and his companions on this chivalric expedition.   What were the fortunes of the young adventurers, or how long they remained abroad, cannot now be ascertained; for the famine, which was making terrible havoc in France, and especially in Bretagne, damped all joyousness of festivity, and filled the pages of the chroniclers with bewailing rather than with the voice of rejoicing.[3]   The lady Beatrice, probably at

[1] Wikes. Gale, vol. ii., p. 54.
[2] Matt. Westm., p. 375.   Annal. lucul., Cotton MS., Nero D. II., f. 169. Villeneuve, vol. ii., p. 25.
[3] Morice, vol. i., p. 192.   Le Baud hist. de Bretagne, p. 244.

the instance of her parents, remained some time longer with them. The visit of the king and queen of Scots was expected in the winter, and they were anxious to have the whole of their family re-united. But if Beatrice had her share in the festivities of this joyous season, she also shared the troubles of the ensuing spring, when the contests between Henry and the barons rose to such a height, that the personal safety of the monarch was endangered.[1] The visit of Beatrice had, however, now been prolonged to a considerable length, and arrangements were made for her departure to Bretagne.

On the 17th of June, 1261, Henry, compelled at length to abandon his favourite scheme of paying his daughter's dowry at the expense of the King of France,[2] formally assigned to his son-in-law 2000 marks, which was somewhat beyond the estimated value of the Richmond estates, to be received in half-yearly payments from his own exchequer.[3] This grant was made at Guildford, but soon after the royal family removed to London, where, on the 14th of July, we find the king, " at the petition of Beatrice, his dearest daughter," granting some oaks in the forest of Windsor to a valet of the pantry of Queen Eleanora, for whom Beatrice had interested herself.[4]

The Bishop of London was appointed to be the guardian of the Princess on her journey to Bretagne,[5] along with a knight called William de Molun, who was to remain in personal attendance upon her for two years.[6] The Viscount of Kent was ordered to give her and her family an honourable reception at Dover, and to provide for their speedy passage.[7] The last of these orders is dated the 21st of July, and we may presume that the party set sail soon afterwards.

[1] Matt. Westm., p. 379. [2] Fœdera, vol. i., pt. i., p. 419.
[3] Fœdera, vol. i., pt. i., pp. 406, 434. [4] Rot. claus., 45 H. III., m. 5.
[5] Rot. pat., 45 H. III., m. 8. [6] Ibid., m. 9.
[7] Rot. lib., 45 H. III., m. 6.

The reception given to the lady Beatrice, on her first arrival in Bretagne, was very joyous;[1] and, on becoming a member of her husband's family, she was met with a warmth and sincerity of affection, especially on the part of the Duchess Blanche, her mother-in-law, which compensated, as far as any thing could do so, for the loss of the home and the friends of her childhood. Several letters, written by Beatrice to King Henry I., are still in existence among the Tower collection, but, unfortunately, some of them are so defaced that it is impossible to make out the connected sense. They seem, however, to contain little more than affectionate inquiries after the health of her father, and warm expressions of willingness to comply with his wishes as far as lies in her power.[2] One of these letters was probably written in the beginning of the year 1262; for, in the latter part of the preceding December, King Henry, writing to the Duke of Bretagne and his son, on business connected with the Richmond revenues, sent a request to Beatrice to write to him immediately, and give him particulars about herself, which he was anxious to hear.[3] Her reply contains an allusion to this request, expresses the greatest joy at the good tidings she has received of him and her dearest mother, and her earnest desire to hear frequently from him.[4]

Beatrice and her husband had a separate establishment at the city of Nantes, whither they resorted whenever they chose to retire awhile from the court; but the harmony that subsisted in the ducal family induced them generally to reside with the duke and duchess. Beatrice continued, in her new sphere of life, to maintain her connexions with her continental relations. Soon after her marriage, she

[1] Morice, vol. i., p. 193, Le Baud, p. 244. Her arrival is assigned, by the latter historian, to an earlier date, but the documentary evidence on the subject is decisive.

[2] See Nos. 419 and 420, Royal letters.

[3] Fœdera, vol. i., pt. i., p. 413.

[4] Lit. reg., No. 419.

received a visit from her half-aunt, the lady Isabella de Croun, daughter of Isabella of Angoulême, by Hugh Earl of March, whose frequent visits at the court of England must have rendered her very intimate with her niece. This lady was accustomed to receive an annual pension from the English king, which the impoverished state of his exchequer had recently prevented from continuing; she had, therefore, addressed a petition to Henry, earnestly entreating the payment of the money which, she assured him, she greatly needed to assist her in furnishing the marriage portion of her daughter.[1] Beatrice warmly seconded this petition in a letter to her father, of which the following is a literal translation :—

"To the high lord and her very dear father, if it pleaseth him, Henry, by the Grace of God King of England, Lord of Ireland, and Duke of Aquitaine, Beatrice, his devoted daughter, wife to my lord John of Bretagne, health and love as to her dear lord, with willingness to do his pleasure in all things.

"I give you to know, sire, that my aunt, the Lady of Croun, has come to see me; and has begged me to pray of you that you would give her a debt which you owe her. And know, sire, that she has great need of it; for a daughter of hers who is married. Wherefore, I pray you, sire, that you, if you please, grant her this debt, and that you so act in this affair that she may perceive that my prayers have availed for her."[2]

We may presume the petition was granted, for we hear no more of the pleadings.

In the July of this year, 1262, Beatrice, who had just completed her twentieth year, became the mother of a son, to whom the name of Arthur was given, and great joy was evinced by the people of Bretagne on the occasion

[1] Royal letters, No. 144. Fœdera, vol. i., pt. i., p. 418.
[2] Royal letters, No. 141. Fœdera, vol. i., pt. i., p. 419.

R 2

of its birth.[1] The child was welcomed, not only by his
parents and grand-parents, but also by his great-grand-
father, Pierre Manclerk, the ex-Duke of Bretagne,[2] father
of Duke John.   This nobleman had succeeded to the
dukedom only in right of his wife Alice, the daughter of
the celebrated Constance of Bretagne, widow of Geoffry
Plantagenet, by her third husband, Guy de Thouars.
After the murder of the unfortunate Prince Arthur, and
the imprisonment of his sister, Eleanora of Bretagne, this
lady was acknowledged duchess : but, on her death, her
husband ceded the reins of government to his son, as soon
as he became of age; and, retiring to the privacy of domestic life, this venerable man lived just long enough to
greet his descendant of the third generation.[3]

The health of Beatrice continued very delicate after the
birth of her infant.   She had an attack of fever, which
lasted some time, and brought her very low; but, at
length, she gradually recovered.   At this time, her mother-
in-law, the Duchess Blanche, wrote to King Henry, informing him that " Madame Beatrice, his dear daughter
and hers, is still enfeebled by her fever, but, thanks to
God ! it is much better, and the physicians say it cannot
last long."   After the usual expressions of good will, &c.,
she concludes with true grandmother's pride by assuring
the king, that " Arthur is a very good child, and very
handsome."[4]   The birth of this infant was followed, in
rapid succession, by that of six other children ; three
sons, called Henry, John, and Peter ; and three daughters,
two of whom were named after their grandmothers,
Blanche and Eleanora, and the third was called Mary; but
the exact dates of their birth have not transpired.[5]

[1] Le Baud, p. 245.
[2] Morice, vol. i., p. 193, and Preuves, vol. i., p. 254.
[3] Lobineau, hist. de Bret., vol. i., pp. 189, 197.
[4] Royal letters, No. 872.   Fœdera, vol. i., p. 464.
[5] Chron. Trivet. MS., No. 632.   Supplement Français Bibl. du roi Paris
sub fine.   Sandford, geneal. hist., p. 93.

Occupied in the unobtrusive duties of domestic life, the lady Beatrice retires much into the shade during the few ensuing years, but we glean a few particulars concerning her from the correspondence of her husband with the royal family of England. Lord John, alike from policy and friendly feeling, kept on good terms with the English court; for he still hoped to obtain the earldom of Richmond, which had been so long held by his family; and for which he was the more anxious, since difficulties frequently arose about the payment of the instalments which he was to receive from King Henry, and they were allowed to fall sadly into arrears.[1] The other part of Beatrice's dower, also, which had been bestowed upon her by her mother-in-law, was unjustly detained in the hands of Blanche's brother, Theobald, King of Navarre; until, at length, Henry induced Queen Margaret of France, whose daughter Theobald had married, to interfere on the occasion.[2] In one of his undated letters to King Henry, John expresses unbounded affection and good will, and a wish to devote himself to the king's pleasure in all things, and promises, if occasion should require, to come and assist him with an armed force; informing him, also, that he and his consort Beatrix are at present residing at Nantes, and are both in good health.[3] Another half-obliterated epistle contains even stronger expressions of devotion.[4]

The troubles that prevailed in England during the year 1264 put a stop for awhile to the correspondence between the two courts. But in 1265, although the king was still a prisoner in the hands of the opposite faction, we find a safeconduct for John of Bretagne to come over to England with his family.[5] They did not, however, avail

[1] Rot. pat., 46 H. III., mm. 14, 11.
[2] Letter of Henry to Queen Margaret, Fœdera, vol. i., pt. i., p. 413.
[3] Lit. reg., No. 873.   [4] Ibid., No. 871.
[5] Rot. pat., 49 H. III., m. 20. Fœdera, vol. i., pt. i., p. 453.

themselves of it till the following year, after the battle of
Evesham had restored the king to the possession of his
throne.   When they were about to set forth, the Duchess
Blanche wrote to King Henry, assuring him of the entire
devotion and obedience of her son, and his desire in every
thing to conform to Henry's wishes ;[1] she proceeds to say
that, thanks to God! Madame Beatrice is very well and
hearty, and growing quite *embonpoint;* she hopes that
the king will attend to the wants of her son John, who is
going over to England, considering how completely he
looks up to him in every thing.[2]

How long John and Beatrice remained in England is
not precisely known.   The grand object of their visit was
accomplished, however ; for, on the 13th of June, 1266,
King Henry formally bestowed upon his son-in-law the
long-coveted earldom of Richmond[3] for which John paid
him the accustomed homage.   The possession, however,
was soon found to be merely nominal ; for, though the
king declared that he had given to his troublesome relative,
Peter of Savoy, lands which ought to have amply contented him in exchange for Richmond, yet his seneschal,
Guischard de Charron,[4] refused, or at least delayed, to obey
the royal mandate to give up the lands to a knight whom the
Duke of Bretagne had sent over to take possession of them ;[5]
and Peter still kept his hold upon them as firmly as ever.

The Princess and her husband were thus left in the
lurch ; and the exchequer of King Henry was in so lament-
able a condition, that the only compensation which he
could offer them was an order that all escheats, wardships
of minors, and marriages of heirs, which devolved of right
upon the crown, should be granted to Earl John, in part

---

[1] Lit. reg., No. 870.
[2] Ibid., No. 872. Fœdera, vol. i., pt. i., p. 391.
[3] Fœdera, vol. i., pp. 468-9.
[4] See rot. pat., 50 H. III., m. 13 dorso.
[5] Rot. pat., 50 H. III., mm. 17, 18 dorso.

payment of arrears.[1] Notwithstanding the manifest injustice thus done to his own daughter, King Henry had actually the weakness to permit Peter to continue peaceably in the enjoyment of his estates, and even to bequeath them to another, whilst his own executors were to receive the revenues for seven years after his decease to pay his debts.[2]

Meanwhile, intercourse was carried on between Henry and the Duke of Bretagne, as appears from a letter addressed by the duke to the king, acknowledging the receipt of one from him, and stating his pleasure at hearing what Henry has said about his son John; but what it was that was said, the decayed state of the letter prevents us from ascertaining; it concludes with the usual assurances of the devotedness of John to the king.[3]

During her residence in England, Beatrice suffered from another severe attack of quartan fever, which had not disappeared when the time arrived for her return to Bretagne. This we learn from a letter she sent to her father soon afterwards. In it she complains that, since she left her father, she has heard nothing certainly of his welfare, which will always deeply interest her; entreats for speedy news, and informs him that she is still ill with the quartan fever, but that it does not now, as it formerly did, harass her incessantly with severe pain.[4]

A few entries, in reference to John of Bretagne, occur on the state rolls of the period, which are curious as an illustration of the manners of the times. A rich merchant

[1] Rot. pat., 50 H. III., m. 4 dorso. Ibid., 52, m. 3. For orders of payments made to John on this account see patent roll, 51 Henry III., mm. 37, 18. Proofs of the poverty of the king occur in an order to sell the royal jewels, which is on the same roll, m. 17.

[2] Clarkson's Richmond, p. 30.

[3] Royal letters, No. 870, Tower.

[4] Ibid., No. 421. Fœdera, vol. i., pt. i., p. 465. No clue can be gathered from internal evidence as to the date of some of these letters; they are, therefore, placed where they best agree with the general tenour of the narrative.

or citizen, for he seems to have held no higher rank, since the appellation of *dominus* is not accorded to him, had recently died, leaving considerable estates to his children, who, being minors, the custody of them and their lands was committed to Queen Eleanora. She was to enjoy their revenues until they became of age, and to have the privilege of marrying them as she pleased. The widow was assigned over to the tender mercies of John of Bretagne, and the right of re-marrying her " as far as it lay in the king's power;"—that is, as far as the weight of courtly authority, short of downright force, would go,— was given to him, not to exercise it with any view to the future happiness of the disconsolate lady, but to promote his own interest by disposing of her hand to the highest bidder, and the sum he thus obtained was to be counted as part payment of a debt owing to him by the king![1] On another occasion, a ward of the crown, having married without leave, was condemned to pay a large fine to lord John, to whom, as previously observed, all similar payments were, for the present, to be made;[2] and again, Clementia, widow of Robert de Swalles, gave him the sum of 400 marks, equal to about £.4000 of our money, that she might be permitted to have the guardianship of her children and the custody of their lands.[3] These are but a few, among innumerable instances that might be alleged, of the nonchalance with which the marriage alliances of royal wards were bought and sold by our monarchs of the olden time.

The year 1268 leads us to a fresh era in the life of the countess Beatrice. Her uncle, Louis IX. of France, commonly known as Saint Louis, had summoned all the peers of France, including the Duke of Bretagne and his son,

[1] Rot. claus., 51 H. III., m. 3.
[2] Rot. pat., 52 H. III., m. 3. Similar entries occur on mm. 5 and 19 of the same roll.
[3] Rot. pat., 53 H. III., m. 28.

to an assembly at Paris, the object of which was undisclosed to any of them, until, in a meeting held in the chapel royal, on the 25th of March, the mystery was solved by the appearance of the monarch, holding in his hands a crown of thorns, advancing to the throne erected for him in the midst of the assembly; whence, after a few moments of silence, rendered more impressive by the deep traces of emotion on the features of the king, he entered upon an eloquent and pathetic detail of the miseries of the Christians in the Holy Land, on account of the rapid conquests made by the Mussulman chief Boudoc Dari, announced that a crusade had been decreed by the pope Clement I., and with enthusiasm proclaimed his resolution to avenge these multiplied injuries. "True servants of the King of Kings," exclaimed he, "follow me, and let us wash out the affronts which the Saviour of man has so long endured. Yes, follow me, to snatch the heritage of the Christians from shameful servitude." Thus saying, he descended from his throne, and, kneeling at the feet of the cardinal legate, who was present, received from him the sacred symbol of the red cross.[1] The whole assembly was electrified at this scene. Touched by the eloquence of the royal enthusiast, and roused by loyalty as well as chivalry, they all, with scarcely an exception, followed his example; and among the number were John Duke of Bretagne, and his son, the Earl of Richmond.[2]

To prepare for a crusade, however, required more than the feverish energy of a momentary excitement. There was the gathering and arming of the troops, the storing up of provisions, the preparing of vessels, and, above all, the procuring the necessary supplies of money; all of which required time. It was, therefore, arranged that

[1] Joinville, hist. de St. Louis Bouquet, vol. xx., p. 299. Villeneuve, hist. de St. Louis, vol. iii., pp. 322-3.
[2] Gaufrid. de bello loco, p. 21. Gesta St. Ludov., p. 56, Bouq., vol. xx.

the expedition should not start until the spring of the
year 1270, and meanwhile vigorous preparations were set
on foot.   Lord John had so long professed unlimited respect for his father-in-law, King Henry, that he thought
it necessary to ask his leave before he set forth on this
expedition;[1] and he, accordingly, went over immediately
with Beatrice to pay a visit to the king.   They arrived in
England early in April, as appears by a grant made to
Beatrice on the 13th of that month.[2]   The object of the
visit was not only to solicit King Henry's permission for
the crusade, but, at the same time, to procure the requisite supplies of money.   In the first of these objects, Earl
John was entirely successful: the solicited permission
was readily granted, for Henry himself had entered warmly
into this crusading scheme.   Soon after the arrival of his
daughter and son-in-law, he held a grand assembly of his
nobles at Northampton, at which his own two sons, Edward and Edmund, both assumed the cross.[3]

The decease of the troublesome intruder upon Richmond,
Peter of Savoy, had recently taken place.   He presumed
upon his right to the last; for, while he left to his brothers[4]
part of the lands given him in exchange for Richmond,[5] he
bequeathed the earldom itself to Queen Eleanora.[6]   She,
however, expressed her willingness to resign them to
her son-in-law, provided she might receive, in exchange,
the revenues of Agennois, and 800 marks annual value of
land in England.[7]   Several letters were written by the

[1] Morice, vol. i., p. 195.
[2] Rot. pat., 52 H. III., m. 18.
[3] Annal. Waverl., p. 224, Wikes, p. 85, Gale ii.   Paris, vol. ii., p. 1055.
Prince Edward assumed the cross as substitute for his father, who believed
himself to have been cured of a serious illness by taking the sacred vows.
See a curious letter on this subject in old French, on the patent roll,
55 H. III., m. 16, and Fordera, vol. i., pt. i., p. 488.
[4] Rot. pat., 55 H. III., m. 29.
[5] Rot. chart., 46 H. III., mm. 3, 1.
[6] Rot. pat., 53 H. III., mm. 24, 13, dorso.
[7] Ibid., m. 24.

king on the subject :[1] and Earl John, in a document dated
from Woodstock the 16th of July, 1268, made a formal
surrender of the lands of Agennois, which he had previously held from his father-in-law, promising to renounce
the homage which he had paid to King Louis for them,[2]
and he was at length put into full possession of the long
coveted earldom of Richmond.[3] Prince Edward, also,
relinquished to him the rape and honour of Hastings, formerly an appanage of the earls of Richmond,[4] which was
confirmed to him by the king, so that his wishes were, at
last, fully crowned.

We must now return to the personal history of the lady
Beatrice. On the 28th of July, 1268, we find the earl
and countess at Geddington, in Northamptonshire, whence
Beatrice, styling herself daughter of the illustrious King
of England, and wife of John, son of the Duke of Bretagne, issued her letters patent relative to the settling of
some lands formerly belonging to Queen Eleanora, but
which the king her father had recently bestowed upon her.
These letters were afterwards duly inspected and confirmed
by King Henry.[5] Towards the close of the year, the
princess gave birth to her daughter Mary.[6]

Although John and Beatrice spent much of their time
at the court residences of Windsor[7] or Westminster,[8] it is
probable, to say the least, that they would visit and reside
awhile in their newly-acquired possessions. The castle
of Richmond, built in the time of the Conquest, was a
strong and noble pile of building. The walls were ten or

---

[1] Fœdera, vol. i., pt. i., p. 476. Royal letters, Nos. 1356-1359.
[2] Cotton MS., Julius E. 1., p. 59. Rot. pat., 52 H. III., m. 28, in cedulâ.
[3] Rot. pat., 53 H. III., m. 13 dorso. See also mm. 23, 5. A letter on this
subject is printed in Champollion's Lettres des rois, vol. i., No. 145.
[4] Always excepting the castle, and advowson of benefices, for which an
equivalent was granted. Rot. pat., 53 H. III., mm. 27, 24, 27 dorso. Ibid.,
2 Edw. I., m. 12.
[5] Fœdera, vol. i., pt. i., p. 477.
[6] Anselme, hist. geneal., vol. i., p. 448.
[7] Rot. lib. scac., 53 H. III., Pasch.   [8] Rot. lib., 54 H. III., m. 11.

eleven feet in thickness, whilst the keep towered to the
height of 100 feet.   It was strikingly situated on an
eminence 40 or 50 feet above the river Swale, which rolled
past its walls; and, although not then retaining all the
massive strength which had distinguished it as a fortress
rather than a castle, still its buildings were numerous and
extensive,[1] whilst the surrounding country, rich in those
bold features of romantic landscape, which still call forth
the admiration of the lovers of nature, presented much
that could gratify the eye.   Earl John seems speedily to
have formed an attachment to his new vassals, for we find
him presenting a petition to the king in behalf of the
monks of Jorvaulx, in Richmondshire, whose goods had
been unjustly detained by his predecessor in the earldom,
Peter of Savoy.[2]

The earl now vigorously occupied himself in raising funds
for his projected crusade, which he at length accomplished
by mortgaging his Richmond estates for the sum of 2000
marks, equal to £20,000 of our present money; and, by a
patent, dated Westminster, January the 27th, 1269, the
king promised him that, should he not live to return from
the Holy Land, his executors should hold the lands of
Richmond until the 2000 silver marks which he had borrowed thereon were discharged.[3]   The king also granted
him exemption for five years from all military service
due to the crown from him in right of his earldom.[4]   The
earl and countess remained in England for more than a
year.   In November, 1269, Earl John, with the consent
of his consort, the lady Beatrice, bestowed some lands on
one of his favourite adherents.[5]   On the 22nd of the same
mouth, we find them at Westminster, where the king, at
the request of his son-in-law, pardoned some fines which

---

[1] Clarkson's Richmond, p. 59.   [2] Royal letters, Tower, No. 128.
[3] Fœdera, vol. i., pt. i., p. 478.   [4] Clarkson's Richmond, p. 31.
[5] Lobineau, vol. i., p. 260.

had been incurred by his servants.[1] The necessity, however, of expediting the preparations for the crusade induced
their return shortly afterwards. Beatrice left her infant
daughter and several of her younger children, whom she
had brought over with her, under her mother's care ; and
they were nursed at Windsor, with the children of Prince
Edward, in the same apartments where their mother had
passed her childhood.[2]

During the absence of John and Beatrice, the Duke
of Bretagne had been equally busy in his duchy in
obtaining supplies of money by means of a capitation
tax,[3] and the Breton lords generally shared the military ardour displayed by their duke and his son, and
mustered in considerable numbers to accompany them.
But gentler and fairer, if not more effective, votaries of
the cross were also gathering around its sacred standards ;
the wives of many of the principal leaders, animated by
the general enthusiasm that prevailed, or touched by a
more feminine, though not less laudable feeling,—that of
reluctance to be separated from their lords during the toils
and perils of the crusade,—determined upon accompanying
them to the Holy Land. Amongst the number were the
Duchess of Bretagne and her daughter-in-law, the lady
Beatrice.[4] Had Beatrice been a less devotedly-attached
wife, the claims of her infant family would have afforded
her a plausible pretext for remaining behind ; but, strong
as were the ties of maternal love, those of conjugal love
proved still stronger ; and, for the comfort of her younger
children, she had already provided by leaving them in
England.

The Breton party proceeded by way of Marseilles, from

[1] Rot. claus., 54 H. III., m. 11.
[2] Rot. lib., 55 H. III., m. 10.
[3] Lobineau says it yielded the then large sum of 8,000 livres. Hist. de
Bretagne, vol. i., p. 260.
[4] Lobineau, vol. i., p. 372. Morice, vol. i., p. 195, and Preuves, vol. i., p. 152.
Le Baud, p. 246.

which place they set sail on the 17th of April, 1270 ; and, after a tedious passage, they arrived, on the 12th of July, at Cagliari, in Sardinia, the appointed place of general rendezvous, whither the whole fleet of St. Louis had already preceded them.[1] Here Beatrice met with other companions in her cousin Isabella of France, eldest daughter of Louis, and wife of Theobald, King of Navarre, who was brother to the Duchess Blanche of Bretagne, and in the consort of the dauphin Philip, and the other French princes who, encouraged by the king, had also joined the crusade. With these royal relatives, Beatrice was, probably, already on terms of intimacy ; for the close vicinity of the French and Breton courts would naturally lead to frequent intercourse.

It could scarcely be expected that the wife of an inferior chief, and one who as yet boasted no independent title, should occupy any prominent place in the accounts of the crusade of St. Louis ; consequently, nothing more individual than a slight sketch of the expedition itself can be given, to form a connecting link in this part of the history of Beatrice... It was resolved that they should first proceed to Tunis, under a hope—fallacious as it afterwards proved—that the sovereign of Tunis, Omar el Maley Moztanca, would embrace the Christian faith.[2] Coasting the shores of Africa, therefore, they passed the rocky platform still strewn with fragments of jasper, which tradition points out as the site of the palace of the unfortunate Dido,[3] and doubled the promontory, where a large circular tower, and the ruins of walls forming an oblong square, were all that remained to show that Carthage *had* been.[4] The crusaders were struck with the

---

[1] Nangis, vie de St. Louis Bouquet, vol. xx., p. 447. Morice, ut sup.
[2] Nangis, ut sup.   [3] Chateaubriand, Itineraire, vol. iii., p. 194.
[4] " Even these ruins have almost entirely disappeared. A few Moorish cabins, a Mussulman hermitage on the brow of the cape, sheep quietly feeding among ruins scarcely elevated above the soil, are all that now remain of Carthage "—Itineraire, vol. iii., p. 185.

beauty of the coast clothed with olive trees; but so far were they from appreciating all that is thrilling in historic associations with these regions, that they even seem to have been ignorant not only of the classical history of the place, but also of the fact that one of the earlier apostolic churches was planted there; for King Louis, in one of his letters, simply announces that they have reached a city which *people call* Carthage.[1]

On the 21st of July, they drew up before the port of Tunis. King Louis, with tender thoughtfulness, ordered the princesses to be all placed together in one vessel, which was to be guarded by part of the fleet while the remainder was in requisition to make good the landing, for symptoms of opposition appeared in the hosts of Saracen troops who were congregated on the beach. Louis, inspired with warrior ardour, called together and harangued his leaders; the royal ship, with streaming banners, entered the gulf, followed by the greater part of the fleet; opposition vanished before their vigorous onset, and a landing was effected.[2] But there was a strong fortress, which commanded the plain selected by the Christian host for their encampment, in the hands of the enemy, and this it was absolutely necessary to master, before the footing which they had obtained could be considered permanent. Accordingly, the arbalisters and other troops destined for the attack defiled before the king, received from him a few words of encouragement and exhortation, rushed on to the assault, and so desperate was their attack, that in a few hours the azure gonfalon, with the fleur-de-lis of France, had replaced the crescent, and floated above the white walls of the Saracen fortress.[3] This stronghold

[1] Michaud, hist. des Croisades, vol. iii., p. 63.
[2] Villeneuve, hist. St. Louis, vol. iii., p. 393.
[3] Nangis, vie de St. Louis, Bouquet, vol. xx., p. 453.   Morice, vol. i., p. 196.
Villeneuve, vol. iii., p. 397.

was now appropriated as the residence of the princesses; who, after having been cooped up three months in their vessels, were at length enabled to land, and the royal daughters of the West took up their temporary abode amidst the relics of the palace of Dido. The army encamped in and about the ruins of Carthage, among the half finished houses which the Saracens were beginning to erect, under the direction of one of their princes, who had proudly undertaken to " rebuild Carthage."[1] But, although the Christian host met with no direct attack, they were harassed by clouds of horse hovering round their tents; and the straggler who wandered beyond its limits never returned again. It was found necessary, therefore, strongly to palisade and fortify the camp, and to appoint a vigilant watch at all points, to guard against surprise. The King of Tunis, so far from fulfilling the fallacious hopes he had held out, even threatened that, in case of an attack upon the city, he would put to death all the Christians in his power; and several skirmishes, some of them of a serious nature, took place.[2]

But an enemy far more fatal than the hostile sword was making deadly inroads upon the host. The burning heat of a tropical climate, combined with the bad water, which was the only beverage afforded them, introduced a fatal epidemic among the troops, which raged even more destructively among the higher ranks, who were less inured to hardship, than amongst the common soldiers. One of the first victims to its deadly ravages was Prince John of France, and the Dauphin Philip was next seized. Meanwhile, the king went from tent to tent, visiting and administering to the wants of the sufferers, till he too was overtaken with the disorder. Painfully intense was the suspense of the whole army, when the illness of their be-

---

[1] Chateaubriand, Itineraire, vol. iii., p. 201.
[2] Morice, vol. i., p. 196.

loved monarch became known; but that suspense was too
soon terminated when the soldiers, whose straining and
anxious eyes were ever bent upon the royal tent, with its
banner of fleur-de-lis, discerned the solemn train of prelates and chaplains proceeding thither, bearing in their
hands the sacred viaticum, for the administration of the
last rites of the dying. A few moments, and the tent
itself was taken down, and the monarch appeared reclined
upon a couch of ashes, attired in sackcloth, the livid hue
of death already on his features, his eyes fixed, his right
hand clasping the cross, and his mind now wandering;
but the ruling passion was still strong: " Saviour," mur-
mured he, " I will worship thee in thy city, I will adore
thee in thy holy temple.   On to Jerusalem!" and sinking
back on the ashy couch which was now his throne, with
a crucifix for his sceptre, and his canopy the sky of Carthage, the good King Louis expired on the 25th of
August, 1270.[1]

His dying couch was surrounded not only by his sons,
but by his daughters and the other princesses, who were
related to his house; and who, kneeling around, overwhelmed with grief, strove in vain to stifle their sobs. At
length the solemn scene was broken in upon by the clarion
voices of the heralds, giving forth the ancient cry of the
French monarchy, " The king is dead, long live the king!"
And well might such a prayer be uttered for him who
became king under such circumstances, for the Dauphin
Philip had been for several days quivering on the verge
between life and death, in the grasp of the very disease
which had deprived him of his father. He did recover,
however, and assumed the functions of his office; but such
was the discouragement occasioned by the death of the
king, and the illness of the troops, that the first use he

[1] Gesta St. Ludov. Bouquet, vol. xx., p. 57.   Joinville, hist. de St. Louis.
Ibid., p. 303.   Nangis, pp. 461, 463.   Villeneuve, vol. iii., pp. 415, 417.

made of his regal prerogative was to sign a truce for ten
years with the Saracens, procuring some trifling privileges
for the Christians of Africa, and to prepare for his return
to France.[1] Amongst those who determined to follow
him in his abandonment of the crusade, was the Duke of
Bretagne.[2]

But there were young and daring spirits among his
gallant band of followers, who set at nought the state
policy of their new sovereign, and glowed with impatient
wrath at the conclusion of a peace, and *such* a peace,
with the infidel; and among these was the Lord John of
Bretagne. Scarcely too was the peace signed when the
arrival of Prince Edward of England, with his wife
Eleanora of Castile, and his brother Edmund, gave a new
impulse to the crusading spirit. Vehement was his indignation when he heard of the truce. " But my dearest
lords," said he, " have we not come here to destroy the
enemies of the cross of Christ, and not to compound with
them ? Far be this from us—let us on; the land is open
before us, and proceed even to the holy city Jerusalem."[3]
The French princes, on the other hand, urged the obligations of the treaty so recently signed.[4] English writers
attribute sordid and dishonourable motives to the French,
especially to Charles of Sicily, asserting that they were
bribed to retire by the payment of a large tribute, to be
annually repeated to the Sicilian monarch.[5]

But the young English hero was above selfish conside-
rations; he refused to share such ill-earned wealth, and
sat moodily apart in his own tent, while the other lords
indulged in their revellings. He found, however, a companion of more congenial sentiments, in his brother-in-

[1] Morice, vol. i., p. 197.
[2] Lobineau, vol. i., p. 262.
[3] Hemingford, Gale, vol. ii., p. 589. Knighton, Twysden, col. 2455.
[4] Hemingford, ut sup.
[5] Chron. Mailros, Gale, vol. i., p. 242. Wikes, vol. ii., p. 93.

law, the Earl of Richmond. Bound to the prince not only by the gentle influence of his wife, but by the laws of chivalry—for he and Edward were companions in arms—he declared his resolution, a resolution sanctioned by his father, to share his destinies, perilous though they might prove.[1] Winter was coming on; and, after the general desertion of the army, it would have been madness for the little band of Christians to attempt to pass it in their present position. They therefore determined to retreat towards the island of Sicily, and there to winter. The fleet set sail on the 1st of December,[2] and on the 3rd neared Sicily :[3] but it was nine o'clock at night before they reached the port at Trapani, and the only mode in which it was possible to land was by sailing in open boats, more than a mile, through a heavy surf, to the shore. This plan was adopted, however, by those of higher rank, and also by the ladies, who all came ashore the same night, and were received, as well as circumstances would permit, while the soldiers remained on board, on account of the difficulties attending the landing of any number of forces in the night season.[4] But a terrible storm arose—many of the French vessels were woefully shattered, and some wrecked; among which were those containing the guilty treasure, which, according to our English chroniclers, had lured its owners from prosecuting the expedition. Prince Edward's ships, either from their superior

[1] Gray's Scalacronica, p. 105.
[2] Hemingford gives an instance of the generosity of Prince Edward on this occasion. As the hosts were embarking, to quit the shores of Africa, it was discovered that there were 200 Frenchmen more than the vessels could conveniently hold. These poor wretches were therefore abandoned by their companions: and, knowing that death, or slavery worse than death, awaited them from the Mussulmen, they filled the air with their cries. The heart of Edward was touched; though he was already on board his ship, he took boat, and, returning to shore, sent them off to be distributed as best they might amongst his own thirteen ships, and he himself was the last man who quitted the shores of Africa.—Gale, vol. ii., p. 589.
[3] Wikes, Gale, vol. ii., p. 93.
[4] Hemingford, Gale, vol. ii., p. 590.

construction, or more fortunate position, entirely escaped damage.[1]

In a few days more, the French king, accompanied by the recreant crusaders, left Sicily on his return homewards. The two English princes, with Beatrice and her husband, proceeded to Messina, where they were kindly entertained by Charles of Blois, the King of Sicily, whose wife, Beatrice of Provence, was sister to Queen Eleanora of England, and therefore aunt to the English princess. Although King Charles was the leader of the French desertion, he yet had generosity enough left to patronize those who, more fearless or less prudential, chose to fulfil and carry out their vows.

We may presume that the Lady Beatrice was not sorry to exchange the society of her French relations for that of her own brothers, and of her sister-in-law, Eleanora of Castile, into whose immediate company she was now thrown. The winter months swiftly glided away, but the joyousness of the party was considerably damped by a letter sent by their royal relative, Henry III., to Prince Edward, informing him of the very infirm state of his health, and that all the physicians then with him despaired of his recovery, and urging upon the prince not to go into regions still more remote, unless he should receive more favourable tidings from him. The letter concluded with a promise to send frequent intelligence of how the Most High shall be pleased to deal with him.[2]

However, either these favourable tidings did arrive, or Prince Edward preferred what he considered as a religious duty, to the obligations of filial affection; for, instead of returning home, or even tarrying in Sicily, the first gentle gales of spring were the signal for departure to the Holy

---

[1] The chroniclers say that his ships were saved because he would not consent to barter the cross for barbaric gold.—Chron. Brute, Lambeth MS., No. 99, fol. 37, col.

[2] Rot. claus., 55 H. III., m. 8, dorso. Date, February 6th.

Land. The party set sail on the 15th of March, 1271,
attended by only one thousand troops; and having first
touched at Cyprus, where they were honourably received,
they proceeded to Acres, the ancient Ptolemais, and
arrived on the 21st, just in time to aid the Christian
garrison of the city, which had scarcely strength to defend
itself against the infidels.[1] This city Prince Edward made
his head-quarters,[2] and here he and his companions
remained five full months, whilst at the same time he was
employing emissaries in all directions to ascertain the
condition of the country, the number and position of the
enemy's forces, &c. Here he was joined by about seven
thousand troops, partly Frisons, who had refused to
return the preceding autumn in the general desertion,
and partly the forces of the Templars and Hospitallers,
and such scattered troops of Christians as remained in the
Holy Land,[3] and also by some Cypriote soldiers, whom
their ancient veneration for the English name had induced
to enlist under his standard.[4]

The prince availed himself of this interval to make his
will, appointing his brother-in-law, Lord John of Bretagne, his principal executor.[5]

The expeditions of Prince Edward and Lord John into
Syria were few and unimportant, and as they were not
accompanied by the ladies Eleanora and Beatrice, who
remained in safety behind the walls of Acre, it would be
irrelevant to our subject to enter upon them. Suffice it
to say, that, after a campaign of nearly a year, occupied
by various skirmishes, the result of which is described as
favourable by the English historians,[6] but rather the con-

---

[1] Wikes, Gale, vol. ii., p. 96.   Continuation of Paris, vol. ii., p. 1007.
[2] Chron. Mailros, Gale, vol. i., p. 241.
[3] Michaud, croisades, vol. iii., pp. 91, 92.   [4] Hemingford, ut sup.
[5] Fœdera, vol. i., p. 495. Given also by Sir Harris Nicolas, in his Testamenta vetusta.
[6] A contemporary chronicler goes so far as to assert that he took prisoner
the two sons of the sultan, but that he generously dismissed them without

trary by the French, the expedition was concluded by a truce for ten years, seven weeks, and ten days, with the infidels; stipulating, however, for certain privileges to be extended towards the oriental Christians and the pilgrims, whose devotion led them to that sacred spot.[1]

The Lady Beatrice had resided with her sister-in-law at Acres, nearly eighteen months, when, about the middle of August, 1272, the party began to prepare for their journey homewards. For some unknown reason they now separated. Prince Edmund took the direct route for England, where he arrived unexpectedly in the middle of December;[2] Prince Edward and his train passed through Sicily and Apulia, to Rome,[3] while John and Beatrice returned home by way of Greece.[4] They seem to have tarried in Syria longer than their companions, so long, indeed, that some uneasiness was entertained by their friends in England about their safety; and at the request of the dowager queen Eleanora, Sir Nicolas de Stapleton was allowed to take charge of carl John's estates, whilst his seneschal, John de Maure, undertook a voyage to the Holy Land, to ascertain the fortunes of his absent lord.[5] Early in February, 1273, however, we find them in the Morea, where the Earl of Richmond founded three chaplaincies in connexion with one of his castles in England.[6] Soon afterwards they safely arrived in Bretagne, where they were gladly welcomed by their parents, as well as by the people, to whom the return of the heir of their duchy, after so long an absence, afforded matter of unbounded gratulation;[7] and once more re-united to her

ransom. — Arundel MS., No. 10, f. 113, College of Arms. Also John of London, No. 20, fol. 37, same collection.

[1] Hemingford, Gale, vol. ii., p. 592.
[2] Annals Waverley, Gale, vol. ii., p. 227. Wikes, Ibid., p. 98.
[3] Hemingford and Wikes, ut sup. Knighton, Twysden, col. 2459.
[4] Anselm., hist. geneal., vol. i., p. 488.
[5] Clarkson's Richmond, p. 31.
[6] Lobineau, vol. i., p. 269.
[7] Les grandes chroniques de Bretagne, p. 275.

young family, Beatrice had time to repose after the fatigues of her long journeyings.

Meanwhile, Earl John was occupied in erecting a religious foundation for friars of the Carmelite order, two of whom he had brought with him from Syria. This was the first introduction of this order into France, and probably into Europe. The earl built them a handsome monastery at Ploermul,[1] which he patronized so warmly, that he afterwards chose it as the place of his own interment, and his mausoleum there remains up to the present time.[2] He seems to have imbibed much of the superstition of the age, and the records of his expedition to the East are rather to be found in the relics which he collected, than in the valorous deeds which he performed. Among these relics was a portion of the wood of the true cross, which he had encased in a richly jewelled cross, and always wore about his person.[3]

The next mention we have of the Earl and Countess of Richmond, is in connexion with the coronation of King Edward I. Although Henry III. had died during the time of the Syrian expedition, it was not until the July of the year 1274, that Edward and Eleanora returned to England. John and Beatrice accompanied them; the King and Queen of Scotland were also ready to greet the new made monarch, so that the family circle, which was to be so soon and so fearfully broken in upon, was once more complete. The beauty of the two royal sisters excited universal admiration, as they shone conspicuously amidst the ceremonials of the coronation.[4] These have been already detailed in the previous memoir. The earl

[1] Lobineau, ut sup. Morice, vol. i., p. 197.
[2] Clarkson's Richmond, p. 33.
[3] This precious relic is particularly mentioned in his will. He bequeathed it to his daughter, the nun Eleanora.—Morice, preuves, vol. i., p. 1186.
[4] Matt. Westm., p. 407. Morice, vol. i., p. 204. Cotton MS., Vespas., A. ii., f. 61 b.

and countess remained at London or Windsor, after the departure of the Scotch king and queen, and King Edward confirmed to his brother several of his previously acquired rights to property in England.[1]

Not long afterwards, the melancholy tidings of the decease of Queen Margaret reached the English court, and threw a sudden damp over the joyous festivities. To Beatrice this bereavement must have been peculiarly painful, as she was then in a delicate state of health, owing to the recent birth of her youngest daughter Eleanora, which took place at this time,[2] and it probably had some effect in accelerating her own death. The last record concerning her is an order, dated the 24th of February, 1275, in which the custody of the lands and heirs of John Peynuer are assigned by the king to his " dear sister Beatrice." This order was given from Windsor, where the court was then staying.[3] Beatrice withdrew almost immediately afterwards to Bretagne,[4] probably in compliance with the wishes of earl John, who might hope that the milder air would prove beneficial to her sinking frame. She seems, however, to have felt that his loving care would be in vain; and, as her end rapidly approached, she made her will, and appointed her mother, Queen Eleanora, and her husband, as her executors,[5] but the will itself is not in existence. She died on the 24th of March, 1275, in the thirty-second year of her age, to the great grief of her relatives, and especially of her mother, who, having just lost her eldest daughter, was the more affected by this reiterated blow.[6] The remains of the Lady Beatrice were, at her own request, brought back to England,[7] and in-

[1] Rot. pat., 2 Edw. I., m. 12.   [2] Anselme, hist. geneal., vol. i., p. 448.
[3] Rot. claus., 3 Edw. I., M. 20.   This was, however, but a renewal of the grant made to her several years before by her father.—See rot. pat., 52 H. III., m. 18.
[4] Middlehill MS., No. 1003, fol. 8 b.
[5] Rot. claus., 3 Edw. I., m. 14.   [6] Matt. West., p. 407.
[7] Middlehill MS., ut sup.

terred in an arch in the north wall of the choir, before
the end of the altar in Christ's Church, belonging to the
Cordeliers, or Gray Friars, in Newgate, London,[1] which
she is said to have founded,[2] and which, during the reign
of her father, she had selected for her burial-place ;[3] but
her heart was carried over by her sorrowing husband to
the continent, and deposited in the abbey church of Fontevraud.[4]

Many were the proofs of affection which the Earl of
Richmond bestowed upon the memory of the wife of his
youth. He presented a golden chalice, costly vestments,
jewels and other gifts, to the friars in whose church she
was buried, and also the more substantial gift of £300, to
aid them in repairing and finishing the nave of the church,
and at his own expense he glazed one of its windows.[5]

By an agreement entered into with the canons
of Egleston, in Yorkshire, the year subsequent to her
decease, he arranged that six monks of that convent
should be constantly resident in the Castle of Richmond,
where they were to have apartments provided for them,
and funds for their maintenance, and there they were
daily to chant masses. The first monk was to chant the
mass for the day, if it were a special feast, and if not,
the mass of the Holy Spirit; the second, fourth, and fifth,
that of the Virgin, and the third and sixth were to perform masses for the soul of the Lady Beatrice, and after
the death of her husband, his name was to be united with
hers in the service. John, however, considerately added,
that, if there should be an occasional failure in the per-

[1] Stow's Survey, book iii., p. 129.   Weever's Funeral Monument, p. 387.
[2] By the French chroniclers : see Morice, vol. i., p. 204.   Uredius, vol. i.,
p. 322, and Anselme, vol. i., p. 448.   But some doubt is thrown over the
authenticity of the statement, from the fact that our English chroniclers do
not mention it.
[3] Her son John was afterwards so liberal towards this church, that he is
called its second founder.   Stow's Survey, ut sup.
[4] Morice, preuves, vol. i., p. 1187.   [5] Clarkson's Richmond, p. 33.

formance of these masses, no strict inquiry was to be made about it, but it should be left to the conscience of the officiating priest, provided always the defalcations were not frequent, in which case the bailiffs and abbots were to make inquisition about the affair. In order to prevent the interruption of these religious services in the time of war, the monks were ordered to leave the castle on the approach of tumults, and to retire for safety to their own convent, where their masses were to be repeated as usual.[1] This benefaction was sanctioned by a patent of Edward I., from which it appears that £30. was the annual sum appointed by earl John for the maintenance of the monks.[2] In 1281, he likewise confirmed some grants, previously made to the church of St. Mary's at York, on condition that prayers should be offered for his soul, for that of his dearest consort Beatrice, and their ancestors and heirs. Some years after her death, we find Edward I. making offerings for her soul,[3] and providing handsomely for her faithful attendants.[4]

By the people of Bretagne the youthful countess was greatly regretted; for the prudence and gentleness of her demeanour had secured her their warm affections, though she did not live to become their duchess.[5] Some years after the death of Beatrice, her husband assumed the title of Duke of Bretagne, on the decease of his father; but, although he survived her thirty years, no second partner was allowed either to fill the place, or banish the memory of his English consort. His last will abounds with affectionate remembrances of her: he bequeaths to the convent of Fontevraud, where lies the heart of his " dear companion Beatrice, whose soul God has taken to himself,"

---

1 Harleian MS., 3674, ff. 70, 71.   2 Rot. pat., 3 Edw. I., m. 30.
3 Copy of the alms' roll, 14 Edw. I., p. 1., Middlehill MS., 1003.
4 Copy of the roll of gifts, 6 Edw. I., p. i., Ibid.
5 D'Argentré, hist. de Bretagne, p. 310.   Morice, vol. i., p. 207.   Le Baud., p. 247.

the annual sum of 100 shillings for anniversaries, to be performed for the soul of his " said dear companion" and his own, still fondly associating his name, even after death, with hers. A similar bequest was made to the church of the Grey Friars in London, where the body of Beatrice was deposited,[1] and also to the canons of the Castle of Richmond, and to the friars minor at Richmond; while, with a regard to the poor, which characterized many of the actions of this prince, he ordered numbers of coats and pairs of shoes to be distributed amongst those who resided upon his different estates, to secure their grateful prayers.[2]

When Pope Clement V. came to Lyons in 1305, to receive the triple crown, Duke John joined himself to the countless throngs who flocked thither on the occasion; and, as one of the most distinguished of the French nobles, he was privileged to hold the reins of his holiness' horse. Some of the spectators, with more eagerness than prudence, had mounted an old wall, in order to witness the cavalcade, when it suddenly gave way, and the Duke of Bretagne was one among the many unfortunate persons who were crushed to death by its fall.[3]

It is more than probable that several of Beatrice's children accompanied her to England on her last visit, since they were retained and provided for, even from infancy, by her own family. Queen Eleanora consoled herself for the loss of her daughter, by lavishing kindness upon her grandchildren, and especially on her namesake, the infant Eleanora. It was at her instigation that she took the veil, along with her cousin the Princess Mary, at Ambresbury, where Queen Eleanora herself had retired;[4] and she assigned the manor of Chadworth, in Berkshire, for the support of her grand-daughter.[5] But, on the death of the nun-queen, in 1291, Eleanora was removed to the

[1] Morice, preuves, vol. i., p. 1187. [2] Clarkson's Richmond, p. 33.
[3] Lobineau, vol. i., p. 291. Colbert MS., 6003., Bibl. royale, Paris.
[4] Chron. Anon., Bib. Reg., 13 E. VI., f. 64.
[5] Monast. Ang., vol. ii., p. 338.

abbey of Fontevraud, of which that of Ambresbury was only a branch. Her predilections for her saintly vocation were so strong, that when, on the news of this intended change of residence being announced to her, she felt some apprehension lest her father designed to withdraw her from the cloister altogether, she took the most solemn and binding vows, before she consented to leave her convent, that her life should be devoted to the service of God in some monastery, and that she would not return to the world. She afterwards became abbess of the monastery of Fontevraud, which she ruled with exemplary prudence for thirty-eight years.[1]

The name of the Lady Mary de Bretagne occurs constantly in the early wardrobe accounts of King Edward I., proving that she was educated with his daughters, and treated, in every respect, with the same kindness and distinction as the princesses themselves; she afterwards became the wife of Guy de Chatillon, lord of St. Paul, and mother of a numerous family. One of her daughters, Mary, was married to Aymer de Valence, and was the Countess of Pembroke, celebrated as

> "The sad Chastillon, on her bridal morn,
> That wept her bleeding love,"

her husband being killed at a tournament held on the marriage day.[2]

John, the second son of Beatrice, was also provided for by his English relations. On the death of his elder brother, Arthur, the earldom of Richmond was granted to him, and he was one of the most able and successful generals of Edward I., by whom he was much employed in the Scotch wars,[3] and afterwards in Gascony.[4] He was taken prisoner at the battle of Bannockburn, and

---

[1] Lobineau, vol. i., p. 270.
[2] Clarkson's Richmond, p. 33. Rot. pat., 14 Edw. II., mm. 4, 15.
[3] Trivet, p. 279. See also wardrobe book, 31 Edw. I., No. 17,360, Addit. MSS., Brit. Museum.
[4] Rot. Vasc., 23-31 Edw. I., m. 22.

remained some time in captivity, owing to the unwilling-
ness of the Scots to accept a ransom for him; and, at
length, to obtain his freedom, King Edward was obliged
to release no less a personage than the Queen of Scotland,
Elizabeth, wife of Robert Bruce, and also the Bishop of
Glasgow, who had fallen into his hands.[1]   He reached a
mature old age, and died childless, in 1334.[2]   Henry died
in England about the year 1284; and his uncle, King
Edward, who was then in Wales, paid the expenses of his
funeral, and had masses said for his soul.[3]   Of the other
children, Blanche, the eldest daughter, seems to have resided altogether in Bretagne; she married Philip of Artois,
Lord of Conches.[4]   Peter died young and childless in
1312.[5]   The eldest son, Arthur, succeeded his father as
Duke of Bretagne; he died very young, but his posterity long retained the dukedom.   To one of his remoter
descendants we shall have occasion to introduce our
readers, as the husband of another of the princesses of
England.

[1] Clarkson's Richmond, p. 34.
[2] Dugdale's Baronage, vol. l., p. 62.   Anselme, hist. gen., vol. l., p. 448.
[3] Elemosyna roll, 12, 13 Edw. I., among the Pell Records now in the Rolls'
House.
[4] This lady and her husband were both interred in the church of the
Jacobins, Rue St. Jaques, Paris, where their figures, carved in white marble
upon a tomb of black marble, long created great admiration.   Anselme,
ut sup.
[5] Ibid.

KATHERINE,

THIRD DAUGHTER OF HENRY III.

Born deaf and dumb—tenderness of her parents—death—funeral—silver image on her tomb.

The Princess Katherine was one of those royal daughters of England of whom little remains on record, save her birth and early death. Yet, unwonted interest attaches to her memory, resulting from her extreme infantile loveliness, and from the circumstance that this royal child was born deaf and dumb.[1] She first saw the light in the palace of Westminster on the 25th of November, 1253, being St. Katherine's day; and from this coincidence of her birth she derived her name, which was chosen for her by the queen her mother, and conferred by the Bishop of London.[2] Queen Eleanora was at this time regent of the kingdom, with her brother-in-law, the Earl of Cornwall, during the king's absence in Gascony; and in one of the State mandates, issued by her in the king's name, when her baby was scarcely a month old, she alluded to its extraordinary beauty. She ordered large quantities of provision of all sorts to be conveyed to Westminster against the purification of the queen, of " a certain *beautiful* daughter who is recently born."[3] This feast was to

---

[1] Paris, vol. ii., p. 879.   [2] Ibid.

[3] If the hilarity of the festival is to be estimated by the quantities of provision, it certainly was a most joyous one; for 14 wild boars, 24 swans, 135 rabbits, 250 partridges, 1650 fowls, 50 hares, 250 wild ducks, 36 female geese, and 61,000 eggs, are among the articles provided. Rot. claus., 38 H. III., m. 15 dorso.

be celebrated on St. Edward's day, January 5th, 1254,
and the king had commanded a large assembly of the
magnates of the land, to congratulate his queen on this
joyous occasion, and a store of the best possible wines to
be sent in readiness.[1]

When her infant was but a few months old, Queen
Eleanora had to leave England, to join the king in Gascony.
Before her departure, however, she took the little princess
to Windsor, and left her under the care of two faithful
nurses, called Agnes and Avisa,[2] to be kept with the other
royal children there.

The king and queen did not return to England until the
commencement of the year 1255, so that Katherine was
more than a year old before her father saw her; but she
was his youngest child, born long after any of the others;
and, even at that early period, her infantile charms greatly
endeared her to him. In the State records, we discover
traces of the preponderance of his affection for this darling
child. By an order dated from Merton, April 2nd, beautiful gold cloths were to be bought, with borders embroidered with the king's coat of arms, and to be made
ready against the king's arrival in London, that he might
offer them in Westminster cathedral for Katherine, the
king's daughter, and his other children; but the name of
Katherine *alone* is specified.[3] It is probable that the
melancholy consciousness of her infirmity had already
reached the hearts of her parents; and that, therefore,
they considered offerings more especially necessary on her
behalf.

In the following autumn, the health of the princess beginning to decline, she was removed, for the benefit of a
change of air, to Swallowfield, in Berkshire, where she
was placed under the care of Emma St. John, lady of

---

[1] Rot. claus., 38 H. III., m. 14.   [2] Rot. lib., 41 H. III., m. 1.
[3] Rot. claus., 39 H. III., m. 14.

Swallowfield. Whilst there, a little kid was ordered to be taken in the royal forests, and brought to her, probably, as a playmate.[1] At first, she rallied considerably, and was so far recovered, that a very favourable report of her was given to the king. Before winter, however, she was sent back to Windsor. In the spring of 1256, she was again taken ill; and such was her father's anxiety about her, that, during one of his temporary absences, he commanded an express messenger to be sent by the queen to bring him news of her. The child again rallied, and, in the joy of his heart, Henry ordered "a good robe of the king's gift" to be delivered to the queen's messenger, who brought "good tidings of the convalescence of Catherine, the king's daughter,"[2] and also that a "silver image, made after the likeness of a woman," and of the size of two other similar figures, which adorned the shrine of St. Edward in Westminster Abbey, should be made as an offering in behalf of "Katherine, the king's daughter, lately sick."[3] After this, we find orders for her expenses,[4] and for wine and other necessaries, not only for her use, but for that of several other children who were there as her companions.[5] Robert Russell, a confidential servant of the queen, was charged with the provision of all that could contribute to the comfort of the little princess. But no cares availed to rescue her from an early grave. She died in the castle of Windsor about the 3rd of May, in the year 1257, at the age of three years and a half. The following quaint couplet was written as a sort of epitaph upon her, by worthy old Fuller :—

Wak't from the wombe, she on this world did peep,
Dislik't it, clos'd her eyes, fell fast asleep.[6]

The death of the little fairy girl, who had twined herself

[1] Rot. claus., 39 H. III., m. 5.
[2] Rot. claus., 40 H. III., m. 13.   [3] Ibid.
[4] Rot. lib., 41 H. III., mm. 10, 14. Rot. claus., 56 H. III., m. 13. Rot. exitûs, 41 H. III. See preface to Devon's issue roll, Edward III., p. 28.
[5] Rot. claus., 41 H. III., m. 14.   [6] Fuller's Worthies, vol. ii., p. 60.

so closely round their hearts, was passionately regretted by both her parents. Queen Eleanora refused all human consolation; and her poignant sorrow brought on a serious attack of illness, that, for awhile, baffled all the powers of medicine: for the seat of her malady was an anguished heart.[1] The king himself, distressed at the indisposition of his queen, harassed with state troubles occasioned by the Welsh incursions, and mourning for his dead infant, was seized with a tertian fever, from which he suffered many days.[2]

The last offices of affection were performed by the king in a manner that testified his love for his daughter. He dismissed her nurses with a present equal to £100 of our money.[3] Her obsequies were performed with much splendour, under the superintendence of the king's almoner, at a cost of £51. 12s. 4d.;[4] and her father ordered a brass image, richly gilt, to be constructed, that it might be placed over the tomb, in Westminster, where she was buried. The preparing of it was entrusted to Master Simon de Welles, and he came to Westminster to commence operations. But the king changed his mind, and determined that a statue of solid silver should be made, to recall more worthily to his mind the features of his little dumb girl. Accordingly, Master Simon's expenses were paid him, and he was dismissed; while William of Gloucester, the king's goldsmith, was charged with the manufacture of the silver image, which was erected at a cost of seventy marks, or £700.[5] The father's love extended, too,

---

[1] Paris, vol. ii., p. 949.
[2] Chron. John Oxford, Cotton MS., Nero D. II., f. 229, col. 3.
[3] Rot. lib., 41 H. III., m. 1.
[4] Devon's Excerpta, ut sup.
[5] Rot. lib., 41 H. III., mm. 4 and 5. Stow, in his Survey, book vi., p. 8, and others, have intimated that *both* the images alluded to were set up over Katherine's tomb; a close examination of the entries on the liberate roll, however, proves the contrary; for, although Welles was ordered to be paid for the brass-gilt image as fast as the king's treasurer saw him progress with it, till the total sum of forty marks had been discharged (m. 5); yet, by a

beyond the tomb; for he gave 50s. a-year to Richard, the
hermit of Charing, as long as he lived, that he might support a chaplain to pray daily in the chapel of the hermitage
for the soul of Katherine, the king's dear daughter.[1]　The
remains of the princess now rest, along with those of two
of her infant brothers, beneath a small raised tomb in the
area or passage leading round the royal chapel, between
those of St. Blaye and St. Benedict, in Westminster Abbey;[2]
but nothing remains of the monument raised by parental
affection to her memory.

subsequent entry, it appears that there was really paid only five and a half marks
for the expenses of conveying himself and his tools to Westminster for the
image he *was* to have made, (m. 4) thus plainly intimating that he did not
actually make it; and the order was immediately afterwards transferred to
the goldsmith; William of Gloucester having failed to account for the large
sums he had received for this and other purposes, his executors were afterwards summoned to a severe account for the same.—Rot. claus., 1 Edward I.,
m. 11.

[1] Rot. lib., 41 H. III., m. 5.　Rot. exit., 42 H. III., Pasch.　The orders for
its payment constantly occur on the issue rolls.

[2] Stow's Survey, book vi., p. 17.

ELEANORA,

ELDEST DAUGHTER OF EDWARD I.

Sources of information—Birth of Eleanora—Removed from Windsor Castle
—Birth of her brothers—Her parents go to the Holy Land—Royal nursery
—Return of the king and queen—Death of Prince Henry—Negociations
for Eleanora's marriage with Alphonso of Aragon—Her position—Retinue
—Education—Library of Edward I.—Eleanora visits Wales—Marriage
embassies—Betrothal—Wars between the King of Aragon and Charles of
Anjou—Eleanora's departure for Spain postponed—Her journeys and oblations—Wardrobe — King and queen abroad — Their presents to their
daughters—Eleanora's letters—Her kindness to her attendants—Return
of her parents—The Aragonese marriage broken off—Eleanora's domestic
life—Influence with her father—Henry Duke of Bar visits England—
Woos the princess—Their marriage—Henry leaves her in England—She
joins him—Duke of Brabant killed at her wedding tournament—Birth of
Eleanora's children—Her husband's war with France—He is taken prisoner
—Eleanora visits her father at Ghent—Curious scene there—Her death—
Burial—Her husband and children.

In commencing the memorials of the daughters of our
first Edward, we enter upon a period in which a larger
number of records bearing upon the domestic history of the
royal daughters of England are extant, than in any other
period in our early history. It is true that, were the contemporary chroniclers *only* to be consulted, they would
present us with scarcely a fact beyond the dates of their
birth, marriage, and death. It is to the State-rolls, to the
collections of royal letters, and, above all, to the wardrobe
accounts,[1] that we have had recourse to fill up the utter

---

[1] As frequent reference will be made to these documents, a few words
about their general character may not be irrelevant here. In the time of Edward I., they contained accounts not only of the expenditure for dress, but of
all the private expenses of the royal family; and many disbursements for the

blanks which, but for the existence of these precious relics of antiquity, would have been inevitable in the biographies of these princesses.

Eleanora, the eldest daughter of Edward I., was not born the daughter of a king, for she first saw the light during the life-time of her grandfather, Henry III. The precise date of her birth is uncertain, but it must have been during the spring of the year 1264. Early in that year, Prince Edward, accompanied by his wife, Eleanora of Castile, returned to England after a short absence; and, with a band of troops which he had collected while abroad, he garrisoned the castle of Windsor, which he destined as the residence of his consort; and here it was that Eleanora was born.[1] She was the eldest child of the prince; the birth of his eldest son, John, being indubitably ascertained to have taken place at Windsor Castle towards the latter end of the year 1266, since entries occur in the liberate rolls for the expenses of Eleanora of Castile during her confinement there.[2]

The infant career of the young princess was a troublous

public service of the State also were made through the medium of the comptroller of the wardrobe. Gradually, however, they became less minute in their details, and assumed more of the character of official documents, their place as domestic records being superseded by the "privy-purse accounts." Of these but few are in preservation. Only one or two wardrobe records have been published. The remainder are principally in the Queen's Remembrancer Office, but there are a few in the Tower and the other record offices; whilst a considerable number, which were purloined by Craven Ord, when he had the custody of the Remembrancer Office, are now scattered abroad in public libraries or private collections. So little regard was, however, paid to such records at one time, that numbers of them have been allowed to decay, or were sold by the government, or have even been used as waste parchment.

[1] Rishanger cont. Paris, vol. ii., p. 993. The chronicle of Peterburgh, Addit. MS. 6913, fol. 220, assigns 1269 as the date of her birth, but this is impossible, supposing her to be, as she is always designated, the eldest daughter of Edward I.

[2] Rot. lib., 53 H. III., m. 1. These orders are also found in the Exchequer liberate roll of the 53rd of Henry III., easter; the date is confirmed by entries in the Chancery liberate roll of the 54th of Henry III., m. 10, ordering the payment of the arrears of a salary of £20 a-year, which the king gave to the valet who brought him news of Prince John's birth, and which, in December, 1269, amounted to £60, being the sum due for three years, thus affording indirect evidence that his birth took place three years before. The same date is also given in the chronicle of Winchester, Cotton. MS. Domitian, xiii., f. 57 b.

one; within a few weeks of her birth the Castle of Windsor fell into the hands of the barons, and her father himself was soon afterwards taken prisoner at the battle of Lewes, which was fought on the 14th of May, 1264.[1]   It appears, however, that the infant princess was still residing with her mother in Windsor Castle; for, about a month after the battle of Lewes, King Henry, then a captive in the hands of the Montfort faction, sent a strict mandate to his daughter-in-law, that she, with her infant daughter, her family, and goods, should leave the castle, and repair to Westminster, till further orders; and, lest she, as a good wife, should be unwilling to take such a step without the consent of her husband, he engages to excuse her with the prince.[2]   The removal to Westminster was accordingly effected; and here the mother and child seem to have remained until the battle of Evesham restored their royal relatives to an independent position.   After this, Windsor Castle was again, as we have formerly seen it during the early part of the reign of Henry III., the nursery of the infant hopes of England; and, during the few succeeding years, two little princes, named John and Henry, became the companions of their sister. They were provided with a suitable establishment, their principal gouvernante being a French woman called Marie de Valoynes.[3]   An entry occurs in 1269 for wine,[4] and another for 400 pounds of wax, 20 pounds of pepper, 20

[1] Cont. Paris, vol. ii., pp. 995-6.
[2] " The king to Alianora, consort of Edward, his first-born son, greeting: Since we will by all means that you retire from our castle of Windsor, where you now abide, we command that you depart from the said castle, with your daughter, John of Westminster your seneschal, William Charles your knight, your two damsels, the rest of your family, your harness, and your goods, and come to Westminster, to stay there until we shall order otherwise.   And this you shall by no means omit, as you love us, our honour, and your own.   Wherefore we engage that we will excuse and hold you clear to the said Lord Edward, your husband.   We therefore receive you, your aforesaid daughter, John, William, two damsels, and family, along with your harness, in safe and secure conduct by these our present letters patent.   Witness the king at St. Paul's, London, the 18th day of June."—Fœdera, vol. i., p. 443.   Rot. pat., 48 H. III., m. 11.
[3] Rot. lib., 54 H. III., mm. 9, 11.   [4] Rot. lib., scac., 53 H. III., Pasch.

pounds of cummin, 10 of ginger, and five of saffron, the gift of the king to the children of his eldest son, then at Windsor,[1] as also frequent payments of moneys for their expenses.[2]

The following year the parents of Eleanora set forth on their expedition to the Holy Land, leaving their youthful family in the care, not of their grandfather, King Henry, but of Richard, King of the Romans, or, in case of his death, of his son, Henry of Germany.[3] Strong presumptive evidence is afforded by this arrangement of the low estimate in which Edward held the character of his father, who would naturally have been chosen as the guardian of the children, had not his feebleness and vacillation caused even his own son to prefer the able and vigilant tutorship of a more distant relative. During the period of their parents' absence, we lose sight of the royal children, since they were removed from the king's protection, and placed in one of the numerous residences of their great-uncle, King Richard.[4]

In 1272 Prince John, who had just attained his sixth year, sickened and died,[5] and his death was speedily followed by that of his royal grandfather, Henry III. On this event, which rendered the young Prince Henry heir apparent to the throne, he along with his sister was immediately removed to the castle of Windsor.[6] A fragmentary wardrobe roll of the 1st and 2nd of Edward I.[7] brings them again in an interesting manner before our notice, and enables us to correct, on authentic evidence, a misapprehension that has existed as to the state of the royal family at this period.

[1] Rot. claus., 54 H. III., m. 11, dated Clarendon, December 7th.
[2] Rot. lib., 53 H. III., mm. 1, 8, 12, 13. Ibid., 54 H. III., m. 11 ; 55, m. 20.
[3] Fœdera, vol. i., p. 484.
[4] Cotton MS., Cleop., A 1, f. 194 b.
[5] Chron. Winch., Cott. MS., Domit. xiii., f. 57 b.
[6] Rot. exitûs et rot. lib. scac., 1 Edw. I., Pasch. Rot. lib., 2 Edward I., m. 2, ap Turr., Lond.
[7] No more definite reference can be given to this document than that it is one among the yet uncalendered and unnumbered wardrobe fragments in the Queen's Remembrancer. It is a small roll, in tolerable condition.

It has been generally supposed that *both* the infant sons
of Edward I. died during his absence from England ; but
the mention of Prince Henry on this roll as the companion
of his sister Eleanora, down to the date of his funeral,
which did not take place till December, 1274, proves that
he survived the return of his parents a few months.[1]   Another child, called "Britton," also had a place in the royal
nursery, but who he was is now impossible to determine ; he
was, however, treated in every respect like the royal children.
From the above named roll, we learn that the widowed
queen, Eleanora of Provence, was a frequent companion of
her young grandchildren.[2]   About Easter, 1274, the queen-
mother removed with Eleanora and Henry to Kennington,
and the following week she took them a short tour through
Isleworth, London, and Stratford, to Havering, but in the
beginning of May they returned again to Windsor. In
June they went to Lutgershall. Several notices of purchases for them occur while they remained there—two glass
cups for Henry and Eleanora, besides zones or belts, and
feather capes ; sugar and oil were sent to Lutgershall from
London for their use.[3]

Preparations were now making for the return of King
Edward ; and Eleanora of Provence hastened on to Canterbury, to meet her son. The children followed her, and the
whole family proceeded as far as Rochester. On August
2nd, 1274, the king and queen once again landed in England,

[1] The generally believed account that Edward received tidings of the death
of *both* his sons, whilst he was in Sicily in 1272, is still farther contradicted
by a document printed in the Fœdera, vol. i., pt. ii., p. 508, relating to a
negociation for Henry's marriage with Joanna, daughter of the Earl of
Navarre, bearing date November 30, 1273, which proves that he was living
at that period, which was after Edward's departure from Sicily.

[2] Though the usual title of mother of the king is not given in this roll to
Eleanora of Provence, who is simply styled "the queen," she must certainly
be the person meant, since all our chroniclers agree that queen Eleanora of
Castile only returned to England at the same time with the king. This
style is easily accounted for when we remember that Edward's mother had
been for many years the only queen in England, and the absence of his wife
seemed to render unnecessary any distinction of epithet.

[3] Rot. lib. scac., 2 Edw. I., Pasch. Wardrobe roll, ut sup.

and joyous indeed was the meeting with their long parted parent and children; the Princess Eleanora was now in her eleventh year, and therefore quite old enough to hail her parents with delight, which would be increased by the arrival also of a baby brother, the young Prince Alphonso, who was born during the preceding year, and who became her constant playmate and companion.[1] The royal family now hastened to Windsor, to prepare for the ensuing coronation.   Orders were given for the robes of the king's children against this festival, and also for roses and other flowers to be bought for decorations.

The partially obliterated state of the roll above quoted prevents the elucidation of more than a few particulars of the royal nursery; there are frequent entries of payments for milk, beer, sugar, spices, oil of saffron, and violets, especially for the use of Eleanora.   The wardrobe entries are not numerous; two dozen golden studs were bought to adorn her robe and those of her brother; shoes with clasps, and worsted hose are named; also furred gloves, having the arms of England wrought on the thumb; one ounce of silk, of different colours, was purchased to make a collar for Eleanora; robes were ordered against the Christmas feasts, and other robes were sent to be shorn.   Shoes were also provided for the nurses of Henry, Eleanora, and Britton.   Mention is repeatedly made of women employed in fetching and carrying water for their baths, and in warming the same.

Young as they were, they were already taught to perform the accustomed services of religion.   They attended service at the great festivals of the church, and paid their offerings regularly: the sum generally bestowed was 4d.

The month of October was spent by the children with their grandmother at her dower residence of Guildford;[2] for, notwithstanding the return of their parents, she was unwilling to relinquish the cheerful society of her juvenile charge.

During this year, the little Alphonso, who was too young to share in the journeys of the other children, resided exclusively at Windsor, and Eleanora frequently stayed there with him,[1] even when Prince Henry was with his parents at court.

As winter advanced, the sympathies of the royal family were deeply excited by the declining health of young Henry. Every means that could be devised were put into operation for his recovery; a number of poor widows were hired to perform vigils and offer up prayers for his amendment; his measure was taken in wax, and sent to all the neighbouring shrines to be burnt, in order to propitiate the saints.[2] Among the numerous remedies applied, two sheep-skins are named, which were bought to be laid over his body, according to the favourite theory of the Galens of the day, who considered that the application of animal heat externally was calculated to promote it internally. But these sedulous cares were vain, for the prince died shortly after at Merton, where he was then staying with his sister and Britton.[3] On the Wednesday after his death they returned to London, and thence to Windsor.[4]

Although the princess Eleanora was now scarcely eleven years old, her hand had long since been plighted in marriage. During a visit paid by King Edward, when on his return

[1] Rot. lib. scac., 2 Edw. I., Pasch. Orders for their expenses while there occur sometimes individually, but oftener unitedly.

[2] The custom of burning the measure of a person in wax is frequently alluded to in ancient domestic records. Instances of it may be found in the issue roll, 34 Edw. I., Easter; in the wardrobe-book of the 28th of Edw. I., printed for the Society of Antiquaries, pp. 97 and 367, and also in that of the 13th, which now forms No. 65 of the miscellaneous rolls in the Tower, f. 19 b. The measures of the king, queen, and their children are said to have been taken, and burnt at a neighbouring shrine as an almsgift of the king. It must have been either a rude image in wax of the person, or, more probably, a wax taper of the same height that was thus consumed.

[3] An order for a marble tomb for him occurs in the issue roll, 3 Edward I., Mich., dated December 7th, (1274).

[4] Rot. lib., 3 Edward I., m. 5. Rot. claus., 5, m. 5, contains an order for bulls and wild cows, to be taken in the park of Windsor, and given for the use of the king's children there.

from the Holy Land, to the Spanish relations of his wife, he
entered into a bond of alliance and amity with Pedro, the
infant of Aragon, by forming a prospective matrimonial
connexion between Alphonso, the young son of Peter, and
his daughter Eleanora. Oaths were taken by both parties
for the fulfilment of the marriage as soon as the young
betrothed had arrived at a proper age, and the dower to be
assigned to Eleanora was arranged with all due formality;[1]
whatever her father chose to bestow upon her was to be
increased a third part by her husband.[2] The negociations
were prolonged during the succeeding years;[3] so that, from
the earliest period at which Eleanora could be conscious of
such a position, she was taught to regard herself as the
plighted wife of the Spanish prince.

In England her situation was no unimportant one. Prince
Alphonso early gave symptoms of that delicacy of constitu-
tion which had already consigned to the grave his two elder
brothers; and, fearful of the mischiefs of a disputed succession, the king settled the kingdom on his daughter Eleanora,
in default of male heirs; so that, until the birth of Prince
Edward, afterwards Edward II., which did not take place
until Eleanora was twenty years of age, the life of a sickly
boy was alone placed between her and the reversionary crown
of England. · Accordingly, we find that, as early as the year
1277, when she was only thirteen years old, she had a complete suite of attendants, consisting, among others, of her
chamberlain, keeper of the hall, groom of the bedchamber,
cook, salterer, shieldman, and sumpterer, or driver of the
sumpter-horse, beside boys and damsels; all these were, of
course, clothed and salaried by the king.[4]

---

[1] Fœdera, vol. i., pt. i., p. 506.   Cotton MS., Vesp., c. xii., f. 45.   This
MS. contains copies by a contemporaneous hand of several of the documents
relating to this marriage, along with many others on Spanish affairs.
[2] Fœdera, vol. i., p. 506.   [3] Ibid., p. 521.
[4] Wardrobe roll, 5th Edw. I., No. 2261, Queen's Remembrancer. Wardrobe book, 6th Edw. I., ff, 7, 19, 29 b, 40, 42, 43, Miscel. roll, Tower, No. 44.
Wardrobe roll, 6 Edw. I., sold by auction by Messrs. Puttick and Simpson,
March, 1849.

Privileges were also accorded to her, on account of her superiority in age to the rest of the royal children; for a difference of at least eight years existed between her and her next sister, Joanna. While, therefore, they remained principally at Windsor or the Tower, she was allowed to perambulate the country, sometimes in company with the king and queen, but occasionally attended only by her own servants, and to take up her residence in one or other of the numerous castles and halls belonging to the king. In the month of April, 1278, she removed from Marlborough to Devizes, where she joined the queen her mother. A suite of apartments in the great tower of the castle was appropriated for her use,[1] but she does not seem to have remained there long. In May she went with her mother from Winchester to London; her equipments being carried with her in two carts; and thence they both proceeded to Glastonbury, whose stately abbey was a frequent temporary abode of our earlier kings.

The employments of the royal ladies are less easily traced out than their peregrinations. Yet, an entry that occurs of the large sum of £4. 3s., paid for a pocket breviary for the queen, proves that Eleanora of Castile was able to read; and the tablets which she always had carried about with her, along with her embroidery frame,[2] would almost afford intimation that she could write too; though, as this is an accomplishment which has not been certainly ascertained to have been possessed by any of our Plantagenet kings earlier than Richard II., perhaps the premises may be considered too slight to draw from them such an inference. A few years afterwards the princess also had writing-tablets for her own use.[3]

If, however, the amount of education bestowed on King

---

[1] See rot. lib., 10 Edw. I., m. 3, where orders occur for sundry repairs to be made about the castle.
[2] Wardrobe book, 6 Edw. I., ff. 8, 12.
[3] Ibid., 14 Edw. I., f. 11 b, Miscel. roll, Tower, No. 66.

Edward's daughters is to be estimated by the modicum afforded to his son, it will not be rated very highly. Prince Edward was sixteen years old before a primer was bought for him.[1] Nor were the inducements to learn to read very strong. In 1296, the royal library consisted only of three volumes, the preciousness of which may be inferred from the fact that they were kept with the jewels; one was a book of chronicles; another a copy of the metrical " Roman de Guillaume le conquerant,"[2] which was bequeathed to the king by his mother, Queen Eleanora of Provence;[3] and a third was the work of Palladius Rutilus, on agriculture.[4] In 1300 the library had received several additions—a book of organ chants, a history of the chivalric deeds of the far-famed Tancred, the hero of the first crusade, and two others of a religious character.[5]

But to return to the princess, whom we left in the company of her mother. Wherever the queen went, she distributed alms among the poor, and Eleanora also gave 10s. in a similar manner, a large sum when taken in comparison with her other personal expenses, which, during the month of June, amounted only to 14s. 9d.[6] Part of the summer of 1278 Eleanora passed at Guildford,[7] but towards the winter she retired to Marlborough Castle, where she spent the Christmas, and remained till the 2nd of March following,

[1] Wardrobe book, 28 Edw. I., printed for the Society of Antiquaries, p. 55; the price paid was £2.

[2] The only copy of this romance now known to exist is in the Bibliothèque du roi, Paris, of which a description is given by M. Paulin Paris, in his work on the romances of that library. In spite of its captivating title, however, the romance is a string of absurd fables, valueless for any historical purpose.

[3] Wardrobe account, 27 Edw. I., No. 2106, Queen's Remembrancer.

[4] Invent. Garderobæ, precipuè de jocalibus. 24 Edw. I., No. 2343, Queen's Rememb. " Unus liber qui incipit ' prologus in cronica'—Unus liber de Romains qui incipit ' Crestiens se voet entremettre'—unus liber parvus qui incipit ' Paladi Rutuli.' " Anything like a comprehensive title-page being unknown at this period, it was usual to designate manuscripts by the initial words. " Palladius Rutilius de re rusticâ" was first published in 1496, under the patronage of Hercules d'Este, and it has passed through many subsequent editions.

[5] Wardrobe book, 28 Edw. I., p. 349.

[6] Ibid., 6 Edw. I., ff. 21 b, 23.   [7] Ibid., f. 29 b.

under the custody of a trusty servant of the king's, named
Henry de Bernham, who received the then exorbitant wage
of 7½d. a day for taking charge of the princess.[1] After this
period, however, we find her more frequently at court.

The wars which King Edward was carrying on with the
Welsh, necessitated his paying frequent visits to Wales, to
superintend the operations of the campaign. Notwithstanding the sternness and even cruelty which marked some of the
public acts of this monarch, his domestic character, if we
except occasional fits of passion, stands out unblemished,
and his affection for his wife and daughters led him to desire
their society, whenever it was practicable without the incur-
rence of personal risk to themselves. Accordingly, in the
year 1282, when he went on his Welsh expedition, the queen
and elder princesses accompanied him. Eleanora had recently acquired a companion in her sister Joanna, commonly
called of Acres, from the place of her birth, who, having
been educated by her grandmother, Joanna Queen of Castile,
had returned to England.

The king's head-quarters were fixed at the castle of
Rhudlan, in Flintshire, which he had strongly fortified, and
where his children principally resided, while the queen occasionally accompanied him farther into the interior of the
country. They held their court, it would seem, with some
degree of state; for mention is made of their chapel, the
equipments of which they had brought with them from
England; and they were also attended by many servants.
Towards the conclusion of the campaign, they returned, by
way of Flint and Chester, to Macclesfield, a journey of sixty
miles, which occupied them four days, as appears from the
entries of the expenses for carrying their *harness*, as their
wardrobe and baggage were politely termed [2]—a strong
contrast to the present rapidity of royal travelling.

[1] Wardrobe fragment, 7 Edw. I., Queen's Rememb.
[2] Rot. Garderobæ Walliæ, 10 and 11 Edw. I , Rot. Misc., No. 57, ap Torr.,
Lond.

The Princess Eleanora had now reached the period at which a royal *fiancée* usually becomes a wife, and the arrangements for her marriage were renewed by her elect bridegroom with some vigour. The young prince had become heir apparent to the crown of Aragon; the death of his grandfather in 1276 having placed his father, Pedro III., on the throne. In January, 1281, ambassadors were sent over to Aragon by King Edward, to treat on the subject of the marriage, and Eleanora herself issued her letters patent, in which she styles herself, "We, Eleanora, daughter of the most illustrious King of England," expressing her belief in the lawfulness and validity of the previous contract between herself and "the noble man, the infant Alfonso, son and heir of the illustrious King of Aragon," and constituting, by express consent of her parents, John de Vescy and Anthony Bek her special procurators, to arrange the ceremonials of the marriage, and to stipulate for the amount of her dower. The document concludes thus: "And we signify this to all whom it concerns by these presents; to which, since we have not a seal of our own, we have requested and caused to be affixed the seals of the most serene Lady Eleanora, by God's grace Queen of England, our grandmother, and of the venerable fathers in Christ, the lords Roger Bishop of London and John Bishop of Rochester."[1]

At her desire, the seals of these prementioned persons were actually appended: the letter is dated from Guildford, February 15, 1281.[2] The princess was at the time on a visit to her grandmother at her dower palace. The dowager-queen seems to have been warmly attached to her grandchild, so much so, indeed, that she, in conjunction with the queen, her daughter-in-law, did their utmost to persuade King Edward to postpone the match, on the pretext that the princess was still young—not a very plausible or consistent one, as urged by them, since Eleanora had completed

---

[1] Royal letters, Tower, No. 1112.   [2] Fœdera, vol. i., p. 614.

her seventeenth year, and both these queens had been married when considerably younger.[1] They induced the king, however, to make an effort to protract the period of separation.

Vescy and Bek were despatched accordingly to Spain; but with instructions likely to prove very embarrassing to ambassadors who had an impatient bridegroom to deal with; for although they were authorized to confirm the marriage treaty, yet they were commissioned to procure the delay of two years and a half, or at least of one year and a half, before the princess was to be sent over to Spain,[2] "because," says the monarch, "the queen her mother and our dearest mother are unwilling to grant that she may pass over earlier, on account of her tender age; and this reason you can assign to the king or his son."

The following spring some objection to the marriage was raised by King Edward, the nature of which is not stated, but it was noticed with vehement surprise in a letter from the Aragonese monarch, who rather haughtily reproached him for his inconstancy.[3] Edward's desire, however, was to retard and not to dissolve the connexion. About the same time, he received a complimentary epistle from his elect son-in-law, in which, though, according to etiquette, he refrained from any distinct allusions to his *fiancée*, he expressed great interest in the health and prosperous state of the king, the lady queen his consort, and their children, and declared how jocund and blithe he had recently been made by the receipt of letters from Edward, containing good tidings concerning them.[4]

The procurators appointed by the King of Aragon were the Archbishop of Taragona and the Bishop of Valencia;

---

[1] Strickland's Queens of England, vol. ii., pp. 68 and 148.
[2] " Two years, if you conveniently can; or, if not, one year from the next feast of All Saints"—that is, November 1st, and the letter was written in June.—Fœdera, vol. i., p. 593.
[3] Fœdera. vol. i., p. 606—date, May 1st, 1282.
[4] Royal Letter, No. 2090.

they communicated with the English ambassadors, and terms were arranged, which met with the full and formal concurrence of both monarchs, as well as of the young betrothed. These were, that an annual dower of 3000 livres Tournois should be assigned to Eleanora. As security for this, four towns were granted to her, with all their rents and revenues, "and with all the Jews and Saracens therein dwelling or thenceforth to dwell," who, it may be concluded by this singular clause, were given up to her tender mercies, to do as she pleased with them, and these towns she was to possess in full and entire dominion : and, in case of her surviving her husband, whether she remained in Aragon or not, she was to retain possession of the said towns, and of two others assigned in addition, until the revenues of them had completely paid off the sum of 40,000 livres Tournois, which her father gave her as her fortune.[1]

The preliminaries being thus settled, the very same day, August 15th, 1282, the marriage was performed by proxy, John de Vescy acting as proxy for the bride, and promising to deliver up her person in due time to her husband. Of these espousals, James, infant of Aragon, younger brother of the bridegroom, sent a formal notification to King Edward.[2]

It is scarcely probable that Eleanora had ever beheld the prince to whom her hand was now plighted by engagements so solemn, and which only waited her journey to Spain for their consummation ; nor is it at all more likely that any confidential intercourse could take place between them in writing, seeing that the love-letters would probably have to

[1] Fœdera, vol. i., p. 613. Cotton MS., Vesp., C. xii., f. 46.
[2] Fœdera, vol. i., p. 615. The documents in the Fœdera relating to this marriage, are taken from an ancient volume in the Chapter House at Westminster, entitled Liber munimentorum. In the index to this part of the volume is a comical figure of a man on horseback, galloping at terrific speed, with long locks streaming behind, and bearing in his hand a banner, with a castle, the arms of Castile, delineated upon it. Beneath the figure is a memorandum that this mark was affixed to the chest where all these deeds were kept, to distinguish it.

be penned by one grave, monkish secretary, and, it may be, deciphered by another. Her cheerful acquiescence in the arrangements made for her must, therefore, have been the result of those notions of passive obedience in reference to matrimonial affairs which then pervaded the females of all classes, but particularly those of the higher ranks, when such a thing as consulting the heart on the subject was never dreamed of.

A sudden change, however, took place in the prospects of the princess, just when she was on the point of leaving England for her new home. To a clear comprehension of this a brief digression will be necessary, which must commence with a glance into the state of the kingdom of Sicily. The wrongs endured by this land of poetry and song, when the tyranny of Rome and the ambition of France forced it to submit to the hated yoke of the French, are well known, and will ever be deeply stamped on the memory by their terrible avenging, when the galled and enslaved Sicilians gave fearful vent to their long-pent wrath in the memorable " vespers of Palermo," in which almost all the French on the island perished in one terrific slaughter. After the first outburst of excitement, the people saw the necessity of seeking a protector against the vengeance of France; and Peter of Aragon, who had married Constance, daughter of their former king, Manfred, was naturally resorted to as their most suitable guardian. His ambition was fired by the prospect of uniting the crown of Sicily to that of Aragon; he set sail forthwith, was welcomed with the most enthusiastic acclamations, and crowned at Palermo, amidst all the vehement exultation of a brave people freed by their own exertions from a foreign bondage.

But Charles of Anjou, the disinherited king, was a near relation and intimate friend of Edward I., for he had married Beatrice of Provence, the king's maternal aunt;[1] and it

[1] L'art de verifier, vol. vi., p. 529; vol. xviii., p. 242.

will be remembered that, on his voyage to and return from the Holy Land, Edward had been hospitably entertained by his uncle, the king of Sicily, and for his young cousin Charles, Prince of Salerno, he had formed a sincere attachment. He could not, therefore, regard with indifference the recent transactions, and policy combined with feeling to prevent his drawing more closely the ties that already bound him to Pedro of Aragon ; although his desire to secure so suitable a settlement for his daughter, and some regard to the obligations to which he stood pledged, precluded any sudden disruption of them.

During the absence of Pedro in Sicily, his wife, Queen Constance, wrote to the English king, earnestly entreating that her young daughter-in-law might be immediately sent over, and also requesting his active interference on behalf of Aragon in the impending struggle. Edward's reply, which bears date January 12th, 1283, from the Castle of Rhudlan, was written with considerable coldness : he positively declined sending the princess at present, alleging the Welsh war, upon which he was then engaged, as his excuse ; and adding that it would be impossible for her to leave England before the beginning of the following year ; and as to the queen's request that he would impede the King of France in any attempted attack upon her lands, he reminded her of the ties of blood and homage by which he was bound to Philip, and refused to do anything that might justly provoke his indignation.[1]

In truth, Edward had already too much upon his hands to render it safe or prudent to excite any commotion against himself in the mind of a monarch who, beside the influence he possessed over the English king by the inextricable meshes of the feudal relationship in which he held him involved, could at any moment have inflicted great injury upon him by a vigorous assault on his continental possessions. These

[1] Fœdera, vol. i., p. 625. Royal Letters, No. 1648, Tower.

Edward was not now in a condition to defend; and it was one branch of the tactics of this able monarch to secure undisturbed peace in his own dominions, while he was engaged in his desolating and successful attacks upon his weaker neighbours.

Meanwhile, the betrothed spouse of Eleanora set forth with his mother and brothers to join King Pedro in his new dominions;[1] but the glittering diadem of Sicily proved indeed "a crown of thorns." Charles of Anjou soon appeared to reclaim his former possessions, backed by all the power of France, and compelled his rival to withdraw. A truce ensued for a short time, the result of a romantic proposition that the dispute should be settled by a personal combat between the two claimants, each attended by one hundred knights; the lists to be held at Bourdeaux, and the King of England to act as umpire. Edward refused the office,[2] but his seneschal was chosen to act in his stead. On the appointed day, Charles and his hundred knights, glittering in superb armour, appeared on the field, which was encompassed with innumerable spectators; and there they paraded all day, amidst the clang of the trumpets of the challengers, which waited in vain for a responsive blast from the other party; for Pedro of Aragon, though to save his knightly honour he durst not be absent from the tryst, had come alone and in disguise, and, having shown himself to the English seneschal, he declared that he dared not trust himself and his troops in a city that was so fully occupied by the French, and then returned secretly and swiftly to his own dominions.[3] Pope Martin IV., who was a Frenchman by birth, and owed his elevation to Charles of Anjou, warmly seconded his cause; and, declaring the kingdom of Aragon forfeit, bestowed it on Charles of Valois, younger son of King Philip III. of France.[4] A furious contest ensued, in

---

[1] L'art de verifier, vol. xviii., p. 242. [2] Fœdera, vol. i., pp. 626, 627.
[3] L'art de verifier, vol. vii., p. 529; vol. xviii., p. 242. [4] Fœdera, vol. i., p. 632.

the midst of which King Pedro died, and his son Alphonso ascended the throne.

Amid the tumult of political conflict, all matrimonial negociations were dropped during several years. This might be partially owing to papal influence, for Pope Martin,[1] and afterwards Honorius IV., who succeeded him, wrote to King Edward, expressly to exclude the relations of the late King of Aragon from a dispensation, recently granted in general terms, to the effect that the sons and daughters of the English monarch might marry with any who were not within four degrees of consanguinity, and enjoined upon him not to form any connexions with such determined enemies of the holy See.[2]

We must now revert to the more immediate history of the lady Eleanora. During the year 1284 and part of 1285 she and her sister Joanna remained almost entirely at court, accompanying the king and queen in their progresses through different parts of England, where their course may be traced by their offerings at religious shrines, as recorded in the *elemosyna* portion of the wardrobe book for the 13th year of Edward I., which is still preserved in the Tower of London.[3] The general amount of the donation made by each princess at every shrine she visited was 7s., equal to about five guineas of our present money, and this sum was frequently offered at two or three places in the same church; besides which, they each regularly gave a penny per day as alms all the year round, and extra donations on the festival days.[4] On the 26th of November, 1284, the king and queen and their three elder daughters paid their devotions at the shrine of Thomas à Becket, or St. Thomas of Canterbury: the princesses offered at three places in the cathedral, that is to say, to three different altars, or sets of relics, the sum total of their gifts

---

[1] MS., No. 8567, Bibliothèque Royale.
[2] Fœdera, vol. i., p. 665.
[3] It forms No. 65 of the miscellaneous rolls.
[4] Liber garderobæ, 13 Edw. I., f. 20.

being 63*s.*; and they again offered at the shrine of St. Adrian, in the same city.[1]

In February, 1285, we find them at St. Edmundsbury, in Suffolk, noted as the burial place of the royal martyr, St. Edmund. During his recent expedition in Wales, the king had made a vow to visit this shrine in case he returned successful,[2] and it was therefore favoured with an unwonted share of patronage. Here their devotion found full scope, for there were in the abbey six shrines, erected by the sagacious monks to gratify the liberal tastes of their votaries, at each of which the king presented an offering; the queen and her daughters only at three.[3] They then journeyed to St. Mary's, of Walsingham, where the ladies remained, while the king proceeded to the cross of Bromholm, where he paid votive offerings for his family as well as for himself.[4] The latter end of April saw them at St. Albans, but they returned to Westminster to celebrate the great festival of Trinity Sunday. The relics, and especially the arm of St. Edward the Confessor, deposited in the abbey, formed the great centre of attraction, and were treated with due reverence.[5] Offerings made by Eleanora in July at Canterbury, in September at Winchester, and in October at Lyndhurst in Kent, complete the account of the regnal year.[6] Eleanora was not, however, satisfied with church oblations; she persuaded the king to make her a present of 53*s.* 4*d.*, to be distributed in alms to poor people, according to her will and pleasure.[7]

Almost immediately afterwards, she, with her sisters, retired from court, as appears by the notice of a messenger called

---

[1] Liber garderobæ, 13 Edw. I., f. 16 b.
[2] Chron. John Oxf., Cotton MS., Nero, D. ii., f. 232 b, col. 3.   Chron. Petrob., Addit. MS., 6913, fol. 258.
[3] Ibid.   Lib. gard., 13 Edw. I., f. 17.
[4] Rot. donorum, 13 Edw. I., fol. 2.   Copy by Craven Ord, Middlehill MS., No. 1003.
[5] Lib. gard., 13 Edw. I., f. 18, b.
[6] Ibid., ff. 19 b, 21, 22.   [7] Ibid., f. 21.

Gervase, who was employed to carry the king's letters to his daughters.[1] Early in the month of December, the three elder princesses undertook a pilgrimage to Glastonbury, the abbey of which was held sacred from its containing the bones of the famous King Arthur. This pilgrimage was evidently considered an affair of some importance, and was probably deemed more than usually meritorious, from its being performed in the depth of winter. The ordinary mode of travelling on horseback was of course out of the question, and the young ladies performed the journey in chariots; a new one being purchased for Eleanora at Cirencester, drawn by several chariot horses, one of which, called Rougemont, was bought for 40s. in lieu of one which had fallen sick, and was tenderly cared for by its mistress;[2] two others were bought, at the prices of 60s. and 106s. The princesses travelled in great state, being accompanied not only by their own servants, but by a number of ladies of honour, who also had pages and maidens to attend them ; and a confidential clerk of the king's was appointed as their principal escort. They seem to have taken up their abode at the abbey itself, and to have been indebted to the monks for their entertainment, since no mention is made of lodgings provided for them. The munificence of these royal patronesses left the worthy fathers no cause to repent their hospitality; for, as the gifts of the princesses during the two days they remained at Glastonbury amounted to 53s., their hosts were no doubt handsomely rewarded.[3] Eleanora and her sisters returned by way of Cerne Abbey, in Dorsetshire, where, on Thursday, December 6th, they offered at the shrine of St. Ethelwold. Journeying on by slow stages, they arrived on the 23rd of the month at Crediton, in Devonshire, and thence went on to Exeter. In this ancient city they were joined by the

[1] Wardrobe roll, 13 and 14 Edw. I., No. 1786, Queen's Rememb.
[2] Wardrobe roll, 14 and 15 Edw. I., No. 1782, Queen's Rememb. Wardrobe book, 14 Edw. I., ff. 2, 2 b, 4 b, 11, miscel. roll, Tower, No. 66.
[3] Wardrobe roll, 14 and 15, ut sup. Wardrobe book, 14, f. 2.

king and queen, and here the royal family celebrated their Christmas festival.

About the middle of January they commenced their homeward journey; on the 17th they passed through Christchurch, Hampshire, and offered at the priory there.[1] In February we find them at Westminster, where orders were given that two barges should be handsomely fitted up, provided with masters and seventy-four bargemen, to take the king and queen and their daughters up the Thames to Brentford, where they stayed one day, Wednesday, the 27th of February, and returned the following day.[2] The season seems uncongenial enough for a pleasure excursion on the water, but many allusions in our old writers tend to confirm the prevalent notion, which we derive from our grandmothers, of the increasing lateness of the seasons. Probably, the latter end of February would be bright spring-time in the thirteenth century. In April the royal family performed a still longer voyage, as far as Gravesend, the king and queen going in boats, and the princesses, having first paid a visit to Langley, proceeding thither in a ship.[3] Some particulars in the wardrobe accounts just quoted afford a curious insight into the minutiæ of the royal expenditure: "To Perrot, the tailor of the lady Eleanora, the king's daughter, for the sewing of two robes of Eleanora and Margaret, daughters of the king, and for the service of valets helping him, and for buttons, thread, silk, gloves, and shoes bought for them, and for bringing these robes from London to the king, and also for soap and other things bought for them, from the 1st of May, in the year 13, (the 13th regnal year of Edward I. 1274-5,) to the present day, 68s. 9d. Also, to the same Perrot, for his expenses during 24 days, when he was at London, seeking robes for the ladies against different feasts, at 2d. a day, 4s."[4]

The provision of new robes for the great religious festivals

[1] Elemosyna roll, 14 Edw. I., Middlehill MS., 1003.
[2] Wardrobe book. 14 Edw. I, f. 7 b.
[3] Ibid., f. 11 b, 12.   [4] Ibid., f. i.

was universal at this period, both for the members of the royal family, and those numerous dependants who received their attire from the royal wardrobe. The term *robe*, though, when used in the singular number, it is, in its modern application, limited to *one* article of dress, formerly included a complete suit, consisting of the tunic, or long under robe, reaching to the feet; the surtunic, which was confined at the waist by a girdle, and descended to the knees; and the mantle, ordinarily of costly material, and furred, which was fastened by men generally on the shoulder, but by females on the bosom, with a jewelled clasp, and swept the ground with its massy folds.[1] The difference in the attire of the two sexes was much slighter than it is at present, and the same names were applied indiscriminately to the garments of both.

In the wardrobe of the princesses considerable attention was paid to economy. Some of the Christmas robes of Eleanora for this year, 1285, were far from new, since it took her tailor seven days to repair them, though they were profusely ornamented with six dozen of silver buttons.[2] Her tailor, Perrot, or Peter, was a very important personage in her household; he attended to her horses and chariots, and provided her with many necessary minutiæ, beside her mere wardrobe equipments; and he also officiated occasionally for the younger princesses, until they were old enough to be allowed a separate officer for themselves. He had constantly a horse and boy to attend upon him, and his wages were 4*d.* a day, double the sum granted to ordinary domestics,

---

[1] An entry in the close roll of the 52nd of Henry III., m. 2, is very decisive on the meaning of the term roba. Johanna, the wife of Ralph de Gorges, is ordered to have "unam robam integram, videlicit tunicam, supertunicam et pallium." On another occasion, when orders for robes had been given without distinct mention of the cloaks, a fresh mandate is sent, that cloaks should be provided without fail, that each of the persons named may receive a *complete* robe.—Close roll, 37 Hen. III., m. 22. When other garments besides these were included, they were always specified, though the term roba was still used for the whole dress: thus, "a hood, with decent fur, and two tunics," are named in the close roll of the 34th of Henry III., m. 18.

[2] Wardrobe book, 14 Edw. I., f. 6 b.

besides 28*s*. yearly allowed for his robes.[1] Whenever he
was absent from court on the necessary duties of his office,
he was allowed 2*d*. a day, above his wages, for his expenses,
that sum being considered amply sufficient for board and
lodging ! The same sum was also given to the charioteers,
pages, and several other attendants of the princesses.

Early in May, 1286, the princess Eleanora and her sisters
went to pay a visit to their grandmother, Queen Eleanora of
Provence, who was then at Dover.[2] They seem to have
remained with her until the embarkation of their parents for
the continent, which took place on the 24th of June following.[3] Several political affairs, particularly the quarrels between Eleanora's plighted lord, Alphonso of Aragon and
Charles of Anjou, called the king into France, where he
remained more than three years. During his absence and
that of the queen, their daughters were the most important
personages in the royal establishment ; for Prince Alphonso,
the heir of England, had fallen a victim to untimely disease
in 1284,[4] and the little Prince Edward of Carnarvon was
but an infant of two years old. His sisters generally took
up their abode with him at Langley, where other children,
wards of the king, were also kept.[5] Nine armed knights
were in constant attendance upon the royal offspring, and
some idea of the splendour in which they lived may be
formed from the fact that their establishment for one year

[1] Wardrobe book, 18 Edw. I., miscel. roll, Tower, No. 70. This book is
not foliated. Wardrobe book, 18, Miscel. roll, No. 71, ff. 2, 37 b.
[2] Wardrobe book, 14 Edw. I., f. 12.
[3] Ann. Waverley, Gale, vol. ii., p. 239.
[4] Matt. Westm., p. 412.
[5] A curious wardrobe fragment in the Queen's Remembrancer, written
about this period, details with great exactness the allowance that was provided for one of these wards, John de Warren. He was furnished with two
robes a year, one at Christmas and another at Easter, "as the sons of great
lords are accustomed to have;" two palfreys ; three sumpter horses, with
men to keep them ; five esquires, who were each of them provided with a
horse and three valets ; for dinner every day his allowance was three penny-
worths of bread, three messes from the kitchen, one pitcher of wine, and two
of beer : his supper provision was rather larger. He was also to have each
night one torch, to burn as long as it would last, and twelve candles.

alone cost the then immense sum of £4,364. 13s. 7½d.[1] Sometimes, the elder princesses wandered with their respective suites to such of the royal residences as best suited their fancy.[2]

They were not forgotten or overlooked meanwhile by their absent parents. Eleanora, as the eldest, and her father's favourite, received special tokens of his regard, in the shape of two costly presents—one, of a golden cup with a foot and cover, value £36; the other, a coronet of gold, adorned with sapphires, emeralds, rubies, and pearls, which had been presented to Edward by the King of France.[3] The queen, too, bought for her daughters small presents of jewellery work at Paris, as tokens of remembrance.[4]

The records of the king and queen during their continental visit, which are fully and interestingly furnished in the wardrobe accounts, afford pleasing proofs of their parental tenderness; for, at all the principal shrines which they visited, offerings were given by them for the welfare of their daughters, who are generally named individually.[5]

During the absence of the king, Edmund, Earl of Cornwall, Eleanora's cousin, was appointed regent of England, to whom the princess addressed a letter, which is still in existence. It is written in old Norman French, of which the following is a literal translation.

" To her very dear cousin, sire Edmund, Earl of Cornwall, his cousin Eleanora, daughter to the King of England, sends health and dear friendship.

" Dear sire, since our lord the king has left with us Monsieur Eustace de Hache, our knight, and he is impleaded on many sides, and is so careful of the service of our lord the

---

[1] Roll of the keeper of the household and wardrobe of the king's children, 15-16 Edw. I., among the wardrobe fragments, Queen's Rememb.

[2] Household roll, Prince Edward, 14-15 Edw. I., No. 391, Queen's Rememb. Wardrobe roll, king's children, ut sup.

[3] Wardrobe roll, 14 and 15 Edw. I., No. 1865, Queen's Rememb.

[4] Wardrobe book, 14 Edw. I., f. 24, miscel. roll, Tower, No. 66.

[5] Wardrobe roll, 17-18 Edw. I., No. 1789, Queen's Rememb.

king, that nothing avails him, since he cannot by any means
depart from us except by the mandate of our lord the king,
we pray you, dear sire, since you are the lieutenant [1] of our
lord the king, that you will command Sir William de Ha-
melton, by your letter, to let him have his warrant of essoin, [2]
so that he may not lose his land in our service, while our
lord the king is out of the land. Dear sire, consent to do
this thing for the love of us, so that he may feel that our
prayer avails for him. Dear sire, know that his day to have
his warrant is this Tuesday next to come." [3]

This letter proves how unflinchingly strong was the loyal
attachment of the gallant knight whom the king had placed
near his daughter, since not even the strongest motives of
self-interest could induce him to relinquish his charge without permission ; and it gives pleasing proof that Eleanora
was not unworthy such devotion, by bringing out the warm
interest she took in the personal concerns of her dependants.
She failed, however, in attaining the object of her petition,
for Eustace's essoin of the king's service was disallowed. [4] He
was not, however, a permanent loser by his attention to the
princess, since, under her auspices, he subsequently rose to
rank and eminence. [5]

Another letter, written about the same time, in Eleanora's
name and that of her sister, Joanna, to the Bishop of Ely, [6]

[1] Used in the literal sense, as " holding the place of the king."
[2] Essoin is the law term for an excuse for absence, alleged upon some just
cause, for one that is summoned to appear and answer in an action at law.
[3] Orig. Letters, Tower, No. 1112.
[4] Parliamentary rolls, vol. i., p. 50 a.
[5] Notice of a relaxation of lands in Warwickshire to this same Eustace,
and Amicia his wife, occurs in the Abbreviatio placitorum. 16 Edw. I., p. 214.
There is also an entry in his favour in the close roll of the 19th of Edw. I.,
m. 6. He was at one time a menial servant of Edward I., but was made constable of the castle of Marlborough, and it was probably in this capacity that he
first attracted the attention of the princess, and was admitted to her service.
—See rot. pat., 24 Edw. I., m. 3. He was summoned to Parliament in the
28th of Edward I., and afterwards became a baron, under the title of Eustace
Lord of Hache. Brevia de veniendo ad Parl.—Cole's selections from miscellaneous records, p. 338.
[6] John de Kirkeby, Archdeacon of Coventry, and formerly treasurer to the
king, who filled the episcopal chair from August, 1286, to 1290.

exhibits the same kindly and condescending sympathy in affairs of their inferiors.

" To the honourable father in God, Monsieur John, by the grace of God Bishop of Ely, Eleanora and Joanna, daughters to the King of England, send health and true love.

" Dear sire, since we understand that peace is not yet made between Monsieur Hugh le Despencer and Monsieur John Louvel the heir, and Monsieur Ralph de Gorges and Sir John Louvel the bastard, for whom we have aforetime prayed you, we pray and require you again, as earnestly as we can, that you, if you please, will take trouble to keep accord among them. And because we see our good friend the Lady de Gorges is so ill at ease in her heart that we have great pity for her, and should be most glad if she were alleviated of the great grief of heart that she has on account of the contest that is among them—therefore, dear sire, we pray you, if it please you, that you will make exertions that good peace be made, and that the thing be brought to a good end; and since we know well that you are empowered to adjust the fines of each party, we beg you that you will do it, for the love of us. We commend you, dear sire, to God, who keep you, body and soul."[1]

The Lady of Gorges here alluded to was doubtless Elena, the mother of Ralph de Gorges, who is several times mentioned as having the guardianship of the king's children in their infancy, and for whom, therefore, Eleanora still nourished a tender respect.[2]

The amiable and compassionate spirit that pervades this epistle is too obvious to need comment. It is worthy of remark that the only letters of Eleanora's now known to be

[1] Orig. Letters, Tower.
[2] Rot. pat., 19 Edw. I., m. 18. Rot. exit., 19 Mich. An entry in favour of Ralph de Gorges and his wife Joanna occurs on the patent roll, 14 Edw. II., pt. i., m. 13 d. Notices of the family occur also on close roll, 40 H. III., m. 3, and liberate roll, 48 H. III., m. 8. The arms of " Sire Rauf de Gorges," six mascles or., on a field azure, occur on the roll of arms, temp. Edw. II., printed by Sir Harris Nicolas, p. 6.

extant, the two above quoted, and another, written several years subsequently on behalf of the Lady Marjery de Combes,[1] were all written, not for any selfish purpose of her own, but to promote the welfare and happiness of her friends and dependants.

Towards the autumn of the year 1289, the eagerly anticipated but long delayed return of the king and queen was resolved upon. Great exhilaration pervaded the royal family at the prospect of seeing their parents; and they hastened to Dover, where, richly clad in robes of cloth of gold trimmed with green velvet, which had been made expressly to do honour to the occasion, they waited the arrival of the monarch and his queen.[2] The delight of this reunion may be more easily imagined than described; for the parents, whom their previous frequent bereavements might well have rendered tremulous, had the satisfaction of seeing their daughters all in blooming health, the younger ones fast rising to girlhood, and the young heir of England, whom they left an infant of two years old, was now become a sportive and healthy boy of five.

While the king was on the continent, he had succeeded in one of the principal objects of his visit—that of procuring first a truce, and then a permanent peace, between his daughter's betrothed, Alphonso of Aragon, and Philip of France.[3] During one period of the negociations, the long-interrupted matrimonial arrangements were renewed. Messengers from Alphonso met Edward almost immediately on his arrival at Paris;[4] the king promised to solicit a dispensation from the Church of Rome, after the creation of the new pontiff, Nicholas IV., and that within three months afterwards the Lady Eleanora should be sent over to Aragon.[5] Soon after this, an interview took place between

---

[1] Orig. Letters, Tower, No. 1639, Appendix, No. xv.
[2] Wardrobe roll, 17 Edw. I., No. 1935, Queen's Rememb.
[3] Fœdera, vol. i., pp. 668, 670, 674, 678.   [4] Lib. gard., 14 Edw. I., f. 16.
[5] Fœdera, vol. i., p. 678. Cotton MS., Vesp., c. xii., f. 45 b.

the two monarchs at Campo Franco.[1] What passed at this
interview with reference to the projected nuptials has never
transpired, but from that time all mention of them entirely
ceased ; and, although the princess remained unmarried till
after the death of Alphonso in 1291,[2] the idea of her becoming Queen of Aragon was relinquished. An aid of 80*s*.
from every knight's fee had been actually granted for her
marriage dower, but it was not collected until some time subsequently.[3]

This may be considered a fortunate escape for Eleanora,
from a destiny which, however splendid, promised but little
happiness. The ambitious character of King Alphonso led
him into ceaseless wars, in which, for the sake of self-aggran-
dizement, he did not hesitate to attack even his own relatives;
and, when compelled by adverse fortune to seek for peace
with France, he purchased immunity from attack for himself
by pledging himself to abandon the cause of his brother
James in Sicily, and to leave that unfortunate people to the
risk of being once more brought under the yoke of their
French oppressors.[4]

The princess Eleanora appears to have been the constant
companion of her parents from the time of their landing in
England. They proceeded from Dover to Canterbury,
where they were met by many of the nobility, and a grand
entertainment was given to the royal family by the monks of
St. Augustin's. A characteristic incident occurred during this
festival. The king sent to invite the archbishop, John
Peckham, to sit at the table and partake of the feast ; but,
it being one part of archiepiscopal ceremonial that the prelate
should have the cross carried erect before him, it was feared
by the abbot and monks that such a display of ecclesiastical

---

[1] Fœdera, vol. i., pp. 686, 687.
[2] Père Daniel says that she was on the point of marriage when Alphonso
died, but this statement is not well supported.
[3] Madox's Hist. of Excheq., vol. i., p. 698. Rot. pat., 30 Edw. I., m. 1.
[4] L'art de verifier, vol. vi., p. 530.

pomp would excite the wrath of the monarch. They had certainly not forgotten the effects of a similar scene upon King Edward's Plantagenet ancestor, Henry II., during the haughty domination of Thomas à Becket. Fearing, then, that evil might accrue, they begged the king to excuse the coming of the archbishop, which he refused to do; but, learning the cause of so unwonted an hesitancy, he ordered his chancellors forthwith to draw out letters, permitting the cross to be borne before the archbishop as usual.[1]

Early in October, we find the royal family taking a water excursion together, which occupied five days. Two mariners of Spalding were appointed, along with other boatmen, to row the king and queen, and their children and attendants, from West Dereham, in Norfolk, to Ditton, in Cambridgeshire, by way of the Isle of Ely.

During the few succeeding years, we find little to elucidate the character or personal history of Eleanora further than her journeyings to and fro, which are traced by her offerings at different religious houses, and her liberality to the poor. In the years 1289 and 1290, Abingdon, Woodstock, St. Alban's, Chester, and Clarendon, were amongst the places visited by the princess.[2] A few particulars occur in the wardrobe-accounts in reference to her expenditure. There are entries for the expenses of Eleanora's bath, for silver buttons, a sponge, an iron spoon, two copper bowls, three pounds of soap, rings and cords for her curtains, keys for her room, cloaks, capes, tunics, surtunics, pelisons, gloves, shoes, a belt decorated with pearls and gold,[3] and a pair of large knives.[4]

In the year 1290, two of her sisters were married; the

---

[1] Chron. Gul. Thorne, mon. St. Aug., Cant.

[2] Wardrobe book, 18 Edw. I., Rot. Misc., 70. Ibid., ff. 2 b, 4. Rot. Misc., 71.

[3] Wardrobe fragment, 17 Edw. I., Queen's Rememb. The date of this document is not given on it, but it is elicited from a mention made of the return of the king to England on the 12th of August, which occurred this year.—See rot. claus., 17 Edw. I., m. 6. Wardrobe book, 18 Edw. I., ff. 2, 7, 8, 13. Miscel. roll, Tower, No. 71.

[4] Wardrobe book, 18 Edw. I., f. 2 b. Miscel. roll, Tower, No. 71.

Princess Mary had long since become an inmate of the cloister, so that Eleanora was left without associate, except in her youngest sister, Elizabeth—between whose age and her own a difference of nineteen years existed—and her brother, Prince Edward. The death of her mother, Eleanora of Castile, also took place in the latter end of the year 1290, and deprived her of the society of a parent whose amiable qualities and maternal tenderness must have peculiarly endeared her to the daughter, who seems, during the later years of her life, to have been her constant companion. Her importance in her father's household was, however, increased by these circumstances. Her train of servants, with the addition of two pages and two postillions, or chariot runners, now consisted of ten men, exclusive of her chaplain, clerk of the stables, and keeper of the chariots, and the keeper of her wines; beside which she had her ladies of honour and waiting-maids :[1] and when she journeyed, her chariots, baggage-carts, saddle-horses, and sumpter-mules, with the attendants, who all travelled with her, must have formed a procession worthy of the rank of the princess royal of England, and the second in succession to the crown.[2]

Her influence over her father, King Edward, was considerable, and appears to have been always benevolently exerted; either to procure alms for the poor, or favours for her friends. Among the latter is particularly named Eleanora of St. Paul, a jewess of London, who became converted to the Christian faith, and who was taken under the special protection of the Lady Eleanora. It was frequently the custom of the Israelitish parents or friends of these converts to a purer faith to deprive them of their whole property, and turn them adrift into the world, and these harsh measures were attempted against the lady of St. Paul. But her princess-

[1] Wardrobe book, 18 Edw. I., ff. 5 b, 26.
[2] The expenses connected with her carriages alone in the bills of smiths, saddlers, &c., from the 12th of August, 1289, to April, 1290, were £123. 5s. 10d. —Wardrobe book, 18 Edw. I., f. 5 b.

friend interfered in her behalf; and the king, at his daughter's intercession, ordered that she should continue in possession of all the property that belonged to her at the time
of her conversion.[1]   Eleanora, with her usual stedfastness of
attachment, ever maintained a watchful guardianship over
her protégée, who soon afterwards became Countess of
March;[2] and the king again granted her ten marks, at the
instance of his dearest daughter, the Lady Eleanora.[3]   To
the princess the king was very liberal in his presents, especially of costly jewellery,[4] for which she seems to have entertained a truly feminine predilection.

The precise period at which Eleanora's marriage with the
nobleman who was ultimately the successful candidate for
her hand, was first projected, is uncertain.   That she remained unmarried longer than her sisters may be accounted
for either on the supposition that she was not considered
disengaged until after the death of Alphonso of Aragon, or
that Edward I. sought for his eldest daughter a union
more splendid than it was her fortune to find.   As early as
the year 1290, a notice occurs of the "Lord of Bar," which
proves that he was on terms of intercourse with the royal
family of England.[5]   Henry III., Duke of Bar-le-Duc, was
the eldest son of Theobald, or Thibaut II., and Jeanne de
Foy, Lady of Puisaye,[6] and inherited the extensive province

[1] Rot. claus., 17 Edw. I., m. 2.
[2] Her husband was probably Guy de Lusignan, brother of Hugh XIII.,
the last Earl March of that house, on whose death Guy became the titular,
though he was never the real Earl of March.   On account of his adherence
to the English interests, he fell under the displeasure of Philip of France,
who bribed him to relinquish his claims on the earldom for the sum of 12,000
livres.—L'art de verif., vol. x., p. 235.
[3] Rot lib., 18 Edw. I., m 1.   Rot. exit., 19 Edw. I., Mich., date, 10th
Nov., 18.   The title of the issue rolls is given for facility of reference,
according to the labels now attached to them.   It will be evident, however,
that, as the regnal and civil years do not coincide, the roll of one term must
include part of two regnal years; this is the case with the rolls of the
Michaelmas terms of Edward I., his accession taking place on the 20th of
November.   The date of the label is generally the latter of the two years.
[4] Rot. exit., 19 Edw. I., Pasch.
[5] Wardrobe book, 18 Edw. I., f. 26.
[6] Duchesne hist. de la maison de Bar-le-Duc, p. 44.

of Bar, which now forms an integral part of the French monarchy. Its position, on the confines between France and Germany, conferred on it greater importance than it possessed from its intrinsic resources; and the feudal supremacy over this province was, at the period of which we are speaking, as well as long afterwards, a subject of warm contention between the French and German powers.[1] The duchy was founded, in the tenth century, by Frederic, Duke of Mozelane, and was originally united with the powerful Dukedom of Lorraine, whose proud dukes boasted their direct male descent from Charlemagne, and looked down with scorn on the Capetian dynasty of French monarchs, as being far their inferiors in the aristocracy of birth.[2]

In the spring of the year 1293, Duke Henry, attended by a large train of soldiers and servants, came over to England; not, as far as can be traced, to fulfil any previously arranged treaty of marriage with the daughter of the English king, but simply on a visit to him, which probably had for its object some political scheme. The Lent season was spent by the king and his family at Norfolk, where the Duke of Bar resided with them; but very few of the nobles of the land attended their sovereign;[3] and it was probably during the familiar access which he enjoyed to the members of King Edward's family at this time of retirement that the Duke was led to desire, and then to solicit, the hand of the princess royal. His request was speedily acceded to; and it was arranged that he should remain in England until the period of his nuptials, which were to take place the ensuing September. Meanwhile, he was entertained with great honour by the king, who took him about with him wherever he went[4]—so that, for some months previous to his marriage,

---

[1] For a full discussion of this subject, see a volume of the Seguier papers in the Harleian collection, No. 4514.

[2] Chatereau, mémoire sur l'origine des maisons de Lorraine and Bar-le-Duc. p. 123. Harl. MS., 4514, art. 29.

[3] Chron. Barthol. Norw.. Cotton MS., Nero, c. v., f. 221 b.

[4] Annal. lucul., Cotton MS., Nero, D. ii., f. 186. Lambeth MS., 419, f. 80.

he was constantly in the society of his future bride; and it
is fair to presume that the union was one of the heart as well
as of the hand.

The ancient City of Bristol was the place fixed upon for
the marriage ceremony. King Edward was determined that
no pains should be spared to do honour to the occasion, and
he summoned all his knights and nobles from far and near
to attend.[1] He himself was present, with the whole of the
royal family. The marriage was celebrated on the 20th of
September, 1293,[2] the Archbishop of Dublin being the
officiating prelate.[3]

The dowry which Eleanora received from her father was
10,000 marks,[4] while her husband provided for her with a
liberality which bore ample testimony to the strength of his
regard. The Castle of Bar, and the revenues of very many
of the principal towns of his dominions, were yielded to her,
with a promise that, should they not amount to the annual
rental of 15,000 livres Tournois, or nearly £4,000 sterling,
he would make up the deficiency;[5] and Edward sent over
four knights to receive seisin of the lands, and examine their
value.[6]

The duke and duchess did not immediately leave England.
In October, Henry, attended by many knights of the king's

[1] Among the recently sorted miscellaneous bundles in the Tower, Np. 135,
is a document containing the names of the knights who were summoned to
be present.—See Archæologia, vol. xv., p. 347.
[2] Chron. Petrob., Addit. MS., 6913, f. 302. Cotton MS, Vesp. A. ii.,
f. 70 b. The chronicle of Bartholomew of Norwich and that of Lanercost
give the 29th of September as the date, but, in the summons sent to the
knights, (see preceding note) the Sunday after ascension day is the day fixed
upon, which fell this year on the 20th of September.
[3] John de Samford, or Saunford, as his name is variously spelled. The
king greatly favoured this prelate. The office of marrying the princess royal
would have devolved upon the Archbishop of Canterbury, but John de Peckham had recently died, and his successor, Robert Winchelsea, was then absent
at Rome, seeking a confirmation of his election. John de Roman, Archbishop
of York, had fallen into disgrace for having excommunicated Antony Bek,
Bishop of Durham, a confidential favourite of Edward I. (see Prynne's records,
vol. iii., pp. 560, 567). The duty, therefore, reverted to the Archbishop of
Dublin. [4] Rot. lib., 21 Edw. I., m. 3. Rot. exit., 21 Edw. I., Mich.
[5] Fœdera, vol. i., p. 798. [6] Rot. pat., 22 Edw. I., m. 21.

household, went to pay a short visit to his brother-in-law, Prince Edward, who then kept a separate court, at Mortlake;[1] and soon afterwards he took his departure alone for the continent, leaving his bride with her father, until fit preparations could be made for her reception. His brother Theobald, who had been educated for the church, remained in England, and King Edward, out of respect for his son-in-law, promoted him to a vacant benifice.[2]

Early in 1294, arrangements were made for Eleanora's departure, which were hastened on account of the prospect of her becoming a mother;[3] and it was of course desired by all parties that the expected heir of the duchy should be born in his future dominions. Accordingly, a safeconduct was sent for, by an express, who was ordered to expedite its arrival as much as possible; and meanwhile the king proceeded with his daughter to Dover, where they arrived early in April. Here Edward appointed the train who were to accompany the duchess, and to remain with her till the beginning of August. The principal of these were, the Bishop of London, the Earl of Hereford, and the Dean of St. Paul's, besides a large company of the knights of his own household, amongst whom we find the name of Eustace de Hache, Eleanora's former friend and protégé.[4] Faithfulness to her early attachments formed one of the prominent features of her character. We have previously noted the tender regard she manifested for the interests of her gouvernante, Elena de Gorges; and her former chevalier was still under her protection, and formed one of her new establishment.

Adverse winds, and the delay of her safeconduct, pro-

---

[1] Household roll of Prince Edward, 21 Edw. I., m. 9, dorso, formerly in the Pell Office, but now transferred to the Rolls House, Chancery Lane.
[2] Rot. pat., 22 Edw. I., m. 21. He afterwards became Bishop of Liège.— L'art de verifier, vol. xiii., p. 437.
[3] Royal letters, Tower.
[4] Ibid. Rot. pat., 22 Edw. I., mm. 19, 20, 21, where letters of protection occur for the above-named persons, and many others.

tracted the period at which the princess was to set sail, for
nearly a fortnight; at length, on Wednesday, April 14th,
she took leave of her father, who had accompanied her to
Dover, and, with a prosperous gale, she and her splendid
suite mounted the vessels prepared for them, and, after a
successful voyage, reached the place of their destination.[1]

When Eleanora was introduced to her new dominions,
she was nearly thirty years of age, and very lovely in person.
She was warmly greeted by her subjects; and Duke Henry,
to do honour to the arrival of his bride, proclaimed a tournament in his capital, to which the chivalry from all parts
were summoned. Very welcome in those days of romance
was the trumpet of the herald that announced to many a
bounding spirit that a fair field was opened for the display
of those warlike accomplishments which were then the ambition and the glory of all—and the call was warmly responded
to. Among the nobles present, escorted by a gallant train,
was John, Duke of Brabant, whose son had recently become
the husband of Eleanora's younger sister. His prowess on
the field of battle, or the jousting plain, had long resounded
throughout Europe; and, therefore, when he appeared,
with his beautiful train of horse, he was welcomed with
great gladness,[2] for he bore the titles of the Flower of Chivalry, and Glory of the World; and it was his proud boast
that he had borne away the palm in seventy tournaments in
France and Germany. Age had not damped the ardour of
the valiant knight; and if we are to believe the testimony of
a contemporary chronicler, another and still more powerful
motive induced him to show his utmost prowess on this occasion; for we are told that the beauty of Eleanora so fired
him, that he determined to distance all his competitors in a
tournament given in her honour, and at which her fair hands

[1] Rot. pat., ut sup. Royal letters, temp. Edw. I. See Appendix, No. xvi.,
where the letter containing these details is printed, as affording a fair sample
of the familiar epistolary correspondence of the times.
[2] Chron. Ducum Brabantiæ, folio, Franck., 1580, p. 12.

were, in all probability, to bestow the crown on the victor.
But though the spirit of the old warrior was as strong within
him as ever, the vigour of his good right arm failed him.
Having selected from the company a knight called Sir Pierre
de Baufremont, whom he thought most skilful at tilting
with the lance, he encountered him; but at the third run
he was unhorsed, and so severely wounded, that in a few
hours it was evident that his career must very shortly close.[1]
The stranger knight, who had been the unintentional author
of the disaster, was filled with dismay, and, in a fit of re-
morse or despair, offered himself a sacrifice to the sword of
justice for the mischief he had wrought: but the dying
nobleman, with great generosity, not only exculpated him
from all blame in the affair, but even bestowed upon him a
considerable present, in token of his free and full forgive-
ness.[2] The death of the Duke of Brabant, which took place
within eight days, at the Castle of Bar, the residence of
Eleanora and her husband, put a melancholy termination to
their wedding festivities.[3]

Bartholomew of Norwich, usually a very faithful chronicler, tells us that in the year 1294, King Edward paid a
visit to his daughter and her husband;[4] but his statement is
not borne out by the authority of the contemporary records.[5]
It does not appear that Eleanora, during the short period
of her married life, ever visited her native country. About
this time she became the mother of a son and heir, to whom
she gave the name of Edward, in compliment to his royal
grandsire. The king gave a present of £50 to the valet of
his daughter for bringing him tidings of the birth of this
boy, who was the second male heir to his crown. His birth

---

[1] Sauvage, chron. de Flandres, p. 70. Labbé, Bibliotheca MSS., vol. i.,
p. 406.
[2] Chron. Wil. mon. Erm. Matthæus, analecta medii ævi, vol. ii., p. 533.
[3] Chron. St. Denis, Bouquet, vol. xx., p. 560.
[4] Cotton MS., Nero, c. v., f. 221 b.
[5] An allusion in one of the royal letters proves, however, that the king
had intended a visit to Amiens, but it was not seemingly accomplished.

was followed by that of a daughter, called Joanna,[1] after Eleanora's favourite sister.

The correspondence between the countess and her father was very frequent; notices of letters and messengers sent to and from herself and her husband perpetually recur.[2]   A collision taking place at this period between the kings of England and France, the Duke of Bar espoused the cause of his father-in-law with great energy, and lent him assistance, which his close proximity to the French territories rendered very effectual.   Furnished by King Edward with ample supplies of money,[3] he armed and led a troop of 1000 steel-clad knights, and a proportionate number of foot, into the adjoining province of Champagne, which belonged to Jeanne, Queen of France, who was in her own right Countess of Champagne.   But the Amazonian queen was not to be thus braved with impunity.   Aided by Walter de Chatillon, the constable of France, she made a rapid and successful incursion into the province of Bar, compelling the duke to hasten back to the defence of his own dominions.   King Edward, unable to afford him any personal assistance, wrote to the King of the Romans, begging his aid in behalf of his son, the Earl of Bar, who had done more for him than any other of his friends in those parts, and was therefore more vehemently charged by the enemy.[4]   This application failed of success.   A battle took place near Comines, in which, after a feeble resistance, the duke was taken prisoner ; and the vindictive queen, roused to ungenerous wrath by the attack made upon her, sent him, loaded with irons, to languish in a Parisian dungeon ; but King Philip of France,

[1] Chron. de Nicholas, Trivet MS., No. 637[17], Supplement Français Bibliothèque du Roi.   This MS. is not foliated.

[2] Wardrobe book, 25 Edw. I., ff. 34 b, 55, 113, Addit. MS., 7965.   Wardrobe fragment, 24 Edw. I., Queen's Rememb.

[3] Rot. claus., 22 Edw. I., m. 1.   Rot. exit., 23, Pasch.   Rot. lib., 25, m. 3, in cedulâ.   Part of his supplies were, however, intercepted en route.   Rot. Aleman., 22-31 Edw. I., m. 17.

[4] Rot. Aleman., 25 Edw. I., m. 13, dorso.   Fœdera, vol. i., p. 867.

rather more merciful than his queen, removed him to a less rigorous captivity, at Bourges.[1]

This took place in the year 1297, scarcely four years after the marriage of Duke Henry. Thus the Lady Eleanora's dream of wedded happiness was shortly and most abruptly terminated. Her position was peculiarly painful—left with two infant children to the regency of a province which lay almost at the mercy of the victorious French. She found, however, an unfailing friend in her father, King Edward; and it was probably his influence, secret or avowed, that secured the duchy from farther intrusion.

The duchess seems to have exerted all the means in her power to effect the liberation of her lord. King Edward, accompanied by his youngest daughter, went over to the continent, and spent the Christmas at the City of Ghent, in Flanders.[2] On his arrival, he was greeted by a present from Eleanora of a beautiful and valuable horse;[3] and soon after she went to Ghent, to visit him in person, doubtless with the view of interesting him in her husband's behalf; but she was never destined to witness his liberation. The king was strangely and even culpably lax in thus neglecting his son-in-law and ally, who was suffering from adherence to his cause; for we do not find that he made a single effort to procure his deliverance. He did, however, grant him the sum of £1500, to be paid by his attorney, but whether for ransom or otherwise is not stated.[4]

The records of this later period of Eleanora's life are extremely scanty: a few particulars still remain of her visit to Ghent. She was there during the Christmas of 1297; and on the new year's day she gave a present of a portable

[1] Chron. Nangis, vol. iii., p. 52. Les grandes chron. de France, edit. P. Paris, vol. v., pp. 119, 120. Guizot recueil de chroniques, vol. xiii., pp. 229, 230. L'art de verifier, vol. xiii., p. 437.

[2] From the dates on the bills of privy seals of the 26th of Edward I. in the Tower, it appears that the king was at Ghent from December 16th to early in February.

[3] Wardrobe book, 25 Edw. I , f. 57 b.   [4] Rot. lib., 26 Edw. I., m. 4.

dressing-box, containing a comb, a mirror silver gilt enamelled, and a silver bodkin, all enclosed in a leather case, to the king, her father. The gift was much valued by him, and he retained it in his possession as long as he lived.[1] It certainly greatly exceeded in value the average of the presents he was accustomed to receive from his daughters: Eleanora had herself, a few years before, been satisfied with a plain gold ring as a new year's token for him.[2] Beside her sister, Eleanora's old companion, Mary of Bretagne, Countess of St. Paul, met her at Ghent. A curious scene took place in the royal palace there, during the residence of the duchess. The king's exchequer, or rather his stock of ready cash in custody of the master of the wardrobe, was very low.[3] In consequence of this circumstance, Robert the panctar, or purveyor of the royal household, whose duty it was to attend to the provisions of the table, was reduced to such extremity, for want of the ordinary payments for household expenses, that he was quite unable to provide bread good enough and in sufficient quantities. The knights, who were accustomed to revel in joyous cheer at the royal board, were highly indignant at this unwonted cutting short of their supplies, and they revenged themselves by a singular manœuvre. They sent into the city to purchase provisions; and, when dinner-time arrived, each chevalier entered the hall, followed by a valet, bearing his mess, "to the manifest contempt," as we are told, "of the king." Upon an angry inquiry being instituted into the reasons of this strange pro-

---

[1] Warbrobe book, 29 Edw. I., f. 148, Addit. MS., 7966. Wardrobe roll, 34 Edw. I., Queen's Rememb. Jewel list, patent roll, 6 Edw. II., pt. 1, m. 3, schedule. Jewel roll, 31 Edw. I., Cole's selections from records, p. 280.

[2] In the year 21. Invent. Jewels, 24 Edw. I., No. 2157, Queen's Rememb.

[3] At this period, almost the whole royal expenditure, whether domestic, political, or military, from the purchase of silk and buttons to the payments of an army, passed through the wardrobe. The office of keeper was therefore responsible and important. Ecclesiastics were frequently preferred to the post: John de Drokensford, who was *custos garderobæ* during this part of the reign of Edward I., was afterwards raised to the Bishopric of Ely.

cedure, the panetar came forward, and proclaimed aloud, in presence of the assembled guests, that it was quite impossible for him to provide the knights with suitable bread, because he could not obtain money from the wardrobe. This made a bad matter worse; the wrath of the monarch was roused at the disgrace which had been inflicted on his regal state: he forfeited the poor panetar his wages for one month, and declared that, if a similar scene were again allowed to transpire, his place should be lost to him for ever.[1] Whether he took as much pains to rectify the cause of this breach of etiquette as to prevent the recurrence of the effect, we are not informed.

The whole household of the king was, it would seem, in a disorderly state; for, by some means, a thief contrived to introduce himself into the private apartments of the Lady Eleanora, during her temporary absence, and purloined from her chamber, whither it had probably been conveyed for additional safety, a splendid cup of silver gilt.[2] The king, however, determined that she should not be a loser by this affair, and made her a present of another cup, which was purchased for her at Ghent.[3]

This was the last token of paternal remembrance which Edward gave his fondly-cherished daughter. She lingered out a few more months of worse than widowhood; when her health, broken by anxiety in behalf of her imprisoned spouse, gave way, and she died in the thirty-fifth year of her age,

---

[1] "Memorandum quod xxviij. die Januarii, in pleno comp., apud Gandaviam, magister Robertus, panctarius regis, ponebatur extra vadia per unum mensem, pro eo, quod die Veneris, xxiiij. die ejusdem mensis, non habuit nec habere voluit panem competentem, pro militibus in aulâ regis serviendum; ob defectam cujus, quidam eorumdem militum panem in villâ emi et per valletos suos in aulâ regis coram eis afferri fecerunt, ad contemptum regis manifestum. Et idem Robertus clamabat, in auditu sedentium, quod non potuit servire milites de pane competente, pro eo quod non potuit habere denaria de Garderobâ. Et memorandum quod ordinatum fuit eodem die in pleno comp. per Thesaurarium et Seneschallum, quod si casus ille vel casus consimilis in posterum contigerit, amitteret servicium regis ex toto."—Wardrobe fragment, 26 Edw. I., Queen's Rememb.

[2] Wardrobe roll, 26 Edw. I., No. 2767, Queen's Rememb.

[3] Wardrobe fragment, 27 Edw. I., No. 2792.

A.D. 1298.[1] None of her own relations appear to have been near her at the time of her decease. The king would not consent that she should be consigned to an unmourned grave abroad; her remains were therefore conveyed to England, and found a resting-place among those of her illustrious ancestors and kindred, in the Chapter-House of Westminster Abbey.[2]

Her husband, after a lengthened imprisonment, was compelled to purchase his release, by humbly entreating pardon from the French king for his past offences, forfeiting part of his lands, and consenting to hold the remainder as a fief of France, which he did by a treaty dated the 3rd of June, 1301[3]—and even these hard conditions were obtained by the intercession of King Edward and his newly-wedded queen, Margaret of France.[4] On the return of the duke to his dominions, instead of being received with joyous greetings, he was upbraided by his people with stern reproaches, for the compromise he had made; and the indignant Barrois assembled to protest against this act, asserting that their prince had no power thus to alienate his sovereignty. But they were little regarded by the French monarch. Duke Henry, glad to escape this tumult of persecution, set off on a crusade, to which he had pledged himself at the request of the French king, to assist in the defence of the Island of Cypress, then vigorously attacked by the Sultan of Egypt.[5] He obtained some advantages in the war, but died abroad in the following year, 1302, and was interred at the Cathedral of Naples.[6] His character seems to have been that of an amiable man, well fitted to secure the attachment of his domestic circle, but inadequate to the emergencies of the station which he occupied.

[1] Chron. Hageneb., Cotton MS., Vesp., B. xi., f. 46.
[2] Stow's Survey, book vi., p. 14.
[3] Chron. de Nangis, vol. iii., p. 53. Duchesne hist. mais. Bar-le-duc Preuves, pp. 39, 40.
[4] Wardrobe book, 29 Edw. I., ff. 29 b, 67, 68.
[5] Duchesne, ut sup., p. 45.　　　[6] L'art de verifier, vol. xiii., p. 437.

Though his father-in-law, King Edward, had done little for him during his lifetime, he professed great regret when the news of his decease arrived. He roused himself to energetic action in behalf of his two grandchildren, Edward and Joanna. The disgust which Duke Henry had occasioned his subjects was such that it was only by the vigorous interference of the king that the lands of Bar were secured to his children.[1] Joanna was sent for to England,[2] where she arrived early in May, 1306,[3] and she was received and treated with all the tenderness due to her near relationship to the royal family : her name, as the " demoiselle de Bar," frequently occurs in the wardrobe accounts.[4] On the 20th of May, when she could not be more than eleven years old, she was given in marriage by her grandfather to John Earl Warren and Surrey, one of the first nobles of the land. Her wedding, of which many particulars remain, was very splendid ; it was celebrated the same day on which her cousin, Eleanora de Clare, was married to Hugh le Despenser. The king gave three cloths of gold to his chaplain for marrying each of these royal brides.[5] He paid also the sum of £37. 4s. 0d. to minstrels, for making minstrelsy before him on the wedding-day. Joanna was a frequent companion of her aunt, the Countess of Hereford, her mother's surviving sister ;[6] and, in the subsequent reign of Isabella, queen of Edward II.[7] Her husband was the last earl of the noble family of Warren, for they had no children. He died abroad in 1361.[8]

---

[1] Rot. pat., 30 Edw. I., m.'7.

[2] Wardrobe roll, 31-34 Edw. I., No. 983, Queen's Rememb.

[3] Wardrobe roll. 34 Edw. I., No. 2637.

[4] Wardrobe book, 34 Edw. I., Queen's Remembrancer, &c.

[5] Wardrobe fragment, 34 Edw. I., Queen's Rememb.

[6] Wardrobe book, 34 Edw. I.

[7] Ward. roll, Queen Isab., 9 Edw. II., Queen's Rememb.

[8] Dugdale's Baronage, vol. i., p. 82.   Joanna's seal, enclosing in the diameter of an inch and a half the arms of her father, mother, husband, and her own, in separate shields, is engraved and described by Sandford. Geneal. History, pp. 122, 139.

The fate of young Edward, Eleanora's son, in some respects strikingly resembled that of his father. After a long minority, in which the reins of government were held by his uncle, John of Bar, Lord of Puisaye,[1] he entered into contests with the Duke of Lorraine, and was taken prisoner; but, at length, being liberated by the intercession of his sister's friend, Queen Isabella of England,[2] by whom, as well as by his uncle, King Edward II., he was greatly patronized,[3] he took the cross, and died abroad of the plague, at Famagosta, in the Island of Cyprus.[4]

[1] Hist. mais. Bar-le-Duc, p. 46.
[2] Wardrobe book, Queen Isab., 7 Edw. II., Queen's Rememb. This book is one among the recently discovered and not least valuable treasures of this office: it is in a good state of preservation.
[3] Duchesne preuves, p. 44.
[4] L'art de verifier, vol. xiii., p. 438. Champier, cronique de Bar.

JOANNA,

THIRD DAUGHTER OF EDWARD I.

Joanna of Acres was the only English princess who first saw the light in a region far away from the land of her fathers—unless we except an infant sister, who is said to have been born and died in the Holy Land.[1] This child must have been born before the Princess Joanna, in 1271, shortly after the arrival of Edward and Eleanora in Syria, since Joanna's birth took place in the spring of the year 1272, soon after which her parents returned to Europe. Joanna was, therefore, the third daughter of Edward I. and Eleanora of Cas-

[1] The reference for this is unfortunately mislaid. It is one of the contemporaneous chronicles in the Cotton MSS.

tile. The sunny East, which gave her birth, also infused its glowing warmth into her mental temperament; and in the wayward energy of her character, she sometimes displayed more of the wild, fitful temper of an Oriental maiden, than that of the milder daughters of the West. She was born at the city of Acres,[1] celebrated in crusading annals, as it has been even in our own times, for its striking and successful sieges. This city had remained in the hands of the Christians since its capture by the hosts of Richard Cœur de Lion; and when prince Edward landed in Syria, he chose it as the most secure asylum for his wife during her residence in the East. From the place of her birth, the princess is usually designated Joanna of Acres. After residing there a few months, she was brought, in the autumn of 1272, to Europe; and, having spent the winter in Sicily, she and her mother, Queen Eleanora, paid a visit to their Spanish relations.

Queen Joanna of Castile became so attached to her little grand-daughter and namesake, that she persuaded her parents to leave the child to be educated under her care.[2] Her nominal tutor was Suerus, Bishop of Calixien, one of the chaplains of the Castilian monarch. He seems to have treated her with the most unbounded fondness, always addressing her as *filiola*, or little daughter;[3] and slight indeed was the restraint exercised, either by the doting grandmother, or the too indulgent preceptor, over the wild young creature, whose impetuous temper required a more than ordinarily watchful and judicious surveillance. But, while Joanna was enjoying the reckless freedom of happy childhood, amidst the vine-clad hills and sunny vales of Castile, her politic father was already occupied in forging matrimonial fetters for her infant hand. France was at this period the great rival power of England; and, in spite of the near relationship of the two monarchs—for they were cousins-

[1] Cotton MS., Claud., E. iii., f. 314, col. 1.
[2] Fœdera, vol. i., p. 559, Royal letters, No. 1115, Tower.
[3] Royal letters, Tower, No. 2239.

german[1]—this rivalry strongly marked their public conduct, and frequently broke out into open war. Under these circumstances, it was obviously the policy of King Edward to strengthen his continental connexions; and, with this view, he sought to cement an alliance with Rudolph, King of the Romans, by a marriage between his eldest son, Hartman, and his own daughter, Joanna. Edward conducted the whole transaction in a most business-like style; he stipulated and succeeded in obtaining for his daughter an annual settlement of 1000 silver marks, from the lands of Hapsburgh, which were hereditary in the house of Rudolph, and 10,000 more from those of the empire.[2] Anxious, too, for the honour of his future son-in-law, Edward obtained from Rudolph a promise that Hartman should be handsomely provided for, and that, in case of his own elevation to the imperial throne, his son should succeed to the dignity of King of the Romans.[3]

The preliminaries being thus arranged and sworn to by the King and Queen of the Romans and their children, Prince Hartman became impatient to have the marriage performed, and wrote to the Bishop of Verdun, a German prelate, who was one of the principal ministers of King Rudolph, to request him to hasten it.[4]

It was therefore agreed that the marriage should be celebrated the ensuing September, 1279;[5] and while Edward requested that, on account of the tender age of the princess, her removal to Germany might be delayed for some time, he invited Hartman to come over to England in due time to complete his nuptial engagements.[6] He wrote to the prince himself, sending him a safeconduct to England,[7] and promising that he should be met at Whitsand;[8] and also to the Bishop of Verdun, requesting him to be present, if possible,

---

[1] Their mothers, Margaret, and Eleanora of Provence, were sisters, being both daughters of Raymond Berenger, Earl of Provence.
[2] Fœdera, vol. i., pp. 536, 555.
[3] Ibid., pp. 536, 554.
[4] Orig. letters, Tower, No. 1118.
[5] Fœdera, vol. i., pp., 548, 556.
[6] Ibid., p. 536.
[7] Rot. pat., 7 Edw. I., m. 19.
[8] Royal letters, Tower, No. 1641.

at the marriage, but, at all events, to send a minute detail of the state of Hartman's lands, that he might arrange the dower of his daughter accordingly.[1] The marriage, as might be expected, met with some opposition from the French court; the dowager-queen Margaret wrote to Edward, entreating him not to let it take place until a truce was accomplished between Rudolph and the Duke of Savoy, who were then at war,[2] but in the king's anxiety for the match her wishes were disregarded.

Although Joanna was only five years old when these negociations were first set on foot, yet, as they had been protracted through two years, she had now reached the mature age of seven, and it became necessary that she should come over to England, to meet her future bridegroom. Accordingly, the king sent two of his most confidential servants, Stephen de Penchester, and Margaret, his wife, to Castile, to conduct the princess home, and to present to Queen Joanna the king's letters, in which he warmly acknowledges "the solicitous and curious education and nurture" she had given his daughter, and requests the immediate return of the child.[3]

Such a request was not to be slighted: Queen Joanna was therefore necessitated to part with her little favourite; and in the spring of 1278[4] the princess arrived for the first time in her father's kingdom,[5] and was introduced to the society of her brother and sisters, to whom she was as yet an entire stranger. Their residence was then in the Tower of London.[6] Joanna's Castilian attendants, two of whom at least had accompanied her to England, were handsomely rewarded by the king—but he immediately dismissed them,[7]

[1] Orig. letters, Tower, No. 1642.   [2] Ibid., No. 1371.
[3] Fœdera, vol. i., p. 559.
[4] Probably about the 5th of May, since on the 5th of November her minor expenses for half a year were paid, amouting to 5s. 3d.—Wardrobe roll, 6 Edw. I., recently sold by Messrs. Puttick and Simpson.
[5] Wardrobe book, 6 Edw. I., f. 45, Miscel. roll, No. 44, Tower.
[6] Rot. lib., 6 Edw. I., m. 2.
[7] Liber garder., 6 Edw. I., f. 45, Rot. Miscel., No. 44, Tower. Rot. donorum, 6 Edw. I., f. 9, copy by Craven Ord, Middlehill MS., 1003.

anxious, doubtless, to remove from his daughter all those to
whose injudicious homage she had been so long accustomed.
Her governess, the Lady Edeline, was, however, excepted from
this regulation; she still remained with her young charge until
after Joanna's marriage,—a period of nearly thirteen years.[1]

The king about this time received a letter from Prince
Hartman, styling himself " Earl of Hapsburg and Kyburg,
landgrave of Alsace, son of the most serene King of the
Romans," full of the most extravagant expressions of subjection and gratitude to his "father and especial good lord."
After acknowledging the receipt of the king's letters, intimating his wish for the completion of the marriage between
himself and his "illustrious daughter," he adds, " Wishing
from grateful to become more grateful, from devoted more
devoted, assembling all the powers of my body and mind, I
rise and bend in most devout acknowledgments, wishing ever
to direct my steps according to the good pleasure of your
paternal mandates, with unwearied promptitude and filial
subjection." We are probably indebted to the pen of "Master Peter, the learned tutor of his boyhood," to whom the
prince refers in the latter part of his letter, for this magnilo-
quent epistle, which has but few parallels even among the
annals of courtly adulation.[2]

The visit of Hartman to England was delayed by the
political struggles in which his father was engaged, and which
prevented his dispensing with the services of a sufficient
number of soldiers as a body-guard for his son; and,
although King Edward wrote to his continental allies to
escort him honourably through their domains, appointed a
fleet to meet him in Holland, and a train of nobles and prelates to attend him on his landing,[3] yet the journey was
never undertaken. Letters of excuse were sent, entreating

[1] Wardrobe fragment, 18 Edw. I., Queen's Rememb. The king presented
her with 100 marks on her dismissal.

[2] Orig. letters, Tower, No. 1117.

[3] Fœdera, vol. i., pp. 563-568. Royal letters, Nos. 1467-9.

the king to believe that the delay proceeded from unavoidable circumstances, not from sloth or negligence, professing the utmost willingness on the part of Rudolph and Hartman to receive the princess as daughter and bride,[1] and promising that she should be nurtured with the same care as the children of the royal house of Hapsburg.[2]

In the year 1282, an accidental death deprived Joanna of her plighted lord.[3] The statement of the chroniclers is that Hartman was drowned by the breaking of the ice while he was amusing himself in skating;[4] but a letter in the Tower collection, written to impart the tidings of his decease to King Edward, gives a different, and, of course, a more authentic account of the disaster. It states that the prince, who was residing at the castle of Brisac, on the Rhine, set out in a boat the Sunday before Christmas, to go down the river on a visit to his father, but that a fog came on so dense that the mariners were utterly unable to steer the vessel. Consequently, it struck upon a rock, and Hartman himself, with most of his companions, found a watery grave.[5]

The details of the Princess Joanna's domestic history, while she was a resident in her father's court, are so similar in their character to those already given of her elder sister Eleanora, that a few brief notices will suffice. In 1280 she was at Windsor Castle, where the younger members of Edward the First's family at that time resided.[6] In the great Welsh expedition, undertaken in 1282, Joanna visited the principality in company with her parents,[7] and was an inmate of Rhudlan Castle when her sister Elizabeth was

---

[1] Orig. letters, Tower, No. 1640.

[2] Ibid., No. 1113. From the advocate of Basle to Edward I.

[3] Fœdera, vol. i., p. 615.

[4] Chron. Barthol. Norw., Cott. MS., Nero, C. v., f. 204. Chron. John Oxf., Nero, D. ii., f. 232 b, col. i.

[5] Orig. letters, Tower, temp. Edw. I. This statement is confirmed in a contemporary German chronicle, Rauch, Rer. Austriac. Script., vol. ii., p. 276. Amongst the royal letters, No. 1470, is one from Rudolph to Edward I., assuring him of his continued friendship, in spite of the death of Hartman.

[6] Rot. lib., 8 Edw. I., m. 3, and claus., m. 10.

[7] Wardrobe book of Wales, 10, 11 Edw. I., miscel. roll, Tower, No. 57

born. Either her turbulent temper must have rendered her a troublesome companion for her brothers and sisters, or the mountain air of Wales was conducive to her health—for the next year we find her alone, with her household, at the Castle of Rhudlan;[1] and again, in the year 1284, she was domiciled at Carnarvon Castle at the time of the birth of her brother, Prince Edward of Carnarvon. She and her youngest sister, Elizabeth, seem to have been the only princesses who advanced so far into Wales. 20d. were offered for her by royal command on the 26th of March, and 14d. the following day, the feast of the annunciation, at different shrines in Wales, besides which were paid the daily alms-offerings of herself, her ladies, and damsels, for one hundred and eighty days preceding.[2] They remained at Carnarvon till May,[3] after which the princess and her brother and sister travelled by slow journeys to Chester,[4] and thence to Windsor. The following year she spent entirely at court, accompanying her parents in their journeyings.[5]

Beside the "ladies and damsels," already alluded to, Joanna had now a full household of her own, nearly equalling, both in number of men and horses, that of her elder sister.[6] Her favourite occupation was embroidery, which she pursued under the tutelage of her Castilian *gouvernante*, the Lady Edeline. Eighteen ounces of silk, of different colours, were bought to assist in the portrayal of those quaint figures of men, and beasts, and birds, which would sorely puzzle the naturalists of the present day to classify and arrange, but in which the limners of the thirteenth century, and we may presume the embroiderers, too, imitated,

---

[1] Writ of privy seal, ordering the delivery of 20 quarters of good wheat for the maintenance of her household at Rhudlan, dated 10th August, 1283.—Royal letters, No. 1114.

[2] Elemosyna roll, 12-13 Edw. I., among the Pell records now in the Rolls House.　　[3] Ibid.

[4] Wardrobe fragment, Edw. I., Queen's Rememb., undated.

[5] Wardrobe roll, 6 Edw. I., purchased for the British Museum, March, 1849.

[6] Wardrobe roll, 13 Edw. I., No. 1785, Queen's Rem. Wardrobe book, 13 Edw. I., ff. 1 b, 4, Miscel. roll, Tower, No. 66.

though they could scarcely rival, the uncouth delineations of the Bayeux tapestry. Beside the usual wardrobe entries for her, were others of plates of gold, pearls, garlands, &c., for her personal adornment;[1] and of cups and pitchers silver gilt, and clasps of gold, wrought with gems, presented to her by her father, either for her own use, or to give away to her attendants, or, oftener still, to offer at the different religious shrines which she visited.[2] A gemmed clasp was a very frequent royal alms-gift; the king and his wife and children presenting similar ornaments, only differing in weight and value, according to the dignity of the donor.[3]

Meanwhile, Joanna was not forgotten by the Castilian relations amongst whom she had been educated. She received an affectionate letter from her old friend and tutor, the Bishop of Calixien, entreating her to use her influence with her father in behalf of two Spaniards, whose names are scarcely legible in the half-obliterated epistle of the bishop, who, he assures the princess, are very well disposed towards the king. He concludes with warm expressions of his continued good will, and his wish to oblige her in every respect.[4]

During the absence of the king and queen on the continent, about this time a quarrel arose among the servants connected with the establishment of the princesses, which threatened materially to interfere with their comfort. The king had left a certain officer, named John de Sutton, in charge to provide all "necessaries, as cloth, fur, wax, spices," &c., for the royal children. In virtue of his office, the said John

[1] Wardrobe book, 14 Edw. I., ff. 5 b, 11 b, Misc. roll, Tower, No. 66. Wardrobe roll, 14 Edw. I., No. 1782, Queen's Rem.

[2] In one year only, (1285) nine of these gemmed clasps were offered by Joanna at Canterbury, St. Edmondsbury, Ely, Westminster, Walsingham, St. Alban's, and other churches or shrines.—Wardrobe roll, 6 Edw. I., ut supra.

[3] On January 23rd, 1285, at St. Thomas's shrine, Canterbury, the king offered a clasp, value £10., the queen one, value £7. 6s. 8d. Prince Edward, then an infant, had one presented by the treasurer worth £6. 13s. 4d. That of the Princess Eleanora was valued at 60s., Joanna's 53s. 4d., and Margaret's 46s. 8d.—Wardrobe roll, 6 Edw. I., ut supra.

[4] Orig. letters, Tower, No. 2239.

visited the fair of St. Botulph, and there purchased large
stores of all the above-named articles; but the seneschal of
the fair, for some unexplained reason, made him restore all
the goods to the merchants from whom he had bought them;
to the great indignation of " William de Picheford, and Edmund of the wardrobe," into whose hands the purchases were
to have been transferred for the use of the king's children.
They wrote an indignant letter to the Earl of Cornwall,
regent of the kingdom, entreating his speedy interference,
and a summary punishment of the insolent seneschal, lest his
bad example should prove a precedent to others.[1]   How the
affair ended, we have no means of ascertaining.

Shortly afterwards, another disturbance took place, occasioned by the petulant spirit of the Lady Joanna, which,
though kept under control by her father, broke out in his
absence.   She quarrelled so vehemently with Egis de Audenarde, whom her father had appointed as the pursekeeper of
his children, to supply them with sums requisite for their
private expences, that she absolutely refused to receive anything more through his medium, and chose rather to run
into debt, and to obtain money where and as she could, than
to compromise her fancied dignity by making peace with her
treasurer.   She appears to have been rather fearful, however, of the effects that were likely to be produced on her
father's mind by this procedure, for she thought it necessary
to send over two ambassadors to the king, with verbal expla-
nations of her conduct.   Her letter of credence to them, the
only epistle of hers now known to be in existence, penned,
of course, in old French, runs as follows :—

" To her very dear lord and father, our lord the King of
England, Joanna, his daughter, gives honour and reverence
as to her very father.

" Dear sire, we send to you our dear *bachelors*, Sir Hugh
de St. John and Sir John Bluet, for business which concerns

[1] Orig. letters, Tower, No. 1634.

us, whom, dear sire, we beg you, if you please, to believe as
to the things which they shall tell you by word of mouth
from me. Adieu, sire. God keep you, and grant that we
may ever hear good news from you!"[1]

The king, on his return, so far indulged her humours as
to discharge for her the debt she had incurred.[2] But arrangements were now on foot, to provide the wilful princess
with a master to the full as determined as herself. Gilbert
de Clare, Earl of Gloucester and Hertford, surnamed the
Red, has already been mentioned in a previous memoir,
as first the companion in arms, and then the rival of the
celebrated Simon de Montfort. After the defeat and death
of the Earl of Leicester, Gilbert was decidedly the first peer
in England; and Matthew of Westminster tells us he was
only inferior in power and dignity to the king himself. Many
little jealousies and disturbances had arisen at different times
between him and the government, which had been temporarily
pacified,[3] but King Edward was anxious to form a more substantial bond of union between himself and his restless subject.

Earl Gilbert had long before been married to Alice
de March, daughter of Guy de Lusignan, and niece of
Henry III.;[4] but, from some unexplained motive, he divorced
his wife, settling upon her a handsome dower, in consideration of her noble birth.[5] His hand was therefore now at
liberty; and, as that of the princess Joanna had also become
disengaged, by the early death of her former lover, a marriage was agreed upon between them, provided the earl

---

[1] Orig. Letters, Tower, No. 1116. This letter is not dated, but it seems
to belong to this period, since, from the omission of the title of Countess of
Gloucester, it was evidently written before Joanna's marriage.

[2] Wardrobe fragment, 17 Edw. I., Queen's Rem. The entry is as follows:
"August 8th, to the Lady Joanna, the king's daughter, for minute expenses
made for her during the three years in which the king was abroad, which
expenses she would not receive from the Lord Egis de Audenarde, who served
the king's sons and daughters, on account of some contention between them,
66s. 8d., by the hands of Edelina her mistress."

[3] Dugdale's Baronage, vol. i., pp. 213, 214.

[4] Chron. Tewksb., Cott. MS., Cleop., A vii., f. 48 b.

[5] Rot. claus., 13 Edw. I., m. 9, dorso. Fœdera, vol. i., p. 654.

could prove to the satisfaction of the king and his council that the divorce between himself and Alice had been formally sanctioned by the church, and could also produce a papal dispensation for his alliance with one who was related, though but distantly, to his late wife.[1] He succeeded in both these points;[2] and, having agreed to confer a dower of 2000 marks upon the princess, the affair was considered settled.[3]

These transactions had taken place in the year 1283. At this time, Joanna was a child of twelve years old, and the projected union was one of mere State policy; but, as the princess sprang up into a handsome and high-spirited girl, she seems to have inspired a warmer feeling into the bosom of her mature suitor, who found in her reckless wildness of temper a fascination which a more sobered character would probably have failed to exercise over him. He condescended to woo the favour of the capricious girl by a series of little delicate attentions, very unusual in the sturdy manners of the times. He made her presents of several costly articles of attire, as appears by a notice of 19s. paid for the sewing of three robes of blue cloth of Tarsus, which the Earl of Gloucester gave to the Lady Joanna and her two sisters; and again for the making of a tunic of tulle silk presented to her.[4] It even seems probable that her bridal wardrobe was principally fitted out by him, for, though in the wardrobe accounts of the year, which are particularly full, there are entries of dresses prepared for her sisters, her brother, and her cousin Mary of Bretagne, against her wedding,[5] seven dresses, twenty-five pairs of shoes at 7d. per pair, and fifteen pairs of gloves at 2¼d., are all that were provided, at the king's cost, for the bride herself.[6]

Just before his marriage, the earl gave her still stronger

---

[1] Fœdera, vol. i., p. 628. [2] Ibid., p. 721. [3] Ibid., p. 628.
[4] Ward. book, 18 Edw. I., f. 7. He also presented her sister Eleanora with a white *robe-de-chambre*. Ibid., fol. 12 b. Wardrobe roll, 18 Edw. I., in the possession of Sir Thomas Phillipps.
[5] Wardrobe book, 18 Edw. I., f. 10. [6] Ibid., f. 7.

proofs of his regard.   He resigned into the hands of King
Edward the whole of his extensive possessions in England,
Wales, and Ireland,[1] of which the king took formal possession, by administrators appointed for the purpose;[2] and
then fresh deeds were drawn up, by which those in England
and Wales were settled upon Earl Gilbert and Joanna, and
their children, if they had any, and if not, upon Joauna and
the heirs of her body,[3] to the exclusion of the Clare family,
for whom the Irish estates alone were reserved—unless the
princess died childless, in which case the whole property
reverted to them.   Gilbert, moreover, rendered himself per-
sonally responsible for all the debts with which the estates
were burdened, freeing the princess from all share of such
incumbrances in case of his decease.[4]

The transactions thus briefly detailed were entered into
with great formality, and they fill several closely written
membranes on the State rolls of the year, in which the long
lists of the lands, castles, and manors of this great earl, extending over several counties, give a vivid idea of his importance.[5]   The king himself thought it necessary to obtain a
guarantee against the ambition of his future son-in-law.   In
giving him the hand of his daughter, he placed him, in her
right, the third in succession to the crown, which was settled
on the prince first, and then on his sisters successively; but
Edward, fearing lest *might* should usurp the place of *right*,
caused Earl Gilbert to take an oath on the holy gospels, in
presence of the Archbishop of Canterbury and the nobles,
to keep good faith towards the Lord Edward, the king's
son, and his heirs; or, in case of his death without issue, to
the Lady Eleanora, whose right of succession he thus

[1] Rot. finium, 18 Edw. I., m. 15.   Liber munimentorum, A, f. 165, Chapter House.
[2] Rot. pat., 18 Edw. I., m. 32.
[3] Rot. Chart., 18 Edw. I., m. 16.   Rot. claus., 18, m. 8, dorso, and m. 2,
cedula.   Rot. pat., 18, m. 27.
[4] Liber munim., A, f. 165 b.   Rot. Cart., 18 Edw. I., m. 16.
[5] They are detailed at greatest length in the fine roll quoted above.

pledged himself to hold sacred. A deed was drawn up to this effect, and six bishops, at the request of Gilbert, affixed their seals to it.[1]

The marriage of the Princess Joanna took place on Sunday, the 30th of April, 1290, when she was in her nineteenth year. It was privately celebrated at Westminster Abbey by the king's chaplain.[2] Her two sisters, Eleanora and Margaret, attended her, and they all wore the rich dresses called *quintises*—but, strange to say, these *quintises* were not new for the occasion, since the tailors of the princesses had been employed *nine* days in repairing them for the wedding. The young Prince Edward, however, and his sister Elizabeth, who were present, were favoured with new robes and *quintises;* and so were also the royal wards, who were all brought to court to witness the festivities.[3] Joyous ones they seem to have been, for a temporary hall was erected at Westminster, and lined throughout with cloth, for the nuptial feast, and there the tables were spread; but the hilarity of some of the guests broke out into such riotousness, that one of them, Foulk St. Edmond, actually broke several of the tables.[4]

The following entries occur in the wardrobe book of the year in reference to the marriage:—

" To Adam, the king's goldsmith, for a magnificent zone, all of gold, with rubies and emeralds, bought at Paris, by command of the king and queen, for the Lady Joanna, against her nuptials, ... £37. 12s. 0d.

" For a head-dress of the same, wrought with rubies and emeralds, ... £12. 10s. 0d.[5]

" On the last day of April, for offerings made at a mass privately celebrated in the conventual church of Westmin-

[1] Fœdera, vol. i., p. 742.
[2] Chron. Brute, Lamb. MS., No. 99, f. 39. Chron. Barthol. Norw., Cott. MS., Nero, C v., f. 205 b.
[3] Wardrobe roll, 18 Edw. I., Middlehill MSS.　　　[4] Ibid.
[5] Ward. book, 18 Edw. I., f. 50 b, miscel. roll, Tower, No. 71.

ster, in honour of the Holy Spirit, at the nuptials of Joanna, the king's daughter, ... 70s.

" In money, given to place upon the missal-book along with the ring with which she was married, . . 40s.

" To Henry, the king's almoner, for a general scramble made on the nuptial day of Joanna, the king's daughter, for the said Lady Joanna, . : . . . . 28s.

" In offering, at a mass celebrated before the Lady Joanna the third day after her marriage, . . . 3s.

" Given the same day to three poor widows, from the three daughters of the king, 1s. each, . . . 3s."[1]

After the marriage of their daughter, the king and queen were anxious that she should still remain at court, to grace the approaching wedding of their younger daughter, Margaret. They made extraordinary efforts to amuse her, for Queen Eleanora gave her five horses to draw her in her state chariot, for five days, that she might perambulate wherever she pleased;[2] but, after the lapse of little more than a week,[3] the young bride chose rather to spend her honeymoon in retirement, free from parental surveillance, and therefore expressed a strong wish to visit the estates of her husband; and at such a time her will was, of course, law to him. They therefore left the court, contrary to the urgent desire of the king and queen. The royal displeasure was oddly manifested against the refractory countess, by the forfeiture of her bridal wardrobe. This appears from a mention of seven robes, made for the Lady Joanna, which the king and queen " took back to themselves, for their own use, against the marriage of her sister Margaret, *because* she left court, with the Earl of Gloucester, to go to his manors."[4] The place of their retirement was Tunbridge Castle, one of the most

[1] Ward. book, 18 Edw. I , miscel. roll, Tower, No. 70.
[2] Wardrobe book, 18 Edw. I., f. 10. Wardrobe roll, 18 Edw. I., Middlehill MSS.
[3] Rot. Cart., 18 Edw. I., m. 20. Gilbert's name occurs as a witness at Westminster, May 5th, which proves that they had not then left court.
[4] Ward. book, 18, f. 10. Wardrobe roll, ut supra.

important of the many fortresses in the hands of the Earl of Gloucester.[1]

Probably, one reason of their departure was a contest agitated between the king and Earl Gilbert, about the nomination to the Bishopric of Llandaff, which was claimed by both parties; and this proud peer ventured to maintain his claims stoutly, against the wishes of his sovereign and father-in-law. With much policy, Edward persuaded him to relinquish his assumed right,[2] and then restored the privilege to him and Joanna, as matter of favour; with the proviso that, after their deaths, it was again to revert to the crown,[3] thus conferring it upon him *de facto*, although not *de jure*. The king added a condition, however, viz., that he should be well assured of the fidelity of the bishop whom the Earl of Gloucester might appoint.[4]

This circumstance is recorded in the patent as well as the charter roll of the year, with a long preamble upon the " fallacious oblivion which ensnares the treacherous memory of man, so that things which are now plain and open, by length of time, become obscure; unless they are established by the authority of writing"—thus accounting for the two-fold and very exact register taken of the proceedings.[5]

The result of this struggle proves how nearly poised were the two powers between whom such a compromise was made, and that the Earl of Gloucester deserved the character given him by a contemporary chronicler, that he was not only strenuous in arms and prudent in counsel, but most bold in the defence of his rights. He had before given King Edward a striking instance of his fearlessness of temper. A quarrel having arisen about his property in some lands, the

---

[1] Ward. book, 18, f. 50. Wardrobe roll, 18 Edw. 1., purchased by Sir T. Phillipps, 1849. In the sale catalogue, it was by mistake stated to be the roll of 6-7 Edw. I.

[2] Liber muniment., A, f. 166 b, Chapter House.

[3] Rot. cart., 18 Edw. I., m. 2. Ryley's Placita Parliament., p. 59.

[4] Rot. pat., 19 Edw. I., m. 1.

[5] Ibid., 18 Edw. I., m. 1 cedula. Fœdera, vol. i., p. 742.

king angrily asked him by what right he held them ; "Behold my warrant!" said he, drawing his sword; "the same
by which you, sir king, obtain from your ancestors, by right
of conquest, two feet of England, and I from my parents
possess a third foot."[1] Either on this or some similar occasion
he so offended the king, that he was fined 10,000 marks for
contempt of the royal authority.[2]

The Llandaff controversy being amicably settled, harmony was fully restored, and the king testified his renewed cordiality, by taking severe measures with some malefactors who
had done damage in the chases of his son-in-law.[3] The earl
and countess now returned to court, which had removed
from Westminster to the Tower. But to be a mere appendage to the train of his royal father-in-law did not comport
with the views of the haughty baron, nor, perhaps, was it
very agreeable to his restless consort. They therefore resolved to retire permanently to an establishment of their
own ; and the mansion of Earl Gilbert, situated in Clerkenwell—then a village at some distance from London, but now
a populous parish lying between Islington and Holborn—
was selected as the place of their retreat. Fitz-Stephen, a
chronicler who wrote in 1190, tells us that "in the north
suburbs of London are choice fountains of water, sweet,
wholesome, and clear, streaming forth from among glittering pebbles, one of which is called Fons clericorum, or
Clerk's well, because in the evenings the youths and students
of the city are wont to stroll out thither to take the air and
taste the waters of the fountain." A priory of the Knights
of St. John of Jerusalem stood there, and also a priory of
nuns, which occupied together twenty-four acres of ground.
Cromwell, in his history of Clerkenwell, says, that possibly
England hardly offered a scene more rich in picturesque

[1] Chron. Lanercost, p. 168, Bannatyne edition.
[2] Rot. claus., 24 Edw. I., mm. 11-10.
[3] Rot. pat., 18 Edw. I., m. 10 d.

situation and rural accompaniments. On every side but that
of the city was spread the prospect of wooded hills and up-
lands, intermingled with luxuriant verdure; whilst the River
Holeburne,[1] whose banks were then clothed with vines,
wound amongst romantic steeps and secluded dells towards
the west.[2]

To this romantic retreat, then, the princess was led, as
her future home. This time no objection was urged by
Joanna's parents against her departure. On the contrary,
the king went to an enormous expense in the purchase of
plate, jewels, and other costly articles of furniture for her.
The list in which they are enumerated is headed thus :—
" To Joanna, Countess of Gloucester, going from the Tower
of London to Clerkenwell now for the first time, to the *hos-
pice* of her husband, as the king's gift for her apparatus."
Among them were one hundred silver dishes, and as many
saltcellars ; four wine, and as many water vases ; two small
dishes for spice and two for fruit ; sixty silver spoons, &c. ;
a large number of bowls of silver, and one of pure gold,
which alone cost £18. 15s. 0d. For her chapel she had also
a flagon, a censer, an alms-dish, made, as was then custo-
tomary, in the form of a ship, and two golden phials, for
wine. Part of her plate was made of the white silver of
Ghent, 300 marks of which had been delivered to the keeper
of the wardrobe for that purpose.[3]

Anxious that his daughter should take her leave of her
friends at court in a manner suitable to her rank and fortunes, the king presented her with forty-six golden cups,
twenty golden clasps, and twenty zones of silk, wrought and
trapped with silver, to give away to whomsoever she pleased.[4]
She had four beds provided for herself, her ladies, and maids,

---

[1] Called Holeburne in domesday-book. Few persons would now suppose
that Holborn derived its name from a stream.
[2] Cromwell's Hist. Clerk., pp. 6, 8, 13.
[3] Rot. claus., 18 Edw. I., m. 8.
[4] Wardrobe book, 18 Edw. I., ff. 49 b, 50.

(among whom occurs the name of Lady Edeline, her former governess) ;[1] a canopy and cushions for her chariot and her room ; napkins, towels, and 346 ells of cloth, uncut; also, one chariot and a long charette, or cart, each drawn by five horses, with suitable equipments.[2] The packing of all these goods and chattels was the next consideration, and one of no small importance. A variety of amusing notices occur of the hampers, and coffers, and baskets, and bags, the horses and sumpterers required to convey them safely from the Tower to Clerkenwell ;[3] one sumpter-horse carried her chapel apparatus, another her bed, a third her jewels, a fourth her chamber furniture, a fifth her *candles!* a sixth her pantry-stores and table linen, and a seventh her kitchen furniture. Truly, no travelling gipsy encampment could present a more miscellaneous assemblage of articles, loading the backs of their wearied beasts, than was exhibited in this curious *flitting*. Whether the princess herself, in her five-horsed chariot, followed, like a good housewife, in the train of her valuables, our deponent witnesseth not. The removal was made early in August. Robert Bareback, clerk of the chapel to the king's daughters, left the other princesses, and, attaching himself exclusively to Joanna, accompanied her to her new home.[4]

The short distance between Clerkenwell and London enabled Joanna to maintain a frequent intercourse with her own family. In her new abode she and her husband gave a splendid feast to her sister Margaret, recently married to John of Brabant, not inferior in gorgeous magnificence to that with which the king himself had honoured the bride on the previous day.[5] In the month of November, the Countess of Gloucester paid a visit to her parents, under the

---

[1] Wardrobe book, 18 Edw. I., f. 51 b.
[2] Ibid., f. 50.
[3] Ibid., ff. 10, 13 b, 50 b. Wardrobe roll, 18 Edw. I., Middlehill MSS.
[4] Wardrobe book, 18 Edw. I., miscel. roll, Tower, No. 70.
[5] Wike, Gale, vol. ii., p. 121.

guardianship of Henry, her waferer; and her expenses were paid by the king.[1]

About this time, Peckham, Archbishop of Canterbury, was inspired with a crusading mania; and he preached with such energy, that many of the noblest of the land caught his enthusiasm, and took the cross. Amongst the foremost of these were the Earl and Countess of Gloucester, who both declared their determination to go to the holy war; but their zeal cooled as rapidly as it had been excited, and they never fulfilled their vow, although many of the barons who had taken the cross at the same time actually joined the crusade.[2]

In the spring of the year 1291, the princess Joanna became the mother of a son and heir. This child, who is said to have been very beautiful, was born on the 10th of May,[3] at Wynchecombe, near Tewkesbury,[4] and received the name of his father, which was given him, at a splendid christening, by the Bishop of Bath and Wells, Ralph de Burnell, who was also the king's chancellor.[5] "Both the parents," says the chronicler Wikes, "delighted with a male child, christened him Gilbert, with inconceivable joy."[6] The king and queen were also much elated at the birth of this first grandchild, yet, so slow were the modes of communication, that it was the 21st of May before the tidings reached the king, then at Norham, in the County of Durham. When William Fitz-Clan, the valet of the countess, did at last arrive to impart the joyful news, he was rewarded with a present of £100.[7]

---

[1] Wardrobe book, 18 Edw. I., f. 52 b.
[2] Barth. Norwich, Cotton MS., Nero, C v., p. 257 b.
[3] In the inquisitions taken on the death of Earl Gilbert, the birth of this child is variously dated on April 23rd, April 25th, May 3rd, &c.—Escheats, 24 Edw. I., No. 107 A, Tower.
[4] Chron. John Oxford, Cott. MS., Nero, D ii., f. 333 b, col. 3. Chron. Hayles, Harl. MS., 3725, f. 17 b.
[5] Cott. MS., Vesp. A ii., f. 70.
[6] Gale, vol. ii., p. 122.
[7] Rot. claus., 19 Edw. I., m. 6.

In the following year, 1292, Joanna went with her husband to visit his Welsh estates, and took up her residence at Caer Philli Castle, which was situated near the River Rimny, among almost inaccessible marshes, in the mountainous districts of Glamorganshire, and was the principal seat of the Clare family in Wales. Its walls were of wonderful thickness, and, from its massive workmanship and vast extent, the castle is generally supposed to have been built in the time of the Romans. The strong round tower was the prison for all the rebels in the neighbourhood. A chapel had been added by its Norman possessors, in which Divine worship could be regularly performed.[1]

But for such a provision, the office of the worthy chaplain, Robert Bareback, had been a sinecure, since rough and rugged were the roads that led, over marsh and mountain, to the nearest church at Llandaff, a distance of three miles; and the young countess was not in a situation to endure much fatigue, for, shortly after her arrival, in the month of November, this mountain fastness became the birthplace of her first daughter, who was named Eleanora, after the queen, her grandmother.[2]

The princess found in her lord an affectionate sharer in her nursery cares. He manifested an unusually tender interest in his children, even when they were very young. Of this a memento occurs in a letter which he wrote, shortly after his daughter's birth, to Ralph de Burnell, the king's chancellor, apologizing for not having attended the king, as he had promised to do, upon a warlike expedition; but stating that, on his return from London to Glamorganshire, he had found one of his children ill, which had induced him to linger in Wales longer than he had intended to do.[3]

[1] Gough's Camden, vol. iii., pp. 121, 125.
[2] Chron. Norw., Cott. MS., Calig., A x., f. 163.
[3] Orig. letter, Tower, temp. Edw. I., written between November, 1292, when his daughter was born, and the middle of December the same year, when Burnell resigned the seals.

During the few succeeding years, two more daughters
were born, who bore the names of two of the countess' sisters,
Margaret and Elizabeth, but the specific dates of their births
are not ascertained.

Joanna amply repaid her spouse for the share he took in
her peculiar department of domestic interest, by entering
warmly into his projects in the management of his estates.
They became involved in a quarrel with the Bishop of Worcester, Godfrey Giffard, by casting up a ditch over the crest
of the Malvern hills, part of which belonged to them, and
part to the episcopal domains. The bishop angrily accused
them of encroachment upon his territories, but was pacified
in a manner rather derogatory to his ecclesiastical dignity,
viz., by a promise made by the earl and countess that a
brace of fat bucks should be sent to him and his successors,
at his manor of Kempsey, every year, on Assumption day,
and a brace of fat does every Chistmas eve.[1]

The same year a contest arose between the Earl of Gloucester and Humphrey de Bohun, Earl of Hereford. It was,
in fact, but the renewal of an ancient quarrel, occasioned by
the encroaching spirit of Earl Gilbert, who had built a castle
on, or too near, the lands of the Earl of Hereford, in Breck-
nockshire. On the former occasion, notwithstanding the
positive orders of the monarch that none of his subjects
should attack each other in a hostile manner, the earls had
proceeded to actual combat;[2] and, therefore, when the
offence was reiterated, it was thought necessary to take
resolute steps to punish the daring miscreants. Both the
offenders were thrown into prison, and the affair was, after
some delay, brought before parliament.[3] Earl Gilbert, as
the aggressor, was compelled to pay a fine of £100 to his
antagonist, and was, moreover, remanded to prison for some

[1] Rot. Cart., 19 Edw. I., n. 32.   Dugdale's Baronage, vol. i., p. 215.
[2] Rot. claus., 17 Edw. I., m. 6, dorso.   Fœdera, vol. i., pt. ii., p. 710.
[3] Rot. pat., 19 Edw. I., m. 20, dorso.   Rot. claus., 18, m. 13 d.

time longer. The castle of Morgannon, the original cause of the quarrel, was forfeited to the king during the life of Earl Gilbert, but, in consideration of his marriage with the Princess Joanna, it was, on his death, to revert to her and her heirs.[1]

The state maintained by the Countess of Gloucester, and the large retinue of servants and attendants by which she was always surrounded, may be gathered from the account preserved of two visits paid by her to the prince her brother, who kept a separate establishment. The first was on Thursday, January 22nd, 1293, when she remained with him until the following Saturday; the second, on the 3rd of May, when she was accompanied by her husband. On both occasions, a "decent company" of soldiers, ladies, damsels, clerks, and squires attended her. They received nothing from the prince's stable, having brought their own horses' provender with them; but their presence at his table nearly doubled his ordinary expenditure, especially in the article of wine, the usual allowance of twenty-two measures per day being increased to forty, or forty-two.[2]

During this year, 1293, the presence of Earl Gilbert was required in Ireland, to defend his numerous estates there against the devastating attacks of the wild native clans He assembled a number of his warlike retainers from among his English vassals, and, accompanied by his countess, set sail about Michaelmas for Ireland; where, by a happy mixture of severity and timely forbearance, he succeeded in taming the turbulent spirit of the people, and triumphed completely over all his enemies.[3]

The king continued, meanwhile, to show his good will to his daughter by presents of extensive lands,[4] wardships,[5] &c.

[1] Ryley's Placita Parliamentaria, p. 74. Baronage, vol. i., p. 215.
[2] Rot. hospitii Edw. fil. reg., 21 Edw. I., dorso.
[3] Wikes, Gale, vol. ii., p. 126. Orig. letters, Tower, No. 1642. During their absence, they appointed two attorneys to attend to their English estates.
[4] Rot. pat., 23 Edw. I., m. 3.   [5] Ibid., 20 Edw. I., mm. 7, 12, ?`

In reference to one of these grants, an odd circumstance transpired; the king had given the wardship of the heirs of Robert de Mortimer to his daughter, and then, forgetting that he had done so, bestowed it afresh on his chancellor, the Bishop of Bath and Wells; but Joanna was by no means willing to relinquish her claim, and the king gave the bishop 500 marks to leave the countess in undisturbed possession.[1]

The next event of importance in the history of the Lady Joanna was the death of her husband, which took place on the 7th of December, 1295, at the castle of Monmouth, in Wales, where the earl and countess were then residing. His corpse was conveyed, on the 22nd of the same month, to the church of Tewksbury, which was the family burial-place of the Clares, and interred on the left hand of his father's tomb.[2] In this stately abbey his figure still remains, with those of several of his ancestors, in one of the richly stained windows which pour their "dim religious light" into that ancient structure. He is dressed in a full suit of rich chain armour; on the breast of the tabard are the arms of the Clare family, or, three chevronels gules; his spear is held in the right hand, and his sword in the left. He wears the ungraceful round Norman helmet, the raised vizor of which exposes to view a set of homely features, but which have not the remotest pretension to the resemblance of portraiture, since precisely the same face is placed on the shoulders of all the generations of the de Clares, whose chivalric forms frown, side by side, from the painted glass, which, enduring in its brittleness, has handed them down unhurt through so many generations.[3]

Though the great earl descended, full of years, to an

[1] Rot. exit., 19 Edw. I., Pasch.
[2] Cott. MS., Vesp., A. ii., f. 71, b.
[3] Carter's ancient sculpture and painting, vol. ii., p. 32. Edward II. offered a cloth of gold on his tomb at Tewksbury on January 17, 1324.— Wardrobe book, 17 Edw. II. The author is indebted to Messrs. Puttick and Simpson for the opportunity of consulting this and several other similar documents, which have recently passed through their hands.

honoured grave, the youthful widow whom he left behind him had scarcely reached the prime of womanhood, for she was only twenty-three years old at the time of his decease. She did not betray any violent grief on the occasion, nor was it likely that she should feel deeply, for her marriage had been one of policy rather than affection, and the extraordinary nature of her marriage settlements left her in a position even more eminent than she had occupied as the wife of the premier peer in England; since the possessions of her late husband were now to revert exclusively to her. Early in January she hastened to court, and eagerly set about the necessary arrangements connected with the enfeoffment of her vast estates. She performed the usual homage to the king, her father, at St. Edmundsbury, on the 20th of January, 1296,[1] and he immediately ordered that all the goods, chattels, and estates of Earl Gilbert should be surrendered to her. Sufficient security was, however, first to be taken for the sums which Earl Gilbert had owed to the royal exchequer, but of those debts, 10,000 marks, which he had incurred as a fine, were pardoned, at the instance of the Countess Joanna.[2] Different sums, amounting in all to £902. 5s. 8½d. were allowed to the executors,[3] and other favours in reference to the collecting of the king's taxes on her estates were granted.[4]

Edward also assigned her the Castle of Bristol as the residence of her children, and gave orders to the constable of the castle to yield up to her whatever apartments she might choose for them and their attendants, only excepting the Tower, and some rooms which were already preoccupied by the wife of one of his faithful servants, then in Gascony.[5] In this arrangement of the monarch to secure his grandchildren more immediately under his own surveillance, is an

---

[1] Rot. claus, 24 Edw. I., m. 11.   [2] Ibid., mm. 11-10.
[3] Orig. letters, Tower, temp. Edw. I.   [4] Rot. claus., 24 Edw. I., m. 10.
[5] Ibid.

implied suspicion as to the capacities of their mother to act
as their sole guardian, which shows that her character for
prudence did not even then rank very high.   During the
remainder of the year 1296, the princess Joanna seems to
have lived in one or other of her Welsh castles, exhibiting
all the external symbols of widowhood.   But it was not the
moody broodings over days of departed happiness that were
uppermost in the heart of the giddy princess.   Among the
retinue of her late lord was a squire, remarkable for his fine
person and chivalric accomplishments, named Ralph de
Monthermer, or, Rauf de Mehermer, as he styled himself.[1]
After the death of the earl, he was still retained in the service of the countess, and her charms so won upon him, that
he even ventured to aspire to the hand of his royal mistress.
Some encouragement must surely have been given him on
her part, before such an idea could have found a place in
his mind.   His suit was favourably regarded, but, low as
the enamoured lady was willing to stoop, she could not consent to wed one who was not even a knight; she therefore
sent her suitor to her father, requesting him as a favour to
grant him the honours of knighthood.   The unsuspecting
monarch complied with her wishes;[2] and then, with a fervour of attachment which scorned all bounds of prudence,
the countess bestowed upon this nameless youth the hand
for which, even then, princes were vainly sighing; and a
private marriage cemented the union of the lovers.[3]

"It is singular," says Sir Harris Nicolas, in his biographical notice of Ralph Monthermer, "that nothing should
be known of the origin of an individual who became the
son-in-law of the King of England, and possessed, in right
of his wife, the powerful Earldoms of Gloucester and Hertford.   Until his marriage with Joan d'Acres, widow of Gil-

---

[1] Orig. letters, Tower, temp. Edw. I.
[2] Chron. Rishanger, Royal MS. 14, C. i., f. 5 b.
[3] Rishanger, Cott. MS., Claud., D. vi., f. 123 b.

bert de Clare, Earl of Gloucester and Hertford, and daughter of King Edward I., early in 1297, his name does not once occur in the records of the period, and it may therefore be conjectured that both his birth and station were obscure, and that he was solely indebted to his splendid alliance for the wealth and honours which he obtained."[1] The precise date of the marriage is not given, but indirect evidence occurs to place it early in January, 1297, when Joanna had been a widow little more than a year.

Daring as was the temper of the Lady Joanna, she trembled to disclose at once to her sire the step she had taken. Some rumours, however—whether set on foot by herself or not cannot be determined—reached him; not of her marriage, certainly, for of that he remained in ignorance some months longer, but of her inclinations on the subject. An instantaneous explosion of wrath followed. Orders were issued to the king's escheators on both sides the Trent, strongly enjoining them that, for reasons which are not specified, they shall forthwith take into their hands the lands, goods, and chattels of Joanna, Countess of Gloucester and Hertford, both in England and Wales, and keep them safely, till they hear to the contrary, and this, as they valued their safety, and would avoid the king's indignation. The usual epithet of the "dearest daughter of the king" is on this occasion withheld from Joanna, and she is merely styled Countess of Gloucester.[2] The mandate bears date from Castle Acre, the 29th of January. One of her faithful adherents, however, Luke de la Gare, who had the custody of her Castle of Tunbridge, resolutely refused to yield it up to the king's messengers, treated their mandate with scorn, and defended his post by force of arms. Edward, enraged beyond measure, ordered all the goods of the brave governor to be seized, and him and his son to be immediately taken and

[1] Siege of Carlaverock, biographical notices, p. 275.
[2] Rot. claus., 25 Edw. I., m. 23.

brought before the royal presence, in whatever part of England the king might happen to be.[1]

Thus, Joanna, from her lofty pre-eminence in riches and power, was reduced at once to complete dependence, until her situation was slightly relieved a few months subsequently by the king's allowing her, from her vast revenues, just enough for the reasonable support of herself and her children.[2]   King Edward's fears had been thoroughly roused; and, to avoid the possibility, as he thought, of any imprudent step on the part of his wilful daughter, he endeavoured to patch up a hasty marriage for her with Amadeus, Earl of Savoy, who had sent to demand her hand.   The arrangements were speedily made, and a letter written, signifying his consent thereto, which bears date March 16th, 1297.[3]

Meanwhile, he had despatched Walter de Winterborn, his own confessor, on the 8th of February, to his daughter, in Wales, to obtain accurate information of the state of affairs.[4]

The princess, however, without informing her father of her movements, had returned to England to consult with her most intimate matron friend, Joanna, Countess-dowager of Pembroke, the widow of William de Valence, half-brother of Henry III., on the course of conduct which it would be prudent to adopt.   Her position was indeed a most delicate one; with the displeasure of her father impending over her, on the one hand—and of the vehemence of that displeasure she had already had fearful warnings—whilst, on the other hand, she, an already wedded wife, was threatened with an immediate foreign alliance.   To add to her difficulties, but little time was left her in which to endeavour to prepare her father for the intelligence that awaited him, for she soon

[1] Abbreviatio rot. Orig., 25 Edw. I., p. 98 b.
[2] Rot. claus., 25 Edw. I., m. 16.
[3] Fœdera, vol. i., p. 861.
[4] Wardrobe book, 25 Edw. I., f. 9 b., Addit. MS., 7965, British Museum.

became conscious that she was in a situation which would render the disclosure of her marriage inevitable.

Joanna ordered her young son Gilbert to meet her at Goodrich Castle, Herefordshire, the residence of the Countess of Pembroke. He arrived there on Monday, February 4th, with his attendants, and the countess herself, with a large suite of servants, joined him on the Wednesday following.[1]

Long and earnest must have been the discussions between the two friends, and very eloquent, probably, the eulogies pronounced by the princess on her husband-lover. There was another person present at Goodrich castle, the Lady Isabella de Valence, daughter of the Countess of Pembroke, who was, probably, overlooked by the agitated princess, but whom she would have regarded with very different feelings could she have foreseen that this young girl was destined to become the second wife of her beloved Monthermer, and under circumstances very similar to those in which she herself was then placed.

It was concluded that the most advisable course would be for the princess to proceed at once to court. She left the principal part of her train with her son,[2] and sent him and her little daughters, who were much beloved by their grandfather, to the king,[3] in hopes that their infant caresses might operate in her favour; and soon afterwards she herself, with but few attendants, ventured into the presence of her father.

---

[1] Wardrobe roll of Joanna, Countess of Pembroke, 1297, No. L. ii., 6, Chapter-house documents. Several of the household rolls of this lady are in existence in the Chapter-house and Rolls-house, all of which are calendared as Queens' household rolls. That they are not queens' rolls is, however, sufficiently proved by the fact that three of them are for the years 1295-1297, when there was no queen, either consort or dowager, in England. Moreover, the rolls are headed " Rotulus hospicii *dominæ*," &c., whereas a queen's style is invariably " *dominæ reginæ*." The name of the "domina" is not given, but they are attributed to the Countess of Valence, from many points of internal evidence, too long to detail at length. The places of the domina's residence coincide with the dower castles of the Countess of Pembroke; the name of Aymer de Valence, and other children of that family, constantly occur as residing with her, &c. The rolls are beautifully written, and in excellent preservation.

[2] Ward. roll, ess. Pembroke, ut supra.   [3] Ward. book, ut sup., f. 33.

On her arrival, the dreaded *dénouement* of course speedily took place. The shock which the intelligence produced upon the monarch and his nobles may be more easily conceived than described. That a princess of the blood royal, and the first countess in England, should, of her own accord, mate herself clandestinely with a simple squire, who had not as yet even won the spurs of his newly-acquired knighthood, was a thing unheard of in the annals of English, and even of European, royalty. The king, in a burst of passionate fury, instantly despatched the unhappy Monthermer to Bristol Castle, and commanded him to be kept in rigorous confinement.[1] He revenged himself upon his daughter, by exacting immediate and rigorous payment of all the sums due to him from the late Earl of Gloucester; availing himself of his present possession of the Gloucester estates to enforce his claims.[2]

The conduct of the nobles at this crisis is thus graphically described by Rishanger: " I will not say that all the magnates of the land regarded this deed with a pleasant mind, but all restrained their lips through fear or reverence —fear, because she was of royal descent, and the daughter of the king—reverence, because she was the principal countess in the kingdom."[3] The subject became one of constant discussion at court, some pleading the cause of the princess, and others taking the opposite side. Among the former party was Antony Bek, Bishop of Durham, a confidential friend and adviser of the king, whose mediation exercised a powerful influence in calming his wrath: on the other hand, one of the nobles, whose name is not given, but who, from the jealous and angry spirit of his remarks, might be conjectured to be some disappointed suitor of the princess, whispered in the king's ear that such a marriage was most adverse to his

---

[1] Chron. Rish., Royal MS., 14, C. i., f. 5 b.
[2] Rot. pat., 25 Edw. I., p. 2, m. 13.
[3] Chron. Rish., Cott. MS., Claud., D. vi., f. 123 b.

honour, since kings, earls, nobles, and barons were all emulously striving to obtain the hand of the princess.

At length, however, Joanna was allowed to plead her own cause with her father; and she argued with all the eloquence of warm feeling. "It is not considered ignominious, nor disgraceful," said she, "for a great earl to take a poor and mean woman to wife; neither, on the other hand, is it worthy of blame, or too difficult a thing, to promote to honour a gallant youth." The boldness of her reply pleased the king: he considered that what was done could not lawfully be undone, and, for the sake of his daughter, he remitted his indignation against her wedded lord.[1] Monthermer was released, and the young couple had the gratification of seeing their union recognised, if not sanctioned.

The reconciliation took place, about the latter end of July, at St. Albans.[2] On the 31st of that month, Joanna's goods and chattels, and also all her lands and honours, excepting the castle and honour of Tunbridge, and her demesnes in Kent, Sussex, Surrey, &c., were restored to her, on condition that she should provide one hundred men-at-arms to serve the king in his French wars, over whom she was to appoint any captain she might think fit, excepting her husband; and also that she should give security for the few debts still unpaid, due from the late earl to the royal exchequer.[3]

The softer and better feelings of Joanna appear to have been wrought upon by the anxieties she had undergone; and, on the very day that they thus happily terminated, she testified her gratitude by one of the few religious acts she is ever recorded to have performed. In company with two of her

[1] Chron. Rish., Cott. MS., ut supra; also, Royal MS., ut supra.
[2] Chron Petrob., Addit. MS. 6914, f. 72 b.
[3] Abbreviatio Rot. Orig., 25 Edw. I., p. 100 b. Palgrave's Parliamentary Writs, vol. i., p. 296. No. 36. A wardrobe fragment of the 26th of Edw. I. mentions the sum of £60 paid to the earl and countess as the cost of the letters obligate drawn up on this occasion. The date is February 6th, 1298.

sisters, she went to the abbey church of Westminster, and there had masses performed for the soul of her deceased mother, Queen Eleanora,[1] perhaps with a half superstitious feeling that to her benign influence she might owe something of the happiness she was now enjoying.

On the 2nd of August, a memorandum occurs that "Ralph de Monthermer, knight, who had married Joanna, Countess of Gloucester and Hertford, the king's daughter, did homage to the king at Eltham, and afterwards to the king's son;" and immediately, at the same place, the countess performed similar homage.[2] After this period, Ralph assumed, in right of his wife, the title of Earl of Gloucester and Hertford, to hold by a service of fifty knight's-fees in Flanders; and, as such, he was soon after summoned to attend Edward, the king's son, with horses and arms, at Rochester.[3]

The earl and countess now resided principally at Marlborough Castle, and here Joanna soon afterwards gave birth to a daughter, whom she named Mary. Her father and brother showed the sincerity of their reconciliation, by presenting small donations, the one of five marks, or, £3. 6s. 8d., the other of £2. 10s. 0d., to the valet who brought them the news of the countess's safe delivery.[4]

The style observed by the princess in her household was not at all inferior to that to which she had been accustomed during the lifetime of her first lord; and it may be well surmised that in the enjoyment of the affection of the husband of her choice, she was far happier than when the seal of her marriage-bond was policy rather than love.

In the year 1299, we find her attending a splendid feast, given by Prince Edward, in the Tower of London, to a

[1] Wardrobe account, 25 Edw. I., No. 2174, Queen's Rem.
[2] Rot. fin., 25 Edw. I., m. 7, quoted by Palgrave ut sup. Trivet's Annals, p. 301.
[3] Parl. Writs, vol. i., p. 297, No. 38.
[4] Wardrobe book, 25 Edw. I., f. 156. Dugdale's Baronage, vol. i., p. 215.

brilliant assemblage of lords and ladies. For this feast extensive preparations were made, and the great chamber in the Tower was cleared of the wardrobe accoutrements which were usually kept there, to serve as a banqueting-room for the Countess of Gloucester and the other ladies.[1] Monthermer was not present, having been employed by the king to conduct some troops into Scotland,[2] where he took an active part in the war, and so won upon the affections of his father-in-law by his chivalric bravery, that the remainder of his wife's lands were restored to him.[3]

The following year, 1300, in the month of January, Earl Ralph was in Ireland, whither he had gone to settle some business connected with his estates, or, rather, with those of his wife. In a charter dated from Kilkenny, the 8th of January, he styles himself "Ralph de Monthermer, Earl of Gloucester and Hertford, Viscount of Kilkenny," adopting the regal plural, and speaking of "our court," and "our seneschal," with all the dignity of an independent prince.[4] Joanna did not accompany him, but paid a visit during his absence to the court of the king, her father. The place of Eleanora of Castile, Joanna's deceased mother, had been recently supplied by Queen Margaret of France, Edward's second wife. One of the many amiable traits in the character of this young queen, was the kindly feeling she ever showed towards her husband's children. On occasion of this visit, she presented silver cups to three of the damsels of the countess Joanna who were in attendance upon their mistress.[5]

Monthermer was present during this year at the siege of

[1] Wardrobe account, 27-28 Edw. I No. 2602, Queen's Rem.

[2] Rot. claus., 27 Edw. I., m. 2.

[3] Rot. claus., 29 Edw. I., m. 1. He was a sort of purveyor-general for the army, and stores of wine, wood, meal, flour, beer, hay, &c., were distributed through his hands.—Wardrobe fragm., 29-30 Edw. I., Queen's Rem.

[4] Lambeth MS., 608, f. 12—transcribed out of the book of the extent of the Earl of Ormond's lands, called the red book, 31 Edw. I.

[5] Wardrobe book, 29 Edw. I., f. 147., Addit. MS. 7966 A., Brit. Museum, date March 21st, in the 28th year.

the Scottish Castle of Carlaverock. This siege has been lately brought into prominent notice by the publication of a very curious contemporaneous account of it, from a manuscript in the Heralds' College,[1] containing a full description of each knight present, with the blazon of his arms. In this interesting document Joanna's husband is thus named: " He whose love was well supported, and brought to an end, after great doubts and fears, until it pleased God he should be delivered therefrom, endured for a long time great sufferings, for the love of the Countess of Gloucester. He had only a banner of fine gold, with three red chevrons. He made no bad appearance, when attired in his own arms, which were yellow, with a green eagle. His name was Ralph de Monthermer."[2]

The banner of Ralph, here described, was the family arms of the Earls of Gloucester, adopted by him with their title. Usually, however, he preferred his own coat of arms, and those are alone engraved on his seal, of which an impression was preserved, attached to the celebrated letter, so well known to the lovers of genealogical or historical antiquities, written in 1301 to the pope, and signed by all the principal nobles of England, remonstrating with his holiness against a pretended claim of his to the sovereignty of Scotland.[3] The obverse of this seal represents Ralph, on horse-

---

[1] Edited by Sir Nicholas Harris Nicolas.

[2] " Celui dont bien furent aidies,
  Et achievees les amours,
  Apres grans doubtes et cremours,
  Tant ke Dieus len voult delivré estre,
  Por la Contesse de Gloucestre
  Por long tens souffri grans maus.
  De or fin o trois chiavrons vermaus
  Il ot baniere seulement.
  Si ne faisoit pas malement
  Kant ses propres armes vestoit
  Jannes, ou le egle verde estoit;
  Et ot nom Rauf de Monthermer."
            Siege of Carlaverock, p. 48.

[3] A facsimile of this letter is engraved in the Monumenta Vetusta, published by the Society of Antiquaries—vol. i., p. 28.

back, in full chivalric accoutrements; and the reverse gives the arms of Monthermer, as already blazoned by our poetic chronicler. The legend is, "S. Radulphi de Monte Hermerii com. Gloverinæ et Hertford"—"The seal of Ralph de Monthermer, Earl of Gloucester and Hertford."

The name of Monthermer stands third in this list of the English nobles, so completely had this child of fortune become indentified with the proud title he now held. Joanna was present at the signing of this document, as appears from the following lines of Piers de Langtoft :—

> "When thei the Chartre in alle had schewed day bi day,
> Sir Roger the erle Marschalle, of Herford the erle Umfray,
> At York thei tok in hand, ther parlement to sette,
> The hie folk of the land, ther alle togidere mette.
> The erle Jon of Surray com with grete powere,
> Of Gloucestre stoute and gay Sir Rauf the Mohermere,
> And his wife dame Jone, whilome Gilberde's of Clare,
> Those banerettis ilkone fro Douer to Durham ware."[1]

On the 4th of October, 1301, Joanna presented her husband with a son, who was baptized, on the 6th of December following, by the name of Thomas. John, Bishop of Llandaff, a prelacy which, as we have already noted, was in the gift of the Countess of Gloucester, officiated at the ceremony.[2] The king gave forty marks to the valet who brought him tidings of the child's birth.[3] A comparative idea of the estimate in which the sexes were held may be incidentally deduced here—this sum was exactly eight times as much as the king had previously given when the announcement was made to him that he had a granddaughter born.[4]

As far as the character of Joanna may at this distance of time be traced, her conduct appears to have been far less exceptionable as a wife than as a mother. We have already

---

[1] Piers Langtoft, vol. ii., p. 301.
[2] Cott. MS., Vesp., A. ii., f. 73 b. Chron. Norw., Calig., A. x., f. 181 b.
[3] Wardrobe book, 29 Edw. I., f. 9 b, Addit. MS., No. 7966 A, Brit. Mus.
[4] See page 348, supra.

seen that, on the death of her first husband, she allowed her
children, still very young, to remain in the castle of Bristol,
committed only to the guardianship of servants, while her
thoughts were engaged with the excitement and difficulties
attendant upon her projected re-marriage. When, however,
the young Gilbert was too old to be abandoned exclusively
to such superintendence, the king, aware that the boy's
mother either could not, or would not, take sufficient care
of him, commanded that, for certain reasons which he does
not assign, Joanna should send her son to court, there to
remain under the tutelage of Queen Margaret.[1] Gilbert,
from the brilliancy of his future expectations, was always
considered a person of consequence, but his three sisters
seem to have lived in comparative neglect—no notices occurring respecting them. Nor were Joanna's children by her
second husband more fortunate. Besides Mary and Thomas,
already mentioned, she had another son, born in April, 1304,[2]
and named Edward, after his grandfather.

It has been previously remarked that Monthermer was in
high favour with the king, who is said to have loved him as
his own son, and highly resented any slight or wrong committed against him. Of these kindly feelings several instances occur in 1302. He had the king's permission, then
very rarely granted, to hunt in all the royal forests in England, and carry away as much game as he chose.[3] Stern
justice was executed against some persons who had seized a
vessel which he claimed as his property;[4] and also on some
malefactors, against whom the earl and countess brought the
charge of having inflicted damage, to the amount of £200,
in one of their chases.[5]

Earl Ralph was also one of the most gallant and successful captains employed by Edward I. in the Scotch war.
During the years 1303 and 1304, we find Joanna accom-

[1] Rot. claus., 29 Edw. I., m. 7.   [2] Rot. exit., 32 Edw. I., Pasch.
[3] Rot. pat., 30 Edw. I., m. 24.   Fœdera, ii., pt. i., p. 54.
[4] Ibid., m. 36 dorso.   [5] Ibid., m. 4 dorso.

panying her lord to Scotland, and she resided some time with him at Dumfernline, where the king, with his young queen and other members of the royal family, had also taken up their temporary abode.[1] Monthermer's establishment was supplied with ample allowance of corn, wine, salt, &c., from the royal stores.[2]

Notwithstanding the large income which the Countess Joanna had at her unlimited disposal, she was sometimes greatly straitened for ready cash, and her father, probably reprobating her extravagant habits, was ludicrously parsimonious in his loans to her, as is evident from entries like the following:

"Lent to Joanna, Countess of Gloucester, the king's daughter, on the 6th of June, at Tynemouth, by hands of her valet, *to be repaid*, . . . 13s. 4d.[3]

"Lent to Joanna, Countess of Gloucester, by the hands of the king's chamberlain, at Dumfernline, January 24th, ... 10s. 0d."

Similar entries occur of ten marks on the 22nd, and 5s. on the 27th, of February, 1304.[4] Although the king was niggardly in his loans to his daughter, he was not so in his gifts. A sum amounting to between £90. and £100. was expended by him in the purchase of jewellery and in different expenses for her.[5]

It must have been in expenditure connected with her own personal gratification that the income of the Countess Joanna was swallowed up, for the expenses of her children's wardrobe, &c., were principally borne by the king,[6] and she gave

---

[1] Rymer collectanea, Addit. MS. 4575, f. 575, British Museum.
[2] Wardrobe book. 31 Edw. I., Addit. MS. 17,360, British Museum.
[3] Rot. Præstit. garderobæ, 29-32 Edw. I., dorso, No. 2144 Queen's Rem.
[4] Ibid.
[5] £63. 7s. 10d. from the 30th to the 32nd regnal year. £8. 18s., and again £20. 13s. 4d., from the 32nd to the 33rd.—Wardrobe book, 34 Edw. I., Queen's Rememb. This is a handsomely bound volume in a case, but is not foliated.
[6] Among the wardrobe fragments of the 35th of Edward I., occur notices of batons, a war-helmet, leggins, greaves, gauntlet, habergeon, saddles and

but little in monastic benefactions. She is recorded to have patronized the priory of Stoke Clare, in Suffolk, which was founded by Richard de Clare, the ancestor of her first husband.[1] She also gave to the monks of Caversham, near Oxford, some land towards enlarging the grounds already granted them by her father, on condition of their praying for her soul and the soul of Earl Gilbert.[2]

But little now remains to be recorded of the Countess Joanna. She was at court in the Christmas of 1305, and received from her father a present of a golden clasp, studded with emeralds.[3] In April, 1306, we find her at a mansion in Essex, where she received a visit from her son Gilbert.[4] In May, 1306, she was present at court, when her eldest daughter, Eleanora, a child of only 13 years of age, was married to Hugh le Despenser, afterwards the unfortunate favourite of Edward II.[5] The last mention that we find of Joanna is early in 1307, when she sent her waferer to her brother, to make minstrelsy before the mirth-loving prince; 20s. were paid to him for his expenses in coming to the prince's court, at Wetherhal, in Cumberland, and returning to his mistress.[6]

But the countess had little further need of his service, for she was fast approaching a world where earthly music can charm no more. She died rather suddenly, at her manor of Clare, in Gloucester,[7] on the 23rd of April, 1307, having

bridles, &c., for Gilbert de Clare; again, of ten pieces of green Tripoli silk for Gilbert and Eleanora, children of the Earl of Gloucester. At one period, Gilbert, with his tutor, formed part of the family of his juvenile uncle, Prince Edward.—See also roll 29-32 dorso, No. 2144 Queen's Rememb.

[1] A cartulary of this priory forms No. 4835 of the Harleian MSS. It notices several gifts from the children of Joanna.

[2] Dugdale's Baronage. vol. i., p. 216.

[3] Wardrobe book, 34 Edw. I., Queen's Remembrancer.

[4] Wardrobe fragm., 34 Edw. I., Queen's Rem.

[5] Wardrobe book, 34 Edw. I., Queen's Rem. £100 were paid to the friars minors of London to redeem the bridal robe of Eleanora le Despenser, which belonged to them as their perquisite.—Wardrobe fragment, Edw. I.

[6] Wardrobe account of P. Edw., last year of Edw. I., Harl. MS. 5001. This is not the original wardrobe book, but a copy in the handwriting of the reign of Henry VII. or VIII. It is not foliated.

Chron. Rob. de Rading, Harl. MS. 685, f. 200 b.

only just completed her thirty-fifth year. The news of her decease reached the king her fatehr on the 1st of May, at Carlisle. He immediately wrote off to the Bishop of London, his chancellor, informing him of the departure of " Joanna, his dear daughter, to God," and commanding that all arch-bishops, bishops, abbots, friars, &c., throughout the realm, should cause obsequies to be performed, and masses to be solemnly sung, with private masses and orisons, for the soul of his daughter.[1]   Not satisfied with this mandate, the king, on the 6th of May, issued another, which ran as follows :—

" The king to the venerable father in Christ, Ralph, Bishop of London, greeting.   Since it is esteemed a work pious and meritorious before God to pray for the dead, that they may be more easily delivered from the snares of sin ; and God, the builder, disposer, and creator of all things, at his good pleasure, hath called to himself from this life Joanna, our dearest daughter, late Countess of Gloucester and Hertford, which we announce to you, not without deep sorrow of heart ; we send to you, praying that you will cause the soul of our aforesaid daughter to be specially com-mended to the most High by all religious and other ecclesi-astical persons, your subjects, through your whole city and diocese, by the singing of solemn masses, and other pious works."[2]

Letters in this form were also written to the other prelates of the kingdom.

On the 2nd of May, Edward himself presented an offer-ing for the soul of Joanna, and on the 3rd and 4th had masses said on her behalf, in his presence, at the church of friars minors in Carlisle.[3]   Whether this unwonted assiduity

---

[1] Writ of privy seal, Royal letters, No. 1643. Fœdera, vol. i., pt. ii., p. 1013.   In spite of the decisive documentary evidence on record as to the period of Joanna's death, Dugdale, with an inaccuracy unusual in him, places it in the latter end of 1307, and, consequently, in the first regnal year of Edw. II.—Baronage, vol. i., p. 216.

[2] Fœdera, vol. i., pt. ii., p. 1016.

[3] Wardrobe fragm., 35 Edw. I., Queen's Rem.

proceeded from the overflowings of bereaved affection, or whether the king deemed that his daughter was burdened with an extraordinary share of those sins for the removal of which he considered such means efficacious, we presume not to decide.

The body of the deceased princess was carried to the Augustine priory of Clare, and attended to the grave by Prince Edward, with almost all the magnates of England.[1] The attendance of so large a train of mourners was an unusual circumstance, and may be considered as a mark of voluntary deference to her rank and talents. More than eleven years subsequently, when her brother King Edward II. passed through Clare, he visited her tomb, presented two Lucca cloths to place over it, and had mass performed in his presence for her soul.[2]

It is questionable whether the husband so dearly cherished was present to soothe the last hours of Joanna's life. Monthermer had been latterly unfortunate in his military career. He had been defeated by the brave Robert Bruce, and compelled to fly for shelter behind the walls of the Castle of Ayr, where he had undergone a close siege, which was only raised by a body of troops sent by the king to his relief;[3] and he is mentioned as being at Athol but a short time previous to the death of his wife.[4] He paid a speedy visit to her tomb,

---

[1] Chron. Dunmowe, Cott. MS., Cleop., A. iii., f. 293. Dugdale oddly blends the account of Joanna's funeral with that of her father, which took place shortly afterwards. The mistake has arisen from the occurrence of an unfortunate blank in the chronicle from which he quotes, which runs thus: "Obiit Johanna de acars comitissa de Clare. Et sepulta est in ecclesiâ fratrum Sancti Augustini apud Clare. Et dominus Edwardus, frater ejus, fuit in præsens, cum omnibus magnatibus fere Angliæ . . . . deceret corpus E. 1 de Karlel usque ad Waltham crucis, cum omni honore. Et ita factum est. Et quod episcopi abbates et priores per baronium tenentes ibidem accederent," &c. After further descriptions of the funeral ceremonies, the chronicle proceeds: "Et post sepultum domini regis Angliæ." From this it is very evident that the latter part of the description belongs to the funeral of Edward I., with the circumstances of which it precisely corresponds, and not to that of the princess, and that the hiatus contained the account of the king's decease.

[2] Wardrobe book, 11 Edw. II., f. 141.   [3] Walsingham, p 105.
[4] Wardrobe book of Prince Edward, ut supra.

however, and gave considerable benefactions to the priory of Stoke Clare, where she was interred.[1]

The favour of his royal father-in-law was not withdrawn from him, however, when the tie that had uuited them was snapped. The king had previously bestowed upon him the Earldom of Athol, in Scotland, when he distributed among his followers the lands of the so-called rebel traitor, Robert the Bruce;[2] but time having shown that such a donation was rather nominal than real, it was transmuted to a gift of 5000 marks, for the purpose of aiding him in the purchase of lands to the value of 1000 marks a year for the support of himself and his children.[3] Edward also remitted all debts due to the royal treasury from the Gloucester estates, even those owing during the life-time of the late Earl Gilbert.[4]

On the death of Edward I., an attempt was made by the officers of the new monarch, who had not yet ascertained his dispositions towards his brother-in-law, to seize the goods and chattels of Monthermer, in distrain for these debts; but the king immediately put a stop to their proceedings, confirmed his father's decrees, and ordered restitution to be made.[5] The same course was adopted by Edward II. with reference to other privileges granted to Monthermer.[6] Dugdale makes an assertion, in which he has been followed by other genealogical writers, that the title of Earl of Gloucester was never given to Ralph de Monthermer after his wife's death; but this statement is incorrect. In all the grants just alluded to, in which Joanna's death is distinctly mentioned, he is styled "Earl of Gloucester and Hertford," and he retained that title till it was assumed by young Gilbert Clare, whose majority, by an edict of his uncle, King

[1] Monast. Anglic., vol. vi., p. 1600.
[2] Rot. cart., 34 Edw. I., m. 1. Rot. pat., 35 Edw. I., m. 4.
[3] Rot. pat., 35 Edw. I., m. 4; and 1 Edw. II., p. 1, m. 19.
[4] Rot. claus., 1 Edw. II., m. 19. Rot. pat., 6 Edw. II., p. 1, m. 4, per Inspeximus. Orig. Letters, Tower, temp. Edw. I.
[5] Rot. claus., 1 Edw. II., m. 19. Royal letters, No. 1644.
[6] Fœdera, vol. ii., pp. 5, 10, &c. Rot. pat., 2 Edw. II., p. 2, m. 24.

Edward II., was anticipated by several years, and at the same
time the king gave him leave to marry whenever he pleased.[1]
It is very probable that the young Gilbert was thus early
installed into his honours from a jealous reluctance on the
part of the nobles for Monthermer to enjoy his honours after
the death of his wife. On the occasion of his necessary re-
linquishment of all share in the Gloucester lands, Edward II.
allowed him 5000 marks a-year in compensation.[2]

Monthermer's first clandestine marriage had succeeded so
well, that, a few years after Joanna's death, he perpetrated,
as already mentioned, a second runaway match, with Isabella, widow of John de Hastings, sister and co-heiress of
Aymer de Valence, with whose mother his first wife had
been on such intimate terms.[3] When the king heard of this,
he fined Monthermer 1000 marks, which he afterwards
remitted.[4] By this lady he had a daughter, who bore the
name of Joanna, and afterwards took the veil at Ambresbury. Isabella is styled by a contemporary writer " Countess of Gloucester,"[5] affording additional proof that Monthermer retained his title by courtesy some time after the
death of the princess. The Lady Isabella survived him.[6]

Monthermer was taken prisoner at the battle of Bannockburn; but, having previously formed, at the English court,
an acquaintance with Robert the Bruce, whose gallant character in many respects agreed with his own, he obtained his
discharge on payment of a ransom, and brought home with
him the king's target, which had been taken in the fight.[7]
He was summoned to parliament as a baron, until the 18th
of Edward II., 1225,[8] when he disappears from the page of

[1] Rot. claus., 1 Edw. II., m. 3.   Rot. pat., 1 Edw. II., p. 1, m. 24.
[2] Rot. exit., 5 Edw. II., Mich., pro anno primo.   Wardrobe account,
temp., Edw. II., Cotton MS., Nero, C. viii., p. 43.
[3] See page 345, supra.
[4] Rot. pat., 14 Edw. II., p. 2, m. 12.   Fœdera, vol. ii., pt. i., p. 403.
[5] Chron de Trivet MS. 632¹⁷, Sup. Franc. Bibliothèque du roi.
[6] Calend. Inquis., post mortem, vol. iii., p. 327.
[7] Walsingham, p. 105, Camden's Scriptores.
[8] Dugdale's summons to parliament, index.

history; and his death is conjectured to have taken place at that period. On the window of Tewksbury church, among the figures of the Earls of Gloucester, is one who wears a tabard simply diapered, without coat of arms, which is generally supposed to be that of Ralph Monthermer.[1] If this conjecture be correct, he was probably interred there, in the family burial-place of the De Clares.

Neither he nor his children cut a very conspicuous figure after the death of the royal lady to whom they owed their elevation. The Lady Mary Monthermer was betrothed by her grandfather, Edward I., when a child of but nine years of age,[2] to Duncan, Earl of Fife; several documents, relating to her subsequent marriage, are printed in the Fœdera,[3] during the reign of Edward II., in which she is called the king's niece. To his two nephews, Thomas and Edward, the king granted during their youth the manor of Warblington, for their support,[4] and afterwards those of Stoke and others in Devonshire.[5] Thomas Monthermer took a share, though not a prominent one, in the political events of the times, and received a pardon for having adhered to the party of the Earl of Lancaster;[6] he was slain in a sea-fight, between the English and French, in 1340.[7] From his daughter Margaret are descended the family of Montacute, or Montague, the present Earls of Salisbury.[8]

Edward, the youngest son of Joanna, was several times summoned to parliament as a baron, and performed military service against the Scots; he died without issue, and was buried by his mother's side in the priory of Stoke Clare, Suffolk.

[1] Carter's ancient sculpture and painting, vol. ii., p. 32.
[2] Royal letters, No. 1736, date October 12th, 1306.
[3] Vol. ii., p. 111.   [4] Rot. pat., 3 Edw. II.
[5] Rot. cart., 3 Edw. II., m. 9. Fœdera, vol. ii., pt. i., p. 91.
[6] Calend. rot. pat., p. 107.
[7] Dugdale's Baronage, vol. i., p. 217. Chron. St. Alban's, Lambeth MS., No. 6, f. 49 b, col. 1.
[8] Harl. MS., 1499, f. 23 b.
[9] Weever's funeral monuments, p. 740.

The destinies of Joanna's children by her first husband were more splendid, but unfortunate.   Her son Gilbert, whose rank and royal descent entitled him to the position of premier peer of the realm,[1] was made captain in the Scotch expedition of 1809,[2] and afterwards *custos regni*.   He married a daughter of the Earl of Ulster, by whom he had one son,[3] who died before him.[4]   He was slain in the battle of Bannockburn in 1314,[5] sacrificed, it was said, by the cowardice of his household retainers, who fled from him when he exposed himself to great danger in the heat of the fight.[6]   He was buried at Tewksbury by his father, and his effigy is also painted upon the window of the abbey.[7]   He left his three sisters co-heiresses of the immense Gloucester estates.[8]   Two of them had the misfortune to become wives to the favourites of Edward II.   Eleanora le Despenser, whose marriage has already been alluded to,[9] was, after the miserable death of her husband, kept a close prisoner in the Tower, until the reign of Edward III., when she was released, and became the wife of William le Zouch, of Mortimer.[10]   Margaret was married, by her uncle, very shortly after her mother's death, to Piers de Gaveston;[11] but, from her unfeeling and capricious husband, she received nothing but mortification and neglect, and she was at length divorced

[1] In the roll of arms of the reign of Edward II., edited by Sir Harris Nicolas, his name is given next to that of the monarch.
[2] Fœdera, vol. ii., pt. i., p. 91.
[3] Edward II. gave £10 in 1311 to the valet who brought him tidings of the birth of this boy.—Wardrobe account, Cotton MS., Nero, c. viii., f. 84.
[4] Dugdale's Baronage, vol. i., p. 217.
[5] In 1324, Edward II., passing through Tewksbury, had masses performed and offerings made at the tomb of his cousin.—Wardrobe accounts, portfolio, 2947, Queen's Rem.
[6] Wright's political songs, p. 262.
[7] Shaw's dresses and decorations, vol. i., plate 28.
[8] Chron. Dunmowe, f. 296.   There are very many entries in the patent rolls of Edward II., about the division and settlement of these estates.—See patent roll, 14, m. 31, &c.
[9] She is several times alluded to in the wardrobe books of Edward II., and twice in that of Queen Isabella, 5 Edw. II., as being a companion of the queen.—Cotton MS., Nero, C. viii., ff. 142, 146.
[10] Dugdale's baronage, vol. i., p. 392.
[11] Chron. Dunmowe, Cott. MS., Cleop., A. iii., f. 293 b.

from him, and married to Hugh d'Audely,[1] who obtained in her behalf the title of Earl of Gloucester. The wrongs endured by this unfortunate lady in her first marriage were among the most prominent grievances which inflamed the wrath of the barons against Gaveston and his weak master, who would thus tamely permit his niece to be insulted; and they ultimately led to the destruction of the favourite. Elizabeth, the third daughter, married John de Burgh, Earl of Ulster, in Ireland. On his death, she was married to Theobald de Verdun, who lived only six months afterwards, and gave place to a third husband, Roger d'Amory.[2] Her daughter, by her first husband, who was also named Elizabeth, became the wife of Lionel, Duke of Clarence, son of Edward III., and the ancestress of the house of York,[3] and by the marriage of Henry VII. and Elizabeth of York, of the present royal family of England.[4]

The following curious dialogue, written during the reign of Edward III., and printed in the new edition of the Monasticon Anglicanum,[5] points out more fully the illustrious progeny of the Princess Joanna. It is represented as taking place at her tomb, of which a rude drawing, bearing, it must be confessed, a closer resemblance to a large wooden chest than to a tombstone, is delineated, with a monk on one side and a layman on the other.[6]

" This dialogue betwix a secular asking, and a frere answering, at the grave of dame Johan of Acres, shewith the lyneal descent of the lordis of the honoure of Clare, fro the tyme of the fundation of the Freeris in the same honoure, the yere of our Lord, MCCXLVIIJ., unto the first day of May, the yere MCCCLVJ.

---

[1] Baronage, vol. i., p. 750; vol. ii., p. 42.
[2] Chron. Dunmowe, ut sup. Chron. Croxden., Cott. MS., Faust., B. vi., f. 103. Trivet's annals, Arundel MS., No. 50, fol. 75 b.
[3] Chron. Dunmowe, f. 306 b.
[4] For much information respecting the Clare podigree, see Dr. Rawlinson's corrections of Dugdale.
[5] Vol. vi., p. 1600.   [6] See Vignette.

"' What man lyeth here ? say me, sir Frere.'
'No man.' 'What ellis?' 'It is a woman.'
'Whos doughter she was I wolde lefe here.'
'I wol you tel, sir, like as I kan;
King Edwarde, the first after the conqueste began,
As I have lernyd, was hir fadir;
And of Spayne borne was hir moder.'
'What was her name?' 'Dame Johan she hight
Of Acris.' 'Why so declarid wolde be?'
'For [because] there she saw first this worlde's light
Borne of hir modir, *as cronicles tell me!*
Wherefore, in honoure, O, Vincent! of thee,
To whom she had singuler affection,
This chappell she made of pure devotion.'
'Was she ought weddid to ony wight?'
'Yes, sir.' 'To whom?' 'Yf I sholde not lye,
To Gilbert of Clare, the erle, by right,
Of Gloucestre.'"

Here follows a long genealogy of the house of Clare, after
which the dialogue proceeds.

"' Now to Dame Johane turn we ageyn,
Latter Gilbertis wife as before seid is,
Which lyeth here.' 'Was she bareyn?'
'Nay, sir.' 'Say me, what frute was this?'
'A branch of right great joy, I wis.'
'Man or woman?' 'A ladie bright.'
'What was hir name?' 'Elizabeth she hight.'"

The remainder of the poem, which is extended to some
length, details the descent of the family down to the marriage of Richard Duke of York with Cecilia, daughter of the
Earl of Westmoreland, and mother of Edward IV. In
their behalf is offered the concluding prayer.

"Long mote he liven to Goddi's pleasaunce,
This high and mighty prince in prosperite:
With virtue and victorye God him avaunce
Of al his enemyes, and grante that he
And the noble Princesse, his wife, may see
Her childres children, or [before] thei hence wende
And after this outelary [1] the joy that nevir shal ende."

These quaint rhymes are a contemporary translation of verses
written in monkish latin, and illustrated by the coats of arms
of the nobles and their wives. They afford a curious specimen of the vernacular English of the period.

---

[1] So in the translation—*outlawry*, as a metaphorical term for human life?
The Latin version has " post *fata* ducens," &c.

MARGARET,

FOURTH DAUGHTER OF EDWARD I.

The Princess Margaret, although the fourth in age of the daughters of Edward I. and Eleanora of Castile, was the first who was born as the daughter of a king, since her elder sisters had come into the world, while Edward as yet only enjoyed the dignity of heir to the throne. Her birth took place at Windsor on the 11th of September, in the year 1275.[1]

[1] Harl. MS., 3846. Chron. Petroburg. Addit. MS., No. 6913, f. 232. Chron. Brute, Cott. MS., Nero, A. vi., f. 27 b.

Of the particulars of her infancy and childhood but little remains on record worthy of notice. She was educated with her sisters, principally at Windsor Castle or the Tower.[1] As she grew up, we find the usual entries for her in the wardrobe accounts; but, since the number and quality of a young lady's dresses and ornaments, the amount paid by her in alms, and other particulars of miscellaneous expenditure, do not, after all, give to her biography much individuality of character, and since what is most curious as affording illustrations of the manners of royalty in the olden time has already been noticed in the preceding memoirs, a few extracts alone must suffice in connexion with the early life of the Princess Margaret.

In 1285, when she was ten years old, she displayed, on one occasion, a more than usually devout spirit, for, after she and her sisters had presented their offerings on the 1st of May, at the great altar of Westminster, and also to the relics of St. Edward, Margaret gave an additional offering of two shillings at the shrine of the Confessor the following Trinity Sunday, which was May 20th.[2] Her journeys this year are readily traced by the number of gold clasps studded with gems, which she is recorded to have offered at the shrines of different saints on certain days. They, probably, afford a fair specimen of her general course of life. She usually travelled in the company of her parents, and always in that of some of her sisters.

On January 23d, she offered at the shrine of St. Thomas, Canterbury; February 20th, at St. Edward's, Westminster; and the 27th, at St. Mary's, Walsingham; April 10th, at Ely; and 17th, at St. Alban's; May 1st and the 20th, at St. Edward's, Westminster. During the month of June, she seems still to have remained at Westminster. On the 6th of July, she offered to St. Thomas, and on the 8th, to

[1] Rot. lib., 6 Edw. I., m. 2. Ibid., 8, m. 3. Rot. class., 8, m. 10.
[2] Wardrobe Book, 13 Edw. I., f. 18 b., Miscel. roll, Tower, No. 65.

St. Augustin, at Canterbury; on the 25th, she was at Chichester. On August 15th, she was present at a general re-union of the royal family at Ambresbury, to witness the profession of her younger sister Mary.[1]

The following occur among other wardrobe entries for her about this time, 1286 :—

" February 24th. To Roger, the tailor of Margaret, the king's daughter, for sewing his lady's robes against the feast of John the Baptist in summer, and against Christmas; also for a knife to be mended, in honour of the blessed virgin,[2] for copper basons, &c.,   .   .   .   17s. 7d.

" February 27th. For silk bought for the embroidery-work of Margaret, the king's daughter,   .   .   8s. 0d.[3]

" 'To William Leybrook, for one new basket of boiled leather, some gold thread, soap, two dozen gloves, basins, golden bowls, and other things wanted for the Lady Margaret, the king's daughter, on the 4th of May, also for plates of gold, pearls, garlands, shoes, &c., .   62s. 10d."[4]

Again, at a later date :—

" To Thomas Caimmill, Margaret's squire, for twelve pairs of shoes, six pairs of gloves, a *barhot* [dress of hairy fur[5]], also for 4 oz. of silk and 200 oz. of gold thread, for a spindle, for the making of garlands and tressures, and for 1 lb. of table-silk, bought for her from Whitsuntide in the 17th year [1289] to February 2d, in the 18th, [1290]   .   .   .   .   44s. 6d."[6]

The mention of the spindle proves that Margaret occupied herself with weaving, probably in silks and gold thread, since no commoner material is mentioned, as well as in

[1] Wardrobe roll, 14-15 Edw. I., No. 1865, Queen's Rem. Jewel roll, 13 Edw. I., British Museum, recently purchased.

[2] So in the MS. What honour was to redound to the blessed virgin from the mending of the princess' knife our deponent witnesseth not.

[3] Ward. book, 14 Edw. I., f. 7, Miscell. roll, Tower, No. 66. Ward. roll, 14-15 Edw I., No. 1782, Queen's Rem.

[4] Wardrobe book, 14 Edw. I., f. 11 b.   [5] Query, a bear-skin—bâr-haut?

[6] Wardrobe book, 18 Edw. I., f. 2. Miscel. roll, Tower, No. 71.

embroidery. In sooth, some constant occupation must have been essential to divert the tedium of leisure hours, even for royal ladies, when the whole world of literature and taste was to them an unknown region, when the varieties of life mainly consisted in their frequent journeyings to and fro, and its business was the arrangement of their wardrobe ornaments.

In one respect, the career of the Princess Margaret differed materially from that of her sisters and most of her compeers; she was never the subject of more than one matrimonial engagement; the *fiancé* of her childhood became the husband of her youth and maturer years; and, although she survived him six years, no fresh offer tempted her widowed constancy.

It has already been noted, that the jealousies subsisting between the courts of England and France induced Edward I. to seek to strengthen his alliances, wherever he was able, with the continental powers, and especially with those whose dominions bordered upon France. With this object, he courted the good-will of John I., surnamed the Victorious, Duke of Brabant, and secured it by promising him the hand of his daughter Margaret, then the eldest princess who was disengaged, for his young son and heir John. The negociations commenced in 1278, when the little princess was scarcely three years old. Her father promised to pay a dower of 50,000 livres Tournois, in four instalments, the last instalment to be due on the marriage of the children. On the other hand, the duke promised, in his own name and that of his son, an annual revenue of 3000 livres Tournois, to be derived from lands conveniently situated in Brabant, and which were to be placed in the hands of two commissioners appointed by the king. In case of the premature death of either of the plighted sposnes, the next brother or sister of the deceased was to take his or her place; but, if circumstances occurred completely to obstruct

any marriage negociation between the two powers, then
the portion of the dowry already paid was to be restored to
King Edward.[1] These arrangements were duly sworn to
upon the holy Gospels, and ratified, not only by the duke
and his son, but by Godfrey, the younger brother of the
bridegroom, and by his mother, the Duchess Margaret.[2]
The dower lands of Margaret were also specifically assigned
to her in the district of Jodoigne, in Brabant.[3]

In 1284, John of Brabant was sent by his father with
many nobles, knights, and clerks, on a special mission to
England. They arrived in London on the last day of
October; their visit only lasted eleven days, during which
time they lived at the king's charges.[4] This was his first
introduction to his young *fiancée*, then a merry child of
nine summers, and more likely to be occupied with her
playthings than to pay much attention to her future husband. That young John, however, professed to be greatly
pleased by his visit, and also gratified with his spouse elect,
appears by the following letter, written a short time afterwards, to his intended father-in-law :—

"To the very high, noble, and puissant prince, his
very dear and beloved lord, my lord the King of England,
John his son and son of the Duke of Brabant, ever ready
to do his will and commandment.

"Very dear sire,—I, who am desirous, as is right, to
hear good news of you, pray and require you that you will
let me know with certainty of your estate, which God ever
keep good and hold in prosperity. And about myself,
very dear sire, I give you to know that I am hearty, which
God ever give me to know concerning you. And know,

<hr />

[1] Orig. letters, Tower, No. 1119, date January 25th, 1279.
[2] Fœdera, vol. i., pp. 551, 553.   [3] Ibid.
[4] Wardrobe book, 18 Edw. I., f. 13 b. These payments are said to be
made for John of Brabant when he *first* came into England; and the date
is ascertained by the mention of Friday as the vigils of St. Martin, a coincidence which transpired in 1284.

dearest sire, that I greatly desire to see you. Dear sire, I pray you to take council that I may marry soon; for I greatly desire it. Command me at your will as your son, and our Lord have you in guard. Dearest sire, as I have no seal, I use the seal of madame my mother.[1]"

About the year 1285, Edward I., anxious still farther to secure the fidelity of the Duke of Brabant, persuaded him to allow his son to come over to England for education; knowing that, by this means, he should have a precious hostage always in his own hands. Accordingly, on the 20th of April, John was sent into England.[2] His youth, for he was only 15 years of age, and that of the still more juvenile Margaret, procrastinated for awhile the time of their marriage; but he was received and treated with all the respect due to his present and prospective position. He was attended by his tutor, Sir Ernulph,[3] and a large suite of servants, among whom were clerks of the household, wardrobe, kitchen, and chamber; valets, a barber, tailor, washerwoman, marshall, palfry-keeper, falconer, couriers, &c.[4] Sometimes he resided with the king, and sometimes with Edward, Prince of Wales, but more frequently was domiciled in solitary state at Langley, Winchester, Havering, or some other of the royal residences.[5]

He appears, however, to have paid occasional visits to his father. A memorial of one of these is preserved in the year 1288; for, at the close of a letter of Duke John about the Bishopric of Liege, the following confirmation occurs :—" We, John, eldest son to my lord duke aforesaid, at the commandment and will of our dear lord and father, and by our own will, praise, agree, approve, and give all things as they are herein inscribed.

---

[1] Orig. letters, Tower, No. 1499.
[2] Wardrobe roll, 14-15 Edw. I., No. 391, Queen's Rem.
[3] Wardrobe book, 14 Edw. I., f. 7.   The tutor died in 1286, and his place does not seem to have been supplied. Ibid.
[4] Wardrobe book, 18 Edw. I., f. 37 b.
[5] Wardrobe roll, No. 391, ut sup.   Wardrobe accounts *passim*.

"In testimony and in security of which things we have appended our seal, with the seal of our dear lord and father, to these present letters. Given in the year of the incarnation of our lord, 1288, Thursday after the octaves of St. Peter and Paul, apostles."[1] The young heir of the duchy had advanced in dignity since the time when he had been obliged to borrow his mother's seal.

The entries in the wardrobe accounts made for the expences of John of Brabant are very numerous, especially in the purchase of riding, hunting, and sporting accoutrements; for, in the chivalrous and manly exercises of the day, he took great delight. A few of these entries may serve as specimens :—

"To Roger, the clerk, for the expences of John of Brabant and his family, viz., the expences of diverse persons going beyond court on his business; of his falconer, squire, and other messengers sent to Brabant and elsewhere; for diverse gifts, oblations, and alms, for the reparation of his robes, the covering and getting up his bed, with thread, silk, &c.; also for six saddles, with their appurtenances, spurs, belts, twelve pairs of shoes, three dozen gloves, vessels for his falcon, &c., &c., £21. 17s. 10d.

"To Roger, his deputy purse-keeper, for the wardrobe expences of John of Brabant and his family, going from court to Havering Bower, and staying there and at Weeley, to hunt, from Sunday after the feast of St. Hilary[2] to Tuesday before the purification of St. Mary,[3] seventeen days, for bread, corn, hay, and other expences, and also for wine . . . . £46. 10s. 11d.[4]

"January 11th. For two gentle falcons, bought at London for John of Brabant . . . £6. 0s. 0d.

---

[1] Heelu's Slag von Woeringen. Codex diplomaticus, p. 461.
[2] January 15th. The feast of St. Hilary is January 13th.
[3] January 31st. February 2nd is the purification of the Virgin.
[4] Wardrobe book, 18 Edw. I., f. 2 b., Miscel. roll, Tower, No. 71.

"To John de Maclyn,[1] violinist of John of Brabant, for one bay horse, bought by him, and given to the said John by command of the king .   .   .   .   40s. 0d."[2]

These last entries bring us down to the beginning of the year 1290, and to within a short period of the marriage of the sport-loving John of Brabant with the English princess. During his five years' residence in England, he had only paid occasional visits to court, and those of short duration. Probably King Edward might be of opinion that, at so early an age, the young couple were better apart; and the predilections of John for the amusements of the field would render a sylvan residence more suitable to his taste. It would not seem that he was a very attentive lover, for, up to the very time of his marriage, he remained absent from his young *fiancée*, partly on a visit to Ambresbury, to Queen Eleanora of Provence, Margaret's grandmother, but principally occupied in hunting in divers parks and forests.[3]

At length, the arrival of the Duke of Brabant, his father, with the principal nobles and ladies of the province, who came to do honour to the nuptials of their future lord, recalled the restless youth to court, for the performance of the ceremony in which he was to bear so conspicuous a part; and the royal family, who had been spending a short time at the Tower, returned in their barges up to the Thames to Westminster, where the marriage was to take place.[4]

The union of John of Brabant with the Princess Margaret was celebrated with great splendour on Saturday, July 8th, 1290.[5] The bridal trousseau and jewels of the

[1] Probably Mechlin, or Malines.
[2] Wardrobe book, ut sup., f. 49. Wardrobe roll, 18 Edw. I. Amongst Sᵣ T. Phillipps' MSS.
[3] Wardrobe book, ut sup., f. 13 b.   [4] Ibid., f. 10.
[5] Ibid., f. 48. Annales, luculenti, Cotton MS., Nero, D. II., f. 182 b., col. 2. Barthol. Norw., Nero, C. v., f. 207 b. Chron. Petrob., Addit. MS., 6913, f. 270, gives July 10th; the chronicle of John of Oxford, Cott.

Lady Margaret were very magnificent. Zones and chaplets of gold, studded with pearls and rubies, and wrought with the leopards of the royal arms in sapphire stones; a clasp, wrought in the form of an eagle; a head-dress of gold, studded with three hundred emeralds, are mentioned among her costly equipments.[1] The king gave 60s. to be placed on the missal with the spousal ring; and he distributed large sums of money in alms to the friars preachers, and others, in honour of the nuptials.[2] The princess was attended by her eldest sister, the Lady Eleanora, whose attire must have been cumbersome in its costliness, since fifty-three dozen silver buttons were purchased to ornament it.[3]

A contemporary chronicler, who wrote in the lifetime of Margaret's son, illustrates his description of her marriage with a drawing of it, in which he represents all the nobles, including the king himself, in full armour, and standing in martial attitudes, whilst the bride and her attendants are placed on [a scaffolding near; wearing the monstrous horned or conical cap, which became prevalent in the succeeding century. He describes the princess as very beautiful, and her bridegroom as "stout, handsome, gracious, and well made."[4]

The valuable MS. chronicle of Bartholomew of Norwich, a contemporary writer, gives a detailed account of the rejoicings at the marriage-feast, which was given by the king at London. Prince Edward, the brother of the bride, was present with a train of eighty knights; but her brother-in-law, the great Earl of Gloucester, was accompanied by one hundred and three knights and six ladies; and her

MS., Nero D. II., f. 233 b., and Matthew of Westminster, p. 414, July 9th, as the date of the marriage, but the authority of the documentary evidence is decisive.

[1] Wardrobe book, 18 Edw. I., f. 49 b.
[2] Ibid., Miscel. roll, No. 70, not foliated.
[3] Wardrobe book, ut sup., fol. 10 b. Wardrobe roll, 18 Edw. I., Middehill MSS.
[4] Klerk Brabantsche Yeesten, Willem's edit., published for the Brussel's Historical Society, pp. 400, 437.

uncle Edmund, Earl of Cornwall, had one hundred knights and six ladies in his train. Many other magnates were similarly, though less numerously, attended, and all in very rich attire. The bridegroom himself had only eight knights, but he was escorted by no fewer than sixty of the fairer sex; and, elegant as was his attire, consisting of the close tunic, loose surtunic with sleeves to the elbows, and capes of vair fur, it was changed three times in the course of the day for a still more costly dress.

Beside the nobility and their attendants, seven hundred and nine knights and ladies led the chorus of rejoicing, first in the king's palace, and then, forming themselves into procession, traversed all the streets and suburbs of the city— a less herculean task in the *thirteenth* than it would be in the *nineteenth* century—accompanied by nearly one thousand of the good citizens of London, who joined in these enthusiastic demonstrations of loyal delight.[1] Their revels seem to have continued even after the close of the long summer-day; for an illumination was got up at the palace in the evening on so large a scale, that four boys had been occupied, during fourteen days, in collecting candles for it.

The nature of the amusements provided for the brilliant company thus assembled appears from some notices in the wardrobe book of the year. From far and wide, both in England and on the continent, were summoned fools, harlequins, harpers, violinists, trumpeters, and minstrels. No fewer than 426 minstrels, partly English and partly foreign, were present; among whom, on the following day, the bridegroom distributed the sum of £100, about £3000 of our money. The fool of the Count of Artois, who came with the Duke of Brabant, had a present of 40s. from the king, the minstrel of Lord William de Fiennes 20s. from Prince Edward,[2] and 40s. were paid to two Welsh trumpeters.[3]

---

[1] Cott. MS., Nero, C. V., f., 207 b.

[2] Wardrobe book, 18 Edw. I., f. 48.

[3] Ibid., f. 48 b.

At the close of the festivities, the Duke of Brabant prepared for his return to his own dominions; but, on account of the extreme juvenility of his daughter-in-law, who had not yet completed her fifteenth year, he consented that she and her husband should remain awhile longer in England. The princess distributed gifts, consisting of zones and other articles of jewellery, to the Brabantine ladies before their departure.[1] Prince John accompanied his father to Dover,[2] from which place the duke set sail for Brabant.

Margaret meanwhile remained with her own family. On the 22d of July, we find her offering with her father, and her sisters Eleanora and Elizabeth, at the shrine and relics at the abbey church of St. Alban's.[3] Careful as the princess usually had been in the performance of her religious duties, yet, on the return of her bridegroom to court, she became infected with somewhat of his recklessness of spirit; and their irreverence occasioned some concern and no small expense to the king. This appears by the following curious entry in the often-quoted wardrobe book of the year :—"Sunday, the ninth day before the translation of the virgin,[4] paid to Henry, the almoner, for feeding 300 poor men, at the king's command, because the Lady Margaret, the king's daughter, and John of Brabant, did *not* hear mass, 36s. 7d.," a sum equal to £27 of our money ; and, not satisfied that the neglect was sufficiently atoned for,. by the king's request, John of Brabant gave an additional sum in alms.[5]

In the month of September, the same year, 1290, John paid a visit to his paternal domains, probably to receive the congratulations of his friends on his marriage ; but its duration is uncertain. His name occurs, along with that of his father, in a grant, confirming some privileges to the citizens of

---

[1] Wardrobe book, 18 Edw. I., f. 53 b.   [2] Ibid., f. 13 b.
[3] Wardrobe book, 18 Miscel. roll, No. 70, unfoliated.
[4] August the 6th, which fell on a Saturday. The translation, usually called the assumption of the Virgin, is on August 15th.
[5] Wardrobe book, 18 Edw. I., Miscel. roll, No. 70.

Louvaine, which bears date Michaelmas, 1290.[1] In 1293, he is frequently mentioned as a visitor of Prince Edward ; in the February of that year, he, along with the two sons of Edmund, Earl of Cornwall, and a large retinue, attended a tournament given at Dunstaple. Thence, on his way to Canterbury, he spent a few days with the prince, as he did also on his return from that city. On Wednesday, June 17th, the prince being at Mortlake, in Surrey, he repeated his visit ; his train consisted of twenty-four grooms and thirty horses, and the two sons of Prince Edmund were again with him. In August, Edward had removed to Winchester, whither he was followed by his brother-in-law and his two companions, and also by many strangers who had permission from the king to hold a hunting match in the neighbouring forest of Ashley.[2] Several other visits to the prince are recorded, but not connected with any particular event, and the roll from which these extracts are taken closes shortly after. Margaret, with one of her sisters, occasionally visited Prince Edward during the year, but not at the same time as her husband.

The marriage of the Lady Margaret did not materially alter her position in her father's court. Her dowry lands, the annual value of which was already increased to 6000 livres Tournois, and afterwards to 8000,[3] were placed by Duke John in the hands of the attorneys appointed by the king, and she and her husband issued, with much formality, their letters patent, authorizing possession to be taken of them in their name. The document is written in old French, of which the following is a literal translation :—

" To all those who shall see and hear these letters, John

---

[1] Codex diplom., appendix to Heelu's chronicle, p. 336.
[2] Household roll of Prince Edw., 21 Edw. I. Devon's excerpta, from the Pell rolls, p. 108.
[3] Fœdera, vol. i., pp. 734, 739.

of Brabant, son to the noble man John, by the Grace of God Duke of Lorraine, and Brabant, and Limburg, and Margaret his wife, daughter to the noble Prince Edward, by the same grace King of England, health in our Lord.

"Know that we have appointed our dear friends, William de Carleton, clerk, and Monsieur Roger de Tilmanston, knight, our attorneys, to receive in our name the seisin of 6000 livres of land, the which our dear father aforesaid ought to deliver to us, according to the agreements made between our aforesaid fathers. And we confirm and establish whatever the said William and Roger shall do in our name concerning this business. In witness of which things we have made these letters patent, sealed with the seal of the aforesaid John, and in lieu of the aforesaid Margaret, because her seal is not affixed, we have caused to be put the seal of the noble Lady Eleanora, Queen of England, wife of our Lord the king. Given at Torpel,[1] the 8th day of September, the year of the Incarnation of our Lord 1290."[2]

The king granted to the Duke of Brabant Margaret's dower revenues for the next three years, to assist him in paying his debts, unless, within that period, he, the king, should accomplish his meditated project of going to the Holy Land; in which case the moneys were to be paid to John and Margaret, for the support of their own establishment; but this proviso had never occasion to be put into effect.[3]

The scantiness of the wardrobe accounts during the few subsequent years leaves us few particulars of Margaret's domestic history. In the March of 1294, she and her brother Edward were seized with fits of tertian fever, which

---

[1] Query, the manor of Torpull, mentioned in Gough's Camden, vol. i., p. 270.
[2] Fœdera, vol. i., pt. ii., p. 739.
[3] Rot. pat., 19 Edw. I., m. 13, in cedulo. Fœdera, vol. i., p. 742, printed from Rot. Vasc., 19 Edw. I., m. 6.

lasted, though with some intermission, for more than a month, but from which they both ultimately recovered.[1]

In Brabant, their future duchess was regarded by the people with great interest—perhaps the more intense from her high rank, and from the curiosity excited by her long tarrying in England. They were anxious that she should become acquainted with their language; and, to tempt her to a study so uninviting as that of the uncouth old Dutch of the thirteenth century, a celebrated Brabançon poet, named Jean van Heelu, a contemporary and friend of the duke, her father-in-law, wrote a long heroic poem, commemorating the war-like deeds of his master Duke John, surnamed the Victorious, in the hope that Margaret's interest in the subject of the verse might act as a spur to conquer the difficulties of the vehicle in which it was conveyed. This poem, after having lain buried for centuries in manuscript in an obscure Flemish library, has at length found an editor in J. F. Willems, and was published at Brussels, in quarto, in 1836, under the auspices of the Belgic government, and of his present majesty King Leopold I.; it forms one of the most interesting of the historical works lately brought out by that government. It is entitled, " *Slag von Woeringen,*" or, " The Fight of Wœringen," one of the Duke's principal battles. The opening or dedicatory stanzas run thus :—

" The Lady Margaret of England, she was plighted to John, son of John, Duke of Brabant. Since she cannot understand Dutch, therefore will I send her a gift of a Dutch poem, by which she may learn Dutch. Hereby send I her a description of her father-in-law, the duke. Never was a more beautiful example given of the great deeds of knighthood. Now beg I her for favour, this noble Lady Margaret, that I may enjoy her kindness, that she will receive graciously that which I have undertaken for her.

---

[1] Orig. letters, Tower, temp. Edw. I. See Appendix, No. xvi.

May God also grant me to bring out the truth of things, for I would adhere to truth, and modestly write the gests, &c."[1]

Truthfulness seems, indeed, to be the leading recommendation of this writer; for he boasts but little of poetic fire, neither does he manifest any great extent of learning. But, while he professes to tell " the truth, and nothing but the truth," it never seems to enter his head that it is also the duty of an historian to tell ." the *whole* truth," for he shows throughout a strong partiality to the Brabançons, and informs his readers, with great *bonhommie*, that "it is not good to relate blameable actions when they can be passed over in silence."[2] In some passages, especially those preparatory to the battle scene itself, he launches out into unusual eloquence. A single specimen, the speech of Duke John to his troops before the onset, is given :—" To-day shall you think of the bold deeds of your ancestors. Never did they fly and abandon their lord. Only act like them, and great glory will be your portion. I boast of you all, and value the services of so many lords, and of you, my good friends; but it is truly *here* that danger begins, for

[1] The verses, of which a translation is given in the text, are added as a specimen of the vernacular Dutch of the period.

" Vrouwe Margriete van Ingielant,
Die seker hevet van Brabant,
Ts'hertoghen jans sone Jan,
Want si dietsche tale nict en can,
Daer bi willic haer ene gichte,
Sinden, van dietschen gedichte:
Daer si dietsch in leeren moghe;
Van haren sweer, den hertoghe
Sindic haer daer bi beschieven;
Want en mach nict scoenres geven
Van ridderscape groote dade.
Nu biddic hare op ghenade,
Der edelre vrouwen Margrieten,
Dat ic hare dogeden moet ghenieten
Dat sigt met ootmoede wille outfraen;
Want om hare hebbict bestaen.
God lated my alsoc volbringen
Na die waerheit van den dingen," &c.

[2] Heelu's chronicle, verses 6395-7.

here will I be left dead, or win the field with honour. I call God to witness that I have desired peace; therefore, God will help us—I will go before you all, for I am the best mounted. Do you watch at my sides and back, firmly and dutifully, that I be not taken either in rear or flank. As to those that shall attack me in front, that is my business; I shall defend myself honourably; but, should you see me fly or surrender, kill me; I command it."[1]

Some account has been given in the preceding pages of the accidental and disastrous death of this gallant duke, while he attended the tournament given in honour of the arrival of the Princess Eleanora, Margaret's eldest sister, in the province of Bar. That event raised John of Brabant to the dukedom, and a deputation was instantly sent over to England to petition the king for the restoration of the prince, and to form his escort homeward. It was not, however, till the spring of the following year, 1295, that the preparations for his leaving England were completed.[2] He set sail in the latter end of June from the port of Harwich, in Essex, with three vessels provided for him by King Edward, which were ordered to be at his bidding till the beginning of August.[3] The king granted him, at parting, £4000, to be received from the customs payable on wools.[4]

Among the records in the Chapter House is his original acknowledgment of the receipt of this sum, dated December 21st, 1295; the seal is still pendant, and elaborately wrought with a figure of the duke on horseback, but, unfortunately, the head and half the body are broken off.[5] Another seal of the duke, of the same date, is, however, engraved in Butken's Annals of Brabant;[6] he wears no coronet; the full, round face is bordered by thick clustered locks, ungrace-

[1] Slag von Woeringen, p. 177, verses 4700, et seq.
[2] Rot. pat., 23 Edw. I., m. 15.   [3] Fœdera, vol. i., p. 802.
[4] Rot. pat., ut sup.
[5] State documents, temp. Edw. I., No. 30, Chapter House.
[6] Preuves, p. 134.

fully parted in the centre ; the left hand holds a hooded falcon, whilst another is seen flying under the nose of his horse, and a greyhound is running below. Thus, in his earlier seal, did the duke choose to perpetuate his love of woodland sports. The seal which he used towards the close of his life represents him in full armour, and without any of these accompaniments.[1] His portrait, as engraved in Barlande's[2] and Haecht's[3] chronicles, and also in Miræus' Annales Brabantiæ,[4] is unpleasing; the face wears a haggard, suspicious, sinister expression; a round cap, turned up with fur, covers the head, and over the rich armour is thrown a mantle, clasped at the throat—a collar of furs and golden chain complete the attire. The knightly sword at his side is accompanied by the gleaming stiletto, an unusual weapon for the warriors of that period. No portrait of him was engraved on his coins; they bore frequently the Belgic lion—sometimes the cross, with the legend on the reverse—" Blessed be the name of our Lord:"[5]

The young duchess did not accompany her husband to Brabant, and nearly two years elapsed after he had left England before she joined him. This circumstance, were no other proof on record, affords sufficient evidence that the marriage of the Princess Margaret was not a happy one; otherwise, a long and self-inflicted separation would never have been undergone by either party. How early the matrimonial infidelities of Duke John commenced remains uncertain, but the profligacy of his after-life is notorious, and this estrangement between himself and his wife leads to the supposition that he had already given her just ground of complaint. It is not always those that have been taught from early infancy to regard each other as the destined companion of after years who form the tenderest

[1] Butken, Preuves, p. 143.   [2] P. 49.   [3] P. 63.
[4] Vol. i., p. 291.
[5] Notice sur les anciennes momoies de Flandres, Brabant, &c., par Fr. Den Duyts, plate vii., Nos. 18-23.

and most enduring attachments. Love, in its fresh and passionate earnestness, delights to invest its object with a thousand attractions, many of which vanish before the cold eye of reality. Yet it is well that the feeling should have subsisted, for it infuses a lingering touch of sentiment into the deep and tender esteem, the confiding friendship which, after the effervescence of passion has subsided, form the beautiful elements of a happy, wedded life. But the Princess Margaret never seems to have won the love of her spouse. Both before and after marriage, his conduct towards her exhibited an indifference incompatible with real affection.

The interval of Margaret's residence in England, after the departure of her lord, was spent partly at the court of her father, and partly at that of Prince Edward, which was kept up separately with great state. But sometimes she chose to be independent of either, and the ever-indulgent monarch provided her with an establishment of her own.[1] One of her favourite residences was the Tower of London, where she spent the spring of the year 1296, remaining there alone for some time after her brother, whose guest she was, had departed.[2]

Meanwhile, Duke John had entered, with seeming ardour, into the political schemes of his father-in-law. England, being then at war with France, he engaged to do service against Philip the Fair with two thousand steel-clad warriors, and he bribed the people of Savoy and Burgundy to enter into a similar confederation.[3] He even professed to have encountered some peril in behalf

[1] Wardrobe book, 25 Edw. I., f. 52 b., Addit. MS. 796, Brit. Mus.

[2] Rot. exit., 29 Edw. I., No. 417. The entry alluded to is as follows:— "To Philip Everden, for kitchen vases, made for the Lady Margaret, the king's daughter, when she stayed at the Tower of London, after the Lord Edward, the king's son, had gone to the coast of the sea, in the quinzaine's of Passover, in the year 24, at which time the duchess was at the cost of the prince.

[3] Rot. Alem., 22-31 Edw. I., m. 18 dorso. Fœdera, vol. i., pp. 808, 820.

of the king, for we find Edward writing to him to express
his regret that he could not afford instant aid to him and
the Earl of Flanders, in the attacks from which they
suffered, but promising to come over as soon as possible,
and share in the good or evil success of the war.[1] For
these services the duke demanded, and Edward pledged
himself to pay, the large sum of 200,000 livres Tournois.[2]
In addition to this, he had, before John left England, bribed him with the sum of 40,000 livres Tournois, in order better to secure his fidelity.[3] For the
ultimate liquidation of these sums, he was even obliged
to pawn some of his jewels to his son-in-law.[4]

Notwithstanding these energetic measures of King
Edward, the allies, whose confederation he had purchased
so dearly, were only lukewarm adherents; and he was
obliged, sorely against his will, to make a truce with the
French king, in which they were included.[5] For the
duke, fertile in resources, had frequently contrived to elude
the demands of Edward, and had maintained a tempo-
rizing policy between the two parties.[6] His distaste for
war speedily procured for him the honourable epithet of
" John the Pacific"—honourable because his love of peace
was not the result of inertness or cowardice, but of an
enlightened conviction of its beneficial results.

The early part of the year 1297 presented a scene of
great gaiety in the court of Edward I., owing to the marriages of several ladies connected with the court,[7] but

---

[1] Rymer collect., Addit. MS., 4575, f. 271. Rot. Alem., 22-31, Edw. I.,
m. 11 dorso.   [2] Rot. exit., 23 Edw. I., Pasch.
   [3] Rot. pat., 25 Edw. I., p. 1, m. 19. Rot. exit., 32 Edw. I., Mich. in
dorso. Rot. lib., 26 Edw. I., m. 7.
   [4] Wardrobe roll, 26-27 Edw. I., No. 2084, Queen's Rem. Among the
Rymer collectanea is a letter of Edward to his dear nephew John III., of
Brabant, about a golden cross and other jewels belonging to Edward I.,
which had been in the hands of his father. Addit. MS., 4579.
   [5] Fœdera, vol. i., p. 838.
   [6] Dewe's hist. de la Belgique, vol. iii., p. 78.
   [7] Wardrobe book, 25 Edw. I., f. 137.

especially of his youngest and favourite daughter, the
Princess Elizabeth, to John Earl of Holland. Margaret
was the companion of her sister on this occasion; indeed,
their intercourse, during the few past years, seems to have
assumed a very intimate character. Being the only two
princesses at court, they were usually together, sometimes
in company with their brother, Prince Edward; they went
together to pay their offerings at the shrine of St. Mary's,
of Walsingham, and again to Langley, to perform solemn
masses for the soul of their departed mother Queen
Eleanora.[1]

The preparations for Elizabeth's marriage were blended
with those for the departure of her sister for the continent. After many delays, it had been determined that
she should perform the voyage to Brabant, under the
escort of her future brother-in-law, the Earl of Holland.
The court were now residing at Ipswich, in Suffolk, where
they celebrated their new year's festival. The king's
new year's gift to each of his three children, then with
him, Margaret, Elizabeth, and Edward, was a clasp of
gold, studded with gems.[2] The Princess Margaret presented her father with a pair of knives of ebony and ivory,
with ferrules of enamelled silver.[3] On another occasion,
she had presented him with a golden clasp.[4] The king
appears greatly to have valued these tokens of his daughter's affection; he retained them in his possession as long
as he lived; and they are enumerated, along with the circumstances of their presentation, in all his subsequent
jewel inventories.

[1] Wardrobe book, 25 Edw. I., f. 7.   [2] Ibid., f. 38.
[3] Ibid., 28 Edw. I., p. 344. Edited by Topham, for the Society of Antiquaries. The original MS. is in the library of that Society. Wardrobe book,
29 Edw. I , f. 148 b., Addit. MS., 7966, A., Brit. Mus., Wardrobe book,
34 Edw. I., Queen's Rem. Jewel roll, 31 Edw. I. Cole's selections from
records, p. 279.
[4] Gaveston's Jewel list, in the patent roll, 6 Edw. II., pt. 1, m. 3, schedule.
It was given by Edward II. to Piers Gaveston.

From Ipswich, most of the orders for the equipments of the Princess Margaret were dated. For her private chapel, she had rich provision of the usual articles of costly plate; chandeliers, patens, chalices, a censer in form of a ship, the vessel for holy water with its sprinkler, the alms-dish, the cross silver gilt, the little bell, and another article called, " *tabula ad pacem*," a tablet of peace, which was adorned with plates of silver and figures, either carved or painted, representing the Holy Trinity.[1] At a certain part of the service, it was usual for this tablet to be carried round the chapel to be kissed by the worshippers; and it was generally formed of a precious stone, richly chased and mounted.[2] The butlery of the Princess was amply supplied with silver cups, plates, and pitchers; for her chamber she had two *lavatoriu*—probably, rather meant to signify sets of washing utensils than baths; while, for her hall, the apartment which served the purpose of the French *salle à manger*, there was rich provision of table-plate, including, among other articles, 120 salt-cellars, and a number of richly ornamented shields of silver gilt. Her kitchen was furnished with plate of equal splendour,[3] whilst the more useful supply of copper pans, brazen bowls, posnets, dishes, &c., was not neglected.[4]

In the articles of her personal adornment, Margaret was both capricious and extravagant. A number of pieces of costly jewellery had been provided for her in London, and brought to Ipswich for her inspection; but she rejected them all, and returned them to the unfortunate jeweller with a haughty message, to the effect that they did not please her.[5] Her trousseau, as it was ultimately arranged, was extensive enough, however, to suit even her fastidious taste; thirty-eight golden clasps, one of which,

[1] Wardrobe book; 25 Edw. I., ff. 134, 135 b.
[2] See Du Cange, article tabula.   [3] Wardrobe book, 25 Edw. I., f. 134.
[4] Ibid., f. 14 b.   [5] Ibid., f. 13 b.

shaped like an eagle, had been presented by her father as a new year's gift,[1] and another of which was adorned with rubies and emeralds—a coronal of silver, a crown of gold of fourteen pieces, gemmed with emeralds and large orient pearls,[2] twenty-eight chaplets of silver, set with pearls, with ornaments of gold wrought in the form of birds, leopards, lozenges, &c., to wear at pleasure on the chaplets—twenty-eight tressures and three coifs, equally rich ; four brooches for her mantle, ten golden rings, one zone of gold, and twenty-three of silver gilt—all these form but a part of the long list of her apparatus.[3]   She had also a seal of gold made for her,[4] a necessary appendage of state to her rank as duchess, and one frequently put into requisition, as would seem by an entry which occurs of 23s. paid for wax to seal her letters,[5] and of payments to messengers to carry on her correspondence.[6]

The king also ordered a new chariot to be made for her, and richly painted ; the trimmings to be of silk, and the chains gilded.[7]   It was to be drawn by six horses ; the chariot provided for her maids of honour by five, and she had two of the vehicles, called long carts, each drawn by five horses, with abundance of sumpter-horses for her luggage.   Six saddle-horses were also purchased for her own riding, and six more for her maids ; but all her equestrian attendants, outriders, palfreymen, sumpterers, &c., were Brabantines sent over by her husband.[8]   Her harness was purchased at a cost of £19. 13s. 4d. ; and, from the circumstance that it was bought of a goldsmith, it must have been very splendid in texture.[9]

The nuptials of the Princess Elizabeth were performed

[1] Wardrobe book, 25 Edw. I., f. 137.
[2] Jeweller's account, 24-25 Edw. I., Miscel. roll, Tower, No. 91.
[3] Wardrobe book, 25 Edw. I., f. 13 b.   [4] Jeweller's account, ut sup.
[5] Wardrobe book, ut sup.   [6] Ibid., ff. 107, 113.
[7] Ibid., f. 15.   [8] Ibid., 25 Edw. I., f. 16.
[9] Rot. claus., 34 Edw. I. m. 4.

On the 7th of January, 1297, at Ipswich.[1] Margaret presented her with a golden cup as a bridal gift ;[2] and the sisters went together on the 24th to St. Edmundsbury, to pay their devotions at the shrine of St. Edmund, to whom they each offered a clasp of gold.[3] This was a sort of farewell pilgrimage on the part of the Duchess Margaret ; a few days afterwards she was to bid adieu to her family. A tone of mournfulness pervaded the parting scene. The king must have felt how completely the happiness of his daughter had been sacrificed to his own political interests, and how utterly inadequate were all the gifts which he lavished so profusely upon her to compensate for sorrows such as she had already endured, and must expect to endure. With a degree of sentiment unusual in his rugged temperament, the king had prepared a parting gift for her. It was a golden pyx, and in it he deposited a ring, the pledge of unfailing love, and placed it in her hands with his solemn benediction when she bade him farewell.[4]

The Princess Margaret, in company with the young Earl of Holland, embarked at the port of Harwich, in Essex.[5] The vessel which was to convey her to her future home was called the Swan of Yarmouth, and was one of the largest ships in the royal fleet. For the greater safety of his daughter, the king had ordered two pilots aboard, and there were on service fifty-three experienced sailors. A large lantern was hung up at night on the mast of her vessel, in order that the rest of the squadron, consisting of six large ships or galleys, and a number of smaller craft, might be able to follow in close and orderly attendance.[6] They were amply stored with provision for the voyage—39 oxen, 4 pigs, 57 sheep, 123

---

[1] Wardrobe book, ut sup., f. 142. [2] Ibid. [3] Ibid., f. 140.
[4] Jeweller's account, 24-25 Edw. I. Wardrobe book, 25, f. 15 b.
[5] Wardrobe book, ff. 14, 31. [6] Wardrobe book, 25 Edw. I., f. 89 b.

dishes of flesh, 10,652 herrings, 293 cods, and 4 barrels of sturgeon, 489 fowls at 2*d*. each, 700 eggs at 8*d*. per 100, and 11 cheeses at 9*d*. each, beside provender for 300 horses, &c.,[1] as also one thousand faggots, cut and carried to the vessel of the princess for firewood.[2] The sum of £300 was paid in cash for her expenses.[3]

Beside the Earl of Holland, Humphrey de Bohun, Earl of Hereford, Lord John of Hastings,[4] and many other lords, attended the duchess,[5] as also her father's clerk, John Lovel, and two other commissioners, who were sent to see that her dower lands were properly assigned to her.[6] Isabella, wife of John de Vescy, is the only female companion named.[7] Special privileges regarding the trade in wool and leather, about which the regulations were then very strict, were granted to this lady, on the ground of her being an attendant of the duchess, but she was not long allowed to remain with her mistress.[8]

The voyage occupied three days;[9] and on the fourth Margaret landed in Brabant, and was immediately escorted to Brussels, the capital, and usual residence of her husband. She was received by him with apparent cordiality ; and in a document bearing date the 14th of February, or St. Valentine's day, he confirmed to his " dear companion dame Margaret" the grant of 8000 livres Tournois, made by his father, and specified the places from which the revenue was to be derived.[10] This confirmation was made in accordance with the express wish of King Edward, who had written to his son-in-law about it,[11] and sent over several messengers to expedite the matter.[12] Soon after-

---

[1] Wardrobe book, 25 Edw. I., ff. 28 b., 31, 33. [2] Ibid., f. 14 b.
[3] Rot. lib., 25 Edw. I., m. 6. [4] Rot. claus., 25 Edw. I., m. 25 dorso.
[5] Wardrobe book, 25, f. 28 b.
[6] Ibid., f. 29 b. Rot. pat. 25, p. 1, m. 20. Rot. Aleman., 22-31 Edw. I., m. 16 dorso. [7] Rot. claus., 25 Edw. I., m. 15 dorso.
[8] Rot. pat., 25, p. 2, m. 9. [9] Wardrobe book, 25, f. 31.
[10] Rot. pat., 3 Edw. II., m. 16, per inspeximus.
[11] Fœdera, vol. i., p. 854. [12] Wardrobe book, 25, f. 33 b.

wards, in the beginning of April, Margaret's English friends and attendants left her and returned home, with the exception of one faithful servant, Thomas de Cummull, who sought and obtained the king's permission to tarry with his mistress.[1]

The city of Brussels, which became henceforth the principal home of Margaret, was anciently distinguished, as it is to the present day, for the picturesque beauty of its situation, on the flank of a range of hills, watered by the river Seine. It had been, from time immemorial, the favourite residence of the Dukes of Brabant, and its castle was founded as early as the year 1040; but the Hotel de Ville, and other spendid buildings which now attract the admiration of the stranger, are productions of a later epoch. For some of its earliest developments of architectural beauty, however, it was indebted to the Princess Margaret, who paid much attention to the decoration of her capital.[2] It was under her supervision and that of her husband that the ducal palace, with its park and fountains, was commenced.[3]

From the time of her arrival in Brabant, the records of Margaret become few and slight. The Brabantine chroniclers scarcely give her more than a passing mention; the neglect of Duke John appears to have been imitated by his subjects, so that the high-born lady, whose coming had, at one time, been so eagerly anticipated, and who had been the inspiring cause, if not the theme, of the greatest poem of the period, saw herself a complete cipher in the court of her faithless lord. She was, besides, doomed to the mortification of being perpetually surrounded with the bastard sons of her husband, all of whom

[1] Rot. pat., 25 Edw. I., p. 2, m. 12.   Wardrobe book, 25 f. 16 b.
[2] Divæus Rerum Brabantiæ, lib. xix., p. 132.
[3] Swertius Monumenta Brabantiæ, p. 7.   Jaques le Roi grand theatre profane de Brabant, vol. iii., pt. i., p. 19.

he openly avowed, giving to each of them his own name, in conjunction with that of their mother, as a distinctive appellation, and treating them, in every respect, as his lawful children.[1] He had also a natural daughter, named, from the place of her birth, Joanna of Vilvorde.

It may be that Margaret wanted energy of character to influence and direct her husband. She bore her destiny, however, with a mild uncomplainingness that raises her character as a wife. Instead of accusing the duke to her father, and seeking redress for the wrongs she endured, she ever espoused his part, and seconded his wishes in the commercial treaties and other affairs that were transacted between them.

In the latter end of 1297, the year of Margaret's marriage, King Edward paid a visit to the continent. On the 5th of September, the duchess sent a messenger to Ardenburgh, to welcome him, and to present him with a horse.[2] The Christmas was celebrated by Edward at the city of Ghent; the Duke and Duchess of Brabant, the Earl of Flanders, and many other nobles, were among the guests; and, at a splendid feast which the king gave, he knighted his son-in-law, Duke John, who, it seems, had not before been initiated into the ranks of chivalry.[3] The duke and duchess remained at Ghent the whole of January. On the last day of that month, Margaret solicited from her father the grant of a bailiwick, in England, for a person named Pierres de Edelinston, whom she patronized; her petition was acceded to, and the king installed her protégé into his office.[4] Soon afterwards, Edward paid his daughter a visit in her own dominions. He was received at Brussels with great honour by the nobles and citizens; and, if we may believe the testimony of a con-

[1] Butken's Trophies of Brabant, i. 369.   Anselme, hist. geneal., vol. ii., pp. 795-6.   [2] Wardrobe book, 25 Edw. I., f. 57.
[3] Spiegel historial van Ludowyk van Veltham, 1218-1316, p. 218.
[4] Writ of Privy Seal, quoted in Madox's Exchequer, vol. i., p. 785, note z.

temporary Brabançon chronicler, he was equally surprised and delighted with the extent of his son-in-law's power. " There were many earls there, who all were liege-men of the duke. On this, the king marvelled sore that so many lords held lands from him. They say the king was full blithe, for he had never known before that Brabant was half so great !"[1]

After the departure of her father, Margaret, now entirely dissociated from her own family, sought in her new situation for such sources of interest and occupation as it was calculated to afford her. She shared, as far as she could, or was permitted to do, in the pursuits and amusements of her husband. Duke John still retained his boyish passion for the chase; beyond the town of Vilvorde, which was eight miles from Brussels, in the direction of Hainault, were some extensive wooded grounds, well adapted for hunting, on the skirt of which rose the small town of Vueren. Here Margaret occupied herself in the re-erection of an almost dilapidated castle, that it might serve as a hunting-seat for the duke, and as a place of retirement for herself, the beauty of the situation having greatly struck her fancy. Under her auspices, the mass of ruins speedily sprang up into a stately castle. The great room she rebuilt on a magnificent scale; and in the grounds, too, she laid out gardens and groves, and framed a beautiful promenade, which extended the whole circuit of the castle—affording a pleasant contrast to the rough, uncultivated ground by which it had been formerly surrounded, and more befitting the feet of a royal lady when she chose to enjoy the summer air in the neigh-

[1] " Daer waren doe vele Grauen twaren,
Die alle't Hertogen man waren :
Daer den Coninc af wonderde sere
Dat van hem hilt d'lant so manich Here.
Om dit die Coninc te blider was,
Want hi ne waende nict vor das
Dat Brabant waer *half* so groot."
Spiegel, ut sup., p. 219.

bourhood of her favourite retreat. Her husband was pleased
with the result of her ingenuity, and the lady Margaret's
walk became a favourite resort with him and his counsellors,
after the fatigues of the council chamber, or the chase.[1]

One of the most striking features of Margaret's character
as a wife is the kindness with which she treated her husband's illegitimate children—a feature the more remarkable,
since several of them were born after her marriage, and must
have been the cause of painful humiliation to herself. A
document is still in existence, in which she calls one of them,
John de Casselaer, bastard of Brabant, " her dear varlet,"
and bestows upon him the forest of Jedoigne in perpetual
gift; but this child was born when his father was very young,
and before his marriage."[2]

In the latter end of the year 1300, Margaret herself became the mother of a son.[3] The birth of an heir to the
dukedom was cause of great rejoicing, and the joy of the
duke and duchess was warmly participated by Margaret's
English relations. King Edward gave a present of one hundred marks, the queen fifty, and Prince Edward forty marks,
to the valet of the duchess who brought the news of her
delivery ;[4] and her sister Elizabeth also gave £13. 6s. 8d. to
another valet sent on the same errand.[5] With her own family,
Margaret maintained frequent correspondence, as appears by
the constant recurrence of payment to messengers backwards
and forwards.[6] Several of her original letters, as well as
those of her husband, are still preserved in the Tower collec-

---

[1] Divæus, p. 132.   Butken, p. 368.   Loyens' Rer. memorab. Brab., p. 17.
[2] Butken, p. 369.   The date 1329 assigned to this deed by Butken is
certainly wrong, since Margaret died in 1318, but we have no means of
ascertaining the true date.
[3] Miræus Chron. Belg., p. 309.   Divæus, p. 132.
[4] Wardrobe book, 28 Edw. I., p. 170.   Rymer Collect., Addit. MS.,
4574, f. 361.
[5] Ward. book, 28, p. 182.
[6] Wardrobe roll, 28 Edw. I., No. 2055, Queen's Rem.   Wardrobe book,
25 Edw. I., f. 22 b; 28 Edw. I., p. 166; 29 Edw. I., ff. 1 b, 66, 66 b, 69,
Addit. MS., 7966 A.

tion; but they are all without dates. Of two of the letters from the duchess to her father, the following are exact translations. The former, written in old French, relates to a delinquent who had sought refuge and protection near the daughter of his sovereign, from a severe, and, as it would seem, unmerited penalty.

" To her very dear and well beloved lord and father, my lord the King of England, Margaret, his daughter, Duchess of Lorraine, Brabant, and Limburg, ready for his commands, wishes health, with all the honour and reverence that she can send him.

" Very dear sire, as Reynald, the Frenchman, of Anglesey, who has served you a long time, has been banished out of your land for the murder of a Frenchman, which he committed in self-defence, I pray you, as much as I can and know how, that it may please you, for the sake of my prayers, and for the service that he has done you, to pardon him his misdeed, which he committed in self-defence; and to grant him your peace, that he may return to your land. Dearest sire, do thus much, that God may be pleased with you for it, and that he may perceive that my prayers have availed for him with you. And our Lord keep you."[1]

The second letter refers to a subject which was the cause of vehement and protracted discussion between Duke John and his father-in-law. The duke had contracted many and heavy debts to certain English merchants, who, having in vain solicited payment, took the law into their own hands, and seized the persons and goods of such Brabançons, both noble and mercantile, as they could lay hold upon, for the satisfaction of their claims.[2] The goods of some merchants of Diest, a town of Brabant, subjects of one Gerald, entitled Lord of Diest, who was not even a Brabançon, but only a friend of the duke and duchess, having been thus appropriated, the duke sent a letter of earnest remonstrance to

---

[1] Tower letters, No. 1122.　　　[2] Rot. claus., 27 Edw. I., m. 10.

King Edward,[1] which was accompanied by one written the same day by the duchess, who, in seconding her husband's entreaties, had also the incentive of personal friendship towards the injured noble. The letter is as follows:—

" To the very high and puissant, her very dear and well-beloved lord and father, Monsieur the King of England, Margaret, his humble daughter, Duchess of Lorraine, Brabant, and Limburg, gives all the affection and reverence that she can send him, with a daughter's love.

" Very dear sire, my lord the duke prays you very affectionately for the people and merchants of the noble man Gerard, Lord of Diest, whom I greatly praise; for, in truth, dear sire, in all my necessities, and on all occasions when I have had need of him, I have found him a good friend and a loyal. Dear sire, know that in no place have his merchants been arrested or detained on account of the debts of Monsieur the duke, even when the merchants of our land have been detained and arrested : so I pray you, dearest sire, that, for reason and right, and also for the love of me, you will command that their goods be restored and delivered them, as Monsieur the duke prays you; by which the said Lord of Diest may profit by my prayers. Dear sire, our Lord guard you. Given at Brussels, the Friday after the decollation of St. John the Baptist."[2]

This epistle affords a tolerable specimen of special pleading; and, as it is written in the old French, which was then the dialect of the court, it was in all probability dictated by the princess herself. Margaret's talents for diplomacy appear to have been considerable, since the king occasionally associated her name with that of her husband, in business negociations.[3] In spite of her interference, however, the English merchants continued their unjust and rapacious mode of repaying themselves the sums owed to them, by seizing the

---

[1] Orig. letters, Tower, No. 1592.   [2] Tower letters, No. 1121.
[3] Rot. pat., 29 Edw. I., m. 34. Fœdera, vol. i., pt. 2, p. 756.

private property of such Brabançons as fell in their way, until Duke John began to make reprisals, and he in his turn seized the goods of William of Doncaster, and other English merchants. At length, " yielding," we are told, "to more salutary counsels"—probably those of his duchess, though she is not named—he sent to offer restitution of the injuries he had committed, provided a fair statement of damages were transmitted to him, and requested that proclamation might be made throughout England to that effect; and that, on his thus satisfying all claims, his men might no longer be arrested.[1] His offer was accepted by the king,[2] and tranquillity for a time restored. It was, probably, on this occasion that Margaret sent another letter to her father, expressing her great delight at the receipt of his letters, from which she finds that the business treated of between him and the duke is completed. The only date given is, Brussels, the Wednesday after the feast of St. Benedict.[3] This letter is written in Latin.

Unfortunately, however, Duke John repented of his compliance with the prudent advice of his wife, and he delayed so long the payment of the stipulated damages, that, in 1305, the king gave formal permission to the English merchants to satisfy their claims as they could—and the disgraceful system of private reprisal was renewed, with the more eagerness, since it was now sanctioned by regal authority.[4] A temporary coolness between the two powers was the natural result, and Duke John entered into close union with the French monarch, pledging himself, for the bribe of 2500 livres Tournois, to become his liege man, and to assist him against all his enemies, excepting the King of England.[5] The peace

[1] Orig. letters, Tower. temp. Edw. I.   [2] Rot. pat., 30 Edw. I., m. 1ʰ.
[3] Appendix, No. XVII.
[4] Orig. letters, No. 2163, Richard de Bermingham to the Chancellor Hamilton. See also No. 2164, a letter from the bailiffs of St. Ives to the king.
[5] Thesor des Chartes, p. 334. This valuable volume, compiled by M. Teulet, contains a list of all the documents in the French archives bearing upon English history. It is not published.

which soon ensued between France and England, however, placed matters on their usual amicable footing.

The year 1307 put a period to the long and energetic reign of Edward I. The following year, his son and successor, Edward II., passed over to France, to celebrate his nuptials with the beautiful Isabella of France, daughter to Philip the Fair. A galaxy of royal and noble personages assembled at Boulogne to grace this marriage; four kings —those of France, Navarre, Germany, and Sicily—and four queens—those of France, Sicily, and the dowager queens, Margaret of England and Mary of France—with innumerable dukes, earls, and barons, were present,[1] and among the rest were the Duke and Duchess of Brabant. The ceremony took place on the 25th of January,[2] after which the duchess Margaret and her husband, along with the French king and queen and many other persons of high rank, went over immediately to England, to be present at the approaching coronation of the bride and bridegroom.[3] This ceremony was performed on the 24th of February,[4] with circumstances of great splendour. Margaret and her husband prolonged their stay in England for a short time longer, since it appears—by an entry of payment for bread dealt out to them and their household, from the king's pantry, from the last day of February to the 5th of March—that they were still in England at the latter date. Their retinue must have been considerable, since, for those five days, their cost, in bread alone, was £6. 15s. 0d.[5]

---

[1] Miss Strickland's Queens, vol. ii., p. 208.

[2] On the festival of the conversion of St. Paul, which occurs January 25th.

[3] Divæus Rer. Brab., lib. xix., p. 139. Annals of Robert of Reading, Cotton MS., Cleop., A. xvi., f. 85; and Harl. MS., 685, f. 199 b. Wardrobe fragment, 1 Edw. II., in a bundle marked W. N. 5319, Queen's Rem.

[4] It was Quinquagesima Sunday, which in 1308 fell on February 24th.

[5] Ward. fragm., ut sup. Philip of France, the Counts of St. Paul's and Drew, are also named in this document. In another loose, dateless fragment, mention occurs of Master John Bust staying at Paris, waiting for a safeconduct for the Duchess of Brabant, but whether that was in connexion with this visit to England, or with one she made to the French court, is uncertain.

The Duke and Duchess of Brabant had long kept up terms of friendly intercourse with the new-made monarch. Towards the close of his father's reign, Duke John had associated the name of "Edward, his most dear brother," with that of the king in his business transactions.[1] Margaret had corresponded with him as prince,[2] and this correspondence continued with great friendliness of feeling on both sides. Two letters from Edward II. to his sister are preserved. The first, partially obliterated, is among the State papers in the Tower; it is addressed to "the noble Lady Margaret, Duchess of Lorraine, Brabant, and Limburgh, our very dear sister."

"Dearest sister, as you prayed us by your letters, we send you herein enclosed the transcript of the assignment of your dowry, and the letters of the same assignment, sealed. We have not wished to send you them, on account of the perils they would incur by the sea. Very dear sister, may our Lord keep you! Given at Westminster, the 25th day of February, in the third year of our reign."[3]

The other letter was written in anticipation of a visit about to be paid by Piers Gaveston to Brabant, in the autumn of 1311. The king entreats Margaret that she will use her influence with all possible efficacy with the duke, or, should he be absent, with his vicegerent, to secure a gracious reception for the favourite, and honourable treatment from the Brabançons, according to the request of the king, and the desire of his heart. This epistle was accompanied by another to Duke John, of a similar tenour, both strongly evincing the passionate attachment of the weak-minded monarch to his brilliant but unworthy favourite.[4]

[1] Orig. letters, Tower, No. 1498, date, Brussels, May 16th, 1303. The Tower collection contains, beside the letters already alluded to, several others from the duke to his father-in-law, but without any particular interest. They are Nos. 1123, 1497-8-9, 1591-2.

[2] Ward. fragm., Queen's Rem. 6s. 8d. is paid to the messenger of the Duchess of Brabant coming with her letters to the prince.

[3] Orig. letters, Tower, temp. Edw. II.   [4] Fœdera, vol. ii., pt. i., p. 144.

The spring of the following year, 1312, a Carmelite friar, named Peter Fleming, and his comrade, are recorded to have come over from Brabant, as messengers to the king, from his sister the duchess.[1]

This is the last notice of any correspondence of Margaret with the English royal family; for, although she lived six years longer, yet the death of her husband, which took place in 1312, reduced her to the rank of duchess-dowager; and as no share whatever in the government was allowed to her, and she had no longer any courtly influence to use, either her intimacy with the king her brother dropped, or, from its assuming a more personal character, it has not been preserved among the State records.

Having thus traced out the details respecting the Princess Margaret, as far as they can be gathered from her English associations, a brief outline of the principal events that transpired in Brabant during the rule of her lord must conclude this necessarily imperfect sketch. The character of John the Pacific stands much higher as a governor than as a husband. It was reported of him that never prince more disliked waging war, but that, when it could not be avoided, he summoned all his energy, and carried it on with such vigour and courage, that his boldness excited admiration in all who witnessed it.[2] He was more frequently called to contend against domestic sedition than foreign invasion. Those struggles which have, at different times, convulsed almost every kingdom of Europe, as the energies of an awakening people strove to free themselves from the shackles of feudal despotism, were rife in Brabant during the reign of John II. The essentially commercial character of the inhabitants rendered them aware of their own strength and importance, and restless under the many disabilities that

---

[1] Treasurer's account, 6 Edw. II., f. 28 b, among the augmentation records at Carlton Ride. This book has been by mistake marked as belonging to the 6th of Edward III.

[2] Barlandu, Chronique de Brabant, p. 51.

óppressed them. This was particularly the case in the city of Brussels itself; and at length, in the year 1306, the pent-up feelings of the plebeiàn party burst forth into a flame, and an open sedition ensued. Duke John was at the Castle of Vueren, but Margaret was at Brussels, when the tumult broke out. She fearlessly showed herself in public, and endeavoured by her entreaties to still the commotion—but in vain.[1] Although the rioters had sufficient respect for her to spare the ducal castle, yet they ravaged the mansions of several of the most obnoxious patricians; and, to give organ-ization and strength to their confederacy, they formally dis-placed the city officers, and created a new magistracy.[2] The wrath of the duke was quickly roused when the news of their temerity reached him; he assembled his forces at Vilvorde, and briskly attacked the mob, who had ventured out with streaming banners to meet him: his rapid charge soon put them to flight—he entered Brussels the same day, took stern cognizance of all that had happened, banished the offending artisans, depriving the plebeian party of the few privileges they had enjoyed, and confirming those of the patricians.[3] He even went so far as to forbid any of the weavers to sleep within the city, since they had been the principal mutineers, and to prohibit all assemblies of the people on any pretence whatsoever.[4] Such is usually the termination of the early struggles of right against might, but how different ulti-mately must be the infallible result!

A dissension of a similar character arose at Malines, over which the Duke of Brabant had recently been made lord, and was subdued with more difficulty. John was obliged to promise the people that they should have a share in their

[1] Divæus Rer. Brab., lib. xix., p. 137. Klerk, Brabantsche Yeesten, p. 429.
[2] Butken's Trophies, vol. i., p. 358. Anselme, Hist. Geneal., vol. ii., pp. 795-6.
[3] Butken, vol. i., p. 359. Barlande, p. 50. Miræus opera, vol. iv., pp. 779, 780.
[4] Gramaye Bruxellæ antiquitates, pp. 6, 11.

own government, but contrived to neutralize the concession
by affixing the punishment of perpetual exile to all who
should be judged guilty of sedition, and by procuring the
immediate banishment of the more obnoxious classes of artisans.[1]

Another occasion soon afterwards arose, which produced
discord between Duke John and his plebeian subjects. A
number of the lower orders in Brabant were seized with the
crusading mania, and had actually taken the Cross, with a
design of marching to the Holy Land, when it was suggested
to them that there were enemies of the Cross nearer home,
as deadly and pertinacious as the infidels themselves, where
conquest would be far easier, and spoil far richer, than in
the East. These were the Jews, who, with their proverbial
instinct, were ever to be found in greatest numbers where
trade was most prosperous. Upon this unhappy nation
the enthusiasm of the crusading Brabançons sought to vent
itself. But Duke John, prompted either by a true-sighted
policy, which enabled him to discover that the Jews were
among the most valuable, because most industrious, of his
subjects, or, compassionating their misfortunes, warmly
espoused their cause, had them all conveyed to the strong
castle of Genap, and, having pleaded for them in vain, he
defended them there against the attacks of the populace,
and finally defeated and punished the crusaders. They indignantly marched to Avignon, to appeal to the Pope against
such unchristian treatment; but the pontiff, Clement V.,
ashamed of the rabble rout, bade them go home and be
quiet.[2]

In his foreign relationships, Duke John was equally fortunate. He had had some contests with the Emperor
Albert of Austria;[3] but that prince was succeeded in 1308

[1] Divæus Annal. oppid. Lovan., pp. 12, 13.
[2] Butken, vol. i., p. 363.   Molanus Militia sacra Brabantiæ, p. 105.
[3] Herman Corner, Eckard, p. 297.

by Henry VII., who had married the lady Margaret of Brabant, sister to Duke John, and who, consequently, confirmed all the privileges of his brother-in-law, and treated him in other respects with much distinction.[1]

Towards the close of his life, the duke was much tormented with the gravel; and, feeling that the disease would terminate fatally, he was anxious to consolidate the regulations for the government of his states which he had made during his life, as well as those of his predecessors. He accordingly assembled his nobles, and likewise the deputies of the cities and towns at Cortenberg, where he established the famous code of laws called, from the place of their institution, the Statutes of Cortenberg.[2] His political views seem to have been modified and matured in his later years. We have seen him a staunch advocate of aristocracy, but his summoning citizen deputies to his congress is a tacit acknowledgment of the principles of a representative government; and the wholesome restrictions which he placed upon the ducal power show that the love of arbitrary rule had been subdued by regard for the general weal. The date of these regulations was September 27th, 1312.[3]

On the 3rd of October following, the duke completed some arrangements with reference to monastic jurisdiction; and, having thus relieved his mind from earthly cares, thought only of preparation for the solemn change which awaited him.[4]

The event which made the Duchess Margaret a widow took place at the castle of Vueren, on the 27th of October, 1312. The complaint from which the duke had so long suffered had become gradually worse, and the difficulty of passing a stone finally caused his death.[5] His body was con-

[1] Butken, vol. i., pp. 333, 362, 364.
[2] Dewes histoire particulière, vol. iii., pp. 175-8. L'art de verifier, vol. xiv., p. 99. Miræus opera, vol. ii., p. 1013.
[3] D'Ewez, p. 178. Butken, vol. i., p. 367. [4] Butken, vol. i., p. 368.
[5] Chron. ducum Brabantiæ, fol., Frankfort, 1580, p. 13.

ducted with great pomp to Brussels, and interred, according
to his previously expressed wish, in the church of St. Gudule,
in the centre of the choir.[1]

Margaret survived her husband only six years. She had
no share in the regency of Brabant, during the minority of
her son, John III., or the Triumphant. The earlier part
of his reign was troublous, owing partly to domestic sedition,
and partly to a fearful famine, the consequence of long-con-
tinued rains, which prevailed to such an extent, that a plague
ensued, which swept away thousands of the wretched people.
In every street, and almost in every house, might be seen
the husband mourning for the wife, the parent for the child,
the brother for the sister—and these miseries continued for
the space of many months.[2] Margaret lived, however, to
see brighter days dawn upon her son. In 1314 he married
Mary, daughter of Louis Earl of Evreux, and made a magnificent entry into Louvaine and the other cities of his
dominions, after which, though still young, he took possession of his estates.[3]

The death of the duchess-dowager took place in the year
1318. The graciousness and frankness of her manners is
said to have greatly endeared her to the Brabançons, by
whom her memory was long cherished with affectionate
admiration.[4] She was buried, by the side of her husband,
in the church of St. Gudule. In 1617, when the archduke
Albert of Austria and his consort, the infanta Isabella of
Spain, then Duke and Duchess of Brabant, visited Brussels,
they raised over the ashes of Duke John and Margaret a
splendid tomb of marble, richly adorned, and upon it a lion
couchant, of gilded brass, holding an escutcheon of the arms

[1] Butken, vol. i., p. 368.   Mirœus Chron. Belg., p. 309.
[2] Divæus Rer. Brab., p. 144.   Barlande, p. 52.   Dewes hist. de la Belgique, vol. iii., p. 148.   Chron. ducum Brab., p. 13.
[3] Butken, vol. i., p. 385.   Anselme hist. geneal., vol. ii., p. 7956.
[4] Butken, vol. i., p. 368.   Anselme, ut sup.   Divæus, p. 132.   Haræus
annal. Brab., vol. i., p. 290.

of Brabant, which were a lion rampant *or*. on a field *sable*. Antony, son of Philip le Bon, Duke of Brabant, who died in 1431, and Ernest, son of the Emperor Maximilian II., Archduke of Austria, who died in 1595, afterwards shared the same sepulture.[1]

[1] Jaques le Roy grand theatre sacré de Brabant, vol. i., pt. 1, p. 187.

BERENGARIA,

Birth and death—Confused statements about the daughters of Edward I.

Of the Princess Berengaria nothing whatever is known, excepting that she was born at Kennington, in the year 1276,[1] and that she died young, the same or the following year. The king paid £6. 13s. 4d., to a "certain woman" who had been "nurse of the Lady Berengaria, the king's daughter."[2] She was buried in the chapel of St. Edward, at Westminster, by the side of her infant brothers, John and Henry.[3]

King Edward had one, if not more daughters, beside those already named, who died in their infancy. Sandford names three, Alice, Beatrice, and Blanche, but without quoting his authorities.[4] An heraldic MS. in the Harleian collection gives Alice, who died at twelve years of age, Katherine, and Blanche.[5] Several chroniclers mention a daughter Isabella, born in March, 1275;[6] but this state-

---

[1] Chron. Winch., Cotton MS., Domit., xiii., f. 67 b.   Chron. John Oxford, Nero, D. ii., f. 231 b, col. 2.   Chron. Petrob., Addit. MS., 6913, f. 286.
[2] Rot. donorum, 6 Edw. I., copy by Craven Ord, Middlehill MS., 1003, f. 7.
[3] Matthew of Westminster, p. 412.   [4] Genealogical history, p. 139.
[5] Harleian MS., 1499, fol. 115 b.
[6] Cotton MSS., Domit., xiii., f. 65 b.   Calig., A. x., f. 138.   Vesp., A. ii., f. 63 b.   The annals of Waverley, Gale, vol. ii., p. 230, give Isabella, born in March, and Alphonso in November of the *same* year, 1275!

ment is inconsistent with the fact that Prince Alphonso was
born in November, 1273, and the Princess Margaret in September, 1275. The queen had a daughter, however, born
at Woodstock on the 10th of May, 1279,[1] who died the
same year, and £7. were expended at her funeral.[2] She seems
to have been the seventh daughter, the date of her birth
occurring between those of the Princesses Mary and Elizabeth ; but the contemporaneous chroniclers omit the names
of several of the royal infants, concerning whom nothing can
be said excepting that they were born and they died.[3]

[1] Cotton MS., Vesp., A. ii., f. 66.   [2] Recepta Garderobæ, 7 Edw. I.
[3] The following list of the family of Edward I. is made out from a careful
collation of every passage referring to them that the author has been able to
discover in contemporary chronicles or records.

	born at		A.D.
Eleanora	Windsor		1264.
John	Kenilworth	10th July	1266.
Henry			1268.
Daughter	Acres		1271.
Joanna	Acres	Spring	1272.
Alphonso	Gascony	24th November	1273.
Margaret	Windsor	11th September	1275.
Berengaria	Kennington		1276.
Mary	Windsor	11th March	1278.
Daughter	Woodstock	10th May	1279.
Elizabeth	Rhudlan	August	1282.
Edward	Carnarvon	25th April	1284.

MARY,

SIXTH DAUGHTER OF EDWARD I.

Mary's biography compiled from records—Her birth—Convent of Amesbury a branch of Fontevraud—Correspondence between Edward I. and the Abbess of Fontevraud—The queen-dowager prevails on the king to send Mary to Amesbury—She takes the Veil—Revenue settled on her—Monastic seclusion in former days as contrasted with the present—Mary's visits to her relatives—Concluding days of Queen Eleanora of Provence—Death of the two queens—Mary detained at Amesbury by her father—Additional income granted—Disputes about the election of the Prioress of Amesbury —Mary made attorney—Her letters to her father—Her visits to court— Offerings—Illness—Debts—Increase of revenue—Extravagance—Love of gaming—Appointed visitor of the convents—Associates with her step-mother, Queen Margaret of France—Attends her at the birth of Prince Thomas—Her excursions—Pilgrimage to Walsingham—Trivet's chronicle dedicated to her—Gifts from her father—His illness—Mary accompanies the queen on a pilgrimage for his recovery—His death—Mary receives Isabella, queen of Edward II.—His kindness to her—Letter from Mary to her brother—Her influence—Wards—Pilgrimage to St. Thomas-à-Becket's shrine—Mary takes charge of her half-sister Eleanora—Visits to the court of her brother—Attends her sister's funeral—Goes to Canterbury with Queen Isabella—Gifts of her brother—Exchange of visits—Deprived of the office of convent visitor—Edward II. remonstrates for her with the Abbess of Fontevraud and with the Pope—Grants her a manor—Her privileges confirmed by Edward III.—Her longevity—Death.

The utility and importance of the numerous and valuable State records of remote antiquity which have been preserved through so many centuries among the archives of England, have frequently been alluded to in the preceding pages. Documentary evidence may indeed be considered the touchstone of all history, by which the truth or falsehood of its statements can alone be tested. In historical biography it is, if possible, of still more value. There is not a character who performed any conspicuous part on the theatre of public affairs, during the reigns of our early Henrys and Edwards, concerning whom some information may not be found on the chancery and exchequer rolls. Though but a few years have transpired since the arrangements of the present record commission have thrown open these treasures to the inspection of the public, yet they have already had their effect upon the tone of historical literature.[1] Of their use in regal biography, it would be difficult to find a more striking illustration than in the details they afford of the nun-princess, Mary. All that we learn concerning her from even the contemporary chroniclers is, that she was born at Windsor, on the 11th of March, the vigils of St. Gregory, 1278;[2] and that in the year 1284 she was veiled a nun at Ambresbury. For any information beyond this, therefore, we are exclusively indebted to the sources above referred to.

The convent of Ambresbury, in Wiltshire, had originally been an independent Benedictine establishment, and owed its foundation to Ethelfrida, the dowager-queen of the Saxon king, Edgar, in the year 980. In the time of Henry II., the conduct of the abbess and her nuns had become so notoriously and openly vicious, that he dissolved the monastery, by dispersing its inmates, and made it a branch of the great French Abbey of Fontevraud, from which, in 1177, a prioress and twenty-four nuns were sent over to take possession.[3] Fontevraud, the burial-place of several of our Plantagenet kings and queens, claimed and possessed many privileges, and special protection, from the monarchs of England. The abbess had her regularly constituted attorneys in England, to attend to her lands and revenues, and

[1] See Sir Harris Nicolas' recent work on knightage as an illustration of this remark.
[2] Chron. Petrob., Addit. MS., 6913, f. 241. Chron. Brute, Cotton MS., Nero, A. vi., f. 27 b. Rishanger, Cotton MS., Claud., D. vi., f. 130, names Woodstock as the place of her birth.
[3] Dugdale's Monasticon, vol. ii., p. 333.

answer all pleas for or against her.[1] Besides occasional munificent donations,[2] she received from the royal exchequer of England an annual pension of £165. 6s. 8d.

From a correspondence, still extant, between the Abbess of Fontevraud and Edward I., it would seem that the idea of making a nun of the young Princess Mary had originated as early as 1282, when the royal child was only four years old. The nuns of Fontevraud, hearing of her father's intentions, wrote to entreat that their monastery might be honoured by the royal selection, and that the princess might be sent to them. Edward's reply to the letter from the abbess and convent bears date March 3rd, 1283, and states that he could not give a certain answer to the request that his daughter should become a nun in their monastery, since she was then residing with the queen, his mother; but that, be she where she would, she should ultimately belong to them.[3] This gracious message called forth the following curious epistle in reply:

"To the right excellent and victorious prince, their very dear lord and good father in God, our Lord Edward, by the divine grace most noble King of England, his devoted daughters and nurslings, sister Gile, humble prioress, and all the convent of Fontevraud, send health, and special orisons to God, that, after a long and victorious temporal reign, he may inherit the glory of a perpetual kingdom.

"Our dear lord, father, and patron;—for the great joy and recreation that you have deigned to inspire into us all, by your sweet and amiable letters, in certifying us, by your great humility, of your estate, which we desire always blessed above all others, we render you our thanks, with

---

[1] Rot. pat., 17 Edw. I., m. 21.
[2] The sum of 1000 livres Tournois were presented to her at once in the year 1290.—Wardrobe book, 18 Edw. I., f. 23 b, Miscel. roll, Tower, No. 69.
[3] Rot. Vasc., 11 Edw. I., m. 5. "Ad hoc, verò, quod nos requisivistis, de nostrâ filiâ in vestro monasterio monachandâ, non possumus vobis modò certum dare responsum, quia non erat nobiscum, sed cum dominâ matre nostrâ Verumtamen, ubicumque fuerit, erit vestra."

clasped hands, as plenteously as we can and know how; and for your good prosperity praise we God our Lord, and thank him as devoutly as we can. So much are we accustomed to the pity and the very great cordiality that you have always shown to us, your devoted daughters, that we again take courage to write to you, and supplicate your excellence, with devout prayers, that you, for God's sake, will deign to keep in memory the sweet and blessed promise that you have long since made to your church of Fontevraud, about our dear lady the demoiselle Mary, your daughter; which promise we have and hold as firm and established; and long, above all other terrestrial desires, for its accomplishment. And with good cause; for, by the will of God, she shall become the light and ornament of your church of Fontevraud, and of all your convent of this place.

"Our dear lord and father, the letters that you have sent us contain, in one part, a mixture of tears and of joy; of tears, because you send us word that it is not in your power to hand over your dear daughter to us, but in the power of our mother and yours, our lady the queen; of joy, because you tell us that she shall be ours, wherever she be. And be it known to your great excellence that if your aforesaid promise be not accomplished, according to our desire, we are in great fear and in great doubt lest our devotion to you should grow cold, and lest we should complain of you to the sweet Jesus Christ, our Creator.

"Sweetest lord and father, hear us for the sake of your compassion, and our prayer, so that we may be at all times still more forcibly and straightly held and obliged more and more towards you, by devout orisons and contracts. Long live and reign the power of our lord the king, for the sake of the sweet Jesus Christ our Lord !"[1]

Notwithstanding the pleading eloquence of this appeal, however, there was another advocate, whose wishes had far

[1] Orig. letters, Tower, temp., Edw. I., uncalendared.

more power over the heart of the monarch than those of the Abbess of Fontevraud. This was his mother, Queen Eleanora of Provence. For her youthful grand-daughter, Mary, the dowager-queen had taken a strong predilection. She had recently been seized with a severe attack of illness, while on a visit to the convent of Amesbury,[1] and it was probably during her indisposition that she formed the resolution of taking the veil in that convent. Having thus fixed upon a quiet asylum for her declining years, she was earnestly desirous that Mary should make her profession at Amesbury, in preference to leaving England for the more distant Abbey of Fontevraud.[2] She had already placed there another of her grand-daughters, Eleanora of Bretagne, daughter of the Princess Beatrice;[3] and this formed an additional inducement to offer to the king, since Mary would find in her cousin a suitable companion in point of rank, though not of age, since Eleanora was much her senior.

Her arguments prevailed, and the king wrote to acquaint the nuns of Fontevraud with his decision. Sister Gile had died in the interim, and been succeeded by the Abbess Margaret de Pasey.[4] She replied to the message of the king, by telling him of the unspeakable joy with which she and her sisters heard that he had decided on making his daughter a nun, and greatly regretting that the princess should be sent to a house which was only a branch, and not to the head of the order; "but since," added she, "we understand that this is done for the solace of the queen-mother, Eleanora, we agree that she shall remain there at present; yet we entreat your royal majesty, by special intercession, that,

[1] Chron. Rish., Cott. MS., Claud., E. III., f. 321 b., col. 2.
[2] Walsingham, p. 13. Chron. Rishang., ut sup. Trivet's annals, pp. 261-2.
[3] For the support of the Breton princess, Queen Eleanora gave her the manor of Chaddworth, in Berkshire.—Monast. Ang., vol. ii., p. 32.
[4] Margaret de Pasey was installed Abbess in 1284.—Gallia Christina, vol. ii., p. 1322. The sister Gile is not named in the list of the Abbesses of Fontevraud: she must have come in between Isabella d'Avoir, whose name occurs in 1276, and Margaret de Pasey.

after the death of that queen, the cause ceasing for which she is placed there, she may then be sent to Fontevraud."[1] Another letter, precisely similar, was also sent to her mother, the Queen Eleanora.[2] This lady, it would seem, was not a partaker of the devout purposes of her husband and mother-in-law in reference to her little girl, but, with the conjugal submissiveness that marked her character, she gave her consent, although reluctantly, to the wishes of her lord. A contemporary writer, whose chronicle was dedicated to the Princess Mary, tells us that "she was veiled nun by her great sire, Edward, King of England, at the wish of her grandmother, the Queen Eleanora, aforesaid, and by the *assent* of the Lady Eleanora, her mother."[3]

The profession of the young princess was appointed to take place on August 15th, the festival of the Assumption of the Virgin Mary, whose name she bore, and who was selected as her especial patroness, in the year 1285, when she was just entering upon her seventh year. Early in the month of July, the royal family left London, and proceeded to Canterbury, thence to Lewes, in Sussex, where they spent Sunday, July 15th; thence to Chichester on the 25th, and from that place to Amesbury, their progress being signalized by offerings in the churches of each place through which they passed.[4] At Amesbury, the king and queen, and the whole of the royal family, even including the infant Prince Edward,[5] with many of the principal earls, barons, archbishops, bishops, and abbots of the realm, were assembled to witness the ceremony of the consecration of the princess. Thirteen young ladies of noble birth were selected as the

<hr/>

[1] Orig. letters, Tower, No. 1646.
[2] Ibid., No. 1645. This latter epistle is copied in the Rymer Collectanea, Addit. MS., No. 4574, f. 427.
[3] Chron. de Nicolas, Trivet MS., 632ᵁ, Supplement Français Bibliothèque du Roi, Paris, sub fine: this MS. is unfoliated.
[4] Wardrobe roll, 13 Edw. I., f. 19 b., Miscel. roll, No. 65, Tower. Jewel roll, 13 Edw. I., Brit. Mus.
[5] Jewel roll, 13 Edw. I., purchased by the British Museum, March, 1849.

companions of Mary,[1] and amidst this stately assembly the
monastic veil was thrown over the heads of these fair young
novices, and the spousal ring placed upon their fingers,
which was to pledge them unalterably to the life thus
selected for them, long before they were of age to choose for
themselves.   The rings were of gold, each adorned with a
sapphire stone, the emblem of purity and chastity, and were
provided at the expense of the king.[2]   Each member of the
royal family presented a costly offering at the altar of the
convent, and the Princess Mary gave an additional offering
of a gem-studded clasp, in honour of her consecration.[3]

King Edward presented his daughter with an annual life
revenue of £100, to be expended for the support of her
chamber in a style befitting her rank.[4]   It was to be paid
in half-yearly instalments at Easter and Michaelmas, the
earlier payments being forwarded through the medium of
Richard, a friar of Amesbury, since the princess had not as
yet clerks of her own to attend to her business.[5]   She had
another allowance, entitled "a fee," of 50 marks per annum,
which she received from the royal wardrobe.[6]   The king,
also, "out of regard to God, and love to his dearest daughter
Mary, whom he had lately caused to be veiled at Amesbury,"
pardoned "his well-beloved prioress and nuns of Amesbury"
the sum of £27. 8s. 0d., part of £30. due to him yearly
from them, for the manor of Melksham, in Wiltshire.[7]

---

[1] Trivet, ut sup.   Annal. Wigorn., Wharton's Anglia sacra, vol. i., p. 508.
Cott. MS., Vesp., A. ii., f. 68 b.
[2] "Jewel inventory, taken at Peterborough when J. de Drokenford succeeded W. de Langton as keeper of the wardrobe."   No. 2157, Queen's Rememb.   Printed wardrobe book, 28 Edw. I., p. 348.
[3] Jewel roll, 13 Edw. I.   Its value was 66s. 8d.   It is mentioned under
date " xv. Aug., apud Ambresburiam" as "firmaculum oblatum per dominam
Mariam, filiam regis, ad idem feretrum, quiâ eodem die, ibidem facta fuit
ipsa monialis."
[4] Rot. pat., 13 Edw. I., m. 6, misquoted m. 11 in Monast. Ang.,
vol. ii., p. 337.
[5] Rot. exit., 14 Edw. I., Mich.
[6] The first payment of it was made at Michaelmas, in the 14th year, 1386,
and regularly twice a-year afterwards.—Wardrobe roll, No. 2474, Queen's
Rememb.   [7] Rot. claus., 13 Edw. I., m. 6.   Ibid., 17, m. 3.

From this time, the Convent of Ambresbury, or Amesbury, as it is sometimes spelled and always pronounced, became Mary's principal residence. Were we, however, to associate with her future existence the ideas of the complete disruption of all earthly ties, the perpetual banishment from society, and the weary confinement to a single solitary spot of ground, which are now the inevitable concomitants of a conventual life, we should greatly err. In these early ages, the monastic vow was rather one of perpetual chastity than of perpetual seclusion, and we have ample testimony to prove that the nun-princess had almost as large a share in the activities of life, and in some of its pleasures, too, as had any of her sisters. This fact may be easily accounted for. When the prevailing, and indeed the only, religion was the Roman Catholic, the force of public opinion was such, that a nun who should dare to absent herself permanently from her convent, and openly to violate the oaths—then considered the most sacred in the world—which bound her to her profession, would at once become the scorn and outcast of society; and thus, although the interior of the monasteries for both sexes frequently presented scenes of disgraceful licentiousness, yet the conduct of the inmates in their external associations was usually marked by strict propriety. But when the adamantine chains of public opinion were snapped, and the strong hold so long possessed by Romanism on the faith and feelings of the people became gradually loosened; when the dawn of a purer faith burst upon the world, then, more tangible bolts and barriers were brought into operation, because it became necessary to seclude, by personal restraint, those who had taken upon themselves the conventual vows. A feeling had arisen, strongly opposed to the fanaticism which burst asunder the hallowed charities of domestic life under the guise of *religion*—a feeling which would secure support, and sympathy, and protection to a self-liberated votary, should she in after life be disposed to retract vows often made too hastily, and sometimes even forced upon the unwilling or unconscious recipient by parental authority.

But, to return to the Princess Mary. The following year, 1286, Mary paid a visit home, and accompanied her family to Walsingham, where they presented offerings at the celebrated shrine of St. Mary, on the 27th of February.[1] A week afterwards she paid another visit to the court, then at Winchester. The following entry of this visit appears in the wardrobe book of the year:

"March 11th. To Walter Langton, for the expenses of the Lady Mary, the nun, the king's daughter, coming to the king to Winchester from Ambresbury, and staying in court four days, in coming and returning,   .   .   63s. 9¼d."[2]

Towards the latter end of the same month, the king visited her at her convent. He went privately, and almost unattended, as we learn from a curious entry of 6d. paid to a guide for showing the king the way from Ambresbury to Stockbridge.[3] Soon afterwards, in the month of May, Queen Eleanora of Provence returned from a farewell visit which she had paid to her relations in France.[4] On her landing at Dover, all her grand-daughters, including her favourite Mary, went to meet and welcome her.[5] They remained with her a short time. In July the aged queen retired to terminate her once brilliant but unfortunate career, in the tranquillity of the priory of Amesbury.[6] The accession of a queen to the ranks of a convent which already numbered among its votaries two ladies of royal, and many of illustrious, blood, was matter of high gratulation to the inmates. Eleanora of Bretagne was almost old enough to

[1] Jewel roll, 13 Edw. I., British Museum.
[2] Ward. book, 14 Edw. I., f. 8, miscel. roll, No. 66, Tower. Ward. roll, 14-15, No. 1782, Queen's Rememb.
[3] Ward. roll, ut sup. Ward. book, 14 Edw. I., f. 9 b.
[4] Cotton MS., Vesp., A. ii., f. 69.   [5] Ward. book, 14 Edw. I., f. 12.
[6] Chron. Rish., Cotton MS., Claud., E. iii., f. 322, col. 2. Annales luculenti, Cotton MS., Nero, D. ii., f. 182. Chron. John Oxf., ibid., f. 233, col. 1.

be the solace of her grandmother's declining years, whilst the little Mary, a sportive child of eight, was to her an object of ceaseless and affectionate interest. The beautiful pattern of active benevolence offered by the remaining years of this dowager-queen is rare indeed, but not unique, since we see it equalled, if not surpassed, in our own times by the illustrious lady who occupies a similar position in the present royalty of England.

A contemporaneous chronicler, speaking of Queen Eleanora, tells us that "she filled her hands with good works; that she spent her time in orisons, vigils, and works of piety; that she was a mother to the neighbouring poor, orphans, widows, and monks; and that her praise ought to resound above that of all other women."[1] Besides other large charities, she distributed £5 in silver every Friday to the poor.[2] Unfortunately, her example, as will afterwards appear, had no influence in disposing her volatile grand-daughter to similar acts of charity.

In 1290 the royal family celebrated their Easter festival, April 2nd, at Woodstock, and the Princess Mary joined them. The king's daughters, with their cousin, Mary of Bretagne, had mass performed for them in the morning of the day, after which they and their maidens presented their Easter offerings. They then distributed among the neighbouring poor 106 ells of cloth, 567 ells of thick russet, and 80 pairs of shoes, the total value amounting to £45. 18s. 10d., which had been purchased at the king's expense, to gladden the hearts of many a child of poverty, at a christian anniversary so exhilarating in its commemorations. The five princesses afterwards removed to Winchester, where, on the 20th of April, they offered in the church of St. Swithin, "at the place where the heart of St. Aymeric lay," and also at the relics in the treasury of the church. Their offerings

[1] Chron. Anon., Royal MS., 13 Edw. VI., f. 64, col. 2.
[2] Chron. Lanercost, Harl. MS., 96, f. 139 b.

were very liberal, amounting in the whole to eight guineas.
On the 23rd of April they offered at the church of St.
Richard, and on the 29th at St. Edward's at Westminster.
All the payments were made at the expense of the king,
their father.[1]   The following day, April 30th, was the wedding-day of the Princess Joanna, Mary's second sister; but
the presence of the little nun is not mentioned either at these
nuptials, or those of the Princess Margaret, which took place
a few months later.

At the close of this year, the royal family of England
were plunged into profound sorrow, by the death of the
queen-consort, Eleanora of Castile.   We do not find that
any of her daughters took part in the splendid funereal pro-
cessions by which the widowed monarch endeavoured to
divert or express the intensity of his woe. About two months
after the funeral he visited Ambresbury, to seek consolation
in the society of his beloved mother and in that of his little
daughter.   He left Ambresbury on the 20th of February,[2]
but was soon summoned thither again on another equally
melancholy event.   This was the decease of the queen-
dowager, which took place on the 24th of June, A.D., 1291,
just five years after her final entrance into the convent.[3]
Her body was embalmed, and preserved till August 15th,
the fête of the Assumption, in compliance with the wishes
of Edward I., in order that he might be present at the
funeral, which was performed with much solemnity.[4]

---

[1] Wardrobe book, 18 Edw. I., miscel. roll, No. 70, Tower, unfoliated.
[2] Rot. claus., 19 Edw. I., m. 8.   Archæologia, vol. xxix., p. 175.—Paper
on the death of Eleanora of Castile, by the Rev. Jos. Hunter.
[3] Trivet's annals, p. 272.
[4] At the conclusion of the ceremony, the king took his mother's heart,
which had been enclosed in a golden case, and presented it to the master
general of the friars minors, with these words: "To thee, as the nearest
relation of my mother, I commit the treasure dearest to me.   Do thou bury
it in London, with honour, among thy brethren, whom she herself loved
most in this world."   It was accordingly interred on her anniversary day,
the feast of St. Andrew, November 30th, in presence of most of the prelates
and nobles of England.—Harl. MS., 96, ff. 139 b, 140 b.

The death of her grandmother was likely to be felt by Mary with more acuteness than that of her mother, for she had been for several years her almost constant companion; but the buoyancy of childhood broods not long over sorrow, however deep, and the tears of a girl of thirteen would probably be soon and easily dried up.

According to previous arrangements, both Mary and her cousin, Eleanora of Bretagne, were, on the death of the queen-mother, to have exchanged the convent of Amesbury for the abbey of Fontevraud. The Breton princess, at the wish of her father, was therefore sent thither,[1] but Mary still tarried in England. The reason of this departure on the part of King Edward from his original intention is not given, nor is any correspondence on the subject preserved.[2] In 1292, the Abbess of Fontevraud came over to England, to solicit from the king the heart of his father, Henry III., which he had bequeathed to her monastery, and which was accordingly delivered to her with much solemnity in Westminster Abbey by the Abbot Walter.[3] Probably one of the objects of her visit was to secure the surrender of the Princess Mary, but the king rather evaded than denied her proposal. He seems indeed to have intended its ultimate accomplishment, for, ever after the death of the nun-queen, the terms employed in all grants to Mary were, that she should enjoy them "as long as she remained in England." Parental affection, however, protracted her departure for awhile; and ultimately the will of the royal nun may be supposed to have been strongly exerted to secure her permanent residence in her father's dominions, where her influence and

[1] Lobineau, vol. i., p. 270.

[2] There is in the Tower collection a letter from the Abbess of Fontevraud, written about this time, praying that the property left to Queen Eleanora might still be continued for the sake of the king's daughter, the Lady Mary. It concludes with eulogistic expressions about the piety of the king and his family.

[3] Fœdera, vol. i., p. 758. An anniversary was regularly performed at Fontevraud for Henry III., King Edward allowing for it £10 annually. In the Tower collection is a letter, No. 1412, from the Abbess Margaret to Edward I., requesting payment of this pension and arrears.

domestic enjoyments were so great. At all events, the idea of her removal was relinquished, and from this period we hear nothing further of it.

Immediately upon the death of her grandmother, Mary's annual income was doubled, £200 a-year being regularly allowed for her support.[1] The following year, 1292, the king granted her forty oaks, as an annual allowance from the neighbouring forests of Chute and Bakeholt, for the fire in her chamber; and the charges of the felling and carriage, which at that time often far exceeded the value of the timber, were to be placed to his account.[2] In like manner, the bailiff of Southampton was ordered to send her yearly twenty measures of wine from the royal stores.[3] The receipt of these articles Mary regularly testified by her letters patent.[4] In these and other grants the princess is usually spoken of as "the Lady Mary, the king's dearest daughter, a nun of Fontevraud, now staying at Ambresbury."

In the year 1293 a quarrel arose between the priory of Amesbury and the maternal house of Fontevraud, about certain rights which were claimed by both, particularly that of electing a new prioress at Amesbury. On the death of the last prioress, the abbess Margaret sent over Johanna de Jeynes, Genes, or Gennes, as she is variously called, "a wise and vigorous woman, in whom she had great confidence," as prioress. She wrote her a letter of recommendation to King Edward, requesting him to confirm the election, and duly to invest the prioress with the temporalities, "in

---

[1] Issue rolls, from the 19th to the 30th of Edward I. See also Fœdera, vol. i., p. 798. Devon's Excerpta, from the Pell rolls, p. 99.

[2] In the 32nd year the expense thus incurred was £5, and in the 33rd £8. —Rot. lib., 34 Edw. I., mm. 2, 1.

[3] Rot. pat., 20 Edw. I., m. 27, in cedulâ. Monast. Ang., vol. ii., p. 337. Fœdera, vol. i., p. 758. Rot. pat., 22 Edw. I., m. 9; ibid., 30, mm. 14, 26, 29. The orders for their delivery recur on the liberate rolls; occasionally they were omitted for a short time, in which case the arrears were always carefully paid up.

[4] See rot. lib., 25 Edw. I., m. 5.

order that she may fully use our right, and correct and reform all those who shall need correction and reformation; and that by her the said nuns and friars may give up their minds to our Lord; since there is no religion without obedience and correction, and it is destroyed by disobedience; and that we ourselves, who are their chief, and that of all the order, may render sufficient account before God in the day of judgment. So please you to do," she adds, "most royal lord and father, that by these good deeds and all others you may come to the joy of Paradise, which God grant you by his sweet pity, so as we desire it. Adieu, very dear lord and father, and may God keep you! Given the Sunday that "Cantate Domino laudem" is sung in the holy church,[1] the year of grace 1294."[2]

Meanwhile, the nuns of Amesbury had elected another prioress, named Margaret,[3] a proceeding which the abbess of Fontevraud took in high dudgeon. She came over to England, and appeared in person to plead her own cause, and to aid her efforts she availed herself of the services of the celebrated Antony Bek, Bishop of Durham. The prioress of Amesbury, on the other hand, chose the Princess Mary, and Peter, prior of Amesbury, aided by Oliver,[4] Bishop of Lincoln, to appear for her—trusting, doubtless, more to the personal influence of the princess than to the business-talents of her pleaders. Indeed, on no other ground can we account for the selection of a girl of fifteen to take part in an intricate ecclesiastic discussion. In the intermediate time, a suitable nun, who was agreeable to all parties, was chosen to attend to the proper religious observances of the priory, and its temporalities were committed by the king into the hands of "his faithful and industrious abbot of Llanelly," until the disputes were settled. This latter

[1] The fourth Sunday after Easter, May 16th.
[2] Rot. pat., 25 Edw. I., p. 1, m. 11, per Inspeximus.
[3] See patent roll, 22 Edw. I., m. 19.
[4] Oliver de Lutton, who was elected in 1279, and died in 1299.

step had] certainly become necessary, since one reason assigned by the king for its adoption was, that "the priory of Amesbury, founded and endowed by our progenitors, the kings of England, and lately enriched by us with ampler possessions, has fallen into such poverty, through constant contentions with the Abbess of Fontevraud, that it can no longer support its wonted state;" wherefore the nuns, prior, and monks were commanded to yield the guardianship of the revenues to the aforesaid prior, in the hope that his vigilant attention would restore order and prosperity to their affairs.[1] They remained in his hands rather more than a year, when the king at length consented to confirm the election of Johanna de Gennes.[2]

The conduct of this lady in the affairs of the convent gave as much satisfaction to the king, on his occasional visits there,[3] as it had previously done to the abbess of Fontevraud; and therefore we may presume that, in spite of the opposition made by Mary to her installation, she treated the princess with proper distinction. So far, too, was the abbess of Fontevraud from resenting Mary's conduct, that she appointed her to act as her attorney in England, partly with a view of conciliating the high-born damsel, whose opposition might be serious to her cause, and partly in the hope that the advocacy of so near a relative of the monarch would be of advantage to her.

A letter from the princess to her father, in her new character, as attorney, seems, from some traces of juvenile simplicity in its style, to belong to this period. The following is a literal translation from the Norman French, in which it is penned.

---

[1] Rot. claus., 21 Edw. I., m. 8, in cedulâ. Rot. pat., 18 Edw. I., m. 14.
[2] Rot. pat., 22 Edw. I., m. 19. The date of the patent for the resignation of the temporalities was June 3rd, 1293 : that for their restitution, June 10th, 1294. See also an Inspeximus in Monast. Ang., vol. ii., p. 338; and Prynne's papal usurpations, vol. iii., p. 769.
[3] See a letter from the king to the abbess of Fontevraud, rot. claus., 25 Edw. I., m. 10.

" To the most high and most noble prince, and her dearest and most beloved lord and father, my lord, by the grace of God King of England, his devoted nun, Mary, wishes health, with all honour and all reverence.

" Dearest sire, we understand that your escheators have seized and placed in your hands the manor of Leighton and of la Grave, with all their appurtenances, on account of the death of a guardian of the said places. And because you know that your ancestors gave them in perpetual alms to the convent of Fontevraud, we beg you, dearest sire, for God's sake and your soul's, that you will place the said manors out of all seisin, if you please, and command the said escheators to go away without taking anything.

" And whereas my lord the Earl of Gloucester has also, for the same reason, seized the manor of Stanvele,[1] may it please you to command the earl and his people that they take away their hands from the goods of my lady the abbess, freely and without damage done. Do as much, most sweet father, for the love of me, that my lady the abbess of Fontevraud may perceive in all things that I am a good attorney for her in this country. I commend to Jesus Christ the soul and body of you !"[2]

A few years afterwards, Mary's name occurs, prefixed to a petition thus headed : " To our lord the king pray Lady Mary, your daughter, and your prioress of Amesbury, and your convent of the same place," and urging upon the king to vindicate the rights of the sisterhood to free pasturage in the manor of Melksham, which had been bestowed upon them by Henry III., and confirmed by the present monarch, but of which his servants had forcibly and unjustly deprived them.[3]

The visits of the king or Prince Edward to Ambresbury, and Mary's visits to them, formed frequent and pleasant

[1] Stavely ?   [2] Royal letters, Tower, No. 1647.
[3] Ryley Placita Parliamentaria, p. 605.

interruptions in the monotony of her existence. On these occasions she always chose that some of her companion nuns should share her enjoyments. Thus, on Friday, June 12th, 1293, we find her visiting her brother at Mortlake, with some of the nuns, and they remained with him till Sunday after dinner. The following September he returned the visit. On Wednesday, the 9th, and Thursday, the 10th of that month, the princess, with the whole convent of nuns and their attendants, were handsomely entertained by him.[1]

The next notice that occurs of Mary is in 1297. On the 9th of March she presented an offering of 7s., and also a gold clasp, in her father's name, at the shrine of St. Edith, at Wilton.[2] On the 28th of April she received letters from the king,[3] and on July 1st, attended by a train of servants and horses, she paid a visit to court, the purpose of which was to take a tender adieu of her youngest sister, Elizabeth, who was about to leave England for the continent, to join her husband, the Earl of Holland. The two sisters resided together for a short time at Langley, while the king was at Westminster; after which they accompanied him to St. Albans, and back again to Westminster. On the 31st of July the princesses had a mass performed at Westminster Abbey, for the soul of their deceased mother, Queen Eleanora, at which they paid 5s. 4d. in offerings. The sum of 9d. was also expended in the purchase of fruit for them from the neighbouring villages.[4] On the 7th of August the nun-princess again departed to her convent. During the thirty-eight days of her visit, the sum of £42. 15s. 7d. was expended in provision for herself and her suite.[5]

The following year, 1298, Mary was seized with a fit of sickness; the nature of her disease is not specified, but

---

[1] Household roll of Prince Edward, 21 Edw. I., Rolls' House.
[2] Wardrobe book, 25 Edw. I., ff. 7, 139, addit. MS., 7965, Brit. Museum.
[3] Ibid., f. 109 b.
[4] Wardrobe roll, 25 Edw. I., No. 2174, Queen's Rememb.
[5] Wardrobe book, 25 Edw. I., f. 27 b.

change of air having been prescribed as a remedy, she left Amesbury for the town of Ditton, in Cambridgeshire, where she remained eighteen days, taking occasional excursions into other parts of the same county. She was placed during this time under the protection of William Lutton, Viscount or sheriff of Cambridgeshire and Huntingdonshire, who was commissioned to provide her with all things needful for her infirm health, and to pay all her expenses, which amounted to £35. 11s. 0½d.[1]

We have already seen with what ample munificence Edward I. had endowed his daughter. Although she had no establishment of her own to support, and her saintly profession excluded her from the heavy wardrobe expenses which were incurred by her sisters, yet her annual income was equal to £3000. of our present coinage, beside her supplies of firewood and wine, occasional presents, and the payment of her travelling expenses whenever she visited court. Notwithstanding this, she was often in debt, and sometimes manifested a criminally heedless inconsiderateness of the sufferings she inflicted upon others by her want of promptness in her payments. There was one Martin of Amesbury, a goldsmith, who had afterwards removed to London, from whom she had purchased many articles on credit. On this account Martin became so much embarrassed in his affairs that he was sent to prison for debt. He of course stated the circumstances to the proper authorities, and the case was referred to the king; when the indulgent monarch himself paid the debt she owed to Martin, who was thereby enabled to discharge his own liabilities, and was set free.[2] To provide, if possible, against the recurrence of so discreditable a transaction, the king, a few years afterwards, enlarged Mary's allowance, by a grant of ten additional oaks every half year,[3]

[1] Ward. account, 24-29 Edw. I., in a portfolio marked No. 2945, Queen's Rememb. Rot. lib., 27 Edw. I., m. 4.
[2] Ward. roll, 27 Edw. I., dorso, No. 2038, Queen's Rememb.
[3] Rot. pat., 30 Edw. I., m. 17; ibid., 34, m. 14.

and by giving her manors, situated in the neighbouring counties of Wiltshire, Dorsetshire, and Somersetshire, or in the Isle of Wight, the annual value of which was £266. 13s. 4d., instead of her former £200., and twenty measures of wine.[1] Of these manors, several were given for her elemosynary charities, but whether their revenues were ever so appropriated is very questionable, since not a memento remains of any benefaction made by Mary on her own account.

The payment of this augmented income was enforced with such strict punctuality, that a female delinquent, who had failed to pay her rental of one mark for some lands she held, was impleaded by the princess, and the king commanded rigorous payment to be made; "since," he says, "we wish our dear daughter to receive all the benefit of our grant, without loss or injury."[2] But still her income was found insufficient to meet her demands; and one of the last acts of the king on behalf of his extravagant daughter was graciously to come to her relief, since she had run sadly into debt to different persons, and bestow on her a grant of £200. from the royal exchequer.[3] It becomes, therefore, a question how such sums were expended by one whose retired situation closed to her so many of the ordinary avenues of female vanity. Instead of the costly tunic, and mantle of cloth of gold or velvet, the loose Benedictine robe of black serge was her constant attire, whilst the long black monastic veil took the place of the costly gemmed coronet or garland. The only ornament ever recorded to have been worn by the nun-princess was a golden clasp, which was perhaps allowed her in consideration of her superior rank.[4] In the furniture of her apartments, however, in the luxuries of her table, and the extent of her stud, Mary rivalled even the rude splen-

[1] Rot. pat., 30 Edw. I., m. 14. Monast. Ang., vol. ii., p. 338. Abbrev. Rot. orig., 30 Edw. I., p. 122.
[2] Rot. claus., 34 Edw. I., m. 3.   [3] Ibid., m. 12, date, April 13th.
[4] Two of these were bought for her from Frowyk, the goldsmith, at a cost of £6.—Wardrobe book, 34 Edw. I., Queen's Rememb.

dour of the court of Edward I. Her bed was hung with velvet and tapestry, and furnished with the finest linen;[1] and the green benches with which her apartment was surrounded on three sides were provided with cushions of the softest down. The linen equipments of her table and pantry were on such a scale, that 102 ells of napkin material, and 100 ells of fine cloth, along with some towels, were presented at one time by her father, the medium of communication being no less a person than his reverence the Bishop of Chester.[2] Her favourite article of diet seems to have been fish, and of this the king frequently presented her with considerable quantities: in one year alone he sent her sixteen sea-wolves to Ambresbury, at another time he sent her two thousand stock-fish, value £6.[3] Other entries occur for the payment of messengers who went to take her fish, where the description of the fish is not given.[4]

The other princesses were content to travel with one or two chariots, and six, or at most eight horses; but, when the Lady Mary made her appearance at court, it was with a train of twenty-four horses, each of which had a groom in attendance, beside the sumpterers who had charge of the luggage.[5] She generally travelled on horseback, but several notices occur of her chariots, as well as of saddles and other articles of horse equipage, bought for her.[6] The pecuniary embarrassments of the princess were owing, however, less to her extravagant personal expenditure, which her large income might have sufficed to meet, than to a love of gambling, a propensity equally derogatory to her high rank and religious vocation, in which she unfortunately indulged.[7]

[1] Wardrobe account, 27-28 Edw. I., No. 1904, Queen's Rememb.
[2] Wardrobe fragment, close of Edward I.'s reign, Queen's Rememb.
[3] Wardrobe fragment, Queen's Rememb.
[4] Wardrobe fragment, 34 Edw. I., and also another dateless fragment, Queen's Rememb.
[5] Wardrobe fragment, temp. Edw. II., in a bundle marked W. N., 5338, Queen's Rememb.
[6] Ward. book, 34 Edw. I., Queen's Rem. Ward. fragm., *passim*. Præstita gard., 33 Ed. I., ff. 2, 3, Harl. MS., 152. [7] Ward. roll, No. 3809, Queen's Rem.

The only presents on record as having been made by Mary
at her own expense were a pair of knives, with enamelled
handles, which she presented to the king as a new year's
gift, in 1304,[1] and a falcon, which she sent to her brother in
1307.[2] The king frequently sent her money or pieces of
plate, to give away to such persons as might have a claim
upon her generosity, which she faithfully appropriated to
their intended use. In spite of her unfitness for so responsible an office, her high birth procured for her the post
of deputy-visitor for the abbess of Fontevraud, to inspect
all houses of that order in England, and administer reproof,
discipline, or correction as she thought fit.[3]

In the year 1299, the second marriage of Edward I.
with the Princess Margaret of France took place ;[4] but the
juvenility of the bride rendered her fitter to be the companion than the step-mother of her husband's children,
several of whom were considerably older than herself.
Soon after her arrival in England, Edward sent for his
daughter Mary to Langley, to introduce her to the queen.[5]
A sisterly intimacy sprung up between these royal ladies,
and they spent a good deal of time together. In 1301,
when the queen was anticipating the birth of her second son,
Edmund of Woodstock, she was anxious to secure the
society of the Lady Mary, especially as her husband was
then absent in Scotland. The king accordingly communicated her wishes to Mary, and she instantly set forth to join

[1] Wardrobe book, 34 Edw. I.
[2] Wardrobe account of Prince Edward, 35 of Edward I., Harl. MS., 6001.
[3] See Appendix, No. xix.
[4] The queen landed at Dover on the 9th of September, and was met at
Canterbury by Prince Edward and many of the nobles of the land. The king
himself was at Chatham on her arrival, but he testified his pleasure by
making a present, equal in value to £60, to the valet of the Lady Matilda,
wife of Lord Henry of Lancaster, who brought him tidings of her landing:
and he gave an additional offering at vesper service in the church there, in
token of his gratitude.—Ward. roll, 27 Edw. I., No. 2618, Queen's Rememb.
He had previously sent eleven pieces of tapestry to decorate the barge which
was to convey her to the shores of her future kingdom.—Ibid., No. 2806.
[5] Ward. account, 27 Edw. I., No. 2106, Queen's Rememb.

her step-mother at the palace of Woodstock—the journey
occupying three long days in June. The young prince was
born on the 5th of August;[1] and in October, after Queen
Margaret was sufficiently recovered to undergo the fatigues
of travelling, the princess accompanied her on a pilgrimage
of thanksgiving, which she made to several famous shrines,
terminating with the cathedral of Hereford. Their journeyings lasted ten days, after which the queen prepared to
join her husband in Scotland,[2] and Mary returned to her
convent, escorted by William de Lutton, one of the king's
confidential clerks, having first distributed gifts of jewellery
to the queen's principal attendants; but these jewels, as
well as the offerings she made at various shrines during her
journey, were all provided by the king, who knew her habits
too well to trust to her own power or willingness to make
such presents as he thought suitable for the occasion.[3]

Mary's communications with her father's court still continued frequent,[4] and her visits seem now to have been
repeated yearly, and sometimes even oftener;[5] but as no
particulars concerning them have transpired, save minutiæ of
expenditure similar to those already given, they deserve
but passing notice. In November, 1304, when the king
went to York, and afterwards to Scotland, he left his queen
at Langley, and Prince Edward with the Princess Mary
were her companions. Part of her household roll during
this period is still in existence, but few details of interest
can be gathered from it, since the sums expended are all
classified under the heads of Dispensary, Buttery, Kitchen,
Saltery, Hall, Chamber, Stable, Wages, &c., and include no

---

[1] Matt. Westm., p. 434.
[2] Chron. Lanerc., Harl. MS., 96, f. 166 b.
[3] Ward. book, 29 Edw. I., f. 156 b.
[4] Wardrobe accounts, 29 Edw. I., No. 1865, Queen's Rememb. Ibid., 30,
No. 1989.
[5] Ward. roll, 29-30, Edw. I., No. 2693, Queen's Rememb. Præstita garderobæ, 33-34 Edward I., Harl. MS., 152, ff. 2, 3, Wardrobe fragment,
Queen's Remembrancer.

particulars of personal expenditure. The household must have been kept up with regal state, for the average expenditure per week was £100.[1]

In the autumn of 1305, Mary took a short excursion, in company with her two juvenile step-brothers, Thomas and Edmund. Young as the children were, they were allowed to eat at the same table as their matronly sister. Robert de Winter, their waferer, had 2s. paid him for serving up wafers at the table of the Lords Thomas and Edmund, and the Lady Mary. On August 22nd they visited Ludgershall, where they remained some time; early in October they went to Reading, and thence to Caversham, presenting offerings at the churches in each place.[2] In November she accompanied her young companions back to court, where Mary, with her sister Elizabeth and her two nieces, Joanna of Bar, Countess of Warren, and Eleanora de Clare, spent some time in the company of the queen, tarrying with her in the different places to which her own inclination or her husband's wishes led her, from November that year to July the year following, a period of nearly nine months.[3] During this time was born the little Princess Eleanora, the youngest child of Edward I., and his only daughter by Margaret of France. In December, 1305, the king, queen, and their whole train visited Amesbury, when Mary sojourned for at least a few days at her convent.[4] On the 7th of July, 1306, she left court for Northampton, whence she set out on a pilgrimage to the two shrines of St. Mary's at Walsingham, and St. Edmund's of Edmundsbury, Suffolk, at both which places she

---

[1] Household roll, No. 2645. Queen's Rememb. The date is ascertained by the mention of Tuesday as the 3rd of November, which coincidence transpired in 1304.

[2] Wardrobe account, 33 Edw. I., recently sold by Messrs. Puttick and Simpson.

[3] Ward. fragm., 34 Edw. I., Queen's Rememb.

[4] Wood and coals were bought for her there, on December 11.—Ward fragm., 34 Edw. I., Queen's Rememb.

was entrusted by the queen with offerings for the health of the infant princess.[1]

So great was the fame of the forementioned shrine, that no one could attain a high reputation for sanctity without having undertaken a pilgrimage thither. A merry pilgrimage, however, was that of the nun-princess; she travelled herself in a litter,[2] and was attended not only by a train of ladies and maidens, but by a number of minstrels, who diverted the party, from time to time, with such snatches of poetry, ballad-chanting, and music, as the genius of the times supplied. She had also her pages and messengers, who went to and from court and elsewhere on her errands. The whole journey, from the time of leaving Northampton to the return to Ambresbury, on the 4th of August, occupied twenty-nine days. The total expense in beer, venison, meat, and fish bought for the table of the princess; grass, oats, and hay for her horses; her oblations and those of the maidens and ladies in her train; gifts to the minstrels, payments to messengers, &c., all which were paid by the king, amounted to £48. 11s. 2d.[3] But even while thus living on her father's liberality, she fell short of money for her private expenses, and sent first a clerk and then a valet from Walsingham to the king to beg or borrow money; through them she received farther gifts of £10.,[4] £5. 4s. 6d.,[5] and 20 marks. She had, probably, been tempted to indulge in her mischievous fondness for gambling.

Mary was a lover of minstrelsy, and always encouraged it as far as she had the opportunity. She was also a patroness of literature; and one of the best chroniclers of the period, Nicholas Trivet, dedicated to her a chronicle, written in old Norman French, and containing much

---

[1] Ward. book, temp. Edw. I., Queen's Rememb.
[2] Ward. fragm., ut sup.
[3] Ward. book, 34 Edw. I., Queen's Rememb.
[4] Rot. exit., 34 Edw. I., Pasch.   [5] Ibid., 34 and 35, Mich.

genealogical information about the family of Edward I. The mention he makes of his lady patroness is as follows: "The fourth [living] daughter of the King Edward Fitz Henry was the Lady Mary, of whom it has before been said that she married the high king of Heaven, and therefore of her it may be truly said, ' Optimam partem elegit sibi Maria, quæ non auferetur ab eâ,'" which is to say, "Mary hath chosen the best part, for this portion, which is God himself, shall never be taken from her."[1]

The annals of this author, written in Latin, have been printed, and are looked upon as good authority for the reign of Edward I.; but the chronicle remains in manuscript; it is headed thus: " Ci comence les chronicles qe ffrere Nichol Trivet escript a dame Marie la fille a mon seignour le roi Edward le fitz Henri." The chronicler prefaces his work with the remark that he has been informed, by several studious persons, that they are weary of the prolixity of histories, and also that there is a dearth of books. Wherefore it seemed good to him to collect accounts of those who have descended from the first father, Adam, extending in a right line down to the birth of our Lord Jesus Christ; so that, by the description which is given, hearts may be more attracted to regard his abridgment, seeing they may understand the thing more easily, and retain it in more vivid remembrance. He promises not to disregard the truth of history, but to show it in due order, according to the descent from Adam, by patriarchs, judges, kings, prophets, and priests, and others of their time, down to our Saviour, and then afterwards the deeds of the apostles, emperors, and kings, down to the apostle, or Pope John XXII.[2] He commences accordingly with the creation of the world as follows:—

" On the first day of time, at prime of day, God created

---

[1] Arundel MS., No. 56, f. 75 b.
[2] This pope was elected in 1316, and died in 1334.

heaven and earth, and the angels of heaven; and made then Lucifer. A short time elapsed, not quite an hour, before he was cast, with all others assenting to him, into hell, which is in the centre of the earth; yet, all the bad angels did not descend with Lucifer into hell, but some remained in the air, some in the sea, and some in the earth."

The history, up to the christian era, is mainly founded on Scripture; afterwards, it contains church history, chronological notices of the popes and emperors of Rome, and also much information about the Anglo-Norman kings of England, including a genealogy of Edward I., back to Adam, our first father, of course tracing him through the favoured line of Seth and Enoch.[1]

One copy of this chronicle is in the Bibliothèque Royale, Paris.[2] Another is preserved among the Arundel MSS. in the British Museum,[3] and a third among the Bodleian MSS., Oxford.[4]

The last notices of the Princess Mary, during her father's lifetime, well accord with those already given. He presented her, as well as each of her half-brothers, Thomas and Edmund, with a new and splendid bed.[5] He pardoned her the annual rental due to himself of £13. 13s. 5d., from a manor which had been yielded to her;[6] and on the 10th of June, 1307, scarcely a month previous to his decease, he gave her, in aid of her expenses, the custody of several manors belonging to her nephew, Gilbert de Clare;[7] which custody had just become vacant by the decease of Mary's elder sister, Joanna, Countess of Gloucester.

---

[1] Arundel MS., 56, f. 74 b. Trivet was also the author of an exposition of the rules of the order of St. Augustine.

[2] MS., No. 632[17], Supplement Français. [3] No. 56.

[4] Rawlinson MS., B., No. 178. This book formerly belonged to the learned Spelman.

[5] Wardrobe roll, 33 Edw. I., No. 2108, Queen's Rememb., Rot. exit., 33, Mich.

[6] Rot. claus., 34 Edw. I., m. 12. [7] Rot. pat., 35 Edw. I., m. 8.

Edward I. was deeply engaged in his last Scotch expedition, when he was seized with a violent attack of the mortal disorder which speedily terminated his existence. The anxiety of the royal family, when they heard of the perilous situation of the king, may be readily conceived. Mary had previously left Amesbury for Northampton, where the queen was staying; and they both, with zealous haste, resolved on an immediate pilgrimage to the shrines of St. Thomas of Canterbury and St. Thomas of Dover, to avert, by their intercessions to those celebrated saints, the dreaded calamity. Queen Margaret took with her her two little sons Thomas and Edmund, and the troop of anxious pilgrims set forth on their melancholy errand. Their agonized pleadings were poured forth in vain; the fond husband and indulgent father had expired before they could have reached the nearer place of pilgrimage.

They were, however, for some time unconscious of their loss. They had left Northampton about the 5th of July, 1307, and the death of Edward I. took place at Carlisle on the 7th; but they were now so far distant, and the modes of communication so tardy, that it was not until they had visited both the shrines with prayers and votive offerings, and were on their return homewards, that the news reached them. The sorrow-stricken queen, unable to bear the society of her infant children, sent them at once to Northampton, where they arrived on the 15th of July. She travelled more slowly to join them there; but Mary did not accompany her. She retired, to hide, behind her convent-walls, her grief for a loss that to her was indeed irreparable. The orphan-princess arrived once more at Amesbury on the 25th of July.[1]

Feasting and fasting, joy and sorrow, the bridal and the burial, follow each other sometimes with fearful rapidity in this ever-changing world. The next event that occurred

[1] Rot. exit., 35 Edw. I., Pasch.

in the life of the Princess Mary was the receipt of a
peremptory summons from her brother, now King Edward II., who had recently celebrated at Boulogne his
marriage with the fair Isabella of France, to set forth immediately to Dover, to meet his young queen on her arrival
in England.[1] Mary had declined the invitation which, as
one of the royal family, she would assuredly receive, to be
present at these nuptials, which were graced by the attendance of so many of the great and noble; but she could not
refuse to welcome home her brother's bride. The royal
party landed at Dover on the 7th of February. Mary did
not remain long with them, but she accepted an invitation
to be present at the approaching coronation of the king
and queen.

The cessation of the special marks of her father's liberality had already affected the exchequer of the princess;
and, as she did not like to apply to her brother for funds,
she was compelled to borrow money from her own clerk,
Gilbert Muresley, to pay the expenses of her preparations
for this important visit.[2] She repaired to London with
more than ordinary state; but the king imitated his father's
generosity in paying all her charges, as well as discharg-
ing her debts.[3] He also confirmed to her, with a slight
exchange of one manor for another, equally valuable, all
the lands she had held during the lifetime of Edward I.,
and ordered her supply of firewood to be sent,[4] and all the
expenses of carriage to be paid, as before.[5] The following year he wrote to the pope on her behalf about some
business of hers which had been long pending, and for the

[1] Ward. fragm., 1-10 Edw. II., Queen's Rememb.
[2] Ward. account, 1 Edw. II., No. 2412, Queen's Rememb.
[3] Ibid. Wardrobe roll of the pipe, Edw. II. and III., anno 1 Edw. II.
These rolls, which are of great size, are stitched together at the top, and not
in consecutive membranes. Each membrane contains the account for one
regnal year. They were formally kept in the pipe office, Somerset House,
but are now deposited in the office of the Exchequer of Pleas, at Carlton Ride.
[4] Fœdera, vol. ii., pt. i., p. 16.
[5] Rot. lib., 3 Edw. II., m. 5. Ibid., 6, m. 3.

forwarding of which she had sent one of her clerks, John le Breton, to the papal court.[1] What the nature of this business was is not ascertained ; it probably related to some renewed contest between the convent of Ambresbury and that of Fontevraud.

Although Mary was never nominally more than a simple nun—though she never seems even to have aspired to the honours of superior of the convent—yet, owing to her birth, her influence at court, and the energy of her disposition, she was looked up to in every case of difficulty or perplexity as the protectress of the priory; and, especially, on the election of a prioress, her wish was first consulted by her sister-nuns, and the negociation of the affair confided to her.   On the death of the prioress Dambert,[2] she wrote the following letter to Edward II. :

" To the very high and noble prince, her dearest lord and brother, my Lord Edward, by God's grace King of England, his sister Mary wishes health, and all sorts of honour and reverence !

" Dearest sire, since a great while has passed since God did his pleasure upon our prioress, we, after her death, sent in all haste to our dear cousin,[3] the abbess of Fontevraud, on my own part and on that of the convent, asking for a lady of this our convent, namely, for Lady Isabel de Genville—whom we understand is well able and sufficient for the office—that she might be granted to us for our prioress.   And we thought, dear sire, that she (the abbess) would have willingly granted us our request, for she is bound to do so, since she was brought up and veiled amongst us, and so she should neither wish nor permit that the church should be so long without prelates.   But as yet we have had no answer; only we understand from

---

[1] Rot. Rom. and Franc., 2 Edw. II., m. 7 d.   Fœdera, vol. ii., pt. i., p. 64.
[2] This name does not occur in the imperfect list of the prioresses of Amesbury given in the Monasticon.
[3] Eleanora of Bretagne.

certain people that she intends to send us a prioress from beyond the sea there, and a prior by her counsel out there. And know certainly, my very dear brother, that, should she send any other than one belonging to our own convent, it would prove matter of discord in the convent, and of the destruction of the goods of the church; which I know well, sire, that you would not suffer willingly and wittingly. Wherefore I pray you, dearest lord and brother, and require you, both for the love of me and of our convent,—which, after God, trusts surely in you,—that you would please to send word to my said lady abbess that she do not undertake to burden our church with any prioress out of the convent, nor with prior other than the one we have now, but that she would grant us her whom we have requested.

"Do this, most dearest brother, that our convent may perceive your aid and sustenance in this case, as they have always done in their needs. May Jesus Christ give you a long life, my dearest brother! Written at Swayneton, in the Isle of Wight, the 9th day of May."[1]

This letter sufficiently illustrates the position of the Lady Mary in her own convent. She preferred the reality to the semblance of authority, and chose rather to enforce the election of a prioress who would, of course, be subservient to her wishes than to become a candidate for the honours herself. She had, however, several young ladies of royal birth who were committed to her special tutelage. One of these was Joanna of Gloucester, the daughter of her niece, Margaret of Gloucester, by Piers Gaveston, who was sent to Amesbury for education, but, dying young, was honourably interred, under Mary's care, in the chapel of the Virgin, at Amesbury.[2] Another was Isabella, grand-daughter of Ed-

---

[1] Orig. letters, Tower, temp. Edw. II. The letter is dateless, but, from its being written at Swayneton, it was probably penned subsequently to 1315, when that manor became the property of the princess in exchange for that of Cotham, and before the year 1317, when Eleanora of Bretagne ceased to be abbess of Fontevraud. See page 440, infra.

[2] Chron. de Trivet, Arundel MS., No. 56, f. 75 b.

mund, Duke of Lancaster, "who," says the chronicler Trivet, "by the assent of her father and mother, was veiled a nun at Amesbury, under the guard and keeping of the very honourable Lady Mary, the daughter of Edward Fitz-Henry." [1]

With the latter of these young nuns Mary made a pilgrimage to the shrine of Thomas-à-Becket. A fragmentary roll, still in preservation in the office of the Queen's remembrancer [2] of the Exchequer, contains some particulars of their journey, which was made a lengthy one, on account of the circuitous route adopted by the travellers. They first paid a visit to court for two days; and on Monday, the last of May, attended by a guide and a military guard, they removed as far as Barnet; thence they proceeded to St. Alban's, and made offerings at the great altar and the other shrines in the conventual church there. They also purchased from "Robert, the draper of St. Alban's," 30 ells of canvass, for which they paid 7s. 6d., and a pair of knives for the princess, price 20s. On the Thursday, they proceeded to Agmondesham, now Amersham, in Buckinghamshire; the following day to High Wycombe—thence to Caversham, in Oxfordshire, where they presented offerings at the church of St. Mary, and at the relics in the chapel, and then enjoyed a pleasure excursion along the river, paying 1s. to two boatmen who rowed them. On the Saturday they arrived at Reading. Here they spent the Sunday, and on Monday went on as far as Newbury. While at this latter place, the princess indulged in her favourite but very unsaintly amusement of dice-playing, and to such a length did her passion for gaming lead her, that, having expended all her own ready cash, she borrowed money from one of her domestics to prosecute her sport. On the Tuesday the two ladies proceeded as far as Andover, which, being within a

[1] Chron. de Trivet, MS. 632ᵛ, Sup. Franc. Bibl. du roi.
[2] Wardrobe account, No. 3809.

few miles of Amesbury, enabled them to pay a hasty visit
to the convent. On the Wednesday they returned by way
of Ludgershall, where they remained in the royal palace
until Saturday. They travelled on that day to Stockbridge,
and having advanced thus far on their journey and passed
over the lonelier part of their route, the guide, by name
Henry, and the troop of soldiers who had been sent by the
king to form their escort, left them. Sunday, June 13th,
they spent at Winchester—on Monday proceeded to Alton
and Farnham, and on Tuesday to Guildford and Kingston;
thus returning, after a fortnight's journeying, very nearly
to the point from whence they started.

The roll, which is very imperfect, does not enable us to
trace their daily progress further. They did, however,
arrive at Canterbury, and presented rich offerings in the
church of St. Augustine's, and also at Christ Church.

The strong attachment that subsisted between Mary and
her father's second wife, Margaret of France, has already
been alluded to. Of the sincerity of this attachment Mary
gave strong proof by undertaking the charge of her half-
sister Eleanora. This child was destined for the cloister,
and she was scarcely a year old when, on the death of her
father, Queen Margaret sent her to Amesbury; where she
resided during the remainder of her brief existence, which
terminated when she was only five years old. Her expenses,
calculated at 100 marks, were to have been reimbursed to
Mary by the king her brother, and he did actually pay 40
marks,[1] but the remainder was long suffered to remain
unpaid—for Edward II. was too profuse to be just—until
at last the princess consented to a transmutation of her
claims in consideration of ten measures of wine which she
was to receive per year.[2]

The visits of Mary to the court of her brother are re-

---

[1] Rot. exit., 4 Edward II., Mich.
[2] Monast. Ang., vol. ii., p. 340.

corded in the 2nd,[1] 6th,[2] 8th, 9th, and 10th years of his reign. The first of these was on the 18th of September, 1309, when the king was at Byfleet, in Surrey, and the queen at Guildford. She was accompanied by one of her nieces, a daughter of the Earl of Gloucester. One object of their visit appears to have been to attend the wedding of the young Gilbert, Earl of Gloucester, the young lady's brother, with Matilda, daughter of the Earl of Ulster, which was celebrated at court on the 30th of September.[3]

Of her visit in the 8th year, 1315, some few particulars remain in an almost obliterated wardrobe fragment, from which it appears that she set forth from Amesbury on the 28th of January for Westminster, and returned thither on the 6th of February: that three knights of the royal household were despatched to fetch her, who also escorted her back; her expences, consisting of payments for meat, wine, herrings, eels, salt, fruits, and fodder for her horses, averaged about 28s. 4d. per day.[4]

The roll of her expences during her visit the following year is preserved, but this also is somewhat obliterated. It appears that Lord John de Brus and a clerk of the king, called William Salford, were sent to fetch her to court. Under their guidance, she left Amesbury on the 27th of April, and passed through Andover and Ludgershall, which latter place she reached on the 1st of May, and paid 4d. to a guide to show her the way thence to Newbury; travelling onward, her route lay through Reading, Staines, and Tottenham; and she arrived at Westminster on the 7th of May.

[1] Præstita garderobæ, 2 Edw. II., No. 2386, Queen's Rememb.
[2] Treasurer's account, 6 Edw. II., f. 28, Augmentation records, Carlton ride, marked 6 Edward III. Rot. claus., 6 Edw. II., m. 16. Fœdera, vol. ii., p. 193. £12. 7s. 3d. was paid by the king for the wages of her people, and for corn, hay, litter, iron-work, &c., while she stayed at Windsor—according to her bill presented in Chancery.
[3] Household roll, 2 Edw. II., p. 2. Copy by Craven Ord, in the possession of Sir Thomas Phillipps, Bart., Middlehill MS., 1003. Chron. Tynterne, Lansdowne MS., 259, fol. 40.
[4] Ward. fragm. in a bundle marked T. G., 9738, Queen's rememb.

Scarcely, however, had the princess reached court when news arrived of the death of her youngest sister, Elizabeth Countess of Hereford. This princess was Mary's last surviving sister, excepting, indeed, Margaret of Brabant, whose distance from England precluded all familiar intercourse; and, touched by the mournful event, Mary determined to pay the last tribute to her sister's memory by accompanying her remains to the tomb. She, therefore, formed one in the party of mourners who travelled from London to Walden, in Essex, to attend the funeral of the countess; and then, under the escort of Lord Geoffry, of Cornwall, and other nobles, proceeded to Canterbury, where she performed what she considered the last duty of affection, by presenting rich offerings for her sister's soul. She purchased two pounds of Paris candles, to burn before some hallowed shrine in her behalf.

Having thus gone through the ceremonials of woe, the princess seems to have thrown off both the semblance and reality of sorrow. Instead of retiring to her convent, or returning with the other mourners to court, she took a tour into Kent; and, on the following Monday, May 31st, as she was at Ospring, she gave a present of 2s. to a minstrel of her brother-in-law, Ralph Monthermer, who had contributed to her entertainment. On the Wednesday, she reached Rochester; Thursday, Dartford; and, on Friday, arrived in London, whither three harbingers had already been despatched, to announce her arrival, and prepare for her reception. Mary had performed this journey partly on horseback and partly in a litter; she had in her train thirty horses for her damsels and her attendants, who consisted of four charioteers, six grooms, two sumpterers, and eight pages; a waggon, drawn by three horses, conveyed her cooking apparatus.[1]

[1] Wardrobe roll of the expences of Mary, the king's sister, No. 2557, Queen's Rememb.

The life of a pilgrim, with all its varieties, its incidents, and its adventures, presented to the Princess Mary so pleasant a contrast to her usual quiet mode of existence at Amesbury, that she never let slip an opportunity of peregrinating when she could find a suitable companion. On her return to court, on the present occasion, her eloquent descriptions of the pleasures of "Canterbury pilgrims" produced such an effect upon the mind of her royal sister-in-law, Queen Isabella, that she was prevailed upon to undertake a journey thither herself, and Mary offered to become her companion. The stately daughter of Philip the Fair and the Queen of England could not, however, visit such a shrine as that of St. Thomas without suitable preparations. Some pieces of cloth of gold, with quantities of spices, saffron, wax for tapers, and other articles were provided for the costly offerings she made at the shrines where she tarried on the road, as well as at Canterbury. Although the princess was but a secondary person on this occasion, she was attended by a numerous train with twenty-four horses, all her expenses being paid by the king, her brother. The pilgrimage was performed in June and July,[1] after which Mary again returned to her convent.

With Queen Isabella the princess seems to have lived on intimate terms; they had previously corresponded together,[2] and, indeed, her fondness for the gaieties of the court would naturally lead her to cultivate the good will of those who were the reigning personages there. Edward II. gave his sister many marks of personal affection, by making her presents of wine,[3] lending her money, &c.;[4] and, when his domestic troubles began to accumulate around him, he

---

[1] Rot. exit., 9 Edw. II., Pasch. Ward. fragm., 9 Edw. II., in a bundle marked W. N., 5338, Queen's Rememb.

[2] Ward. book of Queen Isabella, 7 Edw. II., and Ward. roll, Queen Isabella, 9 Edw. II., Queen's Rem.

[3] Ward. fragm., temp. Edw. II., Queen's Rememb.

[4] Ward. account, 4 Edw. II., No. 3393, Queen's Rememb.

showed a still stronger propensity to cling to her. His communications with her became more frequent,[1] and he gave her several valuable presents, among which was a new year's gift, in 1317, of a golden clasp, adorned with six emeralds.[2] Soon afterwards, he purchased for her fifteen pieces of splendid tapestry, wrought over with heraldic blazonries, from Richard de Horsham, a London merchant, and presented them to her on her leaving Westminster, after a visit which she had paid to him.[3] To complete the equipments of her chamber, for which these tapestries were intended, the king added other tapestries of the same pattern, which he sent after her the following month,[4] and he also sent her a beautiful dorser, or pack-saddle, covered with the same costly material.

In March, this year, 1317, the king visited Amesbury, offering at each of the six altars in the convent church. On his departure, Mary went to visit her niece, Elizabeth de Clare, who had recently become the wife of John de Burgh, Earl of Ulster, in order to be present with her during her confinement, on the transpiration of which event, Mary's valet brought the first tidings of it to the king.[5] She then, as usual with her, escorted the young mother on a pilgrimage of thanksgiving as far as Canterbury.[6] After this the princess paid a visit to court, whence she took her departure on the 30th of May, and on her way home visited the abbey of St. Alban's, where, on the 2nd of June, she offered an onch of gold, adorned with a garnet in the centre, and set round with six emeralds; the king, who had accompanied her thus far, offering at the same time.[7]

One of Mary's principal objects in this visit was to prevail upon her brother to interfere for her with the newly-

---

[1] Ward. book, 10 Edw. II., f. 134, MS. No. 120; and Ibid., 11 Edw. II., ff. 55, 97, No. 121 in the library of the Society of Antiquaries.
[2] Ward. book, 10 Edw. II., f. 180.
[3] Ibid., f. 100.   [4] Ibid., f. 107.   [5] Ibid., f. 99.
[6] Issue roll. 10 Edw. II. Devon's excerpta, p. 133.
[7] Ward. book, 10 Edw. II., f. 181.

elected abbess of Fontevraud, under the following circumstances: The former abbess, Eleanora de Bretagne, had
appointed the princess as her deputy, to inspect all the
houses of the same order in England, and to enforce discipline, and even inflict correction as she found it necessary.
On her death, or resignation, however, the abbess who succeeded her, although she did not herself come over to visit
these alien houses, refused, or at least delayed, to confirm
the office of visitant to Mary. On this the king sent his
clerk, John de Hildesle, over to Fontevraud to remonstrate
with the abbess, but, finding his interference ineffectual, he
wrote a long and earnest letter himself to the abbess, assuring her that no lady in this or any other land could more
effectually execute such a commission than his sister, for
she had not in her visitations and corrections deviated in
the least from the strict law. He therefore entreated her
to ratify the arrangement of her predecessor, both for the
honour of religion, and because a contrary course would
reflect great dishonour upon Mary; urging, as an additional
motive, that a power thus granted might be recalled at pleasure, should she herself wish to perform the office of visitor.
This letter bears date Windsor, May 6th; it was sent by
" Thomas Denart, Dean of Angers," who was to urge the
request.[1] The application totally failed, however, and the
following year Edward wrote to the Pope on the subject,
saying that the affair lay very near his heart, as one of the
most desirable things in the world to him, but that, having
found from his clerk, John de Hildesle, that it is not at all
expedited by the abbess, but rather that it is likely to be
altogether refused, he entreated his holiness, with all possible
affection, to use his influence, that the honour of his

---

[1] Rot. claus., 10 Edw. II., m. 7 dorso, Appendix, No. XVIII. From this
document it would seem that there is a mistake in the list of the abbesses
of Fontevraud, given in the Gallia Christina, vol. ii., p. 1322, and that
Eleanora of Bretagne, instead of ruling from 1304 to 1343, as there stated,
must have either died or resigned in 1317.

aforesaid sister might not be injured by a denial of this concession.[1]   This appeal most likely proved successful, for we hear nothing more of the affair.

About this time the king granted his sister the manor of Ludgershall, valued at £26. per annum, with its military fiefs, church presentations, &c., also ten measures of wine, value 40s. each, and £20. 13s. 4d., yearly revenue, instead of 100 marks, which he had formerly granted for her sustenance.[2]

We have now reached a period at which almost all documentary evidence relative to the Princess Mary ceases. Few of the wardrobe accounts of the latter·part of the reign of Edward II., are in existence, and in those few her name is not mentioned.   On the death of her unfortunate brother, in 1327, and the accession of his son Edward III., the young king confirmed to his aunt the privileges she had hitherto received in gifts of wine, money, &c., from the royal stores.[3]   The orders for the forwarding to her of her sixty oaks and ten measures of wine recur, though with some irregularity, until the 6th of Edward III., A.D. 1332,[4] but no entry is found for her at a later period,[5] from which it may be fairly concluded that this was the date of her death.   She was at this time in her fifty-fourth year, and was the longest liver, as well as the last survivor of the family of Edward I., and Eleanora of Castile.   She outlived her brother, Edward II., six years, and her sister Margaret, the next to herself in longevity, fourteen years.

[1] Monast. Ang., vol. li., p. 340.   The subject of the king's petition is only indirectly alluded to in his letter to the Pope, but the coincidence of dates, and especially the mention of John de Hildesle as the clerk, negociating with the Abbess of Fontevraud, distinctly identify the transaction to be the same with that noticed in the previous letter to the abbess herself.

[2] Rot. pat., 10 Edw. II., p. 2, mm. 20, 19, 18. Rot. claus., 14 Edw. IL., m. 17.

[3] Fœdera, vol. ii., pt. ii., p. 694.   Monast. Ang., vol. ii., p. 340.

[4] Rob. lib., 3 Edw. III., mm. 2, 3, 7.   Ibid. 5, mm. 5, 10.   Ibid. 6. m. 6.

[5] Her name is mentioned in the liberate roll of 7 Edw. III., m. 2, and 9 Edw. III., m. 6, but both times in reference to payments due in the 6th year.

She was interred in the monastery which for forty-eight years had been her principal abode.[1] The hand of Time has been heavy upon this structure, and a picturesque ruin, with its mantle of ivy and wreath of wild flowers, is all that now remains to point out the spot which was at once the abode and the tomb of the nun princess.

[1] Harl. MS., 1808, f. 23.

APPENDIX.

NUMBER I.—*See page* 4.

This letter is without date, but indubitable evidence exists to place it in the year 1225, since the close roll of that year contains a minute and detailed reply to it from Henry III., or rather his council. It is too long to insert in full, especially as it has already appeared in print in M. Champollion Figeac's "lettres des rois, &c.," vol. i., No. xxxv. The bishop commences by complaining of the injury he and his associates had sustained from the severe storms on the 22nd of January, in their passage, and relates the particulars of their journey to Cologne, where they found Henry of Zudenthorp, and John the clerk — of the arrival there of the Master of the Knights-Templars, and the Prior of the Hospitallers—then follows an account of his interview with the Archbishop of Cologne, in which the following curious passage occurs—"Hiis auditis, nuncium vestrum ei exposuimus, dicentes ei quòd vos, tam de maritagio corporis vestri quam sororis vestræ consilio illius perebitis—ad quod respondit consilium suum esse ut talem et tantam oblationem faceremus quod dominus imperator non debeat eam repudiare. Dixit etiam periculum esse in morâ; rex enim Ffrancorum magnam pecuniam ei optulit ut confœderationem filii sui habeat et negotium nostrum impediat. Ex alterâ parte dux Bavariæ venit, cum maximâ pompâ, ad colloquium Ulmæ, et optulit pro maritagio filiæ regis Bohemiæ (quæ est neptis ipsius) xv millia marcarum, ultra oblationem xxx millia marcarum, quam ipse rex Boemiæ prius obtulerat. Sed rex Almanniæ respondit ei quod nunquam eam duceret; prætereà adjecit quod rex Hungariæ misit ad dominum imperatorem et pro maritagio ffiliæ suæ optulit ei pecuniam maximam. Ipse vero non sitit nisi pecuniam, ut illam accumulet; unde consuluit ut nos sub festinatione talem oblationem offerremus, qualem acceptare deberet." The letter alludes in the next place to the delay in the arrival of the chancellor and Nicolaus de Molis, who did not come until the Saturday after the archbishop had left Cologne, and states that they would not go forward to the Duke of Austria till the return of the archbishop, adding, that for reasons connected with the rules of their order, the Master of the Templars and Prior of the Hospitallers cannot stay in Germany longer than till the ensuing Passover; and the bishop concludes by requesting more money to be sent to him by Henry of St. Albans and John de Leyburn. Henry's answer to this letter, dated March 2nd, 1225, is as follows:—

"Rex episcopo Carleolensi salutem. De periculis laboribus et angustiis, quibus vos exposuistis pro nobis, et de hiis quæ nobis significástis grates vobis copiose referimus, quam multipliciter aliàs, sed nunc per indicia, experti sumus certiora. Cum autem accepimus quod magister Domus Templi et Prior Hospitalli Jerusalem in Angliâ morari non possint ultra instans Pascha, quod moleste ferimus, discretioni vestræ, de quâ plene confidimus, unà cum dilectis et fidelibus nostris H. Cancellario Londoniæ, N. de Molis, et speciali et familiari nostro W. de Kirkeham, quem nobis et eis duximus adhibendum, injunctum vobis negocium committimus effectui mancipandum, quod, si in formâ vobis traditâ expediri non possit, saltem per additionem quam per eundem W. vobis duximus exprimendam ad optatum, domino cooperante, perveniat effectum. Et cum insperata mora vestra magnas requirat expensas, Henricus de Sancto Albano, juxta petitionem vestram vobis habere faciat apud Ipr[es] de precepto nostro lx marcas ad expensas vestras. Quia vero audivimus quod H. de Tudenthorp circa agenda nostra se solliciter exhibet, quem in partes Austriæ cum predictis H. cancell. et Nicholao, sicut per eos accepimus proficisci necesse est, non sine magnis laboribus et expensis; precipimus et ad opus suum apud Ipr[es] per dictum Henricum xl marcas assignari, ex quibus tum percipiat de consilio vostro et sociorum vestrorum predictorum partem vel totum prout vestris videritis commodis expedire. Inceptis igitur vestris laudabilibus, juxta quam de vobis gerimus fiduciam, insistere velitis statum vestrum quæ per vos acta fuerunt circa promissa crebris nobis litteris vel nunciis expressuri. Teste meipso apud Novum Templum Londoniæ ii. die Marcii."—*Rot. claus., 9 H. III., pars i., m. 9, in dorso.*

Were other proof needed as to the date of the letter of the Archbishop of Carlisle than that furnished by the specific notice of its contents in King Henry's reply, it might be found in the patent roll of the same year, the 9th of Henry III., pt. 1, m. 9, in dorse, where the credentials of those same ambassadors, addressed to the Duke of Austria and to the Archbishop of Cologne, occur, and in the close roll, pt. 1, mm. 1 and 9, where orders occur for the payment of sums of money to the different personages of the embassy. M. Champollion prints the letter in question, from a copy taken of it by Brequigny from the Collectanea non impressa for the Fœdera, among the Donation MSS., No. 4574, art. 9, where the date assigned is 1236, a year after Isabella was actually married to the Emperor Frederic; but this is only the carrying out of a series of false dates which occur in Rymer, with reference to the marriage of the empress. The whole negociations are placed one year later than they actually took place, although in several instances the dates given in the documents themselves are at variance with those given in the margin. On this, as well as on other occasions, it has been found necessary to collate Rymer with the original documents, in order to disentangle the web of seeming perplexity. M. Champollion alters the date of the letter to 1235; in both cases, the letter is evidently supposed to relate to the marriage of Isabella with the Emperor Frederic. The expressions made use of are rather ambiguous; and supposing Frederic to have been a widower in 1235 — a point on which the contemporary chroniclers are at variance — it might by possibility be construed into a project of alliance with himself; but the following passage, from a contemporary German historian, who wrote his chronicle in 1237, seems decisive on the subject:— "Anno 1225, Henricus rex (Alemanniæ Frederici imperatoris filius) curiam habuit Franchiavort, ubi quidam Episcopus, missus a rege cum cæteris ipsius legatis affuit, laborans ut ipse Rex matrimonium contraheret cum sorore regis Angliæ. Sed cum talis contractus displicuisset principibus nec potuerit habere processum, nuntii inacte revertebantur."—*Annales Godefridi monachi St. Pantaleonis. Freher, vol. i., p.* 394. This passage strongly corroborates the preceding statements, both as to the date and the purport of this negociation.

NUMBER II.—*See page* 50.

Quia sunt alii forsitan qui suggerent domino papæ et Cardinalibus quædam quæ nuper acta sunt a nobis, de consilio magnatum et fidelium nostrorum; volentes ea malitiosè pervertere, quasi sint nobis plurimum obfutura;—nos, ut cautiores vos reddamus ad calliditates eorum refellendas, totam seriem quorundam negociorum hîc duximus exprimendum, ne quid lateat vos, super præmissis, per quod vos vel alios circumveniri contingat. Sciatis ergo quod cùm, tempore legationis domini Norwicensis episcopi, comes marescallus adhuc haberet castra de Merleberg et Lutegareshall, et proponeret in uxorem ducere sororem comitis Roberti de Brus; et essent etiam alii magnates in Angliâ qui nitebantur eum avertere a nobis per confederationes malitiosas, tractatum fuit coram dicto legato et justiciario nostro et quibusdam aliis magnatibus de unâ sororum nostrarum ei concedendâ. Tum quiâ time-

batur confederacio illa cum alienigenis, si duceret sororem comitis
de Brus in uxorem, ne extraneis pateret liberiùs ingressus in An-
gliam, presertim cùm Ricardus marescallus, frater ipsius marescalli,
omnes terras suas haberet in Normanniam—tum quià timebatur
malitia eorum qui cor ipsius a nobis avertere nitebantur, tum etiam
quia sic restituerentur nobis dicta castra de Merlebergh et de
Lutegareshall, quod multum nobis expediebat, ut sic alii magnates
faciliùs inducerentur ad castra nostra; quæ et ipsi tenebant, similiter resignanda. Propter præmissa et tenerum tunc statum nostrum et totius regni, auctoritate dicti legati et consilio talium
magnatum, concessa fuit dicto Marescallo una sororum nostrarum,
ita quod dictus Marescallus fidem dedit de eâ ducendâ, si placeret
nobis et magnatibus regni; et justiciarius noster fidem dedit de
eâ concedendâ dicto Marescallo si magnates regni consentirent; et
dicti legatus et justiciarius noster et alii qui presentes erant fideliter promiserunt quod ad hoc omnem diligentiam adhiberent; et
sic restituta sunt dicta castra in manibus dicti legati, ut si non
perficeretur contractus, infra certum terminum diù jam elapsum,
ipsi Marescallo sine difficultate restituerentur. Postmodum etiam,
cùm hæc essent mandata aliis magnatibus, et nominatim Comiti
Cestriæ, qui tunc reversus erat a terra sanctâ, ipse Comes hoc
valde approbavit et multi alii consenserunt, nemine contradicente,
Postea verò, ortis quibusdam simultatibus, quidam hoc reprobâ-
runt, asserentes, sicut fortè in curiâ ex parte eorum, dicitur—quod
nos majorem thesaurum non habemus quàm maritagium nostri
ipsius et sororum nostrarum. Unde expediret sorores nostras sic
nuptui collocari quod nos magnam haberemus confederationem, in
partibus alienis, et sic tunc temporis remansit negotium illud im-
perfectum. Cum autem nuper idem Marescallus impetrâsset mandatum apostolicum domino Cantuariæ et domino Sarum directum ut
vel facerent eum ab illâ fidei obligatione penitus absolvi, vel
contractum illum confirmari, et importunius instaret idem Marescallus ut altera viarum illarum procederetur,—cùm nollet ulterius
sustinere quin duceret uxorem,—et sicut alterâ vice sic et nunc
timeretur ne idem Marescallus, qui magnæ potentiæ est, tum in
Angliâ quam in Hiberniâ, duceret in uxorem sororem dicti Comitis de Brus, vel filiam ducis Braibantiæ, quæ ei similiter fuerat
oblata, quod propter ea quæ promisimus nobis nullatenus expediret,—vel etiam sororem regis Scotiæ, ubi similiter nobis non
modicum periculum immineret, eo quod quanto vicinior est Scotia
Hiberniæ et terris dicti Marescalli tanto periculosior foret illa
confederatio nobis; et pensatâ strenuitate et potentiâ ipsius Marescalli, et fideli obsequio quod nobis patenter et potenter impen-
dit, presertim circà partes Walliæ et castra nostra, quæ Leulinus
princeps Norwalliæ tenuit, quæ quidem idem marescallus viriliter

ab ipsius manibus eripuit, quæ vix fuissent liberata nisi per poten-
tiam et industriam ipsius; considerato etiam exemplo quondam
regis Franciæ Philippi, qui Comiti de Lemur et Comiti de Puntis
(Ponthieu) et aliis hominibus suis filias suas sorores et neptes
longè libentiùs quam extraneis maritavit, sicut rex Franciæ, qui
nunc est nuper neptem suam, scilicet filiam Guischardi de Belloloco,
comiti Campaniæ in matrimonium copulavit; cùm etiam propter
premissa et magna quæ sperantur de dicto Marescallo, non occur-
reret nobis vel consilio nostro, omnibus circumstantibus ponderatis,
quod alicubi possemus ita ad profectum nostrum et honorem
sororem nostram maritare, nos de consilio talium, habito supra
hoc diligenti tractatu, sine diminutione terrarum, castrorum, vel
pecuniæ, ipsi sororem nostram concessimus juniorem.—*From Royal
Letters, No.* 389, *Tower of London. Original.*

NUMBER III.—*See page* 60.

Rex vicecomiti Gloucestriæ salutem. Scias quod cum dilectas oror
nostra A[lienora], comitissa Penbrochiæ, peteret dotem suam versus
R[icardum] Marescallum comitem Penbrochiæ de terris quæ
fuerunt W[illelmi] comitis Penbrochiæ junioris, quondam viri sui,
in Hiberniâ et in Suwalliâ[1] ita convenit[2] inter eos quod prædictus
comes redderet eidem comitissæ singulis annis quadringentas libras, nomine dotis prædictæ, ad duos terminos, videlicet infra
unum mensem a festo Sancti Michaelis ducentas libras, et infra
unum mensem a Paschâ ducentas libras; et sicut in compositionem
inter eos factam continetur, concessit idem comes quod si, ad
terminos statutos, de prædictâ pecuniâ prædictæ comitissæ non
satisfaceret, sine omni dilatione distringeremus ipsum per terras
et res suas in Angliâ, ad satisfaciendum eidem comitissæ de prædictâ pecuniâ. Et quia idem comes in solutionem prædictæ pecuniæ
terminos suos non servavit, tunc præcipimus quod per catalla
quæ idem comes habet in ballivâ tuâ ipsum distringas ad satisfaciendum eidem sorori nostræ de c et l. libris quæ ei restant red-
dendæ, ne debeat inde at nos clamor pervenire. Teste me ipso
apud Wenlac vi die Junii.—*From close roll,* 17 *Henry III., m.* 9,
in dorso.

NUMBER IV.—*See page* 102.

This letter, addressed by Friar Adam de Marisco to the Bishop of
Lincoln, Robert Grostête, presenting sufficient interest to be ac-
ceptable to the general reader, a translation of it is here given.

"I have long wished, and now at length am able, by the tenor

---

[1] South Wales.　　　　　　　[2] Sic.

of the present letters, summarily to notify, according to the expectation of your reverence, the progress of events that have taken place the last few days, in the court of our lord the king, in reference to the affairs of Gascony, concerning the noble Earl of Leicester. About the feast of the ascension of our Lord,[1] the Gascons, clergy as well as laity, in a numerous multitude, approached the presence of the king, most fiercely accusing the said earl, with malicious compilations of lies, before the king, prelates, and barons, of vexatious spoliations, cheats, and oppressions; and continuing in this manner the efforts of their wickedness, day and night, publicly and privately, up to the feast of St. Barnabas,[2] with the rage of shameless men. To whom favour and audience, both in public and private, not without iniquitous suggesters, were granted, to the surprise of all, especially of those endeavouring after justice and equity. Moreover, the said earl meanwhile frequently suffered reproaches and taunts from the king, before many and great persons, with invectives of the unreasonable; he observing throughout the moderation of gentleness, with the perfection of equanimity, both towards his lord and his adversaries. I know not that, from the remotest times, such manifest frowardness has been shown to any one, whether noble or ignoble. As very few, on account of my Lord of Worcester, Lord Peter of Savoy, and Lord Peter de Montefort, gave support to the faithful one, then the priests who were present, and my Lord of Cornwall, and the other brothers of the king and elders of the council, and also the barons of the kingdom, extolled with lofty commendation the great courage, intrepid fidelity, victorious firmness, and just intentions of the Earl of Leicester. Nor did they omit to engage their help and counsel to preserve the said earl without danger, loss, or disgrace, while I myself said something to some of the great men on the aforesaid matter. But in the midst of so many kind words, real friendship was ever found to be rare. Whither will the cowardice of our magistrates, worthy to be execrated through all ages, lead us? Your provident consideration can, I know, better judge. Whither, I say, but to the dreadful destruction of hopeless subjection.

"When, however, after the daily disturbances of the impious men, it was with difficulty and by laborious entreaties extorted that the Earl of Leicester and many men, who were strong in power and firm in fidelity, reasonable in discourse and unwearied in perseverance, gifted with wealth, experienced in business, courageous in difficulties—as on this occasion the course of affairs strongly showed them to be—and who, as well as their beforementioned adversaries, had come, at the command of the king,

[1] May 9th.　　　　[2] June 11th.

from Gascony, under a safeconduct, were heard, as reason demanded, on the opposite side—the aforesaid Earl of Leicester, in
a clear strain of lucid reasoning, began from his first entrance
into Gascony up to the present day, and showed before the king
and his nobles the course of his conduct, as well in pacific moderation as in warlike labour, for the ecclesiastical dignity and royal
majesty, as well as the security and safety both of clergy and
people, supporting everything with authentic testimony, and con-
futed each accusation worthy of notice made by his rivals, with a
separate answer, of which he proved the truth.

" Moreover, also, the aforesaid men, as well soldiers as citizens,
who had served the King and the Earl of Leicester actively and
strenuously, as well in war as in peace, were furnished with letters
patent of the community of Bourdeaux—in which almost all the
strength of Gascony, both for repressing enemies and protecting
friends, is known to consist—from which authentic writings they
clearly demonstrated, in discreet words, with what evident strenu-
ousness, what prudent circumspection, what just moderation, what
persevering endurance, the said earl had governed the land of
Gascony up to the present time, to the profit and honour of the
king and his heirs, the alleviation of the pious, the castigation of
the rebels, and the salutary reformation of all, even at the cost of
much personal danger, profuse expenditure of moneys, the assaults
of very great difficulties, and the suffering of most painful annoyances. . They showed also to all, by the more efficacious persuasions of plain documents, that the conspiracy of the aforesaid men
against Earl Simon was excited for nothing but because the said
earl did his utmost to restrain the sacrileges, homicides, disturbances, imprisonings, tortures, rapines, frauds, and base practices
which they constantly committed with the most unruly malignity
—neither fearing God, nor reverencing men, and, regardless of
king and law, violating covenants and disregarding natural affection—and because he incessantly strove, now by playing upon
them with terrors, now by alluring them with caresses, now by
governing them by laws, to call them all back to the forms of
pious living.

" Although those who were on the earl's side firmly believed
them, both in their writings and verbal assertions, yet they offered,
either by a corporal duel of any person, or in any other mode
which the court might decree, to confirm each article of their propositions with the undoubted certainty of fixed firmness. In addition to this, they entreated that it might be decreed that an
obligation should be laid both upon themselves and their adversaries, under the security of certain bonds, that in whatever causes
any one should impeach or defend another, they would do it by

law, either before the king, in the kingdom of England, or before judges sent by him into the land of Gascony, and would accept the verdict, if for themselves, or bear it, if against themselves; and on this condition they were willing to renounce their safe-conduct, if their enemies would consent to do the same.

"But, whilst these things were transacted from the beginning to the termination, which, as it was thought, could, with the greatest safety, be adopted in such dreadful dangers from so great causes, the aforesaid earl, with his aforesaid party, despite the rancours of hatred, and despite the attacks of hostility, and despite the dissensions of strifes, was ceaselessly endeavouring, by persevering entreaty, that, by the provident government of his royal highness, the form of peace between himself with his adherents, and his adversaries with their accomplices, which had been entered into a year before, and most firmly fortified as well by the public instruments of barons and priests, as by the solemn oaths of the magistrates and chief men, should henceforth be inviolably preserved by all parties, and that the violators of it should be punished with due reproof. But although all these things were distinctly stated at reasonable length—even to the displeasure of many of our nation—and properly understood, the party adverse to the earl, and still more adverse to the king, neither could nor would agree to any of these things; but with fatal madness, the refuge of the wicked, they totally refused to submit to the task of proving their accusations, or to obey the laws in any impeachment or defence, before any one, either in this kingdom or in their own land, or even to keep the desirable reform of the peace which was made. Their efforts tended to one thing alone, that, in a cause of so great weight, undoubted credence should be given to the lying fictions of their slanders, and that, in every particular touching the present cause, judicial examination should be avoided; and that Earl Simon, contrary to the king's former well-consulted arrangement, should be entirely removed from the custody of Gascony.

"Therefore, when the evident merits of the causes on both sides had been fully heard and weighed by the king and the nobles, the king gave his public sentence upon the controversies of the aforesaid disputes, and was compelled, by the manifestation of the very truth, to say that, on the side of the earl and his party, there could be no room to deny that their very reasonable propositions had convicted the deceitful fables of the liars as cheats; asserting that to those every confidence was to be given, whilst these merited none. This sentence was received with unanimous acclaim of assent by Earl Richard and others, as well by the prelates of the church and nobles of the realm, as by the very counsellors of the king.

" Although, after this, nothing seemed left to do but to promote defended virtue and to punish convicted falsehood; yet, after the interval of a single night, all bonds of justice and equity being violated, fierce threats, rude reproaches, bitter rebukes, and indecent contempt, are heaped upon the earl, the king raging in wrath, and those bad men hissing at him, in their baseness. Right and wrong are confounded; and thenceforth, for several days and nights too, the vexation of intolerable strife is prolonged. The earl, however, diligently tried, as well as he could, amidst such horrid commotions and disturbances, by the means which he thought most available with the king, that, when the strifes of parties were pacified, and both sides reconciled to the earl, he might, by his good will and pleasure, have the royal authority to return into Gascony, to exercise the guardianship of it in justice and judgment, in mercy and compassion, and to do all that in him lay to keep peace with all, in order to preserve the peaceful government of the land of Gascony, as it had been formerly granted to him, for the king and his heirs, in stable security for the future. But if the wickedness of the dissensions should préclude the pacifying of the obstinate, the said earl nevertheless offered that, with a permissive dispensation from the king, he would return into Gascony, with a band of troops and military equipments necessary to so great an undertaking, and would expend as willingly as constantly his own and his friends' lives, labours, cares, and abilities, for the profit and indemnity of the king and his heirs, to humble the rebels, and exalt the faithful subjects. But, if the king refused his consent to both these proposals, the said earl entreated that then, while the prelates, nobles, and counsellors, were together, he might, by the clement exercise of the royal power, entirely renounce the custody of the land of Gascony, with three necessary articles of condition, by a sure declaration of which, made with consultation and deliberation, he might protect himself; namely, that he should not undergo the insufferable loss of his expenses, still less should incur the shameful ignominy of disgrace; and, above all, that those who, by true discrimination and moderation of management for the king and his heirs, in a hostile state, had not ceased to adhere to the earl with person and property, with the firmness of unflinching faith, should not be in any wise exposed to personal danger, or to detriment in their affairs.

" Nevertheless, as he was not able to bring any of these things to effect, at length the king, by his own arbitrary will—for all the rest were torpid, in pusillanimous silence—had certain ordinances, conceived of his own accord, set down in writing, and sealed with his seal. These were, that a truce should be faith-

fully kept between the dissentient parties and between the earl and
his adversaries, till the ensuing purification of the blessed Virgin,[1]
at which time he or his eldest son would go into Gascony, that
then all controversies, whether of strife or war, might be set at
rest by himself or his eldest son—promising the sceptre of Gascony to him who, in the meanwhile, would in the king's stead expedite certain affairs which had arisen, or were about to arise,
demanding the restitution and replenishment of certain castles and
captives, then in the hands of the earl, with many more fooleries,
by all which, unless the Divine Being interpose, he will do much
harm; for his sentence, from beginning to end, tends to his own
disinheriting, the weakening of the kingdom, the confusion of the
earl, and the disturbance of the people.

"All these things having thus transpired, the Earl of Leicester
retired from the king, dismissed with a doubtful leave; and after
his departure, he signified to the king, by his letters patent, that
he was ready to obey his good pleasure, to the best of his power,
as far, at least, as was consistent with the king's profit and
honour. Then, being confirmed by the fear, and animated by
the love, of the Divine name, placing all his hope upon Him, who
does not desert those who trust in Him, disciplined also to obedience by what he had suffered, rejoicing and confiding in the
protection of the Highest, on the fifth day after the feast of
St. Barnabas,[2] he crossed the sea, safely and cheerfully, along
with his eldest son, your reverence's most cherished pupil, and
landed, in the pleasant society of his company, at Boulogne, about
six o'clock; intending afterwards, without any delay, to go into
Gascony, and there, as though he were a deity from Heaven, to
dispense moderation in the affairs of Gascony. For the aforesaid
parties, on leaving the king, took back with them, in their irre-
trievably offended hearts, the discords of hatred, and the fuel of
war, provoked beyond their wont, as it is thought, both against
each other and against their ruler, feeling and openly divulging
their wish for plenty of exiles and calamities to be inflicted on the
nobles of the realm, and the king's counsellors. In reference
to the earl's going into Gascony, his party are much rejoiced, and
the adverse party in the greatest consternation. One of two results of the royal will is expected; for no one knows whether, by
the Lord's permission, the king will undertake something, from
some cause, against the earl, or whether the Lord will prevent it.

"May the wished-for health of your holiness be preserved ever
in Christ Jesus and the most blessed Virgin! I know that there
is no need to recommend to your piety the illustrious earl, the
most devout of mortals, who places special trust for all things in

[1] February 2nd.   [2] June 16th.

your reverence's merits and in the intercessions of your prayers to the son of God. The illustrious lady, Countess of Leicester, presents herself to your most worthy lordship by this present writing, embracing the feet of your paternity with most abundant thanksgiving and humble prayers of piety, recommending her lord, herself, and her children, with her house, and all relating to her, to your intercessions with the blessed son of God, by the holy mother of God, amidst so many fears and dangers.

"Given at Lutton, in Kent, on the Saturday next after the feast of St. Barnabas.[1] The earl and I, after the earl's departure, detained your courier, because, in a case of such rapid variableness, every result of sufficient certainty to be announced being continually in doubt, not only from day to day, but from hour to hour."—*Translated from Cotton MS., Vitellius, c. viii., f.* 30, *b.*

NUMBER V.—*See page* 115.

Li cuens et la contesse de Leycestre dient que cele contesse avoit son doeyre en la tere qui fui Guillame le conte Mareschal, cui ele avoit esté fame; c'est à saveir en la tere de celui conte Mareschal en Irlande et en Westwalles; et dient que li rois à cele contesse dona garde, come à cele qui estoit sa suer et en non-age et veue, et souz son poer et en son reaume et en conseil. Et en cel estat li rois fit saeler dou sael cele contesse, sanz sa volonté et sanz son assentemant, letres, esqueles estoit contenu qu'ele quitoit por vi.ᶜ mars par an tot cele doeyre qui valoit deus mile mars chascun an ou plus. Et celes letres furent saelées xxvi. anz à passez et plus; et par celi fet li roi, cele contesse a esté domagée puis xxvi. anz, en ça que son seignur qu'ele chascun an en mil et quatre cenz mars. Et ce damage il demandent au roi qu'il lur rende et amende par la raison devant dite. Et dient que par celi fet le roi, celui doeyre a esté et est encores encumbrez et enpeschez. Et pur ce et pur les raisons desus dites il demandent al roi qu'il lur rende tant come la devant dite contesse vivra, chascun an mil et quatre cenz mars avecques les vi.ᶜ mars devant diz; ou qu'il lur face la devant doeyre deliverer et lur rende les arrerages. Et cest demande font li devant dit cuens et contesse sauf qu'il ou lor procureor il puissent amender selont raison, si com il lor semblera que bon soit: de la quele demande nos avons baillée la forme as devant diz Conte et Contesse di Leycestre, desouz

---

[1] An incongruity occurs in this date: the writer mentions the arrival of the Earl of Leicester at Boulogne on June 16th, and dates this letter June 15th, since, in 1252, St. Barnabas' day, June 11th, fell on a Tuesday, and the following Saturday must consequently have been the 13th.

non seaus. Date l'an del incarnacion notre seignur mil deucenz cinquante et noef, el mois de Jullet.—*From Conventiones pacis, 43 H. III., in the Tower.*

NUMBER V.—*See page* 148.

Henricus, Dei gratiâ rex Angliæ, dominus Hyberniæ, et dux Aquitaniæ baronibus et ballivis portûs sui Dovorriæ salutem. Cum[1] Alienora Comitissa Leycestriæ, quondam uxor Simonis de Monteforti quondam Comitis Leycestriæ, preparet se ad partes transmarinas transfetare[2]—ut accepimus—per quod, tam in asportatione pecuniæ de regno nostro undique aggregatæ, quam in aliis pluribus posset nobis grave dampnum et dispendium imminere— vobis mandamus quod, sicut vosmet ipsos et libertates vestras diligitis, et sicut ad nos et ad gratiam nostram accessum ullis temporibus habere volueritis, nullo modo permittatis dictam Comitissam aut aliquos de suis aut etiam aliquos alios transfretare in portu vestro vel portibus vicinis,[3] sine licentiâ vel speciali mandato nostro. Et super hiis in quæ dilectus et fidelis noster Petrus de Nevill vobis dicet vivâ voce, ex parte nostrâ, fidem adhibeatis indubitatam.

Teste xxviij. die Sept.

Eodem modo scribitur illis de portibus.—*Royal Letter, No.* 398, *Tower Collection. Original draught.*

NUMBER VI.—*See page* 149.

Venerabili in Christo patri et amico suo karissimo, G. Dei gratiâ episcopo Bathoniæ et cancellario domini regis Angliæ illustris, Edwardus ejusdem regis primogenitus salutem, cum reverentiâ et honore. Cùm ad instanciam carissimæ amitæ nostræ, dominæ Alienoræ Comitissæ Leycestriæ, ad gratiam et favorem nostrum subscriptos familiares suos nominatos recepimus, vos rogamus attentiùs quatinus nuncio ejusdem dominæ comitissæ, latori presentium, litteras domini regis patris nostri, quas eisdem promisimus, super restitutionem terrarum suarum et catallorum et rerum suarum ab isto die inventarum in eisdem per singulis subscriptis vicecomitibus locorum liberari faciatis indilate; et hoc, amore nostri, non omittatis. Videlicet, Vicecomiti Kantiæ pro domino J. de Suares, pro terrâ sibi restituendâ, &c. Datum apud Dovor, xxvi.° die Octobris, anno regni domini patris nostri xlix°. —*From Royal Letters, No.* 399, *Tower of London. Original.*

---

[1] The words "Quia per certis intelleximus quod" are inserted, without erasing the word "Cum."

[2] Corrected into "ad transfretandum, in Francia."

[3] vinis, in MS.

NUMBER VII.—*See page* 155.

Regi Franciæ Rex salutem. Nobiles viros providos et discretos Johannem de Arc. Butelarium Franciæ, Ingerammum de Fenles et Priorem de Valle Viridi pro negotiis Simonis de Monte Forti, filii quondam S. Comitis Leycestriæ, fratrumque suorum, et Alie-noræ Comitissæ Leycestriæ matris eorum, et aliis ad nos a vestrâ serenitate transmissos, admisimus, omni qua decuit reverentiâ et honore. Et nos, qui semper precibus vestris in quantum possumus libenter annuimus, habito super eis cum secretariis nostris diligenti tractatu, vestræ interventionis intuitu concessimus quod terræ quæ fuerunt olim comitis supradicti patris sui, præfato S. restituantur; quarum possesionem ipsum adipisci volumus per procuratorem ab ipso ad hoc specialiter constitutum, cui litteras dabimus de salvo et securi conductu. Et ut de terrarum ipsarum valore certitudo plenior habeatur, volumus dictas terras extendi per unum ex parte nostrâ et alium ex parte dicto S. ad hoc specialiter assignandos; qui, si in extentâ illâ, in toto vel in parte, discordes fortassis extiterint, dicto et ordinationi stabitur egregii principis Regis Alemanniæ fratris nostri, vel illius quem idem Princeps ad hoc duxerit deputandum. Præfatus autem Simon nobis aut liberis nostris vel alteri eorum terras prædictas vendere tenebitur, quandocumque a nobis vel eis vel eorum altero fuerit requisitus; quarum terrarum precii quantitatem arbitrio vestro committimus statuendam. Ita tamen quod, pro marcata terræ, ultra decem marcas per vos dicta quantitas non taxetur, pro quo precio terræ communiter in regno nostro venduntur. Infra vero quantitàtem prædictam, precium per vos speramus esse taxandum, si vestræ serenitatis circumspectio diligenter advertat turbationes et damna innumerabilia quæ sustinuimus hactenus et adhuc etiam sustinemus, occasione seditionis per patrem suum, comitem prædictum, in regno nostro commotæ, et quam idem S., patris inhærens vestigiis, continuavit pro posse, propter quæ exhæredationem non immerito meruit idem Simon. Factâ autem venditione prædictâ et præstitâ securitate de solutione precii, secundum prædictum modum juxta vestrum arbitrium statuendi, infra triennium a tempore venditionis, dicto Simoni precii satisfactio plena fiet. Proviso quod idem Simon vel fratres sui regnum Angliæ vel alias terras nostræ ditioni subjectas nullatenus ingrediantur, absque nostro vel hæredum nostrorum mandato et licentia speciali. Et insuper caveant dicti S. et fratres de dampnis nobis aut liberis nostris, vel etiam alicui de fidelibus nostris quocunque locorum vel terrarum, citrà mare vel ultrà, per ipsos aut alios ad eorum procurationem nullatenus inferendis, et quod colligationes cum inimicis nostris aliquas non inibunt, et si quas cum eis inierunt omninò dissolvent;

super quibus securitas plena præstetur incontinenti per jurisdictionem ecclesiasticam et modis aliis roboranda, prout vestra serenitas duxerit providendum. Ad hoc, de dotalitio comitissæ præfatæ ordinamus et concedimus—sicut aliàs per ipsam comitissam et illos qui tenent terras in quibus comitissa prædicta dotalitium habere se dicit, coram reginam Angliæ, consortem nostram extitit ordinatum—quod ipsa, pro dote suâ in Angliâ, per procuratorem suum, quingentas libras sterlingas recipiat annuatim; cui ordinationi, si dicta comitissa stare noluerit, per procuratorem, cui litteras dabimus de salvo et securo conductu, coram nobis suam justiciam persequatur; quam faciemus ei secundùm legem et consuetudinem terra nostræ, absque difficultate quâlibet exhiberi. &c.

The remainder of the letter treats of indifferent matters. It closes with

Teste rege, apud Strattford, xxiiii. die Junii.—*From Patent Roll,* 51 *Hen. III., m.* 19, *dorso.*

NUMBER VIII.—*See page* 158.

Edwardus, Dei gratiâ rex Angliæ, dominus Hiberniæ et dux Aquitaniæ, dilecto clerico et cancellario suo W. de Merton salutem. Cùm nos, ad instanciam serenissimi principis et consanguinei nostri karissimi, Philippi, Dei gratiâ regis Franciæ illustris, remiserimus Alienoræ, Comitissæ Leycestriæ, omnem indignationem et animi nostri rancorem quos ergà ipsam conceperamus, occasione turbationis dudum habitæ in regno nostro, et ipsam ad gratiam et firmam pacem nostram admiserimus—dum tamen benè et fideliter versus nos et fideles nostros se habeat—ac concesserimus eidem quod jus suum, si quod habeat in hiis quæ clamat versus nos seu alios de regno nostro, juxta regni nostri consuetudines, per attornatos suos prosequatur, vobis mandamus quòd ipsam comitissam, juxta hujus modi gratiæ concessionem admittentes, attornatos ipsius nomine suo plenam in præmissis justiciam fieri faciatis. Datum apud Melun super Sekenam, x. die Aug. Anno regni nostri primo.—*From Royal Letters, Tower Collection, No.* 1130. *Original.*

NUMBER IX.—*See page* 159.

Philippus, Dei gratiâ Franciæ rex, egregio principi carissimo consanguineo suo Edwardo, eâdem gratiâ illustri regi Angliæ domino Hyberniæ, et duci Aquitaniæ, fideli suo, salutem et sinceræ dilectionis affectum. Significamus vobis quod, coram executoribus testamenti inclitæ recordationis precarissimi domini et genitoris nostri Ludovici, Franciæ regis, proposuit Comitissa

Leincestriæ, amita vestra, quod ipsa et Symon de Monteforti, quondam vir suus, paci quæ tractabatur inter dictum patrem nostrum et felicis recordationis Henricum, regem Anglie, genitorem vestrum aliàs, suum noluerunt præbere consensum requisitum ab eis, nisi priùs satisfieret dictæ comitissæ de dotalicio seu doario primi mariti sui, et quod genitor vester concessit quod ipse deponeret quindecim milla marcharum argenti, tenenda Parisiis apud Templum, donec innotesceret quod eidem comitissæ de doario suo satisfactio plenaria facta fuisset. Propter quod, dictus genitor noster dictæ comitissæ mandavit quòd benè poterat esse secura de suo doario, et securè poterat dictæ compositioni suum præbere consensum. Et quoniam dicta quindecim milia marcharum hodie non sunt in Templo Parisiensi, nec fuerunt octo annis vel ampliùs jam elapsis, dieto genitore vestro dictum depositum repetente et etiam assequuto, petit dicta amita vestra ab executoribus antedictis interesse suum, ex eo quod non est sibi satisfactum de suo doario, et quia non durabit depositio quæ facta fuerat ad securitatem sui doarii assequendi. Inde est quià predictum factum nos tangit, et exequutores predictos reddit sollicitos et attentos; pro salute animæ dicti patris nostri, vos attente requirimus quatinus pro exoneratione predictorum executorum et etiam pro commoditate vestrâ, illos qui pro vobis venient ad instans pallamentum[1] nostrum purificationis beatæ Mariæ virginis, bene reddatis instructos de defensionibus et rationibus quæ pro vobis et pro predictis exequutoribus proponi poterunt, ad hoc quod eidem comitissæ, in suâ petitione predictâ, bono modo silentium imponatur. Datum Parisiis, die martis in Octabis beati Dyonisii.—*From Royal Letters, Tower Collection, No.* 1124. *Original.*

This letter is not dated, but internal evidence fixes the date to be the 10th of October, 1273. There were only two recurrences of the feast of St. Denis—October 9th, between the accession of Edward I., in November, 1272, and the death of the Countess of Leicester, in the spring of 1275; and in 1274 the feast and octaves of St. Denis fell on a Tuesday, and therefore there could be no Tuesday in the octaves. The year 1273 is then the only one in which the letter could be written.

NUMBER X.—*See page* 159.

A très haut et très noble prince, nostre très chier neveu, Edouard, par la grace de Dieu roy d'Engleterre, Marguerite, par cele meisme grace roine de France, salut et vrai amour. Chiers niés, la Contesse de Leycestre nous pria et requist à sa fin que nous vous preisons que vous eussiez pitie de li et de son testa-

[1] Sic.

ment, et nous requist ausi que nous preisons de Amauri, son fil
clerc, que vous eussiez pitiè de li et que vous li feissiez droit et ren-
dissiez vostre grace.   Et pour ce que nous li promeismes que nous
le ferions, nous vous priames de......choses, et vous en prions encores que vous vuilliez fere et commander que la besogne qui touche
le testament à la dite dame.:....et délivrée tant comme droiz, et li us,
et la costume du païs pourront doner. Et d......de la......au clerc,
et ..... que heneurs et boen soit, et tant que Diex vous en sache
gré et nous et bones.....: fetes en tant que vous non puissiez
estre blasmez. Et de ces choses, s'il vous plai......vostre volonté
...... le lundi devant la feste saint Denys.—*From Royal Letters,
Tower Collection, No. 1125. Original.*

NUMBER XII.—*See page 209.* .

Margareta, Dei gratiâ regina Scottorum, venerabili viro et
amico in Christo karissimo, domino W. de Mertoun, illustris regis
Angliæ cancellario, salutem in Christo, qui est vera salus omnium.
Quià credimus in nostris justis petitionibus penes vos favorabilius
exaudiri, ideo vestram discretionem pro dilecto nobis in Christo,
domino W. de Swyneburn, tesaurario nostro, quem suis laudabilibus meritis exigentibus, carum habemus et specialem, attentius
duximus exorandam, quatinus in expeditione sui negocii, super
quâdem confirmatione habendâ, secundum cartæ suæ tenorem,
quam inspicere porteritis, partes vestras cum summâ diligenciâ
pro nostris precibus et amore favorabiliùs interponere curetis;
ut, vestrâ mediante diligenciâ, justè se gaudeat assequi quod
desiderat, per quod ad faciendum ea quæ vobis debeant esse grata
arcius teneamur libentius animate.[1]   Valete semper in Domino.—
From Royal Letters, Tower Collection, No. 851. Original.

NUMBER XIII.—*See page 245.*

Excellentissimo domino ac præcordialissimo patri suo H., Dei
gratiâ illustri regi Angliæ, domino Hyberniæ, duci Aquitaniæ,
devotissimus suus filius Johannes, primogenitus ducis Britanniæ,
salutem, cum omni promptitudine servicii et honoris. De vestrâ
per Dei gratiam prosperitate, de quâ me litteratoriè significâstis,
admodum congaudens, sublimitati vestræ significo me, consortem-
que meam, filiam vestram, apud Nannetas, ubi ad præsens moram
trahimus, divinâ favente gratiâ, plenâ vigere corporis sanitate; quod
de vobis mihi semper desidero annotari. Sciatis autem me cum
militibus et armis, in succursum vestrum pro [pos]se meo venire
pri.......quandocunque opus fuerit, et a vobis fuero requisitus.
Statum vero vestrum utinam prosperum et felicem mihi crebrò

[1] Sic.

mandetis, unà cum vestræ voluntatis bene placito; ad quod faciendum operam dabo semper pro viribus efficacem. Benè. et diù valeat in Domino excellentia vestra.—*From Royal Letters, No.*873, *Tower Collection. Original.*

NUMBER XV.—*See page* 301.

Alianor, fille au Rei Dengletere, a son bon ami Sire Johan de Langeton, Chancellier mon seignior le Rei, saluz e bone amour. Nous vous prions chierement por Dame Margerie de Combes que des bosoignes kele a afere de ver vous que vous li serez gracious e eidant en dreiture, por Deu et por lamor de nous, issint kele sente que nostre priere li tiegne lu, e ke nous vous serions tenue a gré saver, et a mercier kant nous vous verrons. Nostre seignor vous gard.—*From Original Letters, Tower Collection, No.* 1639.

NUMBER XVI.—*See page* 309.

A son treschier amy saluz come a sei. Sachez, chier amy, que notre seignor le roy, e touz vos amys là ou nous sumes furent seins e hertiez, Dieu merci, au partir de ceste lettre; porque mon sire Edward e ma dame Margarete sa soer sunt en terteine, puis la feste de la annunciacion notre dame, e ne sunt pas encore perdu acces, mes il sont en amendaunt, Dieu merci. E sachez que ma dame Alianor devoit passer la mer icest Meskerdi devaunt la Pasque, e deverent passer aveak lui levesque de Loundres, le conte de Hereford, le Deen de seint Pool, Monsieur William le Latimer, e Monsieur William de Leiburn, e autre chivalers plusours del hostiel. E le roi retornera be Dovorre iesque a Caunterbury, e sera la icest Juesdi devaunt Pasque, e iloek attendra de vos noveles, por queles Daggemerfeld e son compagnon alèrent nadgueres. Par quei ieo vous pri que au plus tost e le plus sovent qè vous pourez, lui facez savoir les noveles que vous saverez de celes busoignes; qar vous avez tot plein de messagiers devers vous, par queus vous les lui porrez maunder. A Dieu sire qui nous gard. Escrite a Dovorr le Mardi devant la Pasqe.—*From Original Letters, Tower Collection, temp. Edward I.*

NUMBER XVII.—*See page* 393.

Excellentissimo principi domino suo domino karissimo, Edwardo, Dei gratiâ Anglorum regi domino Hiberniæ et duci Aquitaniæ, Margareta, eâdem gratiâ Lotharingiæ et Brabantiæ ducissa, cum omni reverentiâ et honore paratam ad ejus beneplacita voluntatem. Regalis excellentiæ vestræ litteras, cum debitâ veneratione recipimus apud Bruxellam in istâ vigiliâ beati Gregorii, et contenta in eis intelleximus diligenter, excellenti dominationi vestræ significantes quod negotium super quo tractatum est inter nos et dominum nostrum ducem, et de quo quam plurimum nos gaudemus, est perfectum, sicut nostri nuncii plenius vobis dicent. Precipiat nobis vestra regia celsitudo, quia paratæ sumus et esse volumus ad omnia vestra beneplacita et mandata. Diu et prospere vigeat et valeat regius status vester. Datum apud Bruxellam die Mercurii post festum sancti Benedicti.—*From Original Letters, Tower Collection, No.* 1120.

NUMBER XVIII.—*See page* 393.

Rex discreto viro, magistro Thomæ Denart, decano Dangers, salutem. Nuper dilectam consanguineam nostram Abbatissam Fontis Ebroldi, per nostras litteras duximus requirendum ut Mariæ sanctimoniali de Ambresbury, sorori nostræ carissimæ, talem commissionem faceret pro domibus ordinis illius infrà regnum nostrum Angliæ visitandis et correctionibus debitis faciendis ac aliis quæ incumbunt, qualem a predecessore ipsius dinoscitur habuisse; et dilectum clericum nostrum, magistrum Johannem de Hildesle, cum dictis nostris litteris ad eam transmisimus pro dicto negotio prosequendo, et responsionem ejusdem ad nos referendo; cui benevole astitistis, sicut ipse nobis retulit; de quo vobis grates referimus speciales. Verum quia præfata Abbatissa —quorum ducta consilio, ut intelleximus—dictam requisitionem nostram hactenus distulit effectui mancipare, de quo cogimur admirari, præsertim cùm ipsa correctiones et visitationes hujusmodi facere non consueverit personaliter, nec credimus quod aliqua alia domina de religione illâ, de regno nostro vel quivis alius, possit officium illud salubriùs et utiliùs exercere, nec relatum sit nobis quod dicta soror nostra, dum visitationes et correctiones hujusmodi ac incumbentia omnia, sibi, ut permittitur, concessa, exercebat, deviasset in aliquo a viâ juris; vestram dilectionem rogamus et requirimus, ex affectu quatinus pro honore dictæ sororis nostræ ac utilitate religionis ordinis illius, quàm ipsius consideratione, affectu appetimus ampliore, inducere velitis præfatam abbatissam ut nostro desiderio benivole annuat et honore dictæ sororis nostræ quicquam non detrahat in hâc parte. Scitis etenim quod et si talis concedatur potestas, ad voluntatem durat tantummodo concedentis, nec obesse poterit ipsi abbatissæ si ipsa personaliter voluerit visitare aut etiam alias ad hoc constituere personas loco sui. Ceterum in hiis quæ præfatus clericus noster vobis ex parte nostrâ dicet super negotio antedicto, fidem velitis indubiam adhibere. Teste Rege apud Wyndesore, vj. die Maii.—*From Close Roll,* 10 *Edward II., membrane* 7 *dorso.*

END OF VOL. II.

Printed in the USA
CPSIA information can be obtained
at www.ICGtesting.com
LVHW021129300124
770354LV00011B/240

9 781015 887572